PAUL A. BOVÉ, EDITOR

Edward Said and the work of the critic:

speaking truth to power

Duke University Press   Durham and London 2000

© 2000 Duke University Press

Printed in the United States of America on acid-free paper ⊗
Typeset in Quadraat by Tseng Information Systems, Inc.
Library of Congress Cataloging-in-Publication Data appear
on the last printed page of this book.

The text of this book originally was published as volume 25,
number 2 (summer 1998) of boundary 2, with the exception
of the following additional material: Ralph P. Locke,
"Exoticism and Orientalism in Music: Problems for the
Worldly Critic"; Aamir R. Mufti, "Auerbach in Istanbul:
Edward Said, Secular Criticism, and the Question of
Minority Culture" (originally published in Critical Inquiry 25);
and Jacqueline Rose, "Edward Said Talks to Jacqueline Rose"
(a portion of which originally was published in
Critical Quarterly 40, no. 1).

SEAL

CONTENTS

Edward Said and the work of the critic

PAUL A. BOVÉ

Introduction

I am for dialogue between cultures and coexistence between people: everything I have written about and struggled for has pointed to that as the goal. But I think real principle and real justice have to be implemented before there can be true dialogue. —Edward W. Said, "The Limits to Cooperation," in Peace and Its Discontents

I

Said's work embodies three values essential to intellectual responsibility: breadth and depth of knowledge, historical and scholarly rigor, and a profound basis in political morality of a kind that alone makes civilization possible. Minus any one of these virtues, intellectuals become clerks, professionals with specialized interests and career ambitions.

These are character virtues that form a career. They transform works into an oeuvre that depends on and projects the virtues of character, that embodies and forms them. They give the product of intellect shape and focus, and make it into a project that, despite its variations and appearances, has integrity that still needs to be identified and made exemplary.

These virtues have guided Said in a career-long struggle to end conflict and further the effort to build civilizations whose cultures benefit from the coalescence of various peoples and their histories. In the name of justice between equals, dialogue can advance the construction of institutions and the telling of stories that both promote greater understanding and recognize, especially in this age of globalism, the overlapping histories, the shared experiences, of different people. No story is above criticism, especially those that attempt, monologically, to reduce a complex history involving many peoples to the story of the victor. Said has made the Israeli project to absorb Jerusalem culturally into a single national tale that sets aside centuries of complexity, of the presence of other peoples, of the civilizational richness in Jerusalem's history—he has made this effort a particular target of both critique and political advice to those who want to struggle for the city. It would be wrong, I think, to make such efforts on Said's part merely aspects of a local nationalism. Of course, the Palestinian national needs, the struggle of a colonized or occupied people for national determination, cannot be given anything but a central place in all of his work. Yet even this struggle both rests on and gives power to sets of intellectual and cultural virtues that can be found elsewhere and that, in turn, often justify Said's "critique of the colonizers" stories and actions. So, for example, not only does Said frequently invoke the accomplishments of Abbasid civilization as something necessarily forgotten by American war makers intent on barbarizing the basin of the Tigris and Euphrates, a culture of many crosscurrents and inventions, but he also appeals to the historical example of Andalusian society lest we forget that different peoples can share a common history and, together, coexist to produce institutions of civil justice and artworks of extraordinary value and impact. We can say either that the struggles of Palestine have led Said to the Abbasid and Andalusian examples or that, being the erudite scholar of intellectual imagination that he is, knowing of these matters gives weight and force to his political and cultural arguments for the Palestinians and against the Israelis and their American allies. In other words, in the memory of Abbasid and Andalusian cultures, there are reservoirs of intellectual imagination and responsibility that, among other things, as memories, confirm that the present disposition of force need not always be, since it has not always been. At times one feels in Said not nostalgia but, as in Walter Benjamin, more than a little commitment to the values of ruined parts of history that, if we could just remember them at the right times and talk about them in the right ways, might help us now to do better in our own immature and sometimes cruel civilizations. They give us not just utopian confidence but actual knowledge of real, material cultures of coexistence.

So powerful does Said take storytelling to be that he urges it as a form of political action and testimony. Cultures have differing powers; they tell their tales better or worse or simply differently. And these differences have profound consequences in the secular movement of history. When the Israelis besiege and shell Beirut, Said calls for the people to find ways to narrate their experiences, to make the horrible events of their daily lives into experiences by giving them shape as stories that can be shared and remembered, and form a national memory and tradition. Cultures form themselves and, as formed, can claim respect and recognition, especially in conflict with or, better, in dialogue with the peoples of other cultures. Better to be self-representing and to form one's own persistent tradition as part of the effort to throw off subordination. Intellectuals' grand narratives, remembering Abassid and Andalusian alternatives, stand with traditions that have broader and more organic formations—although, indeed, the intellectual's responsibility is to be in relation to those very formations.

The same responsibility obliges the intellectual to assess each and every narrative as it emerges, especially those associated with power; these must be treated suspiciously and, when necessary, bathed in acid so the truths they obscure and the powers they serve stand out. Characteristically, Said has become the most stringent critic not only of the Oslo Accord and hence of the so-called peace process that has renewed the disequilibrium of power in favor of the Israelis in Palestine but also of the stories told by Americans, Israelis, and the Palestine Liberation Organization (PLO) about the "benefits" the "peace process" brings to Palestinians. In other words, although Said's work may study, criticize, and reinvoke the form of grand narratives—most obviously the narrative of empire—as part of the necessary effort to achieve just dialogues among equals, this does not mean such dialogues stand free of critique. Said has made us understand that intellectual responsibility involves becoming a stringent critic of national forms at the very moment of their success. Of course, the Oslo Accord offers little, if any, hope of national self-determination for the Palestinians, and, in fact and principle, the PLO leadership is not a national government since, it is Said's contention, it rests on no popular participatory mandate—nonetheless, the virtue of Said's position is that injustice must be made the object of criticism even, or especially, when it appears in the forms of national identity or national stories. So all of this writing against the Oslo Accord represents a critique of a media- and state-supported monologue of praise for a "peace process" that segregates Palestinians into Bantustans but also stands as the tireless effort to promote another narrative while, organically, aligning itself with the history of Palestinian struggle—a history threatened with oblivion by the narratives of the "victors."

Said's project has always involved a struggle for authority. In many cases, certainly since the publication of *Beginnings*, Said has been involved in recasting the forms of modernity's dominant narratives, their filiative time-shapes and linear structures as much as their deceitful and violent contents, their tales of European supremacy, of the impossibility—as in Conrad—of imagining a world without empire. Said's vision is a wide one. If it is against injustice that he struggles, then we should understand the range and implications of that struggle. It involves, above all, the struggle for the Palestinians, but it also involves a struggle within, for, and against the West that often takes the form of changing the forms of Western narrative. When Said invokes Brahms or counterpoint and Conrad or affiliation, much the same project is at work. It is important to understand Said when he makes these gestures. In certain circles, it has become fashionable simply to bash anyone who attends to figures of "European High Culture" as elitist or "Eurocentric." Such remarks exemplify values even worse than those Said calls "the rhetoric of blame." It is of the essence of Said's virtue that he searches out and does not turn away from the cultural, civil, and political work—wherever it can be found—that embodies either the material forms of human beings living together in everyday lives rich in meaning and accomplishment or the very figures by means of which we can learn how it is possible to think toward living in such societies. Said is not a monologist. The historical mind finds not only the limits of European modernism vis-à-vis empire when it reads Conrad but also the resources for imagining an alternative shape to cultural interaction, for the formation of a culture capable of dialogue when it hears the counterpoints of Bach or Brahms. This is the same consciousness that admires the writing of the Jewish American scholar Sara Roy, or the historical imagination of Ibn-Khaldūn, or the use of Antonio Gramsci by Indian scholars of subalternity. Breadth and depth of scholarship, knowledge, and understanding means a certain catholicism, a cosmopolitanism that roams a world and its historical culture for the pleasure of identifying the resources needed to make interventions so the present society might be transformed to meet a higher set of almost impossible ethical ideals. Intellectuals who can do these things are themselves a resource. It is to the great scholars that intellectuals, no matter how pressing or immediate their concerns, must turn if they are to learn, think, judge, and intervene. Presentism has its dangers, not least of those are a lack of sympathy and a foreshortened perspective that obscures both the long movements of a secular history and the effort and struggle needed to take part in its movements. Often, short perspectives and impatience lead intellectuals to jump to fundamentalist conclusions or to remove themselves into the safe and rewarding confines of mere professionalism. Said, after all, engages figures of intellectual stature not merely because they might confirm some already held assumption but because they offer pleasure to the intellect, knowledge to the understanding, and refinement to the will. Knowing of Andalusian accomplishment, he can turn to the discussion of counterpoint, understanding how peoples fruitfully coexist and judging the likelihood that certain material practices might further or hinder the effort to live productively in peace. There is no disjuncture between the study of Fidelio and the critique of Arafat, and the critic who insists there must be cannot understand the virtue of intellectual responsibility.

Moreover, Said belongs to a great tradition of historical thinkers extending from Vico to Benjamin and beyond. We should always read Said with Benjamin's "Sixth Thesis on the Philosophy of History" in mind: "Only the historian will have the gift of fanning the spark of hope in the past who is firmly convinced that even the dead will not be safe from the enemy if he wins. And this enemy has not ceased to be victorious." Benjamin has put succinctly the political and human fact of Said's commitment to scholarship, memory, and history. The struggle for history is a political struggle, and in this light, Arafat appears as a traitor who has damaged the past as he has the present: He has distorted, lost, and endangered all that was achieved by the *intifada*. His poor political judgment effaces the complexities of material human experience and helps the victor maintain the rule of injustice. The dead will be forgotten; their efforts will be lost; they will be defeated once more: They become what their enemies always called them, "terrorists" rather than "freedom fighters." The future is lost in the battle for the stories of the past.

2

Critics who take Said seriously recognize the central relation between history, narrative, and politics in his work, and they attempt to bring their own study into relation with Said's efforts. In this collection, for example, Jonathan Arac presents us with some of his own arguments on *Huckleberry Finn* and shows us how Said's work can and should matter in the context of American literature, culture, and politics. For just as Said meditates on the quizzical complexities that form the hypotheses of all critical work, so Arac's deeply historical tracings and judgments of the ways cultures work in forming its own icons let us see exactly what the role of criticism should be.

It is Said's particular effect that those who write with him in mind must always confront this question: What should the critic do? In a unique and powerful essay on the problems of land mines and human rights, Barbara Harlow gives one exemplary answer to that question. She enacts in scholarly detail Said's lifelong injunction: Speak truth to power. Like Said, Harlow casts aside "epistemological" worries over what we can know to show that, at the level of politics and history, we can know certain and often quite deadly things—massacres, cover-ups, and the suppression of human rights—and intellectuals must use their special training and knowledge to speak of these matters as they speak about race and stories.

Gayatri Chakravorty Spivak is, of course, one of the leading essayists in the fields of Marxism, theory, feminism, and materialism. With Said and very few others, academics would credit her with the formation of postcolonial studies. Her impact in numerous fields of knowledge has been immense. In this volume, she returns us, topically, to America and, in reading Jack Forbes's *Black Africans and Native Americans*, she examines that most Saidian of all issues: the crossing of peoples and their different histories. Spivak takes Forbes's work as emblematic of the power of Said's *Orientalism* as a beginning, as a setting of an agenda for now nearly two generations of scholars in the social sciences as well as the humanities. Of course, Spivak makes of Forbes's work something very much her own, which, here and now, can be called simply a historical materialist reading of the liberalism that always informs U.S. multiculturalism. As always, however, Spivak forces our attention to the international arrangements of forces and invents for us a new and necessary way to read in light of globalism. Her essay can be importantly placed next to the final chapters of *Culture and Imperialism*.

We need ways to understand Said's importance in so many fields, to so many projects, and in relation to so many other powerful intellectuals and their thought. Mustapha Marrouchi has produced an extended study of essential elements of Said's thinking, especially in relation to Said's historical status as an exile in a metropolitan culture. He weighs Said in scale with Frantz Fanon, Raymond Williams, and C. L. R. James and against those politically unsympathetic critics who do not read Said carefully enough. Marrouchi explains Said's project and the multisided value of his work to his self-created role as a "strategic intellectual." This allows Marrouchi not only to explain why certain self-proclaimed figures of "resistance" misrepresent Said but also to separate him from those Marrouchi calls "his acolytes." This is an important point in understanding a critic who has polemically substituted affiliation for filiation in his thinking. More important, it allows us to approach Said as a figure not to be imitated but read and studied. Like Williams, Said is a brilliant essayist, committed to the flexibility of the form; the author of books who detests dogma; and in what Marrouchi rightly identifies as Said's impatience with the merely abstract, a writer committed to elements of James's feeling for the materialities of life.

Perhaps Said is better known for his fundamental role in the struggles of the Palestinian people, a struggle that has, at times, brought him within the formal institutions of resistance but more often has seen him involved in the intellectual's tasks of speaking truth *against* power and building the severe poetic institutions of freedom and justice. More than any other person, Said has changed, at least to some important degree, the way the U.S. media and American intellectuals must think about and represent Palestinians, Islam, and the Middle East. Rashid I. Khalidi has played a vital role in changing the U.S. understanding of Palestinian history and current realities. Like Said,

Khalidi has thought out the vital role media representations play in U.S. foreign policy, in forming the consensus of empire that, in this case, has cost the Palestinians so dearly. In his essay for this special issue, Khalidi, once more invoking Said's commitment to speak truth to power, analyzes the ways Said has understood, made use of, and changed the American media. Khalidi helps us understand how vital Said's role has been in educating media and scholarly elites; often Said has been almost alone in this effort, but, as a result, many people now better understand the ignorance and prejudice, the workings of "Orientalism" in the U.S. media. And far better than before, we realize the consequences of such habits of ignorance and prejudice. Khalidi notices how Said has brilliantly used the American commitment to "democracy" as a lever to move U.S. media images of the Middle East conflict while letting us also see how, like Gramsci, an organic intellectual, Said's own values are deeply rooted in enhancing popular democratic participation in power and choice.

Of course, the aestheticization of politics has been a problem for intellectuals throughout this century. Kojin Karatani, himself an important theorist not only of the aesthetic but of Japan's status in the history of colonialism and imperialism, argues powerfully that in *Orientalism*, Said has identified and subverted the role of the aesthetic in colonialism. Theorizing the aesthetic as a form of "sadistic invasion" allows Kojin to represent Conrad-like figures — those who adopt an anti-imperial position from within the seeming necessity of empire — as "aestheticentrists" whose own aesthetic commitments require deconstruction. Kojin insists that Said's work lets us realize that aesthetics allows even anti-imperialists to obscure colonialism.

In a very different but related vein of thinking, Lindsay Waters sets out to engage Said's speculations on figuration and representation as the basis for a renewed theory of the aesthetic. Indeed, implicitly accepting Kojin's suggestion that Western aesthetics has been discredited by history, Waters argues that nonetheless Said's work shows the need for an aesthetics and relegitimates the sphere itself. Waters situates Said's work in a contested relation to Adorno as a thinking about pleasure. Waters's essay opens this issue's effort to take seriously the place of music in Said's career and does so by giving attention to Said's own emphasis on the importance of experience, especially, in this instance, the experience by the human of that which moves us — even though it itself is not human.

Such a line of thinking can be, as Waters knows, developed in many directions. Terry Cochran's essay pursues Said's thinking about the inhuman into the equally foundational domain of figuration. Cochran thinks through the theoretical implications of Said's writing to explain how Said has shown, irreversibly, that the conceptual and rhetorical devices for dealing with literature must be applied to all other domains of cultural production and that this fact has serious implications for the organization of knowledge. Cochran's own research into the materiality of knowledge production—especially his thinking about print—form part of the necessary historical context for his reading of Said.

As Cochran takes Said's thinking about music into the topics of figure and materiality, Jim Merod places Said's work into a revealing relation to musical performance. Merod pursues Waters's interest in experience into the central Saidian domain of critical intelligence, taking seriously Said's participation in a "vast" realm of humanistic musical imagination. Merod's interest lies in what seems to be the excessive elements of Said's critical imagination that are played out or elaborated in such things as Glenn Gould's legendary nighttime performances. In other words, in the inhumanity of music, Merod grounds Said's generous and overwhelming humanism.

When W. J. T. Mitchell engages Said in questions about visual art, we begin to grasp, immediately, the very eccentric power that Merod identifies as the center of Said's persistent and expanding civilizational significance. We can read Said's interview with Mitchell for what they say about Goya, Caravaggio, and others, but most important, as Mitchell repeatedly makes clear, is how, in talking about these great figures of our civilization, Said makes us see his own status. It is of the essence that we understand this word *our* as being inclusive. As Mitchell and Said laughingly insist, they are both secular leftists— and feel themselves an endangered species. It is vital, though, for an intellectual such as Said, for whom the greatness of culture matters just because it comes from coalescence and not from difference alone—for just this reason, Goya, although of Europe, can and needs to be read, studied, appreciated, and learned as one important element of a history that exists not just alone but in counterpoint to all others. It is in this sense, in terms of the breadth, rigor, and ethical spirit that motivate Said's generosity, courage, and openness, that we can follow Mitchell in naming Said as part of the same class of figures as Goya himself. Said once insisted that Goethe's greatness lies in his being open to influence. Said has made himself the modern version of this figure, and this extraordinary quality, which is a gift to all the rest of us, needs to be studied and accepted.

Edward Said talks to Jacqueline Rose

JR I wanted to start this evening by way of introduction with Edward Said's own words from two of my favorite books of his. The first from *After the Last Sky*, his extraordinary and eloquent tribute to the Palestinian people:

> Homecoming is out of the question. . . . A part of something is for the foreseeable future going to be better than all of it. Fragments over wholes. Restless nomadic activity over the settlements of held territory. Criticism over resignation. The Palestinian as self-consciousness in a barren plain of investments and consumer appetites. The heroism of anger over the begging-bowl, limited independence over the status of clients. Attention, alertness, focus. To do as others do, but somehow to stand apart. To tell your story in pieces, *as it is*.

The second I take from *Musical Elaborations*, which is his wonderful excursus into modern music which he brings to an end with a celebration of a type of music:

> whose pleasures and discoveries are premised upon letting go, upon not asserting a central authorizing identity . . . an art not primarily . . . about authorial power and social authority, but a mode for thinking through or thinking with the integral variety of human cultural practices, generously, non-coercively, in a utopian cast, if by utopian we mean worldly, possible, attainable, knowable.

I chose these two quotes not just because I like them or because they immediately give you a sense of the extraordinary range of Edward Said's work, but also because I think they give such a strong impression of the affirmative aspect of his work.

In his 1993 *Representations of the Intellectual*, Edward Said described the intellectual as somebody who strikes us with "the unremitting force of his questioning and deeply confrontational intellect" and slightly less flatteringly—he wasn't talking about himself, I should say—of the intellectual whose point was to be "embarrassing, contrary, and even unpleasant." Now, some of these epithets have been thrown his way in his time, so I started with these two quotes so as to convey the spirit—in which I hope this interview and discussion can be conducted—of his positive, inspirational commitment to a future that would be non-coercive, generous, integrally various.

I'm also hoping that we can use this evening as an opportunity to give Edward Said a chance to reply to some of the criticisms, not to say misrepresentations, that on occasion he rather dramatically seems to provoke. I have a personal interest in this. I'm here this evening as a Jewish woman and a feminist with a long-standing commitment to psychoanalytic thinking, and, let's face it, on the surface of it, none of these epithets could be said to apply to you. I'm therefore also hoping this evening that we will have a chance to demonstrate the possibility of undreamt of forms of dialogue across what have often seemed to be insurmountable barriers of historical difference.

My first question is about writing. You've talked about writing all throughout your work, and, at one point, you say: "for man who no longer has a homeland writing becomes a place to live." You also say: "the main hope of the intellectual"—this is a bit surprising—"the main hope of the intellectual is not that he will have an effect on the world, but that someday, somewhere, someone will recall what he wrote exactly as he wrote it." In *Beginnings*, you say the first question—which is why it's my first question—the first question is "Why writing?—a choice is made over the desire to speak, to gesture, to dance." In fact, you do speak and you do gesture. I don't know about dancing.

EWS (inaudible) I don't dance. . . .

JR So, my question is not what it is you write about and why you've chosen to write about those things, but what does writing do for you? Why do you think you do it?

EWS Well, in many cases, at a very simple level, it's because I get pleasure from it. There is something direct about it that gives me a sense that I'm entering the world. I'm one of the few people who doesn't use a computer. I use a pen. I've resisted all of these technological advances, simply because the irreducible pleasure of putting pen to paper with black ink is a way of trying out thought, of expressing ideas, of trying to reach people that I otherwise couldn't reach. In a certain way, it's a refusal of the silence that most of us experience as ordinary citizens who are unable to effect change in a political and economic society that is obviously moved by larger forces than individuals.

But, also, I think there's a certain expression in the writing, of not exactly resignation. Your quote, about the hope of the intellectual that somebody would read their words, I borrowed from Adorno at a time when I felt that things were going very wrong for the Palestinians, and that being left out of the progress of history is a fate which I didn't want to settle for. What I felt that I could at least do was to testify, to be a witness to a certain kind of history and to get it right. I think in the end that is probably the most fundamental challenge of all, to try to get it right, to find words that will fit a situation and that will not change as the situation changes, but which will at least register a reaction to a particular moment that would otherwise go by. I was writing at the time of the Oslo accord when there was universal celebration and people on television were talking about this earth-shaking event, and I was feeling exactly the opposite. I thought this was a very bad moment. From then on, I felt it was important somehow not to let things escape. I've had a lifelong suspicion—well, not lifelong, but for as long as it's been around—of deconstruction: people who say, well, it all depends on how you look. I believe in facts and very often the facts get abused, or left out, or embroidered or hidden or forgotten. So, at that very low level of what could perhaps be called resignation, for me that is what that kind of writing is.

The last thing to say is that, for me, writing is a very varied thing. It depends on the occasion, on what I'm writing and who I'm writing for. There are certain types of writing immediately tied to an occasion and anchored to a deadline; and other kinds of writing that are more reflective and take longer, so the pace of writing is also very important to gauge. My great fear is repeating myself, because in the end, all of us perforce have a repertory of ideas, phrases. For the last few years, I've been writing a column twice a month for various newspapers, not in America, but in the Arab world and Europe. There, the great challenge is to find the right tone for each occasion—it's very very hard—to try, for your reader, to be different, to surprise, above all to raise questions and inspire skepticism. Not to let people feel that there's nothing that can be done. At least, both as a teacher and a writer, you want to try and stimulate or at least involve the reader in a process which you can help along with your own writing.

JR   One of my strongest images of you was, indeed after Oslo, when you were speaking at the School of Oriental and African Studies at the University of London, and you stood in the room—this was the occasion where you gestured—and just drew in the air the roads that were being built through the so-called, about-to-be-liberated, newly independent territories. In a stroke, you demonstrated to me—and it has stayed with me ever since—the economic non-viability of what was happening for the Palestinians. That would be consistent with the life of a spokesperson whose task is, as you have also put it, "the fusing of the moral will with the grasping of evidence," or "speaking truth to power." So, facts, as you've just said. One way I see that aspect of your work is as a sort of enlightenment project, whose aim is to bring critical reason to the court of politics. On the other hand, in much of your writing, especially on literature and music, your passion is for modernism which, by your own account, is skeptical of certain concepts of truth, certainty, and so on. This does not, as I see it, correspond to a division between your writing on culture, say, versus politics, because, even in your political writings, you have talked about the need for us to be—and this is one of my favorite expressions of yours—"receptacles," open so we "could take in as much as the sea" (an image replete with what for many would be seen as the fluidity of modernist writing). So, can you say something about how you square, or how you see the connection between, the enlightenment and modernist components of what you do?

EWS In many ways they're really quite different as you suggest. If you're writing about modernism with all of its skepticism and, above all, irony, then you're really talking about something quite different from what a particular political actor has done, what a political settlement or a political process might be all about. But, what I think connects them—and I've tried to do that—is a certain sense of exploration and provisionality. It's not as if I'm trying, in my writing on politics, to say that it's always fixed in stone. What I say is the result of an effort for me which I'm presenting with every possibility that I'll be proved wrong. There is something about reality which is resistant to that kind of settled analysis, as there is in certain works of literature. For example, I've spent a long part of my intellectual and academic life thinking and writing about Conrad and I've come to the conclusion that I don't really fully understand Conrad and probably never will. Admitting this and going on trying just the same is how I would connect the two parts of my writing. Of course, the tone is different, because the audience is different and because, in a certain sense, the goal is different. In the case of political writing, you have to be more, shall I say, assertive, you have to name names and tell the facts as you see them, which has its own difficulties because there's no situation, whether in my part of the world or in the United States, where you can say what you want. There are always obstacles. Plus the fact that I always have the sense that I'm not really writing in my own language. In fact, I don't really know what my own language is. I use English, but I was brought up speaking Arabic. This kind of uncertainty as to where you finally stand—and I think that a lot of the effort of writing is not to settle too quickly into a position—is unsettling. I feel it as I'm writing although perhaps my readers don't.

I've therefore always been very suspicious of a number of things which I see as ultimately related. Officials. I think officials always lie. I. F. Stone, the great American journalist who died a few years ago and who I knew reasonably well towards the end of his life, used to publish a little magazine out of his home that became very influential in Washington, beginning I think in the Eisenhower years, but especially during the Kennedy and Johnson years, and especially around Vietnam. He was a remarkable reporter, extremely irreverent, and he said that the working rule for the journalist is to assume that every government report is lying. It's certainly true of most journalists—it's the laziness of the twentieth-century journalist—that they repeat the government report. You should always assume that officials representing a position, administrators, people who have authority and power over others, etc., are all involved in keeping their places and their authority intact, and that it is therefore the role of the intellectual, at least as I see it, to keep challenging them, to name names and cite facts.

JR   This is sounding less and less like modernism though? This is sounding more and more like fusing of the moral will with the grasping of evidence.

EWS   Right. Yes.

JR   About fifteen years ago, someone wrote an article about the Middle East in which they envisaged a Palestinian future in which you yourself would be unfurling the Palestinian flag as the president of the new state. Did you ever read that?

EWS   That's the last thing I would want to do. . . .

JR   But should that happen, and of course it's not going to, it would involve you taking on a form of executive and administrative authority. One could at least say that, if you're talking in the realm of politics and saying that everyone else is lying, then you must have the truth? You have to therefore take on a position which you seem very suspicious of. . . .

EWS   No, I'm not saying that I have the truth. I'm simply saying that they don't. I have listened for most of my life to tons, reams of, basically, political untruth of one kind or another, most of it doing abuse to language, which I care about very much. So, it's not that I have the answers which they claim that they have; it's that they are hiding the facts, which is a very different thing, and making promises that they can't keep, effacing bits of history that are embarrassing and complicated. I think it's important to say just that. In the interest of something larger than yourself to which you feel connected—a people, a cause, the silent, the helpless, the oppressed. Those things have moved me a great deal.

Writing about modernism is a totally different thing, because first of all it's much more private. It's a mode of reflection and meditation and perhaps much more uncertain. It's also different, I think, because I think of myself as writing even about modernism or music as a historian, where what you're trying to do is to put the work of art in a larger perspective and connect it to things that normally are not connected to it. In the case, let's say, of opera, it's very interesting to see a kind of politics of the moment, because operas were written for particular occasions in the past whereas most people think of them as classical works—you go to the opera and you wear your tuxedo and all that kind of thing. But, in fact, they were combative in many ways with specific objectives as well as having other aims. And the same is sometimes true of works of literature, which may mean connecting them not just to a cultural and political situation, but also to the privacy of the writer's life.

JR In *Musical Elaborations*, you describe Bach's "Canonic Variations" as "so far in excess of any occasion or need that it dangles pretty much as pure musicality in a social space off the edge." You also use expressions like "self-enclosed," "private," "reflexive." And yet, as I see it, most of your work involves pulling works of literature and cultural art back to their historical and political accountability. So where's "private" in that?

EWS There's been a change. For the last six or seven years, perhaps after I became ill, I got very interested in what has been referred to as "late style." In other words, in the careers of many writers, composers, painters, there's a transformation which has to do with age, which has to do with a new vision that occurs at the end of their careers. The most famous example of this is Beethoven in the last, say, ten years of his life. He was of course deaf, but the deafness can't explain what in fact happened. It is as if Beethoven, who had spent certainly the middle years of the second decade between 1810 and 1816 being a very public composer (for example, his only opera was produced in its third version for the Congress of Vienna, by which time he was the most famous composer of Europe and a celebrated figure in Vienna), suddenly turns away from all that. And what you have is the late work, which is extremely private, very concerned with the medium, really about the technique of music. Most important, they're works that are not unified, the way the earlier works had been, by the force of his personality, by development of the kind that one associates with sonata form. What you have, as you do in the last plays of Ibsen, is a sense of the artist turning inward and examining not only the medium of his art, but also his own work, and turning them inside out. This is true also of Bach's last works, where he's no longer writing for an audience, for patrons, for a court, for the church. He's writing just within the sphere of a fantastic, fantastically mastered sphere of counterpoint, like the "Canonic Variations." That interests me tremendously.

JR   Let me pick up the point about privacy and the changes in your writing. You're writing your autobiography at the moment. I thought everybody here would love to have you talk about that a little bit, if you can.

EWS   It's not really an autobiography. I've resisted the use of that word. I call it a memoir, because, first of all because I'm not really a public figure; it's not "the life and times of," the way a politician would, say, tell the story of what happened during the election of 1997 or whatever. I don't try to account for a public trajectory. But I felt that I had something to understand about a peculiar past. My family was of course Palestinian, but we seemed to live in two or three different worlds. We lived in Egypt. My mother is partly Lebanese, so we lived in Lebanon. This was all during the colonial period. We had an extremely strange — because my father sort of invented it — a very strange, constructed life. I went exclusively to colonial schools, so I know, or knew at the time, a great deal about the Enclosure Act. I was thinking about it when I came down on the plane. I see these pastures, and I remember a question in school that I got a very high grade for: "The Enclosure Act of (I forget what year it was) was a necessary evil. Discuss." I was living in Egypt at the time, but if somebody had asked me about the irrigation system of Egypt, I couldn't have said a word about it. And because my father had lived in the United States for a while and had served in World War I, we, my sisters and I, all inherited an American citizenship. So, here I was, Palestinian, living in Egypt with a very peculiar first name in the circles I moved in (Edward is not your basic Arabic name). I think probably the main thread of the memoir is to trace the effects of this sort of imprisoning or limiting life that I had as a child, perhaps because my family felt that they had to protect me. It was a very turbulent time; I've just finished a chapter on the fall of Palestine in 1948. It really took me a very long time to understand what happened because we never talked politics at home. Right to the end of their lives, my parents were always slightly, I won't say disgusted, but disapproving of the fact that I had anything to do with politics. At the same time my parents, with the best of intentions, were trying to push me in a certain direction, and I felt that I was always going in another way. In a certain sense, the memoir is an attempt to make sense of an effort at self-liberation which didn't completely succeed.

JR   What did they want you to be?

EWS   A doctor, to have a profession, I suppose. And all of my interests were exactly opposed to that. I was a pre-med for a while but I kept breaking the test tubes in the lab and didn't find it interesting so I didn't succeed in it. And then, of course, I started to open towards politics and then also, very important, I found myself much more interested in other parts of the world than just the world I lived in. I think that's been a terribly important thing for me — a certain amount of curiosity which I gained and which I think is also important as a teacher to communicate to my students. It's not just a matter of reading what's on the list, but more a kind of intellectual energy which somehow got released out of that rather imprisoning early period of my life.

JR   What does it feel like to be living in New York as what has become the chief spokesperson in the West for the Palestinian people? How does that work for you, in terms of where you're putting yourself and where you belong?

EWS   It goes all the way from death threats: about ten years ago my office was burned at Columbia University; the Police and the FBI (I was assigned an agent) told me at the time that part of the Jewish Defense League, because the same group were found in the basement of the building where I live, had done this and were threatening to do more. To the more common thing, which is abuse. In New York especially you get a tremendous amount of hate and anger. I remember, for example, one night, it must have been twenty/twenty-five years ago, when I had already been made a professor, and there was a party for a departing colleague. Everybody got fairly drunk. And the wife of a colleague of mine who is herself Jewish came up to me and said—I'll never forget this—and of course she wouldn't have normally said it, because I had run into her on the street, but under the influence of alcohol she felt slightly released: "Young man!" (She was barely maybe ten years older than I am.) "Young man, I want to talk to you about some of your ideas . . . why do you want to kill Jews?" There was an article written about me called the "Professor of Terror." I think now they've gotten tired of doing that, because somehow I've survived it all.

But I think the most peculiar thing of all has been the number of people, mostly Jews actually, who have wanted either to come to my house or to see me at a meal—to see how I "lived." This literally happened to me, I would say maybe half a dozen times. A very well-known Jewish woman psychologist who lives in Boston—we had participated in several seminars in the eighties about conflict resolution—came to New York and rang me from NYU, which is downtown, and said, "Can I come and visit you?" I was taken a bit by surprise and said, "Yes, of course." She came up, entered the apartment, came into the living room where I have a grand piano—"Oh, you play the piano"—looked around a bit more, asked to see my study and then, when I said, "Why don't you sit down? I mean it's a long subway ride from downtown," said, "No, no, I have to go . . . I only came up to see how you lived." Another person at a distinguished publishing house—we were doing a deal or something—refused for weeks, perhaps even months, to sign the contract until I came to Boston and had dinner with him so he could observe me and my table manners.

JR   Let me respond to this with an anecdote of my own.

EWS   Of course.

JR   About three years ago I gave a lecture at Yale University and, the next day, one of the distinguished literary critics at Yale University asked me over lunch if I had "any Jewish blood" in me and when I replied, thinking that it was a strange question but I'd answer it, that as far as I knew I only had "Jewish blood" in me, but why had she asked, she replied, "Because we thought you were Jewish, then we realized you couldn't be, because in your lecture you'd cited Edward Said."

EWS One more story. This is actually quite something; it's poignant. About ten years ago, I went to Emory University in Atlanta to give a series of lectures and seminars. At the last seminar, as I was entering the seminar room, I was stopped by a young man who introduced himself to me as a graduate student of English who was going to attend the seminar and who very much, he said, wanted to drive me to the airport after the seminar. And I said, "Well, that's very kind of you, but it won't be necessary because Professor X is going to do that." He said, "No, listen, it really means a lot to me to drive you to the airport; it really is a matter of some sort of personal privilege." When I asked why (I mean, most people want to get away from that kind of chore), he explained that he had been a student at Columbia in English but had never taken any of my courses: "I went to Jewish school" (since it was a school in New York, a lot of the students came to Columbia), "where the rabbi had said that you were the devil, and we were not to have anything to do with you, so I didn't. But I feel that it was such a stupid and wretched thing to have done that I feel that if I could drive you to the airport it would sort of make up for it."

JR I'm now going to slightly play devil's advocate. I warned you about this question, so you won't be surprised. It's a question about Jewishness and Judaism, because it obviously does shadow your work. There are a number of ironies here. The fact that your present criticisms of the Palestinian authorities have earned you the epithet of "Friend of the Zionist enemy"; the fact, of which people here might not be aware, that, by a historical irony, Martin Buber moved into your house when your family had to evacuate it in 1948. At the end of *Orientalism* you say: "by an almost inescapable logic, I found myself having written a history of a strange and secret sharer of Western anti-Semitism." I would very much like you to talk about the way Jewishness and Judaism or anti-Semitism—of course they're not conflatable—figure in your writing. There are some moments that make me uncomfortable. For example, in *Beginnings* you say after Vico—he's one of your most admired authors— "the crucial distinction is between the gentiles who divine or imagine divinity, on the one hand, and the Hebrew whose true God prohibits divination on the other." You present it as if a lot politically might follow from that. Since I know you are often charged with a much cruder charge of anti-Semitism, which is not what I'm saying here, would you just talk about what Semitism, Semite mean for you and how you do or don't distinguish that from individual Jewish thinkers, scholars, friends, so on. . . .

EWS   Two things to say immediately. First of all, the Semites of course turn up in Vico, but actually Vico is a great Zionist, in the sense that he makes a distinction between the people who have the Book where everything is written, which he calls sacred, and the world of the gentile, or secular world — all, I think, so as to get away from the problems he might have had with the Church, writing in Naples in the early eighteenth century. Since he's interested in historiography and the way history is made, he sets up a distinction between the people of the Book — it could be Christians as well, he says, but he specifically means, in this instance, the Jews — whose history is made for them by God (they're a special case), and the rest of humanity, which is what he's interested in. They're the people that make history possible, because human beings make history. This is what Marx took from Vico — the idea that human beings make their own history.

So, those generic classifications, which one encounters really from the end of the sixteenth century on in European literature, have always struck me: the idea of the Semites, which of course mainly means Jews, but not necessarily, because by the nineteenth century Semite means everybody in the Semitic East. For example, in his *History of the Semitic People* or the *Principles of the Semitic Languages*, Renan talks about Arabic and Hebrew and Aramaic and so on and so forth; all of those languages always struck me as constructions of some sort that were foreign to me because I'd grown up in a mixed environment. The schools I went to in Palestine and Egypt were all full of Arabs, of course, Christians and Muslims, Greeks, Italians, Armenians, Jews, both Oriental (as they used to be called) Jews and occasionally here and there, not too many, European Jews. I saw this kind of construction worked out in the literature of anti-Semitism, for example, and found an interesting parallel between that and the notion of the Oriental, because in both instances Europeans were trying to talk about exotic peoples. In a wonderful phrase, Disraeli asks, "Arabs, what are they?" and answers, "They're just Jews on horseback." So, underlying this separation is also an amalgamation of some kind.

Throughout my life when I've met Jewish people, individual Jews in class, in society and so on, I've always felt a certain kind of affinity. Because in a sense we've been — like now — thrown together, sometimes not too pleasantly and sometimes very pleasantly. It's a very complicated thing, because I'm one of the few people who say that our history as Palestinians today is so inextricably bound with that of Jews that the whole idea of separation, which is what the peace process is all about — to have a separate Palestinian thing and a separate Jewish thing — is doomed. It can't possibly work.

I remember in 1988 I was participating in a forum, organized under the auspices of the Jewish magazine *Tikkun*, in which the Jewish philosopher Michael Waltzer, who is famous in America and a great antagonist of mine, was also participating. He's a man of the left supposedly, but a quite extraordinarily dogged Zionist. It was organized because the Palestinian National Council, of which I was then a member, had just recognized Israel and had spoken about the need for two states for the first time explicitly, and this was seen to be a new opening. I kept insisting that it was not simple. At one point Waltzer said to me: "All right, listen. You've recognized Israel. You obviously have or can have your own state. But don't keep speaking about the past. Let's talk about the future." This is very often said to me by my critics, that I always talk about the past, that I dwell too much on the injustices done to the Palestinians and so on and so forth. The audience was, I would say, about 99 percent Jewish. When he said it, my mouth hung open, but I didn't say anything, because a woman in the audience—I'll never forget this as long as I live, her name was Hilda Silverstein—got up and started—well, it would be too strong to say she started screaming—but she started vociferously attacking Waltzer. She said: "How dare you say that to a Palestinian. How dare you say that to anybody. Because of all the people in the world, we ask the world to remember our past. And you're telling a Palestinian to forget the past? How dare you?" It was an extraordinary thing. And he didn't utter a word after that.

Lastly, not to make this too long, lastly, of course, there is, you know, a, perhaps in the end a deep—and I say this with great sorrow as perhaps the hardest thing to accept—irreconcilability between Arab and Jew which in my generation will not be overcome.

JR   Arab and Jew or Arab and Israeli?

EWS   Well, both. I think it's quite plain. I live in America. It's very hard to find anybody in America who's Jewish who doesn't identify with Israel. And I understand. . . .

JR   I know lots, Edward, I know lots of Jews in America who don't identify with Israel.

EWS   Really? Yes?

JR   Yes. We speak to different people. Clearly, we do.

EWS   Well, let me just finish this, if I may. Because I think a, or the, idea of separation is an idea that I'm just sort of terminally opposed to, just as I'm opposed to most forms of nationalism, just as I'm opposed to secession, to isolation, to separatism of one sort or another. The idea that people who are living together—this happened for example in Lebanon—should suddenly split apart and say Christians should live here and Muslims there and Jews there and that sort of thing is, I think, just barbaric, unacceptable. And yet I think there's a very deep rift caused by real history, and it takes a lot of working through to get over it. There's too much that's gone on between us in this way—between, all right let's say Arab and Israeli. But I feel it very strongly in America. People will tell you, it's an emotional thing—when the pogroms start we need a place to go to. And my answer is, of course, go to Palestine, go to Israel, but don't displace another people when you're doing it. That's the problem. We have been dispossessed. Our society has been destroyed. It's very difficult to forget that. And, lastly, I think the flaw in the peace process, the basic psychological or cultural flaw in the peace process is that Israelis and their supporters, let's leave it at that, Israelis and their supporters have been insulated from the very facts which made their society in Israel possible. With very few exceptions, one of them being, for example, Israel Shahak who, quite remarkable in that respect, is willing to talk about it.

JR   And Leibowitz.

EWS   Yes, I mean you can count them, Leah Zemel, Felicia Lanager, etc. And later in his life, Mattie Peled, who was a general in the Israeli army during the sixty-seven war.

JR   It depends too of course on how you draw the lines. As you know, Ella Shohat has written extensively about the different political configuration you get in Israel if the Palestinians and Sephardic Jews, who are another repressed minority within the Israeli community, should seek some kind of political affiliation, how the whole map would change.

It seems to me that one of the things you've been talking about is what I would want to call, not the irrational, but the non-rational dimension of political identities. In his extraordinary book *The Third Way*, Raja Shehadeh, the Palestinian lawyer working in the West Bank, says of the Israeli: "I dream the dreams that he should have." So there's a quite terrifying and chilling sense of unconscious histories repeating themselves across the red line in Israel and Palestine and through the unconsciouses of the participants. If we go back to your project of speaking truth to power, of making explicit demands, of one injustice being remedied but not at the cost of forgetting the injustice that was done to the Jews; if we assume this could be done rationally, what nonetheless do we do about this non-rational, unconscious, almost pathological dimension of political processes?

EWS   That's obviously a very difficult dimension to existing and working. For example, I've spent a long time criticizing Israel and Israelis, but one must say that Palestinians have a lot to answer for. There's very little real knowledge of Israel or of the need to address a constituency in Israel of conscience, or to try and create one amongst Palestinians. There's either the slavish, "white man's nigger" attitude typified by Arafat and his crew—because the Israelis are more powerful and have America behind them, we have to be their slaves. That's no good. Or there's the view that they are all aliens and intruders. If they go away, like the crusaders went away, that would be the best thing. If they don't, we want nothing to do with them. Neither attitude is OK.

What we haven't done, I think, is to intrude ourselves upon the Israeli conscience: conscience, not consciousness. I mean, they're aware of us—who builds the settlements today, the Israeli settlements? Palestinians build them and the top contractor for the settlements is a Palestinian who is a Minister in the Palestine Authority. That's unacceptable, because there politics and interests are being used to camouflage a really deep complicity which is not the solution. We're in a position of such subordination and such weakness vis-à-vis Israel that our number one priority is to seize and understand ourselves and our history. To this day, there is no decent Palestinian history written by Palestinians. Our own history is unrecorded. There are interesting books, monographs written about the history of Nablus, a short history of Haifa, a little bit here and there, synoptic kind of histories of Palestine, but if you want to look for an authoritative history of the Palestinian national movement, you have to read an Israeli book or an American or English book or German book. But that moment of real self-consciousness is not the consciousness-building of the seventies and the eighties when we thought of ourselves as carrying forth the struggle of Fanon and which dissipated very quickly. You need institutions, you need to build education.

I'll give you another example. Just two months ago, 19,000 public sector teachers in secondary and primary school went on strike. Why? Because they were getting salaries between two and three hundred dollars, which is half the salary of the driver of a Director General in the Ministry—there are now 750 Director Generals in only twenty-six Ministries. They have of course no jobs. They're simply being paid from the public purse to keep them loyal to Arafat. So what happens? The authority refuses to even discuss with them. They pick up twenty-five of the "leaders" of the strike. They jail them. They torture them. None of them—I'm very proud of this as a teacher myself—none of them capitulates. Arafat then says, "Bring them to me." So the twenty-five leaders are brought to his office. Arafat cursed them for one hour, trying to break them, insulting them in the most obscene and filthy language (the correspondent of the *Guardian/Observer*, who is himself not Arab but knows Arabic, rang me from Jerusalem and said, "Did you hear what he did to those twenty-five people? Where did he learn that kind of street language?"). They didn't break. They then accepted a 2 ½ or 3 percent increase in their salaries, but 85 percent of them said that they would go on strike again as soon as the school year was over (exams were coming up). That argues a very poor attitude towards education. Those things have to be addressed. It's a very long and difficult process.

JR   In *After the Last Sky*, you say: "all of us speak of return, but do we mean that literally or do we mean we must restore ourselves to ourselves. The latter is the real point, I think." As you've said many times, Jews all over the world are allowed to return to Israel, but you cannot return. But there you seem to be suggesting more a psychic state of being than a concrete, literal return. Could you say more about what you meant by that.

EWS   I don't know how many people know this, but I'd say probably at least 55 percent of all Palestinians today don't live in Palestine, or in historical Palestine, whether inside Israel as Israeli citizens or on the West Bank and Gaza. So there's a very large community which is made up of refugees of various categories. Some in Lebanon, for example, 300–400 thousand—destitute, unable to work, unable to travel, unable to move. They're the wretched of the earth, and the peace process has nothing to say about them. Eight to nine hundred thousand in Syria of sometimes prosperous, mostly not prosperous refugees, 1.2 million in Jordan, 130–140 thousand in Egypt, and so on throughout the Arab world. In western Europe, the United States, and Latin America there are a fair number of Palestinians, perhaps half a million or more. For most of them, I think, the idea of return, or return—it's very difficult to say this—is unlikely in their own lifetime. And many of the younger generation never lived in Palestine; so either they don't know it or they know it only from their parents. What's impressive is that they still keep the accents, they still keep the sense of where they're from. They may not ever have been there, but they say we're from Nazareth or from Ramallah and so on. So that sense of a tie of some kind is on the one hand metaphorical, but also comes through family who remained and other friends and connections. As against that, Israel has a law of return which entitles every Jew anywhere to become an Israeli citizen. There's nothing comparable to that for Palestinians. And if suddenly by some miracle there was a repatriation allowed for all Palestinians, I don't know—and I don't know anybody who does know—how many Palestinians would actually go back. So, for me, therefore, the question of an actual return is deferred. I certainly won't be able to go back and I'm not sure that I would want to. And maybe I'm not an untypical case; maybe many Palestinians are like that.

But, what return does mean to me is return to oneself; that is to say, a return to history, so that we understand what exactly happened, why it happened, and who we are. That we are a people from that land, maybe not living there, but with important historical claims and roots. Many of our people will continue to reside there. But we have a common self-consciousness of one of the more, in my opinion—not the most, but one of the most—interesting twentieth-century experiences of dispossession, exile, migration. And not only because it's in and of itself connected to the Holy Land, which is saturated with all kinds of significance, but also because it's part of that twentieth-century experience. That's where I feel I have tried to place my emphasis. To speak our case, when we suffer and go through all the terrors of exile and dispossession and the absence of rights. People write me and say, look I don't have a passport; if you live on the West Bank, it says on the passport "Identity unconfirmed or indeterminate"; if you have a refugee's piece of paper in Lebanon, it says, "Nationality: Stateless." The name is never mentioned. When you look and see Palestinians as I do all the time, it's very difficult to say, this is just metaphorical, because it's terrible, it's lived. I think one must never forget that, and that we should try to erect on the ruins of our national history some sense of common purpose, which we still haven't got. We don't know what we are doing.

JR   How compatible would that process be with any kind of statehood? You cite Eqbal Ahmad and use his expression the "pathology of power." Can you envisage a benign, non-coercive form of executive authority? There's a moment in *Musical Elaborations* when you suggest that Strauss's music offers an alternative in its repetitions, in its divagations, in its wanderings, to "more overtly administrative and executive authority." More personally, you have said: "I have never found it interesting to be close to power." Is the idea of a non-pathological authority a contradiction in terms?

EWS   I think it is. I can't imagine it. Speaking in a utopian vein—since you mentioned the Oriental Jews in Israel—I think our best hope is a common struggle with Israeli Jews in historical Palestine to devise a method of coexistence with a minimum of coercion—there's no such thing as no coercion—whether it's through cantons, the way the Swiss have tried to do it, or other ways. But I think the idea of separation or partition, in our time, simply can't work. It simple can't be done, physically. For the Israelis, there's always this tendency to think of us as aliens and therefore the fewer of us around the better, and the best are those you don't see at all. Hence those roads on the West Bank, the so-called by-passing roads. What's so extraordinary is that what the Israelis are now doing on the West Bank and Gaza is really repeating the experience of Apartheid and of what the United States did to the Native Americans. Put them in reservations and or just exterminate them—which the Israelis haven't done, but put them as far away as possible, then the problem will go away. The hope is somehow to break out of those enclosures and to try to work out some method of coexistence with Israelis who are interested in this. I think more can be in time.

JR   Two more questions. This first one I couldn't possibly not ask, although it's almost impossible to ask other than in a tokenist kind of way. How come there are so few women in your writing? All your intellectual inspiration comes from Vico, Auerbach, Spitzer, and so on. I was delighted to find that you'd done some serious research into the belly dancer Tahia Carioca, but are there any women figures from whom you take inspiration? Jane Austen and

George Eliot are not going to be an answer, because F. R. Leavis included them in the great tradition.

EWS   So, you mean, they're OK?

JR   No, so it's not OK. Can you say something about that? Great admirer as I am of yours, as you know, this is glaring.

EWS   Well, you began with Tahia Carioca, an extremely important influence on my early life. Well, no, I sort of resent that in a way, that I have to give a list of approved feminists. . . .

JR   No, I don't want a list; that's not an answer. I want you to say why you think it is that there are so few; to do with your education or whatever.

EWS   Well, certainly that. But don't forget that, for example, in music—actually I've written about this recently—there's this extraordinary masculine world. I remember thinking this when I first encountered the *Great Composers* by Sigmund Spaeth, one of the first books I read about music when I must have been about twelve, who used to be known as the "tune detective." Immediately I saw the title *Great Composers*, I assumed, and I turned out to be right, that they were all men. Growing up, my only encounter with women composers was a film I saw four times, which I reintroduced at a film festival in New York last year, called *A Song to Remember*, in which Katherine Hepburn played Clara Wieck, Clara Schumann. That was my idea of the woman composer, but I couldn't detach it from Katharine Hepburn, because I didn't know any of Clara Schumann's music, except a few melodies that Schumann had written variations on.

And I always went to all-male schools, and the ethos—I think you have to blame this on the British a little bit—the ethos was terribly masculine. In my higher education, there were no women as students, none as professors, neither at Princeton when I was an undergraduate nor at Harvard. My first encounter with a celebrated academic was Jacqueline de Romilly, a classicist who is a member of the Collège de France. I didn't know her at the time but I heard her lecture. I was invigorated by that because it broke the monotony. Then I've tried to educate myself, but too late probably, in the history and writing by women about women of the last few years. But it's true, my experiences, those I feel most comfortable with and have written about mostly, are those defined and shaped by men.

JR   This isn't to let you off the hook, but when my cousin left his primary school on his way to Clifton, his headmaster said, acutely embarrassed: "Now, when you leave this school, you're going to meet other chaps, called girls." So obviously, you had a bit of that.

One final question. The occasion of your being in England is to inaugurate the Empson Lectures at Cambridge University; you've chosen to talk about "Transgression and Authority in Opera." I was fortunate enough to hear the first of these lectures when you gave it at the Collège de France. You talk about Mozart's vision of the "protean, unstable, undifferentiated" nature of human identity, his view that the "stabilities of marriage and the social norms habitually governing human life are inapplicable, because life itself is elusive and inconstant." It seemed to me that you were saying that what Mozart understood about death casts its shadow back across the pretensions, the false and killing certainties of social norms and conventional human arrangements. It seemed a new departure for your work, incredibly moving and quite inspiring. How can that kind of insight be linked into the kind of political vision and hopes you have for the future?

EWS   I don't think it can. But it's there. I know it's there in a sense that I feel—and I don't mind talking publicly about it—have for the last few years felt the impress or weight of mortality. So whatever sense of urgency I feel, whatever sense of hastening towards the end, I think Mozart was right about. It is basically almost Schopenhauerian, that there's a kind of indistinguishable, seething, endlessly transforming mass into which we are going. It really is very much part of what I'm writing about. One of the reasons for this—I think this is the last thing I should say now, so that we could maybe have some questions, if people want to ask them—is that I've become very, very impatient with the idea and the whole project of identity: the idea, which produced great interest in the United States in the sixties and which is also present in the return to Islam in the Arab world and elsewhere, that people should really focus on themselves and where they come from, their roots and find out about their ancestors—the book and television program Roots. That strikes me as colossally boring and totally off the mark. I think that's the last thing that we should be thinking about in a way. What's much more interesting is to try to reach out beyond identity to something else, whatever that is. It may be death. It may be an altered state of consciousness that puts you in touch with others more than one normally is. It may be just a state of forgetfulness which, at some point, I think we all need—to forget.

JR   Thank you. I think we should stop with that and open it up now to questions. I shall relay the questions: How can the amount of financial backing that the United States gives to Israel possibly be justified, even in terms of the language of security that is used to explain a lot of the military investment that goes in from the States?

EWS   I think that's very important. I think the notion of security in the United States, especially after the cold war, has increased. You have to understand how much the United States now spends on defense alone, and defense spending was never an issue during the last election, which gave us Clinton another time. The defense budget of the United States is now five times that of the entire rest of the world's defense budgets. You can imagine how much we're talking about. That argues an imperial vision in which Israel, according to the United States, is a strategic partner of the United States in the Middle East, the only reliable one, because the most powerful, the best air force, nuclear power, and so forth. That's very, very important. And why? Because—and one of the main reasons for the Gulf War speaks to this—because it assures the United States a powerful hold on Middle Eastern oil. Very, very little of our oil in the United States comes from the Middle East, but it assures the United States a strategic advantage over the rest of the industrialized world, namely Europe and Japan. So that's one very important factor.

Number two, just as important, is that there's a sense of shared identity between the United States and Israel for all kinds of reasons, [including] the Old Testament. You have to remember the United States is the most religious country in the world. There was a poll taken a few years ago in which 88 percent of Americans believed that God loved them. So it's very easy to identify with Israel. There's a sense in which there's the errand into the wilderness. Cromwell was a Zionist, for example, and if you look at the early Puritan writings in America, they repeat the idea that the Jews should go back and that there should be this spiritual errand.

But there's also the fact that the Arabs, and especially the Muslims, are perceived still as an exotic, threatening people. I wrote a book about it called *Orientalism* that dealt with that. It's still very much the same, even more so now. They talk about worldwide terrorism. There's much more terrorism in the United States. I mean, this guy McVeigh, who's on trial now in Denver—a white man and a very patriotic American—has killed more people. It has nothing to do with the Middle East, but the notion of terrorism is associated with Muslims and Arabs. And Israel is associated with the opposite. It's Western. Its culture is Western and so forth.

And lastly, there is, as you suggested, a very powerful pro-Israeli lobby in the United States. There's nothing even remotely comparable on the Arab side. There's no Arab lobby. There's no effort made. And, in fact, most of the Arab leaders today are anxious to get into bed with the United States and Israel. There's an objective as well as a subjective alliance between most of the rulers of the Arab world today, whether it's Egypt or Saudi Arabia, or obviously Jordan or Palestine or Morocco, and of course, all of the Gulf. They see a common interest to be preserved between them and the United States because the United States as a status quo of power always has protected, as they did the Shah of Iran and the Emperor of Ethiopia. But even more important than the pro-Israeli lobby, there is a very admirable—because energetic and present in all, many, facets of American life—there's a very large Jewish community in the United States. And there isn't an Arab one like that.

So all of these factors make it possible for this identification of interests, identification of interests with an "s," between the United States and Israel to be so strong, and it continues. It grows more every year. Just one last thing. I just remembered that when Netanyahu was in Washington in March, supposedly to hear from Clinton that he, that the United States, was opposed to the building of that settlement, at the same moment, there was a meeting, the annual convention of AIPAC, the American Israel Public Affairs Committee, which is the chief pro-Israeli lobby in America, at which Gore was speaking on the very day that Clinton was speaking to Netanyahu. His speech was televised nationally; I saw it. He said that the United States supports Israel unconditionally. So what are we talking about? We're talking about a very powerful tie that has taken years to build and for which there is no Arab counter-response.

JR   The question is: Edward Said has said that the role of the intellectual is to criticize authority, but isn't there a point when the previously oppressed take over that authority, when that role of the intellectual should perhaps cease and should become one of support?

EWS   Yes, I think to a certain extent support is warranted, if we're talking about a defensive or weak government that is perhaps just as you said, as a result of the dispossessed taking over, like in the early days after the Algerian victory over France in 1962. One felt that one should support the efforts of a newly independent people who had had 130 to 140 years of colonialism. So the representatives of this revolution needed support. Yes, I think so, in a situation like that. But this is where perhaps we disagree as regards much of the great miseries of the postcolonial world, whether Algeria itself or numerous sub-Saharan African countries, certainly the Middle East, where in my generation, for example, somebody like Abdel Nasser came to power, and I was a great supporter of his—that's where the problem begins. Because support what? Unconditionally? I think the role of the intellectual is never to give unconditional support. I think the difficult thing is somehow to make your stand while giving support, but it's not easy. You said, the easy thing is to just criticize. No, you give support, but you also try and maintain some level of skepticism and detachment, and the integrity of your principles, so that when you see the abuses begin, as they always do, you don't just shut up and say, well, in the name of the country or the name of the revolution, et cetera, I must keep quiet. But you stand out, and you say this, that, and the other thing. And that's always happened, too. We don't know enough about that brief, transitional moment in history after colonialism has ended or revolution has taken place when certain people do do that.

To come back to Abdel Nasser. A whole generation of people who are now in their seventies, who at the time were in their thirties, were imprisoned for many years because they spoke up. And they were themselves nationalists and antiroyalists, they supported the revolution and so on, and they spoke up. They said, this is wrong. You can't have a democratic society and have such a powerful role for the army, the secret police, et cetera. You can't solve, on a theoretical level, all problems by simply using the words, "It's in the interest of the people." And they were punished. He put thousands of people in jail, tortured them, removed six, seven, eight, ten years of their lives for that. Well, you know, it was an important revolution and an important transformation that took place in the Third World when Nasser was in power, but there are all these abuses that also took place, and not enough has been said about that.

JR   One more question: The first point was to say that Israel is made up of many different communities at odds with each other, and the questioner cited Amos Oz talking about it as a patchwork and asked Edward Said whether he could envisage speaking to or working with people like that. The next point refers to people like Hanan Ashrawi who were critical of the Palestinian authority, but who have now gone across, and to ask Edward Said whether he could envisage a more active role for himself in this political process. The questioner ended up by saying he does not believe that Edward Said is as skeptical as he has presented himself this evening.

EWS   Hanan Ashrawi condemned the strike, the teachers' strike, for example. She said they haven't got a right to strike.

The question of the peace camp in Israel is a complicated question and I don't really have time to go into it, but I think there are many different people who talk about peace for whom peace is not the same thing that it is for me. I mean, peace is one of those words that nobody can be against. How could you be against peace? But I remember Amos Oz in particular, because the day of the Oslo signing in September 1993, he and I were interviewed together by Michael Ignatieff. Or rather I was in New York, he was, I guess, here, or in England, in London. And he went first and then I went; we didn't talk to each other. And the last thing he said is this peace agreement is the second biggest victory for Zionism. In other words, he saw it as a great victory for Israel that it had managed to do as well as it did with the peace. So there's that kind of peace, the Peace Now group, which is mostly affiliated with the Labor Party, that produced people like Oz and others, whom I don't feel represent the kind of peace that I want, which is a peace of equals. You know, there's a sense in which when Israelis say, we want peace, I understand this, I'm not condemning it. I'm simply saying it means, let's be done with this problem. Let's end it. I can understand that. But that doesn't mean justice. It doesn't mean dealing with the facts of what Israel did to the Palestinians. I'm not saying the Palestinians are innocent. But it means you have to deal with the realities, which is that every kibbutz in Israel is built on Arab land. And people lived there once and they were thrown away. And Israeli historians, now this is an important point, so-called revisionist historians like Benny Morris, many of them have revealed these facts. But that's not the same thing as when Amos Oz said we want peace as a kind of PR. So I think one has to be very choosy in picking one's partners, and I don't believe there's anything wrong with saying I prefer this type of discourse, this kind of dialogue with X than I do with Y. That's one of the great mistakes the PLO made: they always went with the people who are close to power. The people who interest me are the people who are not in power—like Shahak, whom I mentioned earlier, or Leibowitz—who are not part of the government, people of conscience. And that constituency has to be addressed.

Now, on the Palestinian situation, about what has happened, well, to put it simply, I think that power has corrupted most intellectuals. Again, I can understand it because people need to live after years of occupation. Don't forget that the Israeli occupation still goes on. We're talking about the longest military occupation of the twentieth century; it's thirty years this year, actually. So people have to live; they have to take care of themselves. And what happens is when they join whatever it is, this little authority of Arafat, they become prisoners of it, and their views change because they want to preserve their influence and their prominence and so on and so forth, which is sad. But I think it has to be described as such rather than saying, well, these are the needs and we all have to stand by the leader. I refuse that idea. And they've told it to me many times. You know, now that Netanyahu is here, why don't you stop. You're really helping the Zionists now. I think that's total nonsense because not everything that is being done by the Palestine Authority is good for Palestine or for the Palestinians. In fact, a lot of it isn't. If there's a report about Israeli torture in the prisons, legal torture, and the Palestinians do torture, why are we excused? We shouldn't be. Torture is bad, whoever does it.

I'm not sure I understood what you meant when you said that I'm not as skeptical as I seem.

JR   He wants you to play a more active role.

EWS   No, I said, I'm not interested in two states. I think Arafat and Oslo are the end of the two-state possibility. It simply hasn't worked. There are too many Israeli settlements. They've taken too much land. The most that in their wildest dreams, Israeli leaders, whether of the Left or Right, have said that they're willing to give up is maybe, what, 50 percent of the West Bank? Let's say they give up 50 percent of the West Bank. The settlements will be there. The roads will be there. The Palestinian towns will be divided from each other. They'd be noncontiguous. And 50 percent of the West Bank, the West Bank plus Gaza, is 22 percent of the whole of historical Palestine. And if you take 50 percent of it, you're left with 10 percent. Well, what kind of a deal is that? And anyway, you can't redraw the map because it is just like that. So the answer has to be that we're both condemned to the same piece of land, if you look at it from the point of view of the history of Palestine. Therefore, we should find partners on either side of the divide and go forth. There's no constitution in Israel. I think there should be one. There's no constitution in Palestine either. There should be one there, too. I think basic rights should be defined. I think people can start talking about common rights that entitle Palestinians to the same rights as Israeli Jews, Palestinian Arabs and Israeli Jews, and so on and so forth. It's quite clear from there.

JR   I want to stop there, but by underlining what Edward Said has just said as a plea for forms of connection that seem—as he has said so eloquently this evening—both historically impossible and yet politically vital. And his image of human beings as receptacles that would be open to each other and take in as much as the sea might be the utopian note on which we might choose to conclude this evening.

W. J. T. MITCHELL

The panic of the visual: a conversation with Edward W. Said

WJTM   I thought that we would just start with the motivation for this interview, which was to draw you out about questions on visual arts and the media.
When I first broached the idea about interviewing you about the visual arts,
your first response was that you might have nothing to say.

EWS   [Laughter] It was also my second one.

WJTM   I don't believe it, of course. And on the basis of that, I want to pursue it. I want to know what you make of that as your first—and second—reaction. Why did you seem to want to hold it off?

EWS   Well, because, I will tell you quite honestly, because when it comes
to the oral and the verbal, the auditory and the verbal, I have a very highly developed vocabulary and considerable experience and practice in talking about
them. When it comes to the visual arts, with a few exceptions, in my writing,
I haven't dealt with them, so I feel somewhat tongue-tied.

WJTM   Tongue-tied? This is a novel experience for you.

EWS   It definitely is.

WJTM   What are the specific visual arts that you don't feel tongue-tied
about? You said there were some exceptions.

EWS   Yes, many exceptions, in a sense, as I thought about the questions
you sent me. I can talk with some effectiveness about individual things. But
just to think about the visual arts generally sends me into a panic.

WJTM   Perhaps we should call this conversation "The Panic of the Visual."

Let's start by talking about museums. Are you a regular museum goer? And which museums do you find yourself revisiting most regularly?

EWS   Well, I'm not a regular museum goer, actually. I tend to go to museums if they have shows that are of interest to me, and, occasionally, if I find myself in physical proximity to one, without planning or premeditation, I go into one. That was the case a couple of weeks ago. I was on Fifth Avenue, and I hadn't been to the Frick in a long time, and I said to myself, "Well, let me just go and look," and I did that. That's the kind of thing that I do. I don't visit galleries very often. I might go with a friend to see something specific, but I could go to Paris half a dozen times and not visit the Louvre. But I might go, as I did a couple of years ago, to see something at the Grand Palais.

WJTM   And as you walk into a museum, do you find your steps going to any particular department? Toward painting, sculpture, photography?

EWS   I would say painting and photography more than sculpture. Although, I recall a period about thirty years ago, when I became suddenly, tremendously, involved in Rodin, whose work I had never seen. It must've been more than thirty years ago. And I visited the Rodin museum and started to collect prints of the sculptures I had seen. But mostly it's paintings, and I would say that with very few exceptions, most of my interest is focused on the period, let's say, from the late eighteenth century to the present. I find that earlier paintings, let's say Renaissance paintings, on the whole, don't really excite my visual senses.

WJTM   So historically, basically the same interests that you have in literature.

EWS   Oh, *except* in literature, especially in English, I tend to go back considerably to the earlier periods. I'm very fond of Langland and much of Elizabethan and Jacobean drama. So my range in visual art is less catholic than literature, I think.

WJTM   Now, you mentioned the Louvre before. As you probably know, in recent years, the Louvre has invited a number of people who are not really curators, not experts on visual art, to curate exhibitions. That is, to make some kind of personal selection from their archives. If you could do that, with the Louvre or with some museum, what would you do?

EWS   Well, I haven't thought about that very much. The first name that comes to mind is somebody who has been a great passion of mine for most of my adult life, and that is Goya. And I'd certainly want to do it around Goya and, to a great extent, all of his work. Including the earlier stuff and then the bullfighting pictures and the portraits and then, of course, the rather visionary, and dramatic pictures of his last years. There's something about Goya that strikes me as absolutely essential, at least in my experience.

WJTM   Can you say a little more about that? What is it about Goya?

EWS   I think it's a number of things. One is that there's a kind of freedom and fantasy, and an almost melodramatic sense. You know, like Saturn eating his children, or the various paintings from the house of the dead, *The Disasters of War*, the painting about the execution of May the third—these are very compelling to me. There's a kind of detachment. I mean, they're very involved, very free paintings, in many ways. But I feel the kind of ironic distance that he has at the same time that he's so passionately involved in the subject that he cares about. There's a kind of gentleness in the middle of all the violence that impresses me a great deal. And then, above all, to me, tremendously effective colors. You know the violence of the colors, the swirling of them, the freedom with which he throws them around the canvas. It's very powerful, and they stay in my mind as no other paintings do.

WJTM   As I listen to you talk about this, I can't help associating all the qualities you find in Goya with . . .

EWS   Blake.

WJTM   No. Not really. Perhaps Blake. But, no, with you yourself.

EWS and WJTM   [Laughter]

WJTM   That is, your position with relation to a whole set of very conflicted and even violent situations in politics. Particularly in relation to the Palestinian movement with which you have kind of an ironic attachment, a gentleness and passionate skepticism. Your posture there has been, can I say, Goya-esque?

EWS   Well, you can say that. But, I mean, I'm not saying it. But the other thing that I've also always been very impressed with, especially remembering one of Goya's paintings in the Frick, is his absolutely unreverential quality towards aristocrats and authority. There's always, you know, some gig or some flaw that you see that he seems anxious to point out, even in the kinds of painting that most painters I know of would not actually want to do. I mean going a step in the direction of somebody like Francis Bacon. It's almost like that, but it isn't.

WJTM   Yes. I think that's a very shrewd observation, actually.

EWS   I find that very compelling. That's another thing that I identify with in Goya . . . absolute unwillingness to take authority for anything more than something that is obviously put on and posed and dressed up and self-regarding. One of the things that you notice in all of his aristocrats is a sense that they take themselves very seriously and that they think of themselves as quite grand people. And you get that sense, but at the same time you get—Goya, somehow, I don't know how he does it—some sense of comment on that. You know, the way Glenn Gould played Bach or some composer—you're not only getting the music but also a kind of intelligent commentary on it. And in Goya's case, it's always unreverential.

WJTM   Yes. It's as if he has found some kind of middle ground between realism and caricature . . .

EWS   Yes, exactly, exactly.

WJTM   . . . and is capable of treating people with a certain amount of sympathy and detachment simultaneously. Not turning them into a total stereotype, but certainly not taking them at their own estimation of themselves.

EWS   Exactly. That would certainly be true.

And then I would want to put, since we're talking about Spain, you know, Velázquez, a painter who doesn't really speak to me as much as El Greco does. Particularly in the later paintings, the religious paintings and the still lifes, you know, the landscapes, the *View of Toledo*. There's something quite haunted and almost frightening about them that's always mystified and drawn me to them. You know those great elongated figures, particularly the clerics and the church figures that he was so interested in. All of whom, unlike Goya, filled one with fear and a kind of mysteriousness. To someone like me, who is quite secular and unschooled in the ways of the church of his time, all this suggests hidden labyrinths and the powerful siege of the Inquisition and the ordeals of faith and vision at the same time. So I would sort of associate the two, but then I would go forward to include a certain kind of photography.

WJTM   The most sustained piece of critical writing about the visual arts that I know of by you is probably your collaborative photographic essay with Jean Mohr, *After the Last Sky*. I wondered if you could talk a little bit about the specific relation with photography. When did you . . .

EWS   We've dropped the curatorial question that you asked me?

WJTM   Well, we can stay with it if you like. I actually did have a second part to that which was . . .

EWS   No, no. I was just going to add Picasso, who also means a lot to me, particularly in association with those visionary, unspeakably volatile paintings of Goya. And the almost ecstatic quality that you find in some of the El Greco paintings, you also find in the *Demoiselles d'Avignon*, for example, of Picasso and in some of those Cézanne paintings of the mountains and the scenery around Aix, which have meant a great deal to me. And then, also, the kind of semihysterical paintings of van Gogh, which, you know, have all kinds of literary resonances.

But to get to the reference about Jean Mohr. I never attempted anything like that, and it was, I think, at a period when I had been particularly involved in Palestinian politics and feeling very, very strongly about two things. One was the absence in what I was doing—which was speaking and writing—of any kind of personal dimension to it, and I found myself so involved in the collective and the official and the unofficial that I felt there was something profoundly askew in what I was writing about. And the second thing was a very strong feeling of exile, having been for many years, at that point, about twenty years, involved politically and not having been able to go to the Middle East. This was also during the middle of the Lebanese civil war, so I couldn't go there. And I knew I was unable to go to Palestine, because I was a member of the National Council. I tried several times to go to the West Bank and Gaza, but when friends put out feelers to the Israelis, I was told I would not be allowed in or I would be put in jail immediately, or something of that sort. But I felt very strongly the sense of being unable to connect directly. And it was at that time in the early '80s that I met John Berger. I had written a review of the book he did with Jean Mohr, *Another Way of Telling*, which impressed me a great deal because it was really about the way one could narrate with pictures.

WJTM   Yes.

EWS   Jean is a rather taciturn, modest man, and he said, "You know, I have an archive of eight or nine thousand photographs of Palestinians that I've been taking since I worked for the Red Cross, beginning in 1948." So I remember visiting him and going through this archive. And then there was another event, at that time, perhaps the climax of the whole thing, which was this 1983 UN conference on Palestine, for which I was a consultant. So I suggested, having seen his pictures, to the organizers in Geneva that we hang some of his pictures in the entrance of the UN in Geneva, and they accepted, but they said that the only way they could get the Arab states to agree to this, was, ironically, that we not have any captions. I tell this story at the beginning of *After the Last Sky*.

WJTM   I remember it well.

EWS   So there's that sense of the silent pictures without a commentary, which itself would be intrusive and political from the point of view of the Arabs. I was considered to be a kind of unguided missile. They thought I might say the "wrong thing." So I felt compelled, in a sense, to do the book. And so we spent, or, rather, I spent weeks and weeks making a selection of the photographs from his enormous archive. And he didn't demur. I mean, it wasn't his choice, it was my choice. Occasionally, he would say, "Well, I'm not so sure I see this picture quite the way you do." And I wasn't really looking for pictures—this is very important—I wasn't really looking for photographs that I thought were exceptionally good, as opposed to ones that were not exceptionally good. I was just looking at photographs that I felt provoked some kind of response in me. I couldn't formulate what the response was. But I chose them. And then, looking at the photographs and having them spread out all over the floor for weeks on end, I then began to group them in series. And I couldn't, at that point, tell myself or anyone else what the series were, but they seemed to belong together. Then I broke them down into four groups with series within them. And I felt that I was actually doing it in a kind of abstract way. That's to say, I was really working according to principles that are much easier for me to deal with within the nonrepresentational art of the Islamic world. You know, where there were certain kinds of patterns that you could see that were not representational in the sense, you know, that they had a subject, but they had some motif and rather a musical motif. And so I decided that I would do the book in four parts. Then I devised topics for each of the parts and proceeded accordingly. The last thing was that I arranged the pictures on the page in a particular way. At the top of the page, on the side of the page, lengthwise, full length, framed, unframed, that kind of thing.

WJTM   I don't think I fully realized the extent to which this whole procedure was almost a musical operation.

EWS   Yes, yes. Because I couldn't find a simple scheme for it that had a kind of narrative, or even a philosophical equivalent.

WJTM   Yes.

EWS   And so I ended up calling the first one "States" and the second one "Interior," and the third one "Emergence" and the fourth one "Past and Future," which are, you know, fairly innocuous and abstracting. I tried to fill them with the sense of the primitive meaning of those things, in terms of Palestinian statements, the state of Palestinian life, the people. In the second part, for example, inside their houses, how they inhabit these displaced places. The first picture, for example, which I thought was a wonderful photograph, was of a doorway in a refugee camp in Jordan, which had lots and lots and lots of scribbling and writing over it and a little child peeking through the door. And that struck me as the perfect example to start the thing off, because it all really had to do with the min al-dakhil, which is "from the interior" and what that means to Palestinians.

WJTM   Yes. So in some sense there were photographs that you thought were just marvelous images in themselves for pulling out some essential feature . . .

EWS   Yes.

WJTM   . . . of Palestinian identity.

EWS   But I couldn't, and I still can't, with any certainty, talk about them with any confidence, talk about them as photographic objects. I couldn't analyze them. I was really more interested in how they corresponded to or in some way complemented what I was feeling. And, of course, underlying the whole thing was the theory that I had written about in an essay that had appeared in the *London Review of Books* called "Permission to Narrate." And I talked about the difficulties of Palestinian narratives . . . that is to say, we didn't have and couldn't formulate a linear narrative in the national sense for all kinds of reasons. There were too many obstacles, we were too divided over this and that, and the absence of a center made our lives essentially fragmented. And so, you know, departing from that, then I said, well, I can't tell a story in a traditional way or in an accepted way. And I had to do something else.

WJTM   Was the dating of the photographs important to you? Did it matter to you whether a photograph came from 1965 or 1975?

EWS   No. I didn't find that at all important. I found, instead, that what was important was the face. I would look at it, and if the face said something to me, then I might, or might not, ask Jean who the person was, and he would inevitably then tell me who the person was and what his story was — why he took the picture or what was interesting about him. But that wasn't always the case, and I chose a lot of the pictures precisely because you couldn't date them. There was a kind of, a kind of . . . how shall I put it? There was a kind of . . .

WJTM   Unknowability?

EWS   Yes. Exactly.

WJTM   On the issue of the unknowable: I think one of the most intriguing and moving moments in that book for me is when you describe looking at the photograph of a woman who's shown in a very close-up portrait. She has her chin in her hand, she's looking directly at the camera . . .

EWS   . . . and her face is full of lines.

WJTM   Yes. You start talking about the picture of her as something that captures our life at home.

EWS   Right.

WJTM   And then I believe that it was your sister, or perhaps Mariam, who said to you, "No, that's Mrs. Farage."

EWS   Yes, exactly.

WJTM   And there was this moment in your text where you pause and realize you'd been caught with the unknowable suddenly turning into the knowable . . .

EWS   Exactly.

WJTM   . . . and it really threw you off . . .

EWS   Also, feeling at the same time that, as I said, something had been lost.

WJTM   Yes.

EWS   I was interested in the slippage between not recognizing her and then recognizing her, or, you know, suddenly because somebody said that that's who she was and then I remembered her. And then realizing, in between the two sensations, there was this quite real face, and in that face was something that I couldn't describe. I remember then dividing that photograph off from the rest of the chapter, the end of the chapter called "Interior."

WJTM   Are there going to be any photographs or other kinds of illustrations in the memoir that you're working on?

EWS   Yes. Last week, I talked about this with my editor, my English editor, who was here, and we were working on the manuscript. I mean, I've turned in about one hundred thousand words of it now, and so we have a pretty good sense of how it's going to end. And, hopefully, of when it's going to end. And we thought that it would be necessary to have some photographs of a rather personal time from my past. I don't really know how some of them got here, but there are a lot of photos sitting in big boxes in one of our cupboards that I've seemed to collect over the years, beginning with pictures from the late '30s right up until the present.

WJTM   And do you think you'll be addressing those or talking about them?

EWS   I do it in a funny way in the text. In other words, there are certain things . . . For example, since you mentioned it, this morning, I was working on one of the great characters of my memoir, which was my father. We had a very, to me, painful and quite traumatic relationship. He was a very laconic man. I never knew really very much about his past. But, in addition, he was always there on top of me in the sense that he was trying to make me do certain kinds of things, all that had to do with my body. I mean, I felt that from the age of eight—seven or eight—that there were many things wrong with me. Until I was twenty-one, he totally dominated me. I remember when I graduated from Princeton, we went to New York. He'd always been, since I was a boy, complaining about the fact that I had very bad posture. He was always after me for that. And then we went from Princeton to New York to shop in Manhattan. I don't remember exactly where, but he bought me a truss, which I wore—I mean, it was straight out of Freud! . . .

WJTM   [Laughter]

EWS   . . . which I wore to keep my back straight. And we were that kind of thing. There was always something wrong. In the passage I'm writing now, about things from that same time, when I found out in 1961—I remember the moment very, very well—that he had melanoma, which ultimately killed him . . . I mean, it took hold and then metastasized into lung cancer and all the rest of it. When I realized that he was going to die—and that's the passage I'm writing now—it was like the earth fell out from underneath me. I realized also the particular kind of affection I had for him and the relationship that we had. I have a picture of my father and me from 1937 or 1938. I was a tiny child. It's a picture on the beach in Alexandria. He's standing behind me, or rather sitting behind me, and I'm standing. And, you know, he's sustaining me, on the one hand, and yet one could also see the power and the authority which dominated me at that time.

WJTM   Are there other kinds of images that take you back to these formative moments?

EWS   Yes. I had wanted to mention that because of your having sent me these questions about visuality—arts, media, experiences, memories—that the visual culture that did surround us was almost all nonancient Egyptian, non-Pharaonic, and almost always Islamic. There were no museums in Jerusalem, and, in Cairo, my experience was more with architecture and patterns and designs that were ultimately calligraphic than with perspective and the representation of a figure, and with iconography of the sort that one finds in Western pictorial traditions. So the painterly and the picturesque were, to me, very obscure. There were no keys to them.

Then, there were two very powerful visual experiences of my youth, and I remember them very well. One of them was the wax museum, to which we would go often because I was so fascinated by the scenes from Egyptian history. You know, the opening of the Suez Canal, the dynasties. This was during the monarchical period. They were lifelike figures, and I remember looking at them—I was very small, five, six, seven at the time—and always expecting them to move and say something, and, of course, they didn't. But I kept going back. A close friend of my parents, a historian, who lived in Beirut, would come to Cairo once a year or twice a year. I remember one of the great pleasures of those days was to go to the wax museum with him and have him make the speech and make the figures seem to speak.

WJTM   Yes.

EWS   That was very important. And the second visual experience that was fascinating to me were the exhibitions in the Agriculture Museum, which must have been built by the British, a series of three huge buildings in Giza. The central building had exhibits of all the various wheat, sugarcane, and agricultural products, and instructive displays about Egyptian ecology, as well as birds and animals, and so on. But what fascinated me the most were the glass cases with exhibitions of various diseases, not lifelike images but anatomical representations of the human body. I would go back to them time after time after time to look at bilharzia, elephantiasis, and things of this sort.

WJTM   Were these pictures of people afflicted with . . .

EWS   But they weren't pictures only. There were pictures and models.

WJTM   I see.

EWS   And they gripped me with, of course, a terrified fascination.

WJTM   When you say "models," you mean models of the bacteria, themselves?

EWS   Of the . . . let's say . . . I remember, for instance, an abdomen afflicted with elephantiasis . . . not only elephantiasis, but yaws. You would see the front of it and then a cutaway, so you could see the inside, that kind of thing. They were like medical models.

WJTM   Yes, yes.

EWS   I was extremely taken with these and, of course, read the inscriptions many times over and felt myself to be threatened by them because they seemed to be all around. Aside from that, it wasn't until I came to Europe for the first time in the early '50s that I went to art museums. Before that, museums simply weren't part of my experience at all.

WJTM   So this does certainly make plausible some of your reticence, your feeling that you came late to the Western art traditions.

EWS   I came very late. And, of course, there was such a heavy emphasis upon the writing and the reading on the one hand and the musical on the other in my efforts.

WJTM   Yes. I find your account of the Agricultural Museum in Giza particularly fascinating, since it seems like the most unlikely impressive visual experience for a child. Do you think that that has resonated in any way for you later? What does it connect to for you now?

EWS   It may be that the influence and the images are now coming back to me partly because of my disease, you know and the visualization one has of it. But the idea that one's body conceals within it, in a way that becomes more and more visible, the progress of a disease, a dread sort of decomposing, or degenerative or distorting process, is to me, extremely compelling. And I remember very well, for instance, also, in my youth, seeing a movie of *The Picture of Dorian Gray*.

WJTM   Oh, yes.

EWS   I was in my early teens at the time, and I don't know whether you remember the film, but George Sanders was in it, and Dorian was played by Hurd Hatfield. The painting, which was revealed in the last part of the film up in the attic, as he went on and became more decadent and more degenerate, and he remained as beautiful as ever, the painting aged and became decomposed. There was a painting which I researched, and it was by Ivan Albright— do you remember him?—an American artist of the '30s and '40s who was fascinated by images of decomposition and disease. They commissioned him for this film. I remember this because it resonated with my experiences at the Agricultural Museum.

WJTM   Perhaps this also links back to your fascination with Goya and with El Greco, both of whom represent the deformation of the body . . .

EWS   Yes.

WJTM   . . . so vividly.

EWS   Absolutely.

WJTM   Now, I want to ask you about the first time you *saw* an opera, as opposed to hearing one on records, and what the effect was of encountering opera as spectacle for the first time? Was that an important experience?

EWS   Well, I remember exactly the first opera I saw. I must have been about, twelve or thirteen. It was in Cairo. There was a season of Italian opera every year in the winter. I think it must have begun around January and ended at the end of February for two months. My parents had a subscription. I was taken to the opera for the first time to see *Andrea Chenier*, which is, in my opinion, a third-rate opera by a fifth-grade composer [Laughter] called Giordano. I'd never heard of him or the opera, but I remember the first question I asked my parents, and I think maybe it was my father: "Do they sing all the way through, or is there any talking?" And they said, "No it's singing all the way through, no talking." So I was fairly intimidated by this, because I didn't know Italian. And when we went, I was much oppressed by the notion of listening to an opera, to music, to words I couldn't completely understand. But I remember being completely overwhelmed by the spectacle for which I wasn't at all prepared. I mean, I thought it would be just people. I hadn't seen performances or attended performances of oratorios and various choirs. That would have been the limit of my musical experiences. But to see it . . . I remember the man who played Gerard, who was the baritone villain in the opera, Gino Bechi, who was a famous Italian opera singer of the '40s and '50s. Doing the kinds of things on stage that Douglas Fairbanks would do in a movie—fencing, then sliding across the table and doing it while singing all the time. It immensely pleased me. At the same time, I thought the music was uninteresting. I remember also later finding in our record library his big aria, which was called "Enemy of the People," sung by somebody else—I don't remember who, it wasn't Bechi—and listening to it over and over again for sort of confirmation and reliving of this opera that I'd seen only once. Of course, the last thing that really impressed me and gripped me, I should say, about the experience, was that it was so rare. It wasn't something you could go back to, the way you can play a record over again. It wasn't something you could look at again the way you could look at a painting or an object. It was "in time," and it was a very fine moment, and the only way you could recapture it was by memory, and my musical memory was quite formidable in those days. I was able to play over bits of it again in my head, and it wasn't until I came to the United States as an undergraduate at Princeton that I was able to make the further connection with the score.

WJTM   So what do you think is the importance for you of the spectacle in opera? Is this something you find relatively dispensable?

EWS   Not at all. In fact, in recent years, I've become almost obsessed with it. That is to say, I realize that most of my own experiences, most, but not all, of my own experiences of opera going have been ones in which the spectacle is absolutely essential. I have always been immensely troubled by the original idea of that setting and even the direction. The visual elements of the opera were meant simply to be a kind of background to the singer. Throughout my early years of opera going, both in Egypt and at the Met, I remember distinctly the immense power of going to Bayreuth in 1958—I was twenty-two at the time and had just graduated from Princeton—and seeing the effect of this rather more integrated, this rather more interpretive notion of direction and theme in use by the Wagner brothers. I mean, there was a programmatic side to it, that is to say, they wanted to strip away from *The Ring*, from, lets say, all the Germanic and realistic, in the verisimilitudinous sense of the word, baggage of the opera. So there were no helmets, there were no spears, there were no chariots, there were no fur coats, no huts and all the rest of it. It was very abstract. Most of the effects were achieved by lighting and this quite remarkable notion of a disk on which the actor stood, which sometimes would break in half, would sometimes tilt, would sometimes be flat, depending on the action. I thought that kind of spectacle was what I had always missed in representational and eurythmic interpretation. And ever since then, I thought them out. I mean, I've always tried to find directorate and theme designers who think of those visual and dramatic aspects of the opera as equal with the musical, and that's why I've developed such an interest in opera. It's to see the integration of the visual, the dramatic, the musical, and, of course, the historical. I mean, how does history get into these things?

WJTM   Perhaps this is a good time to bring up the question I raised with you about Foucault and his theoretical statements about exactly this problem. I'm thinking particularly of Deleuze's account of Foucault as a thinker whose analytical categories are fundamentally divided between the seeable and the sayable, or the articulable and the visible. Are these distinctions that make sense to you and that you feel are useful?

EWS   Well, I've always felt that when Foucault spoke about epistemology, he certainly didn't have in mind the kind of epistemology one associates, let's say, with Kant or even Wittgenstein. There is, however, a distinctly theatrical component in his work, as if epistemology were a theatrical instrument of some sort.

WJTM   Yes.

EWS   And I recall, in particular, in *Les Mots et les choses*—and I think I was one of the first people to write about it after it came out in France—I remember reading it with tremendous excitement and realizing that Foucault's epistemology always had a kind of visual correlative, the notion of the table, or the tableau, the notion of the theme, the notion of transparency, and so on, which you couldn't always yourself visualize.

WJTM   Right.

EWS   But at least there were hints towards a fundamental dimension of display or theatricality in Foucault's work. And then, in The Archaeology of Knowledge, The Order of Things, and Discipline and Punish, it struck me there that he was particularly anxious, actually, to begin with the visible—in other words, it was the visible that made possible the sayable. For instance, the dismemberment of Damiens, the regicide, which opens the book on the prison, and then, of course, the whole notion in The Archaeology of Knowledge of the archive, which brings to mind, as I think it was intended, scenes from some of Borges. And in the rather special status, which was half seeable, half sayable, of the enoncé, or the statement, and then, in The Order of Things, where he was dramatizing himself, where he talks about standing in a place and speaking in a particular way, I find that all very much part of this kind of combination theater and speech, which was quite remarkable, quite unique.

WJTM   Right. And I take it that what Foucault means by the "heterotopia" is the conjunction of these modes of expressions, the seeable and the sayable . . .

EWS   Yes.

WJTM   . . . modalities that are not exactly commensurate, in that one can't just be straightforwardly substituted for the other.

EWS   Not at all, not at all. I mean, that's why I said correlative, not in the sense of interchangeable but in the sense of one doing something that the other can't do . . .

WJTM   Exactly.

EWS   . . . and if you remove one, then something is missing in the other.

WJTM   Let me take you with this topic to a slightly different territory, and that's the question of space and geography—place, landscaped territory—and the whole issue of the time-space problematic in your own work. I don't exactly have a formulated question about that . . .

EWS   No, but it's, you know . . .

WJTM   . . . it's clearly very important to you.

EWS   It's very clear in my mind.

WJTM   Okay. Please proceed.

EWS   I once evolved a kind of typology, a kind of pedagogic typology of thinkers who proceed according to temporality and are gripped by it, and that would include, of course, the Hegelian tradition, the deconstructive tradition—people like de Man, Derrida, Lukács, and so on—and then what I call the spatial tradition, including figures like Vico and Gramsci. I find it in the Italian materialist tradition, going back to Lucretius, but including Vico and Gramsci. And there the conception of society is essentially territorial, and therefore, in criticism and philosophy, there's a whole question of how you cover one with the other, and how you move between different segments of a contested geography. And then I realized that I belong firmly in the second camp, because a lot of my work really deals with geographical demarcations, geographical spaces.

WJTM   Yes.

EWS   In a way, I think it's part—at least in my own experience—of the universality of the Palestinian experience, which is also about territory and contested space and dispossession, which means you have to do certain things because you don't have the space or the place. It's hard to regain some substitute or equivalent for space if you don't have it. And the relationship between language and space becomes an issue, above all, the notion of writing and distance, which very much informs my thinking about matters of exile and displacement.

WJTM   So earlier, when you talked about narrative and the Palestinian lack of a narrative, would you put that on the same side as the lack of the place, the lack of . . .

EWS   Absolutely.

WJTM   . . . the space?

EWS   The narrative here is a function of speaking from a place.

WJTM   I see. So narrative for you is actually a kind of spatial notion.

EWS   Absolutely. Not a temporal one. I mean, obviously, it has temporal elements—it would be silly not to acknowledge that. But it's principally, for me, the possibility of producing a territorial object, if you like, or a territorial location, as in *Robinson Crusoe*, where, in talking, he revisits, he repopulates, he reenacts both the shipwreck and the establishing of himself on the island. That's the core of it.

WJTM   Could you say something now about visual imagery and your long-standing commitment to secular interpretation—to a secular politics. Like all leftist critics, including myself, you're . . .

EWS   Our number is dwindling . . .

WJTM   Well . . . [Laughter] We'll survive somehow. You've often used concepts like fetishism and idolatry to talk about certain kinds of identity politics, certain kinds of nationalism. I wanted to ask if you have any kind of theoretical reflections on the notions of fetishism and idolatry—that is, the moment when an image becomes an end in itself, becomes personified, becomes mystifying. Are there any limits to your secularism? Do you have any fetishes or idols that you know of?

EWS   Well, as few as possible. Let me start in a kind of humdrum way. I'm very interested in certain kinds of objects, both visually and tactilely, especially fabrics, particularly the fabrics out of which clothes are made. These materials obsess me. I mean, I'm always interested in finding out . . .

WJTM   I've often remarked that your suitcase is at least three times as big as mine when you go on a trip.

EWS   That's something else . . . [Laughter] . . . but, I mean, I'm really choosy about the concept of the suitcases . . . [Laughter] . . . of the sizes.

WJTM   Me, too, but it's because you need all these fabrics with you, right?

EWS   Yes. I don't know. I don't really understand what the origin of it is, but I have a fantastic interest in them and, of course, in style and fashion. I've always been interested in that. I know a great deal about it—costumes. But it goes back, I suppose, to the sense of engagement with those wax figures. For me, they were lifelike, but foreign and strange. I recall that when I became interested in painting, I was also very interested in the texture. I mean the physical texture of what the painter was trying to do. And one of the fascinations I had with Rodin, for example, was his representations of gowns, of folds, of density, of material. That was very interesting.

WJTM   Yes, this is all beginning to come together for me, because I see this as also linked to your interest again in Goya, and the way the integument of the body, even the flesh itself, seems to become part of the paint and to flow off the frame of the body.

EWS   Exactly. I mean, you could call that a fetish if you like, but what's important for me about it is that it's not inaccessible, it's not like a precious object. I've no interest in jewels, for example, at all. I mean, they don't say anything to me. And decoration—in the tradition from which I come—is very interesting to me, but it's decoration of a fairly consistent kind. It's arabesque, it's floral rather than animal—that sort of thing. I'm fascinated by that. One of the ways I listen to music is to listen to that, as well. That's why I'm particularly interested in counterpoint. It's patterns against each other, with each other, not alone. The other thing has to do with the way I grew up and the place I grew up. Certainly after Palestine, well, even in Palestine, I was always conscious of prohibitions on places and objects to which I couldn't go. I mean, Jerusalem, for example, is a very hieratic and ritualized city, where one could go to certain places but one couldn't go to others. Particularly in places like the Holy Sepulcher, where I was very early made aware of not being able to go in or not being welcome into the Greek Orthodox, or the Catholic, or the Armenian Churches. It was a church of many divisions, and some of them were accessible and others were not. So there was always a sense of prohibition and remoteness in those places. The same in Egypt, where we were foreigners, basically. There was our familiar space at home, but once you came out of the house, the city was divided—this was during the monarchy—into areas that were hierarchical—where the king was and where the aristocracy lived. I remember one of my earliest experiences, which had a lot to do with the writing of *Orientalism*, when I was walking in the Gezira Club of which we were members. It was a famous enclave built by the British. The members were mostly foreign, although there were some local members. I was thrown out by the secretary, who was a friend of my father's. I tried to say to him . . . He said, "Don't you know that Arabs are not allowed here?" And I said, "Yes, but we're members." And he said, "Don't argue with me boy, get out!" It was that sense of forbidden space that really sowed, I think, the seeds of my rebellion against the hieratic and the fetishistic and the ritualized and the idolatrous. I felt the need always to go against those prohibitions and those statutes and those forbidden places. The urge to enter those places usually cost me quite dear, going into places where I wasn't wanted, which is what I felt I was doing in *Orientalism*.

WJTM   Your idea being to bring some illumination into those dark or inaccessible places?

EWS   Illumination, but also some disposition to mock them and to show that they were, after all, constructions, and not divinely endowed or somehow spontaneously created. You understand what I mean?

WJTM   Yes. Growing up a Roman Catholic, with veiled tabernacles and sacred icons, how could I not?

EWS   And that's why I've always been so interested in Vico, because Vico was the first writer who taught me that human history is painstakingly made the way you might make a model, or an object, and not endowed with any particularly sacred quality, and therefore, it was the province of the philosopher or the scientist to be able to look at any part of human history with the same secular scrutiny without regard for idols. That's why he was a great admirer of Francis Bacon. I remember I first read Bacon when I was a freshman or sophomore at Princeton, and he fascinated me with the notion of the idol and the tribe and the cave and so on and so forth. So the notion of de-idolizing has always been very important to me.

WJTM   But at the same time, it sounds to me as if you're conceding, at least to the possibility of a certain limited fetishism in yourself that you don't see as equivalent with this mystified, dominant ideology.

EWS   You know, I'll tell you . . . Ever since I got ill, I realize that all this stuff that I care about—for example, my interest in the piano, in my piano . . . I don't use, as you know, computers; I use pens, and I have a very large collection of pens. All these objects that mean a lot to me I feel are easily dispensable tomorrow, because I realize how transitory it is, and I find myself, in a funny way, sort of living the way that passage describes—you know the passage, I've quoted it many times—from Hugh of Saint-Victor, where the person who is the stranger everywhere is somehow at home but not loving the world too much—you know—you're moving on.

WJTM   Yes.

EWS   I have that sense, actually, quite strongly developed, perhaps since I've been ill.

WJTM   Edward, there is one long, last question I want to ask you about the way you reconcile your aestheticism with your politics. I'm thinking of the way you negotiate the tension between your identity as a "high-modernist aesthete," which I take is not an insult for you . . . [Laughter] . . . and your role as a committed political activist. One of the things that's always struck me as remarkable about your career, your writing, is your ability to somehow negotiate the tension between those two things in a marvelous, intricate way. How do you conceive of the relation between art and politics? You consistently affirm a respect for the formal autonomy of the arts and resist reductions of artistic forms to political or ideological issues.

EWS   Right.

WJTM   Yet it's clear at the same time that all your criticism insists on the interweaving of aesthetics and politics, and I wanted to ask how you feel, on reflection, you've negotiated this tension, and also to ask you, more personally, whether you've ever felt baffled or torn by your dual commitments to art and politics, or whether it has just seemed that they are, in your experience, one and the same thing?

EWS   Well, it's certainly not the latter. They're not one and the same thing. And *baffled* is an excellent word for what I often feel with an art whose ideological or political origins are simply irreconcilable with the aesthetic object. The example that always comes to my mind is Wagner. There's no question at all that Wagner was a horrible person in every conceivable respect. But it's very, very difficult to negotiate the leap that you must make between his overt, explicit, endlessly repeated sentiments on the one hand and his music on the other. There's a, there's a . . . you could call it a mystery, you could call it fundamentally irreconcilable . . . there is something there that simply defies comprehension. I think that's probably true of other individual works and artists and their political background. On the other hand, I mean, I don't see how one could write about somebody like Wagner or Delacroix, for example, without taking into account the political context from which they emerge. So what I try to do—whether successfully or not, I can't tell—what I try to do is, in the re-creation of the work or the interpretation of the work, dramatize and present the circumstances—I mean the political circumstances, the historical circumstances, cultural circumstances, ideological circumstances—and try to make the work more interesting as a result without reducing it. I mean, it's much easier to see this in the rereadings of texts for me or in the restaging and reconceiving of musical works, because there you can actively intervene to point the work in a particular direction, to stress certain things, to connect, as I tried to do with Jane Austen, some of the problematic aspects of her tacit endorsement of slavery, not at all to blame her but to connect her to an emancipatory strain of interpretation that comes after her with West Indian writers themselves. To read her along with C. L. R. James, along with the history of colonialism, the history of slavery and so on, trying to reunderstand that history, which in the case of her novels, is occluded or at best marginal. So, that's what I try to do. It's very hard, but it seems to be the most interesting thing about the criticism and interpretation of great works of art.

WJTM   I agree. It is very hard, and I'm struck by the fact that you, of all people, experience it as hard, because you seem to pull it off with such virtuosity so many times, and I think the rest of us are all looking to see how you do it.

EWS   Yes. But I don't think there's any method or secret. There isn't any clue or pattern to it, except the basic one, which is that a great work of art is not an ideological statement, pure and simple.

WJTM   Right.

EWS   And vice versa. I mean, no ideological statement, pure and simple, can become a great work of art. I mean, it's very difficult. You know, it is as Sartre says about Paul Valery: that he was a petit bourgeois. But not every petit bourgeois is a Valery.

WJTM   [Laughter]

EWS   And that's very salutary to keep that in mind. And I think the final point, perhaps the most interesting point, is that there is a pleasure, there's a satisfaction of it's own, that comes with working through this particular type of irreconcilability. And that's why Adorno interests me so much and why the Hegelian tradition has always made me feel suspicious, because there's always the subsumption of contradictions and irreconcilabilities in the higher synthesis, and I don't believe in that synthesis at all. So then you have to have a certain amount of skepticism, too . . .

WJTM   . . . and a certain kind of willingness to stand on very precarious ground . . .

EWS   Oh, absolutely.

WJTM   This is why, for me, the figure of the tightrope walker . . . You're capable of falling . . .

EWS   A walker, or the other one that I like is the circus performer who has whirling plates on those rods, which he has to keep twirling around, otherwise they'll fall . . . and there are always too many, and they are always in danger of falling. But, I mean, if that's not what we're doing, then what the hell *are* we doing?

WJTM   [Laughter] Dropping plates, breaking china everywhere, I suppose.

EWS   By the way, have we finished?

WJTM   No. I wanted to follow up just one more step with this fascinating discussion and that's to push a little further to each side of the art/politics division. Would you agree that if you're not capable of mediating or somehow serving these two masters that it's going to be in some way reductive to both your appreciation, your understanding, of art and the quality of the politics you profess? I think it's obvious with the artistic side that if you simply reduce art to ideology, it's not very interesting.

EWS   No.

WJTM   But I wonder about the opposite side. Suppose politics is just politics. Or is nothing but the art and craft of producing power. To what extent does politics need your kind of aesthetic sensibility, your kind of formalism, to be authentic politics?

EWS   Now, that's a very good question, because, in the end, you see, if you get stuck in the trap into which Foucault inserted himself and was never able to get out except by exiting through subjectivity and the care of the self and all the rest of it, which to me, is uninteresting, then you have to regard politics as not just the production/reduction of power but also as constituting a very complex and rich tapestry of historical experience. Most of which, alas, in the writings of political scientists and polemicists, simply is never given a chance. That's why, for example, I am much more interested in the politics of loss and dispossession than I am in the politics of triumph and fulfillment. I wrote a couple of years ago a long essay on lost causes, and it's clear that you can regard politics that way. I mean, you could look, for example, at E. P. Thompson's *Making of the English Working Class*, which is a history of loss, but out of it comes ennobling and interesting experiences of the sort that don't make it into Parliament or don't necessarily get recorded by historians. So politics has to be more than just the struggle for power. It's a struggle for fulfillment, it's a struggle for recognition, it's a struggle for acknowledgment, it's a struggle for survival, it's a struggle for betterment and liberation. That's what interests me in the end, not the people who are plotting a coup. I mean that sort of Blanquist view of politics. But the process by which civil institutions are built—usually subverted and corrupted, at least in my experience of the politics of the Third World—with a renewed commitment to ideals of human emancipation, enlightenment, and community—it seems to me, in the end, that that's what it's all about. Now, of course, in that there is a terribly important role for the aesthetic. Not as an illustration of it but as part of that same struggle.

WJTM   Central to the practice itself.

EWS   I mean, that's the kind of politics that interest me.

WJTM   As you're speaking, I'm reminded of William Blake's name, his proper name for the artist and prophet. You remember the name of the character? His name is "Los."

EWS   Oh, "Los." Yes, very good. And, of course, reversed, it's "Sol."

WJTM   The traditional Apollonian artist who's above it all . . .

EWS   No, of course, one isn't above it. I mean, I don't believe that one is above it.

WJTM   Right. You are with Blake's Los, the prophet, down in the basement.

Race before racism: the disappearance of the American

Some years ago, I wrote an essay on a singular book that I seemed to have been saving for just this occasion: a tribute to Edward Said. Jack D. Forbes's *Black Africans and Native Americans*, an ambitious and impressive book, seemed to sketch a disappearance of the "American," as much as *Orientalism* had sketched the appearance of an "Orient."[1] Of course, Said is a ground-breaker in our discipline; Forbes belongs to the group of social scientists who have been chipping away at the monolithic Eurocentrism of their disciplines for at least the last twenty years, during the two decades after *Orientalism*, as it were.[2] Therefore, I speak of Forbes in tribute to Said.

How does Forbes restore the American moment in the history of Europe, North Africa, and the Americas in the last five hundred years (321–22)? "American" in this book means "Indians in the colonial era and 'African' . . . [means] presumably unmixed sub-Saharan Africans" (192). Working this out in your head each time "African-American" is used is like a child's lesson, by rote, of the unlearning of Eurocentrism. Forbes makes us rehearse the new meaning of the phrase relentlessly. By the time we come to the following statement, in the closing pages, we know what he means: "*American survivors and African survivors . . . have merged together to create the basic modern populations of much of the Greater Caribbean and adjacent mainland regions*" (270; author's emphasis). It is a mark of the intellectual boldness of *Black Africans and Native Americans* that the "adjacent mainland regions" happen effortlessly to include both the

Americas. The book has earned the right to this bravura gesture, an undoing consonant with the doing of *Orientalism*.

The book's strengths *are* in some sense its weaknesses. There is a certain panoramic quality to the book, its theses stated over and over again. Lists—of runaway slaves, by color, in Valencia (44), of registered slaves in Seville (107), or of slaves sold in Las Palmas (154–55)—proliferate, interspersed with striking single examples: "a pale-colored woman with chestnut hair . . . reportedly seen among the Americans of Vinland . . . in c. 1006" (18); Paul Cuffe, the early-nineteenth-century "American-African mixed-blood" (58); the two "Americans from Newfoundland . . . that [Thomas] More 'had probably seen . . . ' prior to . . . the publication of *Utopia*" (54); the Surinamese boy, "captured in 1775 on a raid against the rebel leader Bonny . . . [who] could not bear to be touched by any white person" (63); the "*esclava lora* named Catalina from Mauritania" (139); Elijah Bass of South Carolina (197); and many, many others. Thus the book not only gives a sense of swarms of people moving over great expanses, it also guards the complementary sense of the starkly singular. The many citations of the usage of racially descriptive terms give us an additional sense of the precarious dynamics of language. I never tired of this multitudinous aspect of the book. It is, however, possible that a more rigorous reader might find the book somewhat repetitive, confusing, and insufficiently theorized. But then, *Orientalism* has had its detractors as well. For this reader, *Black Africans and Native Americans* has the virtue of the watershed.

Forbes's book attempts to show, in its opening chapter, that there was sufficient contact among Africans and Americans, and Americans and Europeans, before Columbus. Columbus represented a rupture, because he returned, and because he "was singular in that he was, from the first, a dedicated slaver and exploiter with an extremely callous and indifferent attitude towards culturally different human beings" (22). One misses the common Marxist argument that he represents a rupture also because he suited the world historical moment. But perhaps that argument is made in the breach.

The second chapter summarizes trans-Atlantic slavery and interaction after Columbus and comes to the conclusion that "*two* great mixed races have developed in the Americas. The one in which African ancestry is strongest we can call 'Eastern Neo-American' because it is most characteristic of the eastern half of the Americas. The other one, in which American ancestry is strongest, we can call 'Western Neo-American' because it is most characteristic of the area from Chile and parts of Argentina to western North America" (64).

The last chapter deals with African American contacts in the modern period and, in its conclusion, simply states the book's main objective: to break through the isolation of the contemporary Native American: "The ancestry of modern-day Americans, whether of 'black' or 'Indian' appearance, is often (or usually) quite complex indeed. It is sad that many such persons have been forced by racism into arbitrary categories which tend to render their ethnic heritage simple rather than complex" (271).

The intervening seven chapters are about words: *Negro, Black, Moor, Loro, Pardo, Mestizo, Mulato, Mustee, Half-Breed, Zambo*, and, finally, *People of Color*. *Mulato* occupies the three middle chapters of these seven. Forbes worries the word as a dog does a bone. He gets behind dictionaries to capture the elusive lexical space between meaning shifts by sheer empirical obstinacy. He teases out usage to show the emergence of juridico-legal practice and rational classification. This is an invaluable quarry, on the level of aggregative apparatuses (power) and propositions (knowledge), for a future Foucauldian who will dare to try to take these further below, into the utterables (*énoncés*) that form the archival ground level (not ground) of knowledge and the nonsymbolizable force field of power.[3] I cannot readily imagine such a person, for the *pouvoir-savoir* (ability to make sense) in question involves "300 to 400 years (twenty generations) of intermixture of a very complex sort, [and] varying amounts of African and American ancestry derived at different intervals and from extremely diverse sources—as from American nations as different as Narragansett or Pequot and the Carib or Arawak, or from African nations as diverse as the Mandinka, Yoruba, and Malagasy" (270–71).

For the perceptive reader, then, Forbes's book at once opens the horizons of Foucault's work, shows the immense, indeed perhaps insuperable complexity of the task once we let go of "pure" European outlines, and encourages a new generation of scholars to acquire the daunting skills for robust cultural history, a relay where Said is a stalwart teammate.

I am not particularly troubled that Forbes does not align himself with the critique of European humanism, as indeed Said does not, either.[4] As Said has argued in "Traveling Theory," political writing in the United States is usually better off without such alignments.[5] Forbes sets up, for example, an opposition between "evidence" and "myth," as does Said between "world" and "text": "I have provided a critical and theoretical basis upon which a new approach to this subject can be erected, a basis informed by the empirical examination of the evidence relating to the meaning of ethnic terms in given spatial or temporal realms as opposed to simply making deductive assumptions based upon myths of the recent past or of the present" (269).

The critique of humanism would honor this impulse and, sensing and guarding its political importance, would still question the adequate justifiability of the binary opposition between myth and evidence, and would question further the vanguardism of theory and the stability of evidence as such, without questioning the usefulness of evidence. Such a critique would interrogate the complicity between the *faith* in theory, truth, and evidence on the one hand, and the *fact* that the racial other has been legally described as incapable of truth telling, of giving, precisely, evidence (198, 214). We must not lose sight of the importance of reclaiming the place of giving evidence—of telling truths—of the importance, even, of truth; but in the process, we must not, paradoxically, advance that very vanguardism of truth-evidence-theory that can generate oppression in its name, again and yet again. And I believe Said can, by the same impulse, be asked to honor the double bind of responsibility and accountability to *radical* alterity, even as he reminds us of the importance of "work, intention, resistance, effort, or conflict." [6]

Like Said, Forbes does, in practice, go a long way to support such questioning. Here, let it suffice to say that those of us who share an interest in the critique of humanism would do well simply to add projects to Forbes's own sense of the vistas opened up by his book. Sometimes this sense appears incidentally—"the impact of Americans upon Portuguese life has not been studied although Camoens in his epic poem *Lusiadas* refers to the *tristes brasis* (sad Brazilians) arriving in Lisbon" (39); "in Africa itself, the impact of Americans and part-Americans, whether from Brazil or elsewhere, remains also to be studied" (60)—but usually it appears almost ritually at the end of each solid chunk of work, each sprawling chapter:

> It seems clear that many persons of Native American ancestry, in whole or part, have been at times classified as "negroes" or "blacks," in the several languages reviewed. This is a matter of considerable significance for the scholar seeking to understand the actual ethnic or racial identity of non-white persons in the slave trade, in the American colonies and in the United States over the centuries. . . . This necessity for radical reinterpretation will become still clearer as we proceed to discuss terms used for brown colored persons. (91–92)
>
> Thus we have a sequence in which first the Europeans began with very general color terms . . . ; second, when they coined many more color terms . . . ; thirdly, when they invented or adopted terms for various mixed-bloods . . . ; fourth, when they attempted by means of such terms to individually categorize most types of mixed-bloods; and, fifth, when it all became so very complicated that they fell back upon very general terms such as *pardo* or made ones like *mestizo* very nebulous. Finally, all of this occurred within a reality where the great mass of colonial people probably used all these terms in pragmatic ways based upon appearance and culture rather than upon actual ancestry. (130)

It is typical of the panoramic construction of the book that this degree of abstraction is undone and concretized, again, some thirty pages *later*:

It would appear that in the Indian Ocean area, at least, the Portuguese were developing a system of nomenclature directly analogous to what the Spaniards were doing in the same time period. That is, *mestizo* was being restricted to part-American or part-Indian mixed-bloods while *mulato* was being used for part-African mixed-bloods. But even as in the Americas *mulatos* were also of American-African mixture, so too in Asia it would appear that *mulatos* could be of African-Asian mixture. This same development does not seem to have occurred in Brazil where, as noted earlier, *mestiço* generally retained the very broad meaning of "mixed." (167)

This leads to an important generalization of work to come: "It would seem that we have established a good case for a reinterpretation of the early colonial history of the Caribbean, other parts of the Spanish Empire, and Brazil. If, as we have shown, *mulatos* in the first century of colonization were principally of American-African descent, then, of course, the formative character of the slave cultures (plantation and otherwise) and of the early 'free colored' cultures must be re-examined" (181). Nearly forty pages later, another step forward: "It would seem that those many students of North American history and society who have been fascinated solely with the Black-White nexus or who have conceived of Black and Native American history as being two largely separate streams are going to have to re-examine their assumptions. This will have great implications for the study of the diffusion of central traits in areas as diverse as folk-tales, music, social structure, folk language and religion" (219).

I treasure the moment in Toni Morrison's *Beloved* when the gang of runaway slaves find a camp of sick Cherokee, for whom a rose was named. Decimated but stubborn, they were among those who chose a fugitive life rather than Oklahoma. The illness that swept them now was reminiscent of the one that had killed half their number two hundred years earlier. In between that calamity and this, they had visited George III in London, published a newspaper, made baskets, led Oglethorpe through forests, helped Andrew Jackson fight Creek, cooked maize, drawn up a constitution, petitioned the King of Spain, been experimented on by Dartmouth, established asylums, written their language, resisted settlers, shot bear, and translated scripture. All to no avail.[7]

"Scholars" may not perceive the connection. But a writer of Morrison's sensitivity does, and it is not news to most African Americans (192). It was a television version that decided to erase Alex Haley's discussions of his Native American ancestry. And Forbes wants the right, for Native Americans, to a full entry into the contemporary political descriptive "people of color" and not just as ethnographic curiosities for Claude Lévi-Strauss or Jean-François Lyotard to unearth as models for the times.[8]

Forbes comments in passing on the contribution of sanctioned ignorance to this state of affairs: "White people often do not actually know the correct ancestry of non-whites but simply make guesses (which doubtless are often very inaccurate)" (232).

> The "tunnel vision" of seeing pre–Civil War "free persons of color" as simply a stage in the evolution of modern-day Afroamericans must be revised in favor of a more complex analysis which recognizes the tri-racial origins of the population and which also sees their relationship to both contemporary Afroamericans and Native Americans and their relevance to comparative research with similar populations elsewhere in the Americas. . . . The archaeology, ethnology, art, oral literature and documentary records must all be examined from Iceland and Ireland to southern Africa with a view to the discovery of evidence relating to American influences. The task has hardly commenced. (264, 265)

I, too, am ignorant, although I seek no sanction. Scholars hound the groundbreakers. I can only point at some of the ways in which *Black Africans and Native Americans* touches some concerns from which culture studies are veering away and expands on the implications on some of the positions quoted above. I will speak first of its paradoxical empirical deconstruction of lexicographic ground, its textualist critique of classificatory rationalism. Second, I will touch on its relationship to subaltern studies, its demonstration that the history and semiotics of hybridity do not begin with colonialism. Third, I will comment on its intervention in the politics of identity. Finally, I will point at the work it assigns to feminism.

First, then, the empirical intuition of affirmative deconstruction. The early Jacques Derrida criticized Lévi-Strauss for apparently solving philosophical problems with a precritical quantitative empiricism.[9] I do not think Forbes is a candidate for such a critique; he is, rather, the man who *does* compute the distance from Piccadilly to Liverpool Street by Einsteinian physics, or, rather, puts that physics to the test of the timetable.[10] It is as if Forbes concludes that the reality of the body (race as visible mark of human difference) and the soul (*ethnos* as the felt signature of human identity) is textual, simply by piling em-pirical example on empirical example to stage the shifting of meaning. The dictionary was a sort of paradoxical authority for Freud's uncanny: that the *Heimlich* and the *Unheimlich* come together in the speculative asymmetry of the *Un*. No such theoretical neatness for Forbes. We are left with the rocking back and forth of the vocabulary of racism until the very confusion mocks the struc-ture of reference.

Preto in Portuguese dictionaries from 1592–1784 (73–74, 118–20), *Moor* from 1571–1913 (81–83), and *mulato* in the dictionaries of various languages from 1592–1824 (168–79) are three examples among many. Forbes sees the dictionary (by definition the white dictionary, but that is another matter) as a testament of desire and difference: "The problem is, of course, that Santamaría wanted to force the term to conform with prevailing white dictionary definitions when, in fact, he had the knowledge that it did not and told us as much. As we shall see below, more recent Spanish usage in the Americas does *not* conform with normal modern dictionary definitions either" (177).

He sees the dictionary, therefore, as insufficient, a record of symptoms, condition, and effect of meaning: "It seems clear that the terms under review went through several changes of meaning which the above dictionary definitions do not completely clarify. Therefore, I will proceed to non-dictionary definitions to round out the picture" (222). Stepping out from his stance in front of those bound books, the dictionaries, he in fact begins to read the world as a library. "Rounding out" the picture is creatively to blur its outlines: "Of course, dictionaries are usually from 50 to 100 years behind the actual speech practices of people, it would seem, and European dictionaries often were especially slow in reflecting usage in colonial areas. We must, therefore, look at a few examples of actual practice to understand the meanings of *mestizo*" (128).

The proliferation of examples leads to a sense of social polysemy. This empirical proof of textuality can take on board the more risky notion that "examples of actual practice" are not identical with practice, that practice cannot be infinitely repeated as the same.

From this proof it is but a step to the critique of rationalized classification, where the risks of "Legal Definitions" are repeatedly disclosed, shading off and out into "Extra-Legal Definitions" (such as Runaway Slave Advertisements) and "Definitions by Inference" (195–218). Forbes fits the defining impulse to the Linnean aura of the eighteenth century: "In 1735 Carl Linnaeus published the first edition of his *System of Nature*. . . . Human beings were divided into two species, *Homo Sapiens* and *Homo Monstruos*. Within *Homo Sapiens* were placed: (1) wildmen, (2) Americans (copper-colored), (3) Europeans (fair), (4) Asians (sooty), and (5) Africans (black). *Homo Monstruos* included Patagonians and flat-headed Canadians (both American groups) as well as 'Hottentots' and Chinese" (103). Here, since the agency is European, the Foucauldian project can be expanded with greater ease. But even these "systems[,] developed some 200 or more years after the commencement of miscegenation[,] must inevitably be extremely flawed, since an individual might well look 'black' but possess American and/or European ancestry, might look 'white' but possess American and/or African ancestry, or might look 'Indian' and yet be part-African or part-European" (104–5). It is for us to insist that there is no such thing as a classification grounded in a temporally immediate visual access. And indeed, within its own conceptual protocol, the structure of this book offers us a web of words and terms, discontinuous in meaning—patched with history—a much mended textile center for which the historical account is no more than a frame.

"The concept of mixture" is, for Forbes, something like the writing in general that straddles the narrative-historical cut of racism and inscribes identity:

> The same process which led to the concept of a number of biologically separate "races" then resulted in a desire to chart out what might happen when persons derived from these so-called biological groupings inter-mixed with each other. . . . This concept of mixture is, I believe, very significant for our analysis of the terms used for intermediate colored people, . . . because these terms did not imply interracial mixture nor did they, in fact, make any assertion about ancestry. It seems that the mixture of native and foreigner, of tame and wild, was of some significance but the concept that racial differences (in the modern sense) were more important than other differences (nationality, religion, being a stranger) did not apparently exist. (106, 101)

I will discuss some implications of this passage at greater length in the context of the beginning of history. Following the uncertain thread of empirical deconstruction here, let us consider the possibility that the generality of the concept-metaphor of mixture leads Forbes to propose mixture at the origin, where mixture becomes a catachresis, since its possibility cannot be derived from an unmixed prior moment (let us track this with Said's implicit undoing of the unitary "Orient"):

> Nor can anyone reasonably equate the brown-skinned Berbers of North Africa, the Native Americans or the Canary Islanders with such a concept [as "mixed"]. Certain Spanish writers have attempted to regard Muslim loros as being the product of intermixture between black Africans and "white" North Africans but the color of the ancient Egyptians, 5,000 years previously, would have doubtless fallen within the loro range. One cannot assume that brown-skinned peoples are hybrids, since, in fact, white and "black" peoples may have diverged from an original brown-intermediate human stock.[11] (111)

I believe it is these unacknowledged philosophical sympathies that allow Forbes to treat a gap in evidence as "proof": "A strong case exists for the evolution of muwallad (or maula-muwallad) into later mulato. A gap of documentation exists from about 1317 to the early 1500s, time enough for the change from *mulado/mulad* to *mulato*" (147). Notice the significant verb *to exist* being used for both *case* and *gap*, the proven and the absence of proof. On the next page, we jump over this gap into a methodological necessity: "It seems clear that we cannot further clarify the origin of *mulato* until we examine other evidence relating to the use of the term in early modern times. As we shall see, there is a possibility that *mulato* went through several fairly significant changes in meaning during the sixteenth century" (148). The next step, taken at the beginning of the next chapter, is to leave behind the question of origin altogether: "At this point it seems best to leave the subject of the origin of the term *mulato* in order to proceed with explicit definitions and actual usage, prior to 1650" (151). I have already noted that *mulato* is the most important racial marker for Forbes's study.

It is not surprising that there is not a single "poststructuralist" book in Forbes's bibliography. Yet such is Forbes's sense of the deconstructive (he never uses the word) nature of his undertaking that he summons Ludwig Wittgenstein on color to be his witness that the perception of color, and indeed color words, are not grounded, although to summarize Wittgenstein's radical inconclusiveness, he quotes the altogether more foundational Josef Albers, who takes for granted the physical being of color, however inaccessible: "Color is almost never seen as it really is" — would Wittgenstein's passage, quoted immediately above this, endorse that it *sometimes* is? — "as it physically is" (95).

Again, Forbes's own conclusions are more in keeping with deconstruction, never answering the ontophenomenological question most important for his book ("What is color?") resolutely in the affirmative, recalling the Nietzsche of "Truth and Falsity" [12]: "To be colored, to have color, is to be visible. But what, indeed, is color? Is it a 'sensation' similar to hot and cold, sweet and sour, hard and soft, and so on?" There follows a statement of two alternative canceling positions, in a passage introduced by "Some would say." Then comes the sentence of Nietzschean cast: "In the mind, in some manner, the message is decoded and transformed into a colored, presumed representation of the object." What "manner" is it? "It is the representation in the mind which is colored, not the object itself." What is it "to be colored," then? And then a couple of sentences that are rather close to the early Derrida, even invoking the *ce qui reste* or "what remains" that remains from the ruins of the ontophenomenological answer. It is almost as if, if one speculates the origin of identity, one is bound to be washed up on the uncertain shores of deconstruction: "By means of color, we experience visibility, differentiation, spacing, and forming as a mental function. Of course, one problem with this type of analysis is that it fails to deal with the question of what is left of an object after color is removed." It is characteristic of Forbes's intellectual style that he puts a practical lid on the problem, by himself and via Hattersley: "But however we analyze the perception of color we find that it is an extremely complex interaction which cannot be separated from habits of the mind which may be labeled as 'cultural' (social) or 'individual.' Hattersley argues that . . . 'There is a strange psychological law. . . . Things that are alike in some ways are actually alike in all ways until it is proved otherwise. . . . The law of similarity is strongest with respect to things we ordinarily pay little attention to' " (98).

Again and again Forbes shows the connection between fear of resistance on the one hand and shifts in meaning in racial descriptives on the other. As a result, the pores of his book are filled with accounts of subaltern insurgency. His book does not concern itself with the most problematic aspect of South Asianist subaltern studies: the call for a historiographic restoration of subaltern "consciousness." In fact, as I have suggested, even the possibility of subaltern identity is shown by him to be thoroughly textualized and dispersed among many nations, many cultures. Yet Forbes's work, in the constant invocation of historical figurations cunningly obliterated in the interest of dominant history, belongs with the work of subalternist historians. Forbes is not afraid to speculate where necessary: "*Negros ladinos* had already been prohibited in 1526 and, most likely, *mulatos* and *loros* were now [1530] simply being added to the list. . . . It may well be that many *mulatos* in Spain by 1530 were half-American (or half-*canario*) and were regarded as being especially dangerous because of their potential connections with both rebellious native groups and with Africans. . . . In 1585 a report to the Chichimecos noted that they [rebel Americans] were going about armed, on horseback, and carried with them 'very skillful *mestizos* and *mulatos* who lead them' " (161, 165). But there is no doubt that, in 1503, "further shipments [of Negroes to Haiti from Seville] were suspended because of the troubles which were produced when the Africans united with the island's American rebels. . . . Slave rebellions took place on Borinquen in 1522, on Haiti in 1527, in Panama in 1531, at Amatepeque in Mexico in 1537, and in Peru (as noted earlier). In 1538 slaves and French pirates sacked Havana. From 1533–43 the American cacique Henríquez led a major joint rebellion of Americans and Africans on Haiti" (185, 188).

I have often wondered if subalternist work can ever be global, since it is so much a rejection of world systems theory.[13] Forbes's book shows me the immense excitement and difficulty of "internationalizing" subalternist work from below.

One of the consequences of this enlarged subalternism is a quiet demonstration that not only does history not begin with colonialism but that the *pouvoir-savoir* of the great diasporas, the movement of peoples across land, has not always been "racist" in the contemporary sense: "This issue is especially important in relation to the assumption fostered by some scholars that Black Africans did not experience American acculturative influences until arriving on American soil, but it is also significant in relation to the assumption that one can (or could) examine West African cultures through twentieth-century fieldwork and assume that what one finds is (or has been) largely unaffected by external influences" (61).[14]

In North America itself, "another association gradually arose . . . and that was between 'negro' and 'slave' " (84). Forbes offers us a set of conclusions that might surprise many:

> It seems highly likely that pre–Civil War society was much more ethni-
> cally diverse and culturally pluralistic, at least in so far as non-whites
> were concerned. . . . "Free Negro" implies, I think, a much more cultur-
> ally and ethnically unified group of people, *and also one thoroughly circum-*
> *scribed by the black-white conflict.* . . . I believe that the evidence indicates that
> the "free people of color" generally consisted in all non-European per-
> sons of whatever racial ancestry except: (1) unmixed Indians living on a
> federal reservation or when living as independent nations; (2) unmixed
> Indians living in recognized Indian towns in a few states such as Massa-
> chusetts (but this is only a partial exception); and (3) free persons of
> unmixed African ancestry according to the usage common in many
> southern states. . . . Thus we cannot suppose that the "free colored"
> population was a "fixed" entity. (263; my emphasis)

This important passage will relate to the emergence of the other in today's black-white (or different-same) liberal multiculturalism, as well as to the fact that the claim to the phrase "people of color" may be possible precisely be-cause it has a flexible prehistory. I have not the expertise to check out the substantive accuracy of the passage, nor the accuracy of such statements as, "There was apparently no concern or need to identify persons of 'mixed race' [in the Christian Middle Ages] since the concept of 'race' (as we know it) did not exist and 'race' mixture among human beings was not an existent con-cept" (100), or that "in the 1200s–1400s in the Mediterranean region . . . no association of color with servitude existed, since most slaves were European or North African" (102). But I have no doubt that the exercise in historiciz-ing rather than essentializing racism is absolutely crucial, and I am persuaded that Forbes gives us a model of the scrupulousness with which it must be per-formed.

I will speak more of this in connection with trends within the current metropolitan politics of identity. Here let me point out that Forbes's position does not go against contemporary antiracist struggles; it only undermines the universalizing of race as a radical intellectual category. (In this he seems less extreme than Colette Guillaumin's groundbreaking work precisely because it is more empirical.[15] This is marked in Forbes's respectful situating of the African American movement in the accepted sense: "The latter half of the nineteenth and the first half of the twentieth centuries saw many persons equating 'colored' with 'negro' and 'negro' with 'colored,' at least in the United States. Such usage arose not only from white racist efforts to place all non-whites (or at least persons of African ancestry) in a single catch-all category but also from Afroamerican efforts to secure internal unity. . . . We must avoid the mistake of reading back into the past contemporary definitions" (262; my emphasis).

Forbes shows European colonialism as inaugurating a displacement in the discursive text of racism: "Ancestry-based discriminatory practices . . . arose primarily in the colonies" (102). This is, in a certain sense, a bit of the pretext of Orientalism. "Racist caste systems" correlate "with the rise of overseas colonialism" (125). "The appearance and evolution of the term mestizo in both the Spanish and Portuguese Empires reflects the kind of caste-like and racialist social orders which evolved in the colonies" (130). "As a reflection of the developing colonial caste system in 1571 negras, free or slave, and mulatas were prohibited from wearing gold, pearls, or silk but an exception was made for those married to Spaniards" (163).

The idea of "caste" and a "racial caste system" is favored by Forbes to describe developments under colonialism for the consolidation of what we today recognize as racism and is brought forward in his current work.[16] His general point is that the nomenclature of preracism and racism is nonscientific and fluid, as in all caste systems, leaving room for mobility. It needs to be said, however, that the actual caste system of India is so fine-tuned and rationalized an instrument of social functionalism that the use of the term should perhaps be modified.[17]

Forbes lifts the historical amnesia from contemporary metropolitan cultural politics of identity. M. Ackbar Abbas, the Hong Kong–based cultural critic, speaks of the disappearance of identities in the new nomadism of the Asia-Pacific rim.[18] Forbes gives us an account of the disappearance of the Native American moment, looking backward at 1492. Every rupture is a repetition.

The "agitat[ion] for the termination of the Gingaskin Indian Reservation in Northampton County" in Virginia in 1780, because the absorption of Americans was being coded as extinction, has something like a relationship with "more recent attempts to allot and acquire Indian lands" (88). Later we read that "whites often tried to deny their Indianness" (90). People of American descent who were imported from the Caribbean or exported to Jamaica were reclassified as "Black" (231). Forbes shows how Americans get lost in censuses, in translation, and in so-called de-tribalization (see, for example, 117,

172, 242–43, 247). It is a tribute to his sense of history that Forbes, himself a Native American, sees the "authentic" Native American as a millennial imperialist construction. The product of this insight is a wonderful call to postcolonial solidarity, characteristically made in the name of a black historian: "In an article published in the *Journal of Negro History* Johnston remarked: 'Where the Negro was brought into contact with the American Indian the blood of the two races intermingled, the Indian has not disappeared from the land, but is now part of the Negro population of the United States.' The latter statement might offend many Indians today, who still survive, of course, in great numbers as Native Americans, but nonetheless the significance of Johnston's thesis as regards the extent of Native American–African intermixture remains before us" (191).

This point of view is to be contrasted with the persuasive and representative view that the Indian population dwindled, was exported, and was replaced by Africans and imported slaves from the West Indies.[19] We have seen that it is in the pores of these arguments that Forbes discovers the survival of the American, in the male and female line.

The historicization of racism, the deconstruction of the disappearance of the American, and the empirical establishment of textuality question the politics of identity on both sides, be it the Brazilian or U.S. demand to be recognized as "white" cultures or the politics of alternative identities subsumed under multiculturalism. By focusing on the vast heterogeneity and textuality of the description of mixed groups, Forbes shows that the emergence of the other, as the other of the white, may be, at best, an unwitting legitimation by reversal of the very dominant positions it is supposed to contest.

We know about Daniel Defoe's representation of the representation of colonial power in simulation in *Robinson Crusoe*.[20] What are we to make of the monolithic "othering" of the other of Europe in representation as such? Are we to caricature it ourselves by defining ourselves as the other (of the white dominant in metropolitan space)?: "It would appear that both Americans and Africans began to appear in exotic pageants and entertainments staged in London during the seventeenth century. It is not always possible to clearly ascertain the ethnicity of the performers, since Africans were sometimes dressed up as Americans, or perhaps vice versa" (56).

What are we to make of the Spanish official in the early 1560s who "was using 'white' and 'black' in the sense of 'us' and 'them,' that is, those who could be counted on to support Spanish control and those who, because of their status, might aid an enemy" (78–79)? In the discontinuous narrative of the development of racism, how are we to compute the relationship between that usage and the 1854 California State Supreme Court statement that "expresses a strong tendency in the history of the United States, a tendency to identify two broad classes of people: white and non-white, citizen and non-citizen (or semi-citizen)" (65)? Are we, once again, to become complicitous with this tendency by identifying ourselves, single ethnic group by single ethnic group or as migrant collectivity, only as the other of the white dominant? Shall we, "like so many Europeans, [remain] utterly transfixed by the black-white nexus either as 'opposites' or as real people" (172)? Given that, in the literally postcolonial areas such as Algeria or India, white racism is no longer the chief problem, Forbes's historical reasoning is yet another way of bringing together the intuitions of global resistance.

Because North Africa, Brazil, and the Spanish Empire are important areas for Forbes's argument, the heterogeneity of the Islamic world, so often ignored in contemporary discussions of racism in general, is minutely disclosed in Black Africans and Native Americans. The phenomenon of slavery in Islam is introduced early on (26). Soon we become aware of the specificity of Islam as opposed to the more amorphous sources of enslavement: "It is not possible to tell whether a given loro (for example) is from the Americas, from the Canary Islands, from northern Africa, from India, or from Spain itself. The major exception is when an Arab or Islamic proper name accompanies the color designation" (40).

A new phase in the narrative of heterogeneity is introduced when we learn that part of "the Inca nobility . . . were . . . 'shipped to exile in Spanish Sahara' . . . after the abortive Tupak Amaru rebellion in Peru in 1781–3" (59). We are taught to ask new questions: Why were Muslim slaves called negros if they were not black (76)? We are taught to discover new connections; contrary to some established opinions, Forbes makes a convincing case that the crucial descriptive mulato is a displacement of the Arabic muwallad-maula (141–50). The importance of Islam in discussions of imperial formations is illustrated here from below. We are used to such discussions from above, where Islam is the conquering power.[21]

In conclusion, a word of lament, yet once again, about the absence of a feminist impulse in many radical texts. (My friend Said routinely invokes feminism. But beyond drawing a dubious parallel with anticolonialism—as in his conversation with Catherine David at documenta x in 1997—he withholds interest.) The Native American woman, being legally free, was the enslaved man's access to "freedom." And slavery itself is "matrilineal." These two facts provide the motor for a great deal of Forbes's narrative of interaction. Yet Black Africans and Native Americans, so resourceful and imaginative in probing the pores of the hide of history, never questions the catachreses hidden in them. It is correctly mentioned that Native American practices included the thought of "individual freedom [and] utopian socialism" (266). But it is not noticed that there is feminism in those practices as well. What is it to define as "free," *after* enslavement, genocide, colonization, theft of land, tax imposition, those women who had, before these acts (masquerading today as social cohesion), been culturally inscribed as "freer"? What is it to become, then, a passageway to freedom after the fact?

(Forbes is able to deconstruct "free" in the field of race: "It has commonly been assumed by many writers that the so-called 'free' people of color living in the United States prior to the Civil War were always of African ancestry and that the words 'Negro,' 'Black,' and 'African' or 'Afro-American' can be freely substituted for 'colored.' My research questions this assumption and also the assumption that such persons were 'free.' In fact, they were 'restricted' subjects of the British Crown and, later, of the United States. Their social character also requires empirical study rather than *a priori* assignment to a single racial or social category" [239].) What is the "meaning" of matrilineage in slavery, mentioned in parentheses—"(generally slavery was inherited in the female line)" (240)—where lineage itself is devastated? It is, of course, not surprising that there are no adequate answers to these questions. The record would have been more complete if there had been a single acknowledgment of that loss.

This is not a text of critical race theory. It is a bold book by someone who has suffered definition. This is an effort by a Native American to open up the definition of both *native* and *American* until they lose their outlines and become ethicopolitically productive. In the process, this effort shares some flaws of passionate revisionary texts: the historical imagination reaching beyond mere contextual scholarship, in this case Spain and Portugal. Scholars have caviled at Said as well, to their detriment. Indeed, just as Said is brilliant in teasing out the patterns in the representation of Islam in *Covering Islam*, but is perhaps not as adroit in noticing where religion, with the withdrawal of all other possibility of agency (institutionally validated action), becomes the only agential mode left, so also Forbes, obsessed with dephenomenalizing color, ignores precisely religion as agential recourse of last resort, privileging the immanence of racialization in the interpretation of data.[22]

Indeed, *Columbus and Other Cannibals*, the book written for an implied "American" reader and more lyrical in idiom, has something like a relationship with the impassioned good sense of *After the Last Sky*, although the latter is characteristically more cosmopolitan in tone, anchored in the visible archive of a present.[23]

The organic intellectual, in the service of a paradigm shift, is sometimes forced out of scholarly distance. In praise of such destinerrance—errancy underived from proper destination, I offer Forbes's book, with respect, to the better maker.

JONATHAN ARAC

Criticism between opposition and counterpoint

My title signals a line of thought that has been provoked by the recent work of Edward Said. I will begin by reflecting on some of the terms he deploys to characterize the activity of criticism, and then I will explore their uses as a perspective on my recent book, *"Huckleberry Finn" as Idol and Target*. This consideration of Said's work and my own proved surprisingly timely, as I was completing this essay, with new developments in the public sphere of my home state, Pennsylvania. I will conclude with these recent developments.

Said has long insisted that the fundamental role of the critic is opposition. As he puts it in the introduction to *The World, the Text, and the Critic*, "Were I to use one word consistently along with *criticism* (not as a modification but as an emphatic) it would be *oppositional*."[1] Not all who know Said's later work realize that much the same view was expressed as early as 1975. In the conclusion of *Beginnings*, Said writes that Michel Foucault and Gilles Deleuze demonstrate that the intellectual's work is "adversary" in its effort to "controvert the dynastic role thrust upon him by history or habit." Thereby, he argues, Foucault and Deleuze participate in "the adversary epistemological current found in Vico, in Marx and Engels, in Lukács, in Fanon, and also in the radical political writings of Chomsky, Bertrand Russell, William A. Williams, and others."[2]

Including both revolutionary activists and scholars from the disciplines of rhetoric, psychiatry, linguistics, philosophy, and history, this is a notably heterogeneous listing of oppositional figures. It conforms to no known orthodoxy of its time or since, but, in retrospect, its trio of "political" writers, along with "epistemological" theorists, suggests two points. First, as early as 1975, when Said had won renown only as a leading figure of the emerging theory movement, he was already looking to the political concerns that have accounted for a substantial part of his writing in the last twenty years, and he evidently understood those concerns as intimately related to his work as a theorist. Second, Chomsky, Russell, and Williams were known as major scholars who wrote against the American war in Vietnam. Because Said is such a cosmopolitan polymath, it is still a fairly unfamiliar point that the debates of U.S. politics in the 1960s helped to form his intellectual commitments and style.

Said has recently acknowledged the formative impact of oppositional American writers of the 1960s in his introduction to *Representations of the Intellectual*. Here he defines the appeal he found in James Baldwin and Malcolm X: "It is a spirit in opposition, rather than in accommodation, that grips me, because the romance, the interest, the challenge of intellectual life is to be found in dissent against the status quo at a time when the struggle on behalf of underrepresented and disadvantaged groups seems so unfairly weighted against them."[3] This emphasis on the imbalance in representation recalls Said's attention to problems of the mass media in many essays and several of his books, notably *Blaming the Victims* and *Covering Islam*.

In *Culture and Imperialism*, Said considerably complicates—ramifies and nuances—the notion of oppositional commitment. He expounds what he calls "contrapuntal criticism." He explains his term, which is the adjective formed from *counterpoint*, in this way: "In the counterpoint of Western classical music, various themes play off against one another, with only a provisional privilege being given to any particular one; yet in the resulting polyphony there is concert and order, an organized interplay." Of course, the *counter* in *counterpoint* is a term of opposition, and in the musical technique of counterpoint, such phrasings as "note against note" occur; Said argues that "in the same way" counterimperial themes may be read against the thus far predominant interpretations of many great works of Western culture.[4] Nonetheless, the direction of meaning here seems to me quite different from adversarial opposition. One could map the terms onto the polarity of late Freud: Oppositional criticism is aggressive; it cuts. Contrapuntal criticism is loving; it joins. As Said says in *Culture and Imperialism*, "My principal aim is not to separate but to connect," his reason being precisely that "cultural forms are hybrid, mixed, impure."[5] But opposition is hard to imagine except as a gesture of separation. He continues, "I do not mean what people mean when they say glibly that there are two sides to every question." He associates "barriers and sides" with "theories of essentialism and exclusiveness." All of these "give rise to polarizations."[6] But so may opposition.

In a 1993 interview, during which he looks back from the '90s on what is his most famous and influential book, *Orientalism* (1978), Said recounts how he came to contrapuntal criticism. In a self-interpretation that not all readers would agree with, he explains that in *Orientalism*, "the heroes are basically the novelists"—Gustave Flaubert notably. But, he points out, "there's an ambivalence," because "you could be an imperialist and an orientalist and also a great writer." He goes on, "That's really what I'm interested in, the coexistence of these two things." His interest makes him ask, "What does one do in the face of that?" He sees the main traditions of literary study as having worked "to separate . . . completely" the great writing from the bad politics.[7] In contrast—or is it opposition?—to these traditions, contrapuntal criticism brings the writing and politics together. In *Culture and Imperialism*, Said goes to great lengths to differentiate his position from what he calls the "politics of blame," in which a past writer is condemned for having participated in the evils of slavery, imperialism, and so forth.[8] Instead, he argues, one needs "many voices"—as in musical polyphony—to "produc[e] a history." British novelists of the nineteenth and early twentieth centuries, such as Jane Austen, Joseph Conrad, and Rudyard Kipling, are writers whom he "love[s] and admire[s]."[9] This ambivalence, and the commitment it entails to develop critical resources to honor the love, not simply to castigate the politics, have set a distance between Said and much of the work in colonial discourse theory that *Orientalism* inspired.

Said is rightly recognized as a critic and theorist who has been continuously and fruitfully concerned with the relations of culture to politics—especially at the level of the state. His powerful challenge twenty years ago to what he put down by means of scare quotes as so-called left American criticism is a landmark but by no means an isolated point in his work.[10] Yet the tension between opposition and counterpoint may be illuminated by a distinction between politics and culture. I say a distinction; may it even be an opposition? Our intellectual life struggles to find sufficiently complex and nuanced terms for relationships, no less than William Wordsworth did in the nineteenth century when he argued that views which "seem opposite to each other" may have "a finer connection than that of contrast."[11] Similarly, in *Beginnings*, Said values Foucault's work for developing terms such as "*adjacency, complementarity, and correlation*" to define "relationships" that are not "linear."[12]

In the last pages of *Representations of the Intellectual*, Said examines the works of Arab intellectuals in the West in the wake of the Gulf War. His purpose is to illustrate the harm it does when an intellectual signs on to the service of any "god-term" (to gloss Said by a phrase from Kenneth Burke).[13] The disabling problem is that "because you serve a god uncritically, all the devils are always on the other side." The critical thinking Said recommends tries to get beyond sides. Instead of the binary oppositions that establish the structure of Orientalism, one would "think of politics in terms of interrelationships or of common histories such as, for instance, the long and complicated dynamic that has bound the Arabs and Muslims to the West and vice versa." He continues: "Real intellectual analysis forbids calling one side innocent, the other evil." To develop this thought, he adds, "Indeed the notion of a side is, where cultures are at issue, highly problematic, since most cultures aren't watertight little packages, all homogeneous, and all either good or evil." [14]

Notice what has happened in Said's sequence of four sentences. The complexity of culture is adduced to criticize a political choice. It would be too simple to say what is nonetheless unavoidable here: Perhaps culture more readily allows for ambivalence, or polyphony, than politics does. One may reject the politics of blame because Austen, Conrad, Kipling, and company are dead, but even in the realm of culture, the politics of current criticism may require some decisiveness (a term, one will recall, that etymologically means "cutting from"). To conceive of culture as all-embracing points in the direction of various moments in recent criticism that deny or minimize the possibilities of opposition. I am thinking of Foucault's polemical assertion that Marx was at home in the nineteenth century "like a fish in water," his "opposition" to bourgeois economics simply contained within the era's larger structure of possibility. I think, too, of Walter Benn Michaels, who argues for the foolishness of imagining that Theodore Dreiser could stand "outside capitalism" so as then to "have attitudes toward it." [15]

Said may approach such historicist totalization when, in an interview, he characterizes Conrad as follows: "He couldn't understand, as no one else in his time could either, that it was possible for natives to take over the governance of their own destiny. I'm not blaming him retrospectively. He lived in essentially a Eurocentric world. For him, although imperialism was in many cases bad . . . nevertheless there was no alternative to it." [16] This is, to us now, what Said calls the "almost tragic limitation" of Conrad, even as Conrad has also achieved "the most formidable work of the imagination by a European about Africa," a work that therefore demands engagement by later, postcolonial writers, such as Chinua Achebe in *Things Fall Apart* and Tayeb Salih in *Season of Migration to the North*.[17]

The motif of the "alternative"—what Conrad tragically lacked—is crucial in what Said demands of the intellectual. Some alternatives, it seems, are too big to be imagined even by a great writer such as Conrad, but other alternatives, even if lesser, may be brought to bear by intellectuals, and in doing so they define their oppositionality. In an interview, Said names one kind of work for "the secular intellectual, in opposition." This work is "to provide alternatives: alternative sources, alternative readings, alternative presentation of evidence."[18] To be in opposition, in this sense, is not simply to choose one side of a preexisting polarity. To provide—find, construct, invent—an alternative is an action simultaneously creative and oppositional. In politics and culture alike, it adds another voice. It complicates what had seemed a totality by confronting it with something discrepant from itself.

For Said, a crucial instance of such a false totality is the affirmative nationalism endemic to modern states in their political and cultural self-representations. The task of "modern critical consciousness . . . of oppositional criticism" is to challenge that "hegemony."[19] The opposition here is exercised by a force within the nation that constitutes itself as somewhat different from the nation—for instance, citizens of the United States who refuse to be wholly accounted for by "Americanness." Said ends one of his best-known essays, "Traveling Theory," by asking, "What is critical consciousness at bottom if not an unstoppable predilection for alternatives?"[20] These alternatives, we have seen, regularly take the form of what he calls "oppositional knowledge." The purpose of such knowledge is highly activist: namely, "to challenge and change received ideas, entrenched institutions, questionable values." And it is crucial for Said that such knowledge emerges not from what he calls in many negative usages *system* or *method* but rather from "historical research."[21] So our critical use of history is a resource for our present alternatives.

The distinction that I referred to earlier between culture and politics is one that we may find hard to make and yet that is also extremely important. At the end of my book on *Huckleberry Finn*, I insist on the distinction. At the time of Twain's death, William Dean Howells had memorialized Twain as "the Lincoln of our literature,"[22] and I have come to believe that much of the energy of what I call hypercanonization (I will return to this term) has come from those who would rather play out racial issues only in literature, treating the political questions as already taken care of—as if, for example, we no longer need affirmative action provided that Huck is in every classroom. So I oppose this displacement of politics into literature—not that it is a betrayal of literature but that it is a corruption of politics. I conclude my book by asserting that if we really want to fight racism, then "the Lincoln of our literature must yield to the Lincoln of our politics."[23] In other words, *Huckleberry Finn* in the classroom is not appropriately used to fight racism. I had earlier argued that to say everything might *be connected* to politics was not the same as saying that everything *was* political. This little verbal nuance—connection, not identity—is all the difference between metonymy and metaphor.[24] Said's work, I have been arguing, through its inventive attention to tropes and modes of discourse, enlarges our resources for describing relations in terms that are different from the same-versus-not-same, is-or-is-not, binary logic of identity.

To amplify further our range of terms, I cite a program Said set out for the renewal of Arab intellectual life. He speaks of developing a "critical language" that will be capable of "two things." The first is "to assess and critique power" — that is, a political thing. The second sounds cultural: "We need a language of appreciation, care, and attention" that will not be based on orthodox religious values.[25]

In my book on Huckleberry Finn, I do refer to Said's contrapuntal criticism, but I did not write the book as a whole to illustrate his critical procedures. I am using this essay to think back over what I did to see how it may be illuminated by the suggestions Said makes. It is in the very last chapter that I invoke his notion of counterpoint. I do it to open the geopolitics of Huckleberry Finn to a perspective beyond that of American nationalism, even when the nationalism is so capacious as that of Ralph Ellison. My further exercise of care and attention to Twain's book comes in earlier chapters, as I try to develop alternatives to the by now terribly standard ways of treating the two most discussed pages in this very much discussed book.

The opening page of chapter 19 sets forth how Huck and Jim "put in the time" as they made their escape downriver on the raft. This passage has been highlighted in critics' discussions of Huck's American "vernacular" language. I try, instead, to analyze the style in a way that opens up Twain's relations with European art prose practices of his age, from Flaubert to the decadents. This analysis goes beyond the nationalist bounds within which so much discussion of Huckleberry Finn has confined itself, and it resituates the argument for vernacular in relation to global processes of creolization, another instance of the connections between culture and imperialism.

Then the even more famous passage: In the middle of chapter 31, Huck drafts a letter to Miss Watson about how she could recover her escaped slave, Jim, but he finds that he cannot send it and decides, "All right, then, I'll go to hell." This passage has been highlighted in countless critics' discussions of Twain's moral vision. (I can't help remarking on the dangers of disciplinary narcissism when so many English teachers have decided that the greatest scene in American literature is one in which a solitary writer broods over the composition and revision of a document.) The major point in my book was to open that passage to a range of alternative voices that Twain's technique did not allow to come into play and that in this context function oppositionally. My argument is that Twain deliberately simplified and restricted Huck's resources by eliminating from his consciousness the languages of Christian love and of republican equality. By this means, Twain makes Huck's decision seem a miracle of the human heart. Huck's discovery of his power to be in opposition achieves tremendous comic power, but it wholly obscures the actual alternatives by which individuals in American history came to act against the system of slavery. This restriction is part of Twain's literary art, but it tells very gravely against the long-repeated claims that this scene is the moral high point of American literature.

So I have opened up lines of counterpoint which restore *Huckleberry Finn* to a history that diverges from the consensus of liberal nationalism. But this goal of superior critical care, this dimension of counterpoint, was, in my intention, very much subordinated to opposition—opposition not to Twain's book but to the traditions of criticism that have made it play so large and yet so limiting a role in American life. My book, as I reimagine it in the light of these reflections, counts as a critical genealogy of the hypercanonization of *Huckleberry Finn*, of how it became an indispensable element of the liberal imagination.

As a work of criticism, my book has a strong animus. I am fed up with reading that *Huckleberry Finn* is the "quintessentially American book" and that it is a "devastating attack on racism." These terms are not good descriptions of the book, and they are not the best terms for appreciating the book. I do not argue that *Huckleberry Finn* is racist or un-American. Rather, I explore how Twain's book came to be endowed with the values of Americanness and antiracism, and with what effects.

In the later 1940s, there began a process I call hypercanonization. That is, within the canon of American classics that was defined in the academy at this time, *Huckleberry Finn* was placed at the very top. Academic excess would not itself be important, but in this case the academic judgments fueled newspaper and magazine articles when public controversy arose about the desirability of *Huckleberry Finn* as required reading in junior high schools. The excessive media response in defense of *Huckleberry Finn* I call idolatry.

My book details and analyzes the emergence of hypercanonization in the academy—it occurred in the years 1948–1964—and demonstrates its role in idolatry, largely since 1982. Like much of Said's writing, mine is a work of academic scholarship and critical argument that aims to provide oppositional knowledge. I hope it may be useful for parents who want to fight the idolatry that routinely answers them when they complain that their early teenage children are being made to study and admire a text in which the title character, hero, and narrator, Huck, hundreds of times uses the term *nigger*. I do not want to ban *Huckleberry Finn*. I *do* want to see fairer, fuller, better informed debates when the book comes into question.

As a road map, let me offer a very brief historical sketch of the reception, by literary authorities, of Twain and *Huckleberry Finn*. Twain is widely valued nowadays for his opposition to the established culture of his time; we recall that library committees refused to allow their libraries to carry *Huckleberry Finn* because of its unsavory setting and uneducated language. But there are higher authorities than library committees. Twain was greatly admired by, and his career supported by, the two most important and prestigious editors of the leading high-culture magazines of his time. In the 1870s, Howells, as editor of the Atlantic Monthly, wrote highly favorable reviews of Twain's work and actively recruited Twain for his pages. In the 1880s, Richard Watson Gilder, as editor of Century magazine, made recruiting Twain a top priority, and Gilder published three excerpts from Huckleberry Finn. Twain's relation to the genteel tradition may be less opposition than counterpoint.

As of the middle 1930s, one hundred years after Samuel Clemens had been born, fifty years after Huckleberry Finn had been published, twenty-five years after Twain's death, the image of Twain held a privileged place in American cultural memory, but Huckleberry Finn had not yet become one of the great books of the world. Twain was part of the atmosphere of American culture, not someone whose standing depended on closely attentive reading of whole works. In the last years before his death in 1910, Twain had already been widely identified in the United States as "our" Mark Twain and represented by cartoonists in imagery that made him equivalent to the national icon of Uncle Sam.

After Twain's death, Huckleberry Finn was admired by innovative writers as various as Gertrude Stein, H. L. Mencken, Sherwood Anderson, and Ernest Hemingway, but for the culture at large it was a beloved boy's book. The several decades after the Second World War transformed the cultural standing of Huckleberry Finn. In the 1940s, it became what it still remains: a universally assigned college text and the focus of a huge amount of academic scholarship and critical discussion. My research indicates that the turning point was 1948, with the first college text of Huckleberry Finn, introduced by Lionel Trilling. Scholars and critics established terms for valuing Huckleberry Finn as a masterpiece of world literature and as the highest image of America. This is the process I call hypercanonization.

There is no sign that hypercanonization is diminishing. In 1990, The Heath Anthology of American Literature was published, in two volumes. This fifty-eight-hundred–page collection avowedly grows from the radical concerns of the 1960s, and it asserts its commitment to feminist and multicultural transformations of the canon. The anthology enforced its principles so strongly that in its contemporary literature section, out of over fifty poets and fiction writers it included who were younger than John Updike—that is, at the time under sixty years old—only two—Thomas Pynchon and Michael Herr—were white males. Yet in this same volume, which reaches from the Civil War to the present, Twain occupies nearly 10 percent of the total pages. No other writer of the nineteenth century has eighty pages; no twentieth-century writer has even fifty pages; William Faulkner has twenty-five pages; and Huckleberry Finn is printed in its entirety.

The formation of academic hypercanonization took place from 1948 to

1964, a period coinciding with the onset of the cold war and the emergence of the Civil Rights movement. It ended with the passage of the most important Civil Rights legislation since the Reconstruction, but also with the simultaneous erosion of the cold war liberal coalition. In 1948, Harry Truman so effectively co-opted the Civil Rights concerns of Henry Wallace's third-party candidacy that Strom Thurmond, then the Democratic governor of South Carolina, led southern "Dixiecrats" in protest out of the party convention. In 1964, things went the other way. Lyndon Johnson was so worried that Barry Goldwater might exploit what was already becoming known as "white backlash" that Johnson refused to accept the challenge to the establishment convention delegates by the Mississippi Freedom Democratic Party. In addition, the impact of the war in Vietnam, and the beginning of violent urban agitation by African Americans, further contributed to end this historical phase. Yet the hypercanonization persists; I think it is a wishful residue of values that were once connected to concrete struggles to improve the life of the United States.

There is a painful paradox that mobilizes my book. When, in 1948, Trilling declared and reiterated that Huck and Jim formed a "community of saints,"[26] a new moral value was attributed to Huckleberry Finn and to America at a time when an increasing number of white people wanted to believe that racial prejudice was a thing of the past. Yet this interpretation of Huck and Jim, by idealizing their relation, powerfully invites complacency. When readers, teachers, and critics follow Trilling in identifying the relation of Huck and Jim as the pinnacle of human community, it is as if an imaginary "we" uttered in self-congratulation: "Americans have spiritually solved any problems involved in blacks and whites living together as free human beings, and we did so already by the 1880s; all that remains is to work out the details." But many African Americans have not wanted to join that "we." No sooner had Huckleberry Finn begun to achieve hypercanonization, in part because it could so effectively serve as an icon of Civil Rights consciousness, than it also began to be challenged in the schools by African Americans—the very people on whose behalf, it was imagined, the book was functioning. If Civil Rights meant anything, shouldn't it mean that African Americans would have a real voice in public definitions of what counts as a model of enlightened race relations?

What distresses me in these controversies in the media is the structure that I call idolatry—the journalistic by-product of hypercanonization. News about African American protests against the required place of honor held by Huckleberry Finn in the classroom—especially at the junior high school level—began to appear in the press as early as 1957, in the very midst of the first phase of southern white protests against school integration, but only in 1982 did this topic first become big news, rapidly reaching television. John Wallace, an African American educator—he was based at the Mark Twain Intermediate School in Fairfax, Virginia!—denounced *Huckleberry Finn* as "racist trash" —above all for its several hundred uses of the word *nigger*.[27] And the fight was on.

Idolatry continues in the rhetoric with which newspapers frame stories about challenges to the hypercanonical status of *Huckleberry Finn*. In the summer of 1995, the museum housed in the mansion that Twain built in Hartford, Connecticut, held a workshop for schoolteachers. Look at the headlines: in the *Pittsburgh Post-Gazette*, "Mark Twain Museum Mounts *Huckleberry Finn* Defense"; and in the *New York Times*, "Huck Finn 101, or How to Teach Twain without Fear." The *Post-Gazette* casts the workshop as "coming to the rescue" of beleaguered teachers, and the *Times* explains that "for the lovers of Mark Twain, the event is a pre-emptive effort to bolster the nerve of teachers." In the *Post-Gazette* story, a display quote from a scholar proclaims, "It's a weapon in the battle against racism that we can't afford to take out of our classrooms."[28]

Why must the book be rescued from African American parents and students for their own good? Why must they be the objects of preemptive cultural strikes? Why is it so obvious to so many authorities that their complaints cannot be taken seriously? Why must parents and students be told repeatedly by authorities that they are bad readers rather than being acknowledged as voices in a genuine debate over what works against racism in the classroom? In a theoretical essay on class and the category of race, the African American historian Barbara Jeanne Fields has argued that "ideology" does not consist in "the 'handing down' of the appropriate 'attitudes' " but rather in "the ritual repetition of the appropriate social behavior."[29] Applying her view to the controversies over *Huckleberry Finn*, what counts, I'm afraid, is not the attitudes of interracial good feeling that the book supposedly teaches but rather the opportunity the book provides for the incessant reiteration, the ritual repetition, of practical behavior: When blacks complain about *Huckleberry Finn*, the authorities proclaim that they are wrong.

This is what the idolatry adds up to. Liberal white American opinion identifies with the wonderful boy Huck. Even though his society was racist, he was not, and so "we" are not. For African Americans to challenge this view is to challenge "us," just where "we" feel ourselves most intimately virtuous, and it is also to challenge Twain, and thereby the America he "quintessentially" represents. I am trying to construct an alternative to this structure.

Most school instruction does not treat *Huckleberry Finn* simply as an excellent aesthetic object. If it were read and taught only for pleasure, there would be much less passion in defending its classroom role. The identification of a book not just with a nation but with the *goodness* of the nation makes controversy so painful. Why can we not allow our *selves* to be better than our masterpieces? Toni Morrison has recently argued that every time *Huckleberry Finn* is removed from a classroom, Jim is reenslaved: "The cyclical attempts to remove the novel from classrooms extend Jim's captivity on into each generation of readers." [30] In contrast, I look forward to a time when we can leave this classic behind, that is to say, when we and our children live by standards that Twain and his society could not yet imagine, and when it no longer matters to anyone whether Huckleberry Finn is required or not. It can then be loved by many without being imposed on all.

Recently in Pennsylvania—unbeknownst to readers of the New York Times national edition—it all began to happen again, but with some differences. On Monday, 2 February 1998, kicking off Black History Month, the State Conference of NAACP Branches issued a proclamation from the steps of the statehouse, asking that Huckleberry Finn no longer be required in schools. I have not had the chance to read the full document but have learned from news sources its major concerns, which arise from the word nigger.

I found it very heartening that the document, to my knowledge, avoided the rhetoric of blame. It did not brand Twain or the book as racist. It simply insisted that the book created intolerable classroom situations. Moreover, to my understanding, this is not a First Amendment issue of book banning. The NAACP is very clear that it is not concerned about libraries, even school libraries. Its concern is educational policy: the place of mandatory honor that the work holds in many curricula. If one believed the line on political correctness that generated so much heat a few years ago, then one would imagine the NAACP as the massed forces of groupthink mobilizing against Twain's masterpiece of the free spirit. But the NAACP is not a very powerful body, and Huckleberry Finn is a very powerful book. And much of its power in the culture, and especially in the schools, comes from the belief that it is a "weapon against racism." So when such a group says it is not, I think we need to pay attention. But look at the offensively dismissive front-page headline in the state capital newspaper: "Group Tries to Sell Huck Finn Up the River." [31]

The first story in the Pittsburgh Post-Gazette came off the Associated Press wire, and it, too, shows the idolatry that I wrote my book to oppose, the utter failure of cultural authorities to be responsible and accurate in their own statements, even as they criticize others for being unsophisticated or anti-intellectual. In this case, the American Library Association (ALA) was the establishment source to which the Associated Press turned. Here is what Judith Krug, the director of the Association's Office for Intellectual Freedom, told them. They report her opinion that Huckleberry Finn is "a classic that benefited students so long as they place it in its proper context." Then they quote her example of context: Twain "wrote this book as a cry against slavery and he did it in the context of the world at that time." She continued, "Jim's name is Nigger Jim in the book because that's exactly what he would have been called at that time."[32] In other words, just like many students, the ALA Intellectual Freedom officer speaks as if slavery still had defenders when *Huckleberry Finn* was published, twenty years after the Civil War ended. And like many cultural authorities before her, Krug seeks to minimize the impact of the term *nigger* by implying—some authorities assert outright but wrongly—that the term meant nothing special in the 1840s, when the book's action occurs, or in the 1880s, when Twain wrote the book. Worse still, yet most common, she uses her authority to tell the world that Jim is named Nigger Jim. Of course, Twain never uses that formulation, but one would never know it from the public record—including the work of many distinguished professors, some very recent. So the decades-long pattern that I had analyzed in my book still exercises force.[33]

I had the chance to speak my mind. I was interviewed both by local TV news stations and by the *Pittsburgh Post-Gazette*, the major Pittsburgh newspaper, and the reporters actually made use of what I told them. In addition, I published an article in the Sunday opinion section of the *Post-Gazette*. You already have the gist of my views. As the primary intellectual authority consulted, I could affect the overall coverage. I gave the paper the name of a high school teacher whose class on *Huckleberry Finn* I had visited, and she became the lead for their big story. My background interview laid out historical contexts from three periods—Huck's time, Twain's time, and the last fifty years of hypercanonization. So alternative knowledge was brought to the discussion.

My greatest pleasure in the events to date is the character of the headlines in the *Post-Gazette* once its reporters took over the story. The first is a big front pager: "A Word of Caution about Huck." In all my research covering the last fifty years, I had never seen a headline so big yet so temperate for a story treating challenges to the centrality of *Huckleberry Finn*. The headline that the copyeditors wrote for my opinion piece was in the same vein: "*Huckleberry Finn* Not Required Reading"; in the subhead, they used the word *perhaps*.[34] I believe that my intervention in this public debate has offered an alternative that has helped to diminish polarization and to attenuate the usual shrill defensiveness.

This episode has helped me understand what had earlier seemed a puzzling emphasis in Said's model of the intellectual. In an article for the *New Left Review*, he uses the stirring big words of the "secular, oppositional intellectual," but the role he defines for them—for us—is cast in a very different idiom: We need to be "informed and effective wet blankets."[35]

TERRY COCHRAN

The matter of language

I

Perhaps more than any other critic in the last half of the twentieth century, Edward Said has consistently engaged historical issues that stress the overlap between literary concerns and political interests. In Said's case, this critical orientation or necessity has generated endless controversy and reaction from across the political and literary spectrum, seemingly giving credence to his assertion that literature, politics, and criticism are inextricably linked. More precisely, however, Said's most profound contribution to contemporary thought may reside in his painstaking demonstration that the conceptual tools of literary understanding are not only applicable to other cultural domains and productions but are necessary for coming to terms with their emergence, historical significance, and political economy. In this context, for example, Said straightforwardly proposes a conceptual model that involves thinking "both in political and above all theoretical terms." [1] This theoretical reflection incorporates and draws its impetus from literary thinking, which since the invention of writing has been central to forming political hegemonies and to the unfolding of human traditions, as well as to the historical continuity they provide. Ultimately, yoking the theories of literary and linguistic production to analyses of political interests inevitably leads to questions about potential materialist understandings of history.

Before broaching these implications for both Said's criticism and for critical thinking at large, the reference to literature and literary understanding requires further consideration. Elaborating a materialist understanding of written culture, including its ideas, concepts, and linguistic presuppositions, necessarily departs from the operative notions of literature in modernity. The term *literature* bears the burden of its institutionalization in the epoch of modernity and, in its nationalist versions (for example, French literature, Spanish literature, and so on), has been the linchpin of cultural hegemony since the beginnings of literary history in the late eighteenth century. In the modern structure of the university as it was consolidated in the following century, literary disciplines and, later, departments became identified with ahistorical humanist values, that is, universal qualities to which all human beings in all historical times should aspire.[2] Despite the contemporary weakening of these ahistorical claims, literary culture and understanding continue to play an important, though widely unacknowledged, ideological role in constituting collective consciousness. In virtually all present-day literary histories, the Renaissance marks the moment when literature—that is, secular writing—became the vehicle both of abstract universal values and of the national or communal identities that claim to share them. Consequently, every cultural group striving for national or communal hegemony in the epoch of modernity has elaborated a secular literary tradition, complete with historical account, grammars of the literary language, and dictionaries.[3] Inevitably in the service of a given collectivity, literary scholars—who have gone under many names, ranging from philologists to humanists, from intellectuals to literary critics—have reinforced the institutional scaffolding of literature by creating critical editions of canonical works, reinterpreting their meanings, and generally underscoring their importance for universal values (thus the category of *Weltliteratur*) and for the evolving collective consciousness of a people. In sum, the claim of literature as the bearer of universals effaced its political aspect and veiled its hegemonic role, just as the amalgamation of humanism with literature (the backbone of the "humanities") served to isolate it from political economy and epistemological claims.[4]

Against this schematic backdrop, Said's own literary and critical practice, which closely follows contemporary developments of literary understanding and involves divesting literature of its ideological blinders, on the one hand, and reintroducing literary reflection as a basis for critical thought, on the other, becomes more urgently visible. In the twentieth century, the place of literature in the overall production of culture has undergone radical transformation, and the literary premises of modernity are under increasing scrutiny. Mass production, which has characterized literary dissemination since the early diffusion of print technology, has spread to other material cultural domains that include painting, photography, film, television, radio, and software. In other words, literature and the literary tradition no longer single-handedly dominate cultural production, and the economic force of the cultural commodity has upset the well-policed conjuncture of literature, universalism, and humanism. Without this privileged ideological investment, writing — shorn of its grandiose literary claims — takes its more modest place alongside other sectors of culture. This historical situation, which is as much a product of political and economic transformation as a result of technological and cultural change, casts an entirely different light on literary reflection and on the conceptual concerns that constitute it.

Questioning the historicity of writing or literature is not an idle task. Across diverse historical epochs, the terms, concerns, and objects of (literary) reflection or interpretation seem to vary greatly according to social, political, and material factors. For example, the fundamental historical conditions of biblical times certainly moved particular textual problems into the foreground and had an obvious effect on the means, procedures, and outcomes of interpretation. The elements determining the parameters of reflection are undeniably distinct if the text exists as words baked in clay, carved in stone, written on parchment, or printed on paper; if the words are deemed to originate in a deity's voice, an emperor's court, or the activity of an autonomous individual; or if the text is recognized as belonging to a homegrown or foreign tradition. The way in which these factors are combined, in conjunction with others, including the size of the potential public and the institutions that produce, preserve, and perpetuate the meaning of the respective text, help configure the historical limits of interpretation in addition to the hegemony they institute.

At the same time, however, the general questions that underlie literary reflection, that is, reflection on writing (or, more generally, on inscriptions resulting from human intervention), are always of the same order. They derive from a fundamental, almost scientific formulation: How does one determine the meanings of an object (in this instance, a written text) that exceeds the empirical moment of its origin? It was produced, and its existence as a material object (and the kind of material is important if only because it defines its period of empirical accessibility, if not legibility) outlasts its author or creator. A number of concerns and categories of thought have emerged to come to grips with this massive question: concerns such as the relationship of the inscription (text) to the collectivity sharing its language, its pertinence to the present, its place in the network of other extant writings (both similar and dissimilar), and its contribution to human understanding at large. Despite superficial differences, these concerns have — aside from the evident historical divergences alluded to above — remained constant since the advent of writing and attest to the daunting difficulties of any literary reflection as well as to its continued relevance. Just as the physicist uses "idealized experiments" [5] to describe and understand the workings of what has come to be called "nature," the (literary) theorist constructs discursive models to depict the polyvalent relationships between language, the interactions of human consciousness, and the world. In contrast with theoretical physics, however, acknowledging the idealizing or even ideological aspect of literary understanding as an object of reflection necessarily introduces questions about extraneous interference; this interference, which in shorthand can be called the "political," encompasses constraints such as force, power, and the implementing dictates of an institutional or individual agent.

A relative awareness of the historical production of ideas has been an essential component of critical thought since the nineteenth century, particularly with the rise of literary hermeneutics. This awareness constitutes the landscape within which Said's critical project is initially inscribed. In elucidating the historical bases of ideas, for example, Said sketches the paradigmatic nature of the literary tradition and its concomitant critical framework: "Each age, for instance, re-interprets Shakespeare, not because Shakespeare changes, but because despite the existence of numerous and reliable editions of Shakespeare, there is no such fixed and non-trivial object as Shakespeare independent of his editors, the actors who played his roles, the translators who put him in other languages, the hundreds of millions of readers who have read him or watched performances of his plays since the late sixteenth century." [6] This passage, which appears in Said's text as an illustration, advances various notions that bear closer inspection and that run counter to the universalist or ahistorical bias of modern literature. Furthermore, elaborating the stakes bound up with the name and interpretation of Shakespeare offers an important glimpse into the unique linguistic and historical perspectives that orient Said's work.

In the terms of literary thought, "Shakespeare" is a figure that happens to be a proper name. The figure of personification has long been an object of consideration in the tradition of literary reflection, beginning with classical manuals of rhetoric (such as those by Aristotle, Cicero, and Quintilian); often described by the term *prosopopeia*, it took its place alongside a host of other very technical terms of signification, the majority of which have today become archaic.[7] Understanding personification as a technical or formal linguistic element is deeply ensconced in the literary tradition, both in theory and in practice, and typically follows the dictates of commonsense realism. On coming across a proper name, marked in English with a capital letter because of its conceptual importance, readers immediately personify it by assimilating it to personal experience and to empirical individuals they have actually met. "Shakespeare," a group of letters printed on a two-dimensional page, suddenly has arms, legs, a point of view, and so on. Most literary debates, whether among specialists, in the popular press, or in the classroom, tend to turn around what kind of attributes—attitudes, actions, creations—can be justifiably assigned to a figure.

Yet, rather than pursuing the formalist aspects of personification, Said offers a larger perspective that stresses how the figure—in this case, Shakespeare's name—comes to be and how it is deployed in time. The presuppositions are as easy to enumerate as the repercussions are far-reaching. As a name whose object rests out of reach, whose meaning can only be grasped through the mediation of countless descriptions and qualifications that are themselves no less linguistic than the name itself, Shakespeare and whatever its reference participate in a very precise linguistic economy. Its primary characteristic can best be grasped in contrast to an idealized referential situation. In a straightforward act of referentiality that takes place in an ideal present, a living individual points to an object and utters "Shakespeare." Referentiality is seemingly complete and utterly realized: It is guaranteed by the individual who serves as a relay for the one-to-one correspondence. This classic model of referentiality lays out the elements but displays little communality with the complex discursive networks that give a semblance of life to historical and literary figures. Moreover, in returning specifically to the Shakespeare figure, the presumed empirical moment when the name William Shakespeare was bestowed on a newborn adds nothing whatsoever to our understanding of the figure and can only be rendered present by yet another layer of language (and, in any event, Shakespeare scholars continue to discuss the empirical identity of Shakespeare, including his authorship of various literary productions). For a figure to signify as a figure, for it to take on the trappings of existence, that from which it derives must be absent—preferably for good.

Though less palpable, historical reality, which is given substance between the lines of written texts, is just as real as the most mundane of physical objects, and this notion of the figure extends rather than truncates or diminishes reality. On the contrary, maintaining that language operates according to figurations, it presents a model of the way that language intervenes temporally and spatially (given that absence connotes both aspects) to mediate between understanding and the empirical. This basic linguistic model sustains even the most rudimentary historical interpretation of literary texts and has been institutionalized in the form of hermeneutics.[8]

Said's remarks on the Shakespeare figure implicitly describe this hermeneutic version of literary understanding. The "object" of the Shakespeare figure has no fixed identity, no inert existence cut off from Shakespeare's multiple receptions that vary geographically and chronologically, in space and in time.[9] At the same time, however, Said's characterization underscores the empirical presupposition that provides a methodological framework for interpretation: Shakespeare doesn't change, but his identity is inexhaustible and never ceases becoming manifest in new facets. Whatever Shakespeare's empirical existence, it can never be known directly and is tributary of the collective idea that historical actors and discourses make of it. Although this basic theory of literary understanding may no longer do justice to the collective idea of Shakespeare that is today in full expansion, spreading throughout the globe and traversing all media, its conceptual and methodological reign in the epoch of scriptural dominance has been incontrovertible. In this sense, it constitutes the touchstone of literary—and, by extension, cultural—critique at the present time.

Whereas Said's comments on Shakespeare succinctly summarize the traditional model of literary understanding, the continuation of the passage extends that model to include institutional—and, implicitly, political—aspects: "On the other hand, it is too much to say that Shakespeare has no independent existence at all, and that he is completely reconstituted every time someone reads, acts, or writes about him. In fact, Shakespeare leads an institutional or cultural life that among other things has guaranteed his eminence." [10] In other words, the Shakespeare figure exists beyond the individual realizations that accrue historically. From this perspective, the point of reference for Shakespeare is not a fictional and unreachable place somewhere in the distant past; instead, the institutions of knowledge and culture guide, however unobtrusively, the figure's ongoing realizations, the multiple meanings that can legitimately be attributed to it. Shakespeare's life is *real* and can never be reduced to some form of arbitrariness: There is no *mere* interpretation. The immaterial figure, the idea of Shakespeare, comes about and subsists in conjunction with material interests fueled, channeled, and guaranteed by institutions that go from the micro level of textual debate, to reigning interpretations in the respective disciplines of knowledge, to macro views of historical understanding and potential interpretation.

2

In view of its peculiar relationship to history, writing (literature in the broadest sense) offers a synthesis of the material and immaterial tensions between historical understanding and contemporary transformation, individual action and collective intransigence, the political status quo and revolution. Other means of recording the sediments of human thought and deed—means spanning the gamut of twentieth-century media—operate along the same axes as writing, but scrutiny of those processes of marking the world has, for obvious technological and historical reasons, been intertwined with literary understanding. Because of his efforts to render an account of these tensions,

Said's many critical texts that treat questions of literary theory—including *Beginnings* and *The World, the Text, and the Critic*—incorporate an interest in and a response to wide-ranging political concerns. But *Orientalism*, undoubtedly Said's most widely read and influential work, stands as his sole extended systematic treatment of the links between the theoretical and the political, between the literary and the cultural. A work of ongoing relevance to understanding the underside of literary traditions, *Orientalism* results from important deliberation on the historical capacities of language and on the political force of its deployment in institutions and knowledge production.

Instead of simply presenting a counterstory of the "Orient," *Orientalism* analyzes the idea of the Orient as it was linguistically asserted and historically elaborated. There are evident parallels between Said's characterization of the Shakespeare figure and the idea of the Orient, initially a vague notion that is given body through numberless supporting texts that describe, personify, and endow it with intention. As with all knowledge, figures or ideas clasp together material and immaterial aspects; they undergird all historical understanding or interpretation. Without the material—for example, writing—the idea dies with the mind that thinks it; without the possibility of thinking beyond the material, it is impossible to actuate past legacies, to render them pertinent to any given present. In regard to the Orient, *Orientalism* attempts to lay out the parameters of this complex but absolutely necessary interaction between the material and the immaterial: "The Orient was almost a European invention." [11] Volumes could be appended to this qualification, this "almost," without ever exhausting the subject. Because it emerges from historical awareness, it is not merely an invention or phantasmatic projection, nor is it an unambiguous, objective portrayal of what it names.

Like any linguistic figure, the idea of the Orient possesses historical dimensions that exceed the ideal referential model I sketched out earlier. In *Orientalism*'s introductory chapter, Said elucidates the presuppositions of the study: "I have begun with the assumption that the Orient is not an inert fact of nature. It is not merely *there*, just as the Occident itself is not just *there* either" (4). Informed by an understanding of the specific linguistic character of writing, the figural model *Orientalism* endorses, no matter how scientifically rigorous its application, contrasts with a model construed on the basis of an empirical knowledge of nature. The Orient, whether idea or referent, is not "there," the object of a pointing finger that indicates it for a present and discerning public. Although the "nature" model of knowledge may have useful applications in specific contexts, its potential for explaining the figuration of written language is severely limited owing to the infinite variables involved and to their immateriality. In the case of the figure (of the Orient, for example), understanding is not a matter of clear and transparent perception, as if one were present before an object and had the power and voice to express it unequivocally.

Grasping the workings of this figuration, whose implications for historical understanding go well beyond the sense of any particular figure, is fraught with difficulties. These obstacles come less from the enormous quantity of material than from the intricacy of analyzing historical figures that provide the very means of thinking. *Orientalism* hints at the historical magnitude of the problem: "Therefore as much as the West itself, the Orient is an idea that has a history and a tradition of thought, imagery, and vocabulary that have given it reality and presence in and for the West" (5). As an idea that takes form in time, the Orient is a product of historical accretion; once transcribed, it served as a virtual point of reference for competing and coalescing discourses that flesh out its skeletal figure. The reality of that Western Orient is that of institutions whose domain is largely immaterial, even if the authoritative actions that reveal its reach have visible consequences. Yet not unlike the figure of Shakespeare, which both channels and derives from countless institutional—and, today, commercial—forces and structures, its historical existence is unassailable. Although in *Orientalism*, Said's object of analysis is specifically defined, the economy of signification he delineates extends beyond any specific object. The "West" no less than the "East" (as well as any personified collectivity so common in literary and historical discourse) necessarily participates in the same economy of meaning. From the perspective of institutionalized knowledge, the figure belongs to a configuration merging multiple series of interwoven vocabulary, a plethora of images, and historical accounts to marshal them into coherence. Moreover, as Said's remarks suggest, the figures tend to be defined in conjunction with other figures, supplementing, opposing, and becoming assimilated to them, thus increasing the labyrinths of signification and the convoluted imbrication. Therefore, to read, interpret, and explicate this institutionalization, the process whereby a figure comes into existence, involves deciphering the "whole network of interests" (3), coming to terms with the concomitant "constellation of ideas" (5), and confronting the "sheer knitted-together strength" (6) of discourses holding the figure in place.

While the economy of the figure undeniably endorses the proverb that "history is always written by the victors," its force is more epistemological than physical. In the encapsulated view of the proverb, control of the past, its sequential unfolding and meaning, follows on bodily subjugation. The figural understanding of history, on the contrary, places struggle at the heart of the signifying process as well, which cannot exist in isolation from its respective medium. The most controversial upshot of this way of perceiving struggle in language revolves around affirmations of historical truth. As Said comments, cultural discourse circulates "not 'truth' but representations" (21). In-jecting reflection on language into the historical equation indicates to what extent the Orient, even as a historically delimited category, becomes an epis-temological question in addition to and alongside physical domination, just as knowing and knowledge reveal their political significance.

The nature of language, its ephemeral orality and its inability as writing to transport to succeeding epochs whatever empirical meaning it might have expressed, imposes strong limitations on notions of historical truth. In this sense, Said's grappling with the question of Orientalism cannot be separated from this larger investigation of the historical and linguistic sediment of knowledge. Applied to the figure of the Orient, Said's words constitute a gen-eral commentary on this tangle of conceptual relationships: "Its objective dis-coveries—the work of innumerable devoted scholars who edited texts and translated them, codified grammars, wrote dictionaries, reconstructed dead epochs, produced positivistically verifiable learning—are and always have been conditioned by the fact that its truths, like any truths delivered by lan-guage, are embodied in language" (203). History involves institutions, ideal projections, and a complement of presuppositions, but its economy is de-termined by a linguistic process and the material of its inscription (printed words, for example). Without this rigorous scaffolding, historical truth is a meaningless concept, and the scaffolding is bound into form by language. Language, inseparable from its materiality, is the common denominator for these disparate elements that extend from the political to the theoretical. Ulti-mately, the entire edifice of historical understanding rests on the efficacy of the model of signification attributed to language.

3

Although this fundamental reflection on language has far from dominated historical thought in the West, it has been a recurring theme among theorists at least since Dante, who addressed issues of the political repercussions of language. In evoking this tradition, Said cites briefly Nietzsche's "On Truth and Lie in the Extramoral Sense" (203); although Said does not dwell on this text, mention of it has become de rigueur for both critics and supporters of Orientalism's claims.[12] In effect, Nietzsche's text advances a surprisingly com-plete hypothesis about the historical and political workings of language; it renders explicit the entangled political and epistemological ramifications of critical practice, including that which characterizes Said's Orientalism.

Circulating judgments about Nietzsche display such tenacity that they fre-quently replace reading of texts attributed to him. Evoking the "Nietzsche" name in describing individuals or their writings suffices to demean their motivation or challenge the validity of their analyses. Nietzsche's essay on truth and lying, which examines the representational capacity of language in isolation from the historical contingency of moral judgments, is often cited precisely in this context. For example, Jürgen Habermas considers Nietzsche (along with the Marquis de Sade) as one of "the really nihilistic *dark* writers of the bourgeoisie." [13] The italicized *darkness* summons images of the closed room where nefarious events occur, as well as the opposite of "enlightenment," the eighteenth-century ascendancy of reason. In a similar vein, as one of Said's critics affirms in referring to this essay to prove Said's irrationalism, antihumanism, and antihistoricism: "In a Nietzschean world, virtually anything is possible." [14] Although the grounds for this boundless possibility are not rendered explicit, this sentence accurately iterates the standard allegory attached to Nietzsche's name.

However, before writing Nietzsche off as an irrational thinker of mythic proportions, it is essential to consider the text on truth and lying in its entirety (the essay to which the two extant sections belong remains unfinished). This partial essay, which Nietzsche drafted in the context of teaching classical rhetoric and pre-Platonic philosophy, presents a coherent hypothesis about the way language functions as a means for producing knowledge. Although all interpretation—whether of history or of the empirical world—depends on hypothetical presuppositions, the assumptions leading to understandings or interpretations of human culture (writing or other material forms) are of a different order than those of experimental science. Whereas the latter must by definition admit of empirical verification, no matter how idealized the hypothesis and how tenuous or refracted the link established between the idea and its experimental realization, the presuppositions of cultural interpretation can be judged only according to the efficacy in producing a framework for further interpretation. Unlike scientific understanding, which has a built-in linearity running from relative human ignorance to greater magnitudes of human knowledge, cultural understanding (which encompasses all thought relating to historical artifacts, products of human activity and inscription) exhibits less fixity in projecting the origins and finalities of the collective human species. Presuppositions about historical knowledge (and, therefore, literary and cultural understanding) are distinguished by how they conjecture the relationship between a human origin and its projected end, whether as divine creation awaiting its conclusion in a final judgment, as human consciousness moving toward absolute knowledge by virtue of its own efforts, or as successive social formations marching inexorably toward a classless society. This larger set of concerns forms the context for Nietzsche's comments on the veracity of language, which propose a novel hypothesis about its epistemological role.

For all its supposed irrationality, Nietzsche's essay proceeds methodically and analytically, staking out a series of philosophical positions by referring to the assumptions underlying Western views about the role of language in engendering human knowledge. In this sense, the basic elements of the essay are not new; its novelty results, rather, from taking those observations drawn largely from political thinkers and placing them into an immanent model of historical explanation. The ironic opening of the essay, which recounts a fable about how "clever beasts invented knowing" and thus paved the way for their subsequent death, underscores the fictional, narrative nature of all conceptions of the emergence of human consciousness.[15] This beginning, no less than the first gurglings of language itself, can be recaptured only in the form of a story; in any subsequent historical moment, humans are unavoidably left with nothing more than a process of institutionalization already under way. Nevertheless, how one thinks of this "origin," even if one denies it entirely, has a decisive impact on the historical, linguistic, and cognitive potential of the human agent. For Nietzsche, that moment of emergence is irrevocably and, in fact, structurally lost, and all recuperations that claim a simultaneity for language, human consciousness, and subjective intention can only be ideological, subordinate to and supportive of historical interests. In offering a different hypothesis of the irruption of language, Nietzsche provides the backbone for an immanent historical understanding that draws its impetus from the disparity between an unknowable origin, without an identifiable author, and a full-blown human reason enjoying the unacknowledged benefits of sociopolitical institutions. This historical conception rests squarely on Nietzsche's materialist view of language that stands opposed both to the positivist belief in history as a homogeneous continuum and to Heidegger's philosophy of history characterized by efforts to catch glimpses of an overlooked Being.

In Nietzsche's hypothetical reasoning, the contrast between truth and lie, which has been at the core of moral critiques of the essay, comes to be as a by-product of sociolinguistic institutions. Laws of truth emerge alongside linguistic legislations. At this point in the argument, Nietzsche reformulates the themes of the essay in a more precise fashion: "And besides, what about these linguistic conventions themselves? Are they perhaps products of knowledge, that is, of the sense of truth? Are designations congruent with things? Is language the adequate expression of all realities?" (81; 878). In the logic of the essay, the upshot is that language, knowledge, and the sociopolitical are inseparable, and no single element enjoys even relative priority. Examining these questions in reference to their historical import occupies the remainder of the essay. In the context of contemporary critique, this batch of questions can be restated somewhat differently: What theory of language would enable one to account for the role that language itself plays in producing knowledge, on the one hand, and in setting up the sociopolitical institutions that monitor such knowledge, on the other?

To address this issue, the essay posits that at the heart of human society lies a basic forgetfulness of the epistemological situation in which language evolved. A far cry from Heidegger's dire warnings about the forgetfulness of Being, this assertion is nonetheless commonplace among Western thinkers whose concerns combine political and linguistic deliberation. Prominent in this tradition, for example, are Dante and Machiavelli, who stress opposing aspects of the question. For Dante, whose philosophical role in providing arguments for modern national languages has long been recognized, this original forgetfulness (*oblivio*) anchors the secular process of human action and linguistic change: "All our language—besides that which God created at the same time as man—is subject to the reworkings of our free will (*beneplacito*), after that confusion which was no more than a forgetting of previous language." [16] In the post-Babel world, after the divine gift of language that could only be the perfect expression of reality, language is as unstable as human action is fickle; Dante's well-known proposal to counter this deleterious tendency calls for instituting a grammar of an idealized Italian language belonging to no particular community. In this way, an (institutionalized) sphere of collective culture and sociopolitical writing could be demarcated.

For Machiavelli, "forgetfulness" occurs as a result of active struggle between societies or between human beings and the elements of nature. Thus, instead of a passive forgetting, the inability to ascertain, much less to represent past plenitude with any certainty—such as the creation of the world around five thousand years ago, in Machiavelli's example—results from an active effacement or annihilation, something like the historical rewriting that takes place in twentieth-century dictatorships. When a new religion emerges —a new cultural hegemony, as we would say it today—the first task is to eliminate the preceding religion, a goal easier to accomplish if it is simply a matter of substituting a new language. In this way, Machiavelli concludes, human and natural events (such as floods, plagues, and so on) "wipe out the memories of things," "extinguish" the old institutions in favor of the new.[17] As is customary in Machiavelli's straightforward analyses, historical outcomes are determined by relations of force in which the struggling actors can be readily identified.

Despite obvious distinctions between Machiavelli's and Dante's orientations, their shared historical conception, as well as its political implications, are specifically modern; the questions they raise about culture, its social and conceptual institutions, and the need for a collective written language have furnished the parameters for modern political thought. Writing in the shadows of this tradition, however, Nietzsche expands this historical conception to include the notion of knowing, that is, language as an institutionalized process of knowing, which is consequently also subject to historical transformation rather than just a means to record history. This contrast between Nietzsche and the tradition from which his considerations emerge succinctly illustrates the point of contention between interpreters who endorse Nietzsche's materialist view of language and those who exempt the faculty of human knowing from the forces of history. In its simplest terms, Nietzsche's view of language is summed up in his definition of the word: "What is a word? It is the copy in sound of a nerve stimulus" (81; 878). Words are not initially products of a masterful consciousness but are born out of interactions and result from nerve stimuli, out of the purview of a controlling human mind. This hypothesis is obviously unverifiable to the same extent as any other story about the origin of language, even those based on the most rigid belief in a one-to-one correspondence between a word and a thing.

Once again, though, Nietzsche's hypothetical discourse on language and knowing does not appear out of nowhere, and, as in the case of forgetfulness, his particular inflection is significant. Jean-Jacques Rousseau, another thinker whose writings traverse many domains along the literary-political axis, pursues a similar series of conjectures. His *Essai sur l'origine des langues* tells the story of what he calls the figural origin of language.[18] This much debated text offers an example of Rousseau's hypothesis of language formation, and the components of this account are easily summarized: One human being sees another and, having no inkling of their resemblance, names him a "giant" (because his apprehension at seeing someone else for the first time leads him to believe that the other was much larger, stronger, and so on, than himself); after recurring sightings of the other, however, he realizes their similarity and invents a new name to describe them both; at this point, human beings have a word, *giant*, with no referent, even though it was the first word.[19] After elaborating this example, Rousseau makes the following observations: "This is how the figural word is born before the proper word, when passion leaves us starry-eyed and the first idea it offers us is not that of truth. . . . With the illusory image offered by passion being the first to show itself, the language corresponding to it was also the first invented; then it became metaphorical when the enlightened mind, recognizing its prior error, employed its expressions only for the same reasons that produced it."[20] Despite its being heavily marked by eighteenth-century notions of language and signification, the fundamental components of Rousseau's linguistic understanding differ only slightly from those of Nietzsche (even if Nietzsche might have been shocked to see this affinity, given his constant ridicule of Rousseau).[21] What for Nietzsche is an utterance provoked by a nerve stimulus becomes in Rousseau's description the result of an involuntary passion. Just as with Nietzsche's nerve stimulus, inciting a reaction akin to a protozoon's response to an electric shock, the passion depicted by Rousseau takes place spontaneously, gratuitously, without the intervention of thought. This intense reaction of passion transpires according to an unpredictable logic of its own, not reducible to an economy of truthful representation. With the engagement of reason (that is, the enlightened mind: l'esprit éclairé), the linguistic irruptions of passion, along with the resulting idea and the experience prompting it, are deemed erroneous or flawed. At that moment, subsequent to the mindlessness of passion, all enters into order: Truth opposes error, and proper meaning wins precedence over the figural. Redressing this disjuncture, which is recognized only as it is established, creates the linguistic space of metaphor.

In paring away the divergent dramatization, Nietzsche's version seems to endorse similar conclusions: For reasons that become clear as its argument unfolds, Nietzsche's essay stresses that the very distinction between truth and error comes from the legislated regulation of reference. But Rousseau's portrayal of figural languages as error, which an enlightened mind will later correct, privileges individual consciousness and experience, no matter how much a traumatic experience and the resulting expression might disrupt its placid serenity. In tracing the further implications of this involuntary model of linguistic emergence, Nietzsche assigns the production of concepts to the linguistic process itself rather than to individual consciousness alone, thus dispelling any ambiguity about the absolute privilege of individual reason. As part of the linguistic process, any utterance is caught up in the formation of concepts: "Every word instantly becomes a concept precisely insofar as it is not supposed to serve as a reminder of the unique and entirely individual original experience to which it owes its emergence; but rather, a word becomes a concept insofar as it simultaneously has to fit countless more or less similar cases—which means, purely and simply, cases which are never like and thus altogether unlike" (83; 879–80). In addition to echoing Rousseau's account of the repeated experiences necessary ("après beaucoup d'expériences") to realize the error of the word *giant* and invent the category of "man," Nietzsche's analysis takes up the terms of Aristotle's logical conception of language, which forms the basis of Western linguistic thought.[22]

Contrary to Aristotelian logic, however, which derives language from assumptions about the essences of things and about its capacity to absorb and represent them, the conceptualization inherent to language in Nietzsche's essay does not owe its existence to a presumed essence. As the essay continues, even the "contrast between individual and species is something anthropomorphic and does not stem from the essence of things" (83; 880). This anthropomorphism, the figural dimension of language that creates an interface between consciousness and reality, is closely intertwined with the conceptual categories of human thought that builds on the individual's particularizing experiences. This anthropomorphic impulse permeates language as a network of meaning production and surfaces repeatedly as obligatory for linguistic analysis (a tendency reflected in both Aristotle's and Rousseau's use of the human figure in analyzing the links between thought and language). Rather than attributing human specificity to the ability to use language, a historically common assertion, Nietzsche emphasizes the capacity to manufacture concepts, a by-product of the amalgam between thought and language: "Everything which distinguishes man from the animals depends upon this ability to volatilize perceptual metaphors (*die anschaulichen Metaphern*) in a schema, and thus to dissolve a figure (*Bild*) into a concept" (84, 881).[23] Ultimately, this human penchant to conceptualize operates by virtue of language, which is of a wholly different order than what it expresses. Nietzsche characterizes this disjuncture as mimicking a "suggestive transference, a stammering translation into a completely foreign tongue."[24] Language, and the thought it permits, dissipates this incommensurability, just as the translation replaces the original it can never equal.

In its own highly original way, the essay on truth and lying presents a model of historical and linguistic knowing with a defined set of presuppositions. This insistence on a model does not signal the relative interchangeability of historical models and their consequent interpretations. All models or groups of assumptions cohere with compatible interests and historical constraints, including socioeconomic and cultural formations, even if the dominance or hegemony of certain models is not wholly arbitrary. In this sense, the Aristotelian idea that essences—by definition intangible and invisible—underlie appearances, a model that requires a reinforced and extensive network of institutions to guarantee the proper correspondence between essences and appearances, meanings and expressions, tends to produce regular and stable views of history that proceed in orderly fashion toward an orderly and fulfilling end. In the same way, Nietzsche's model also has a highly charged historical component, even if it stops far short of identifying the historical with the breezy narrative claiming to represent it.

4

The extreme importance of this fragmentary essay for Said's work and for contemporary critical thought generally derives more from the consequences of Nietzsche's formulations than from the formulations themselves. As Nietzsche's essay makes clear, in stretching this linguistic model along a time line, history—and, no less significantly, concomitant human consciousness —becomes a never-ending process of sedimentation: "Even the relationship of a nerve stimulus to the generated figure is not in itself a necessary one. But when the same figure has been generated millions of times and has been handed down for many generations and finally appears on the same occasion every time for all humankind, then it acquires at last the same meaning for human beings it would have if it were the sole necessary figure and if the relationship of the original nerve stimulus to the generated figure were a strictly causal one" (87; 884). This description contains the nucleus of a theory of history that resembles more a radical materialism than an empty denial of external reality. What is arbitrary at some long lost beginning, what is not necessary in itself (an sich), takes on a historical necessity through time. Historical necessities exist, but only as the result of history itself. The figure— of thought, of expression—cannot be divested of its history any more than a language can be freed of its meanings and still remain a language. The gradual naturalization of these figures, that is, the (tools of) thought they render natural, makes human consciousness possible; at the same time, they pose formidable obstacles for any theory of history that would not place human consciousness at its conceptual center. A rigorous materialist theory of history would inevitably have to take into account the matter of thought, which means integrating consideration of language while refusing to grant absolute primacy to human consciousness and to the theories of representation and causality that such primacy involves.

This theory of language—what I have called Nietzsche's model of historical understanding—surrounds and traverses the passage Said cites to indicate the theoretical underpinnings of his investigation into Orientalism. This passage, certainly the best known paragraph of the essay and perhaps of Nietzsche's work as a whole, both summarizes the essay and, because it is torn from the carefully constructed argument, misrepresents it: "What then is truth? A mobile army of metaphors, metonymies, and anthropomorphisms: in short, a sum of human relations which have been poetically and rhetorically intensified, transferred, and embellished, and which, after long usage, seem to a people to be fixed, canonical, and binding. Truths are illusions which we have forgotten are illusions; they are metaphors that have become worn out and have been drained of sensuous force, coins which have lost their figures (Bild) and are now considered as metal and no longer as coins" (84; 880–81).[25] The problem with truth is that it is inextricably tangled up with language, but the result of this observation is to historicize rather than relativize truth. Language, and the concepts that feed on it, definitely establish truths; but truths are also the product of historical forces and live on by virtue of social, political, and linguistic institutions, among others, whose longevity masks the figuration at the basis of all language. This model of language and consciousness, which presupposes that the economy of language is fundamentally metaphorical and figural, opens up new avenues of historical critique that extend to the concepts themselves. Institutions—understood in the broadest sense—efface that figuration into invisibility, just as time erodes the face of a coin; from this perspective, historical understanding calls for recovering those figures and deciphering the forces that promoted their disappearance.

In the last twenty years, since the publication of Said's *Orientalism*, the theory of history put forth in Nietzsche's essay has had significant reverberations in contemporary criticism. Whatever their ultimate goals, however, these reactions end up at the very least nodding to the political implications of this materialist view of language. In an important essay on anthropomorphism, for example, Paul de Man remarks on Nietzsche's definition of truth: "Tropes are neither true nor false but are both at once. To call them an army is however to imply that their effect and their effectiveness is not a matter of judgment but of power. What characterizes a good army, as distinct for instance from a good cause, is that its success has little to do with immanent justice and a great deal with the proper economic use of its power." Although de Man primarily seeks to read the figures of Nietzsche's text and to show how the anthropomorphism of its language plays out its assertions, his comments are revealing of the dual power that inhabits language. De Man refers to this power as "epistemological" and "strategic," tied simultaneously to the production of knowledge and to persuading, to convincing, to provoking actions. In other words, as a product of ongoing institutionalization, language enforces, cajoles, and convinces, but its power is also more insidious because it lurks in its concepts, in the very matter of thought. Conceptually, this power is an antecedent to judgment, which acts in the name of that power even as the judge can do little more than assert his or her impartiality.[26]

Nevertheless, this powerful paradigm of historical understanding, grounded in the linguistic matter of concepts, carries within itself the mechanism of critique. In Nietzsche's text, this critique has to do with metaphors, those figures always caught up in the process leading to concepts: "The drive toward the formation of metaphors is the fundamental human drive, which one cannot for a single instant dispense with in thought, for one would thereby dispense with man himself. This drive is not truly vanquished and scarcely subdued by the fact that a regular and rigid new world is constructed as a prison from its own ephemeral products, the concepts" (88–89; 887). At bottom, the human linguistic process portrayed here, certainly anti-Aristotelian and contrary to beliefs in mystical essence, exceeds the concepts that would channel and master it. In that sense, it is a theory concerned with production cutting across concepts that accrue to themselves universality while denying—or forgetting—the historical force necessary for them to come into being. Because figuration belongs fundamentally to language and, consequently, to human thought, the social and cognitive power of institutions lives by the same process that enables unmasking, however fleetingly, the power they conceal.

In effect, this conception of historical and linguistic matter acknowledges a wholly different form of power and no longer relegates discursive and cultural expression to simply a secondary role vis-à-vis executive force. This basic force of linguistic figuration, of the formation of metaphors, underscores the importance of the matter of history—inscribed almost exclusively on paper prior to the late nineteenth century—and of literary reflection. It is not happenstance that Nietzsche was trained as a classical philologist, the nineteenth-century equivalent of a literary critic; nor should it be surprising that Antonio Gramsci, the twentieth-century thinker who has most deeply analyzed the historical ramifications of cultural production and who has also been a fundamental reference for Said, was a university student of literature who concentrated on linguistics. Gramsci's view of metaphor displays interesting affinities with that of Nietzsche, despite their wide differences of historical vision. In clarifying the use of the term *immanence* in materialist theory, Gramsci characterizes the status of metaphor: "All language is a continuous process of metaphors, and the history of semantics is an aspect of the history of culture: language is both a living thing and a museum of fossils of past life and civilizations." [27] This historical sedimentation, inscribed and reinscribed in the ongoing elaboration of figures, provides the stuff of thought, of its hegemonic force, and of the critique that sifts out the interests that cover up their figural nature.

In Gramsci's speculations, the overlapping effects of the linguistic and the political receive greatest emphasis. Gramsci links these disjunctures between reigning metaphorical languages to the emergence of new worldviews (or new world conceptions: He refers to a "nuova concezione del mondo"), thereby moving the historical question into the foreground. Contrary to Nietzsche, whose concern with the power of ideas and concepts takes a largely epistemological turn, Gramsci focuses, in his work, on the historical significance of historical transformation and of the ideologies in subsequent world orders. Language is "always metaphorical. Although one may not be able to say exactly that every discourse is metaphorical with respect to the thing or material object indicated (or to the abstract concept), so as not to enlarge too much the concept of metaphor, one can nonetheless say that present-day language is metaphorical with respect to the meanings and ideological content that the words have had in prior periods of civilization." Despite Gramsci's hesitation about putting into question the empirical model of language deriving from Aristotle, the historical trajectory he describes clearly operates according to a historical model of meaning production: There is no pure essence hiding and waiting only to be discovered. The explicit recognition that metaphor is also a concept uncomfortably dovetails with language's ineluctable production of concepts and introduces an irony that Nietzsche would have, no doubt, appreciated. But Gramsci's notion of succeeding worldviews, with their concomitant hegemonies and supporting constellations of ideas, gives this theory of history an overtly political face. While the primary outcome may be to radicalize historical understanding, to question universals presumed to continue unscathed by history, in practice this linguistic materialism hints at a new mode of historical intervention.[28]

At the edge of the twenty-first century, the question of historical intervention takes on unforeseen meanings, largely because of the historical conjuncture itself, the clash in worldviews and the technological means that diffuse them. In his careful reading of the established truth about the Orient, a reading that entailed laying bare the gradual evolution of the idea into the status of an existing thing whose ideological foundations have been forgotten, Said's analysis has done considerably more than dispel illusions. In his drive to unite the theoretical and the political, Said's work has made contributions to both realms; his portrayal of certain tendencies of historical intervention could very easily apply to his own work: "The critique of objectivity and authority did perform a positive service by underlining how, in the secular world, human beings construct their truths, and that, for example, the so-called objective truth of the white man's superiority built and maintained by the classical European colonial empires also rested on a violent subjugation of African and Asian peoples."[29] But, even more importantly, his work has irrefutably demonstrated that institutions are more than simply the buildings that have doors, locks, fenced-in lawns, and local police. They are also nonempirical institutions composed of language, concepts, and figures.

In responses begins responsibility: music and emotion

"*Teamwork,*" *Koteks snarled, "is one word for it, yeah. What it really is is a way to avoid responsibility. It's a symptom of the gutlessness of the whole society.*"—Thomas Pynchon, The Crying of Lot 49

He who would only recollect is a voluptuary, but he who wills repetition is a man.—Søren Kierkegaard, Repetition: An Essay in Experimental Psychology (*Lowrie transla-tion*)

I

One of the most pressing issues at the present moment in the field of criti-cism and aesthetics is the question of feeling. There was, until very recently, a "taboo on the sensual," as Adorno remarked. Adorno, himself an inconstant lover of the sensual in the arts, was given to saying things such as "the force of pleasure" in aesthetic response "has an infantile quality."[1] If understanding and even encouraging a "New Robustness," as art historian Joseph Leo Koer-ner calls it, is on the agenda of a small but growing number of critics, there is still a fair amount of resistance to any such move by moralists of both con-servative and progressive political orientation who are convinced that wanton violence and pleasure in the arts begets wantonness in the beholders of the arts.[2] For such people, art can be and ought to be uplifting. And so we find philosophers, such as Martha Nussbaum, devoting a great deal of attention to setting before us the ideas of Hellenistic philosophers, who hold that the right philosophy is all one needs to free oneself of harmful emotions.[3]

That the emotions are involved in our experiences in art is not a matter of doubt to the ordinary person who listens to rock or goes to a thriller or a gothic movie precisely in the hope of undergoing turbulence of a level that would cause the rider of a jet plane to panic. But at finer seminar and editorial tables, the emotions are still frequently unwanted guests, treated as if they were illegal immigrants trying to take jobs away from the righteous, upstanding citizens of reason, the ideas. A great deal of the blame for this inhospitality could be leveled at our ruling concepts of what Art with a capital A is and ought to be. We still have not sufficiently outgrown "the concept of art, . . . a category which the nineteenth century, to a previously unimaginable extent, but hardly more justification at bottom, imposed on the creations of intellectual productivity."[4] Those who think of themselves as endowed with especially fine artistic consciences have hurled down, from the altar of art, curse upon curse on the emotions, like Prospero railing at Caliban, until the moment he comes to acknowledge Caliban and all he represents. Those dominating the arts scene have, to a too great extent, operated like Prospero before he takes his turn.

Edward Said has never played the role of a lordly Prospero out of touch with the feelings of Caliban and locked in splendid and lonely isolation. If this is true—as I believe it is—it is due in no small part to the fact that Said, unlike some other great critics of the twentieth century, such as Georg Lukács, has never made the aesthetic experience serve ideology. At a meeting of the Modern Language Association to discuss the merits of his then recent book *Culture and Imperialism* in Toronto in December 1994, Said was critical of some of the words said in his praise by admirers who thought he was saying that politics trumps all other concerns. He said, "I have heard that there are some philosophers who think that the age of grand narratives such as the narrative of liberation is over. I disagree. That narrative still holds great power for me. But if that narrative does not have room for all the small narratives of liberation such as those I feel when reading a novel or listening to a work of music, then I want no part of it." One reviewer of *Musical Elaborations* sensed embarrassment in Said in the face of his own musical experiences, but I think this misreads Said.[5] Said says that, of course, he realizes the dangers involved for someone (who is attacking the ways in which the arts have been made to appear autonomous from other social practices) to be emphasizing privacy and pleasure the way he does, most especially in chapter 3 of *Musical Elaborations*, a chapter entitled "Melody, Solitude, and Affirmation." He says this because both privacy and pleasure are "replete with the historical and ideological residue of that bourgeois individuation now either discredited or fully under attack."[6]

Said defines the intellectual as a person who tells the truth to power. He takes this even further, into what is sometimes more touchy and difficult terrain, in insisting by his own actions that the job of the intellectual is to tell the truth to his followers and to himself. If these aesthetic experiences that he has take a particular course, his job as philologist, first of all, is to try to understand them and to faithfully record them. The account of a set of aesthetic experiences that Said gives us in chapter 3 has many virtues, but they all flow from his will to account, with almost total absorption, for the minute details of the experience.

Because idealism and high modernism exiled feeling from arts talk for nearly two centuries, we do not have the words to talk about our experiences of art. In refusing to look down from the heavens of high theory on the sentient creature who undergoes a musical experience, I think Said has done real theoretical work. For two centuries, we have for the most part valued the intellectual over the sensual, moralized the arts, devalued the role of the recipient of art in artistic judgment, and promoted the notion of the work of art as an organic whole whose workings can be understood fully in terms of its internal organization. The first line of Marcel Proust's *Contre Sainte-Beuve* reads: "Chaque jour j'attache moins de prix a l'intelligence." "Every day I set less store on intellect." Proust's words form a line of light, a beacon to guide us home! "The truths of intellect are less precious than those secrets of feeling." Intellect and theory become names for what obstructs us from understanding the workings of art if we do not understand what Proust calls "this relative inferiority of the intellect." [7] Note the word *relative*. It is not that we can do without theory or the intellect. It is foolish to suppose we must choose either theory or feeling, abstraction over community. Theory becomes the problem if we believe in a discursive solution for problems. As Miguel Tamen writes, "Being a critic for Said means primarily describing oneself in a position of empirical dissatisfaction without for that matter having to produce complete explanations of the causes or of the remedies for such dissatisfaction." [8] Theory and the intelligence still have their necessary roles to play. As Proust warns, "If intellect only ranks second in the hierarchy of virtues, intellect alone is able to proclaim that the first place must be given to instinct." [9]

Said has refused the name of theorist.[10] Not for him the somber clothes of the literary theorist, who might well be a Puritan divine rather than an enthusiast of the arts. Not for him what I might call art-theory black but a brighter plumage. Walter Benjamin writes, "Gray is all theory; green, and not only green but also red, yellow, blue, is the golden tree of life. In our predilection for the various shades of gray . . . running to black we find an unmistakable social reflection of our tendency to privilege theory over all else in the formation of intellect." Always stylish, Said clearly pays attention to appearances. As Paul Valery has said, "Man is himself, is man, only at the surface."[11]

People who profess to pay no attention to appearances are not to be trusted. One risk Said takes in this third chapter is that of appearing to attend only to surfaces and thus seeming to be the voluptuary Kierkegaard speaks of. His book is so full of glittering appearances by stars such as Alfred Brendel and Glenn Gould, and by colorful figures such as that captivating captive of Cairo, the exiled Polish Jew, Said's piano teacher when he lived in Egypt, Ignace Tiergerman, that one might take the essay as a grand display of cosmopolitan culture. This would be to cheat oneself of learning one of the many things that can be learned from Said, especially if one is interested, as I am, in the nature of the aesthetic experience and most especially in the experience of music. As Simon Frith argues in his recent *Performing Rites*, "The question underlying the last two hundred and fifty years' debate about music remains: What does a listener to music actually do?"[12] This cunning essay of Said, an essay that evinces real humanist sprezzatura, says something very important. Its significance, I think, is hardly hinted at by its assured tone. There is no heavy breathing, but the "labor" he emphasizes in the title of the book in the word *elaborations* is all there.

The exile of feeling is more significant, I believe, than the exile of evaluation that Barbara Herrnstein Smith has analyzed in her *Contingencies of Value*.[13] Although they go hand in hand, feeling is even more basic than judgment, because it is or ought to be the basis of evaluation. "After Beethoven," writes Said, "music veered off from the social realm into the aesthetic almost completely" (12). Aesthetics, which (if the name of this area of inquiry is to be of any significance) ought to be about feelings, was hijacked about the time the Jena Romantics dispersed to other places and other jobs. Friedrich Schlegel ended up working for one of the Kissingers of his day, Klemens, Fürst von Metternich! These were the thinkers who tried, I think, most seriously to develop the project contributed to by a host of thinkers in the eighteenth century to understand (the way people like Karl Philipp Moritz and the group involved with the journal *Gnothi sauton: oder, Magazin zur Erfahrungseelenkunde*, published from 1783 to 1793, did)[14] what it is that things can do to provoke responses within human beings. How can a mere thing strike a mortal so strongly as music can do?

My ulterior motive here is to enlist Said in an effort to revive aesthetics after a hiatus for several centuries in the inquiry into aesthetics, despite the efforts of people such as Benjamin, Theodor Adorno, and Paul de Man to resituate the field back on earth by shifting attention back to feelings. Interest in such matters among what some would call analytic philosophers has not been strong.[15] Although Said's chapter features much musical notation, professional musicological analysis is not what Said wants to offer nor what he provides, for the same reasons that in literary studies he prefers the critic to the theorist. He means to give an exemplary reading not of music but of someone attending to music. That is the only score he wants to settle. He wants to attend to that experience as closely and finely as Glenn Gould does to a Bach score, note by note, avoiding legato, avoiding articulation. He wants to see musical experience in the light of all the other experiences or the relative paucity of experience at the present time. Music is too important to us all to be left as the exclusive preserve of the musicologists. There is a role to play for what Said calls the "rank outsider" (xvii), because "music's autonomy from the social world has been taken for granted" for too long (xvi). As Said's much admired mentor, R. P. Blackmur, writes, "Criticism, I take it, is the formal discourse of an amateur." No more, no less. Such critical practice does blend intelligence with feeling in the way Proust desires and is truly theoretical. As Said comments, writing about Blackmur, "I do not think it is wrong to call the form of this apprehension of intellect and experience fundamentally theoretical." [16]

2

It might be helpful if I survey Said's chapter, highlighting certain elements in it: Said begins by talking about musical experience as an experience prompted by recollection, a recollection that is bound to actual material reality. The text to initiate his discussion comes from Proust, of course, and he points out that Proust is not suggesting that what is recollected is some prior experience itself, as if recollection could give us direct access to past experience, but rather an object, "the very object in which experience seems to be lodged" (74). He says "such objects acquire an immaterial existence when they mix indissolubly—the word is Proust's—into the general mixture of other thoughts and sensations of that time" (74–75). Next, he talks about the individual as a function of that object, the work of music, that precipitates the experience of subjectivity. A "precarious singularity," that of the individual composer, performer, or recipient, "attaches to the uniqueness of music itself" (75). This attachment is in evident need of explanation because, as Said says nicely, of the "muteness" of music (75).

Artworks such as music offer us the illusion of unity and completeness, but in fact they await completion in the response of the auditor who might respond in enthusiasm, forgetfulness, other recollections, distraction, or boredom. Artworks offer us "illusions of aesthetic unity" (75). A peculiarity of music that differentiates it from some other arts, though certainly not from sports events, such as football games, is that the experience of music is subject to time. We listeners are compelled to rigorous and linear attention by the sheer unfolding quality of the work of music in time. Music has an "ineluctable temporal modality" (76). We must, if we would experience it, submit to "the tyranny of its forward logic or impulse" (76). However, although musical events are one-time occasions, they can return to us in memory.

At this point, Said gives an extended example of the way recollection might work in order to see what questions this process might lead to. The musical experience may be unique and occur at one time, but it has a sort of "extendable" nature. He recounts listening to Brendel perform Brahms's Theme with Variations for Piano. As I have mentioned, I am interested in the way Said might provide us with a vocabulary for talking about the emotions we feel when undergoing a musical experience, so I note the way he discusses the "unexpected pleasure" that came to him when he recognized how the piano work of Brahms, which he did not at first think he knew at all, recalled Brahms's String Sextet in B-flat, to which it is indeed related. This pleasure, partly because it was unexpected, made him "unusually attentive" (80) to the work. And then he was "reminded spontaneously" (83) of Nimrod's variation in Elgar's *Enigma* Variations. The words he uses to describe the music are not technical but rather are words that give labels to emotions, "sweetness" (81), "noisy aridity" (81), "satisfying and affirmative" (82), "expansive, serene, even assuredly satisfied" (83), and so on.

And for a while reading Said, I am transported back to the romantic period, thinking about Samuel Taylor Coleridge and his lyre, a symbol of the human soul being played on by the object world of the winds that blow across it through an open window:

> And thus, my Love! As on the midway slope
> Of yonder hill I stretch my limbs at noon,
> While through my half-clos'd eye-lids I behold
> The sunbeams dance, like diamonds, on the main,
> And tranquil muse upon tranquility;
> Full many a thought uncall'd and undetain'd,
> And many idle flitting phantasies,
> Traverse my indolent and passive brain,
> As wild and various as the random gales
> That swell and flutter on this subject Lute! [17]

Although this comparison is useful in a loose sense because it does suggest that Said is indeed picking up the eighteenth-century talk about the aesthetics that Coleridge is calling on in his poem, I would not push the comparison too far, because I think Said is pursuing matters in a different way and to much different ends than Coleridge. The voice in Coleridge's poem speaks as if it were ashamed of attending to an account of feelings, "these shapings of the unregenerate mind" (line 55). And the bias of the poem is toward a totality—it speaks of "the one Life within us and abroad" (line 26) and "one intellectual breeze" (line 47) that animates all things human and inhuman—a totality that Said would find stifling.

As Said continues to recount all he recollected when prompted by Brahms, Brendel, and the piano, he again marvels that such "speechless, contentless eloquence" can have such an effect on him (86). Music is mute, for all its noise. Artworks are the children of silence, even musical artworks. Said cuts off his "inventory" (86) of fleeting feelings, acknowledging that, of course, he could go on, but the point is not to give an inventory of recollections but to give us an adequate display of the associative power of his mind. Giving us a sense of the power of his mind alone in isolation is not his point at all, even though a quick reading of his disarming text might give one such an impression. The imperial, Prospero-like power of his individual mind is beside the point. It is put aside or off center by this flooding ensemble of recollections as they consolidate and converge, mounting enough force to strike him physically. "The music itself was affirmed for" him, and he likewise was affirmed for the music (88). The way in which he is affirmed is not an intellectual matter, because the music hits him "in a muscular-nervous way," which was confirmed for him when he found himself able in short order to play the Brahms variations himself on the piano with "an almost total absorption in the notes" (88). The anamnestic intoxication with which he undergoes music gives him knowledge felt along the bone.

This experience leads him to question such talk about music that makes the composer into the absolute genius of the set of activities that go into the making, performing, hearing, and recollecting of music. The distinction between composing and interpreting music is useful, but only up to a point, and then it can be positively misleading. Interpretation is the equivalent of composition or must be of equal interest to the critic. Exploring why and how this must be so leads him into a discussion of what he calls, following Raymond Williams, "the structure of feeling" (91). He suggests that while purely musicological analyses of the structure of a work of art may not tell us all there is to know about it, structure is still of prime interest—the structure of feeling, the process of gaining experience, into which the objective, material piece of music leads us. He contrasts a performance by Maurizio Pollini of Bach's *Well-Tempered Clavier*, which was done the way it was for reasons purely internal to the professional behavior of pianists so that it would be maximally different from Glenn Gould's interpretation of the work, to the practice of his piano teacher in Cairo, Tiegerman. Here, too, Said tells us that his thoughts and his chapter are not being guided by the all-controlling mind but by promptings of a physiological sort. He uses language such as "I found myself recalling—I mean the word literally" (91). Just as the individual listener is the ultimate ground for the experience he or she will have listening and engaging music, so the individual performer must be for the playing of music. The nature of the musical performance can only be theorized at ground level in the midst of "the difficulty" Said remembers he once had when trying to play Brahms and having "to separate the actual music from the large mass of the score's many notes" (91). One who is "blasé" (91) does not demonstrate the proper aesthetic attitude and does not submit to undergoing the trial by feeling in detail, on the ground, for example, the "structure of feeling" that might be provoked in you "if you really *know* about" a work of music and its composer (91). If one has knowledge and is part of this "structure of feeling," then one relies on the canon, but such performances in effect exist "beyond the canon" (91).

The structure of this feeling encompasses the resolutely individual performer or listener and also, nonetheless and paradoxically, the social. Such behavior gains value to the extent that it can turn itself resolutely to its own goals and not those of the crowd. It has nothing to do with an effort to conform to the expectations of other people. Said confesses again that what he is describing is something he finds difficult to express. Again and again in this chapter, he has confessed that he feels himself walking on thin ice, yet he feels compelled by the rightness of his conviction of his overall picture of things to move on as if in imitation of the performers and composers whose work he most admires and whose persistence in their very singularity is the source of their making the music of their own music, as he calls it.

Said's grasping for words is not pretense, and the words he finds are, I think, valuable, because they provide a report, as it were, from the borderlands of aesthetic experience. This is a place many of us get to but most of us have very few ready words to talk about what we experience, and we find ourselves, all too often, if not all the time, even more mute than Said finds music itself to be.

He then attempts to explicate the paradoxical phrase "the music of his music" (93) by reference to the word *melody* (92). Melody may be the most elusive of basic musical categories. Proust finds music in literature, and what he says about the music he finds there may illuminate Said's idea of melody: "When I began to read an author I very soon caught the tune of the song beneath the words." He must be in a state of drifting consciousness to do so, he writes, and when he is, he has the capacity to plumb the depths of an artwork to reach its inner, hidden melody.[18] Melody, according to Said, is "an expandable notion" and ought to include "all those things that go into making up the particular idiom, or aesthetic statement, of composers or even of styles" (94). He defines melody "as a name both for an actual melody and for any other musical element that acts in or beneath the lines of a particular body of music to attach [key word, I think] that music to the privacy of the listener's, performer's, or composer's experience" (96).

He then discusses the set of circumstances—historical circumstances—that have made it so difficult to speak about melody the way he wants to speak about it. He acknowledges that Adorno had reason to rail against the ravages of "regressive hearing" and all the "continuous noise pollution all around" us (96), but maintains that the abstracting of the high art of classical music from history has had an effect almost as oppressive as that of a country forced to live with *The Sound of Music* as its one sound track—a musical imprisonment that the Austrians know something about. There might be a certain justice to this turn of events in a way analogous to Dante's meting out justice in *The Inferno* according to the logic of the *contrapasso*: The guilty are dosed with just the medicine they prescribed to others for the rest of eternity. The revolution in "art music," now cut off from popular forms and all the other sounds of life that led to the apotheosis of the sonata form, has made for a music of control, in Said's view, which works to too rigid a logic of development and produces a music to which one cannot dance, a music one has to listen to sitting rigidly in concert halls, all hushed and still as if his or her passions could never be aroused.

Said admits to caricaturing the music of Beethoven and his followers—he knows what Charles Rosen has written about the sonata—but he sees that a kind of "marble curtain" (my phrase) fell on classical music when the sonata form gained hegemony (100–102). It is a music of control that does not condone elaboration. The sonata movement within a larger work may have been intended originally as a place for free elaboration, but with the triumph of the sonata (thanks to Beethoven), the possibilities for elaboration and improvisation seem to have gone, only to return to Western music in the ranks of respectability with jazz, a history very odd to think about when we recall Adorno's love for Beethoven and hatred for jazz. Once "classical music" came to dominate high music, then the sort of improvisation allowed for in Bach's *Musical Offering* was out of style in new music. Said contrasts this royal absolutism in music with other forms of music, such as the classical Arabic song, which has "an aesthetic whose hallmark was exfoliating variation" (98). He finds musical death in the Austro-Germanic tradition but also signs of vitality even in the "magisterial narrowing of focus" and "majestically slow and inward self-contemplation" of Olivier Messaien and Richard Strauss (103). What distinguishes such music is its own internal consistency and its beautifully, radically elaborative "letting go" (105), as he characterizes Strauss's *Metamorphosen*. Such music is exemplary not because of the composer's absolute control but because of the composer's willingness to elaborate in a way that bears comparison to the music of classical Arabic song, the songs of Umm Kalthoum. Such work, such elaboration, is part of the work, Said wants to believe, of building a civil society from the ground up, not from the top down. The chapter ends by emphasizing a strong distinction between control versus elaboration. By the work of "elaboration," this labor, the enjoyment, the pleasures, and the pains of music could become contagious and metastasize throughout society. It is a hopeful picture. In ending the chapter the way he does, with this jump to the notion of how an elaborative art fosters a civil society, is Said giving us his own version of a humanism not altogether different from that of Nussbaum? But I am allowing myself to slip from description to interpretation. Let us move on.

3

In Said's spirit, I would like to elaborate on what he has said in chapter 3 of *Musical Elaborations*. I want to explain why I find this essay—and a critical essay it certainly aims to be, nothing more and nothing less—so worthy of attention.

Said's hypothesis is right: By understanding the workings of the individual in the experience of music, we can also gain a much richer sense of why music and all the arts are necessarily social. He claims earlier in the book that the musical performance "is both a private musical experience for performer and listener, and a public experience too" (12). These experiences are "interdependent and overlap" (12). There are historical and political reasons for trying to separate the two, but—he stresses—"they *are* together" (37). "The inner life," asserts Emmanuel Levinas, "is the unique way for the real to exist as a plurality." Beginning with the individual may seem to be beginning at the furthest remove from the social that Said certainly wants to comprehend. But by beginning with social explanations, one can become stuck in a kind of sand trap of self-confirming hypotheses about art, as the work of Pierre Bourdieu gives ample evidence. But Bourdieu is not alone in that trap: One wants to show the shallowness of bourgeois taste without risking falling victim to the blandishments and baubles that seem to please the bourgeoisie, so one ends up roughly where one begins, lambasting the petite bourgeoisie with their Disneylands and leaving the haute bourgeoisie feeling quite smug and superior in their expensive seats at the opera house. The pleasures of the bourgeoisie are only cheaply emotional and not powerfully intellectual. Yes, but . . . ? One does better to look into the emotions, because the emotions are arguably—so Annette Baier does indeed argue—"history-laden states of mind." And the idealist and modernist conviction that life should be led according to the dictates of reason so that Spirit can permeate all and that "man" should not be "alienated" from the Spirit may conform to long-term Western values such as those propounded by the Stoics, whom our contemporary Nussbaum promotes. But, on the other side, we might just listen to David Hume, who urges us to believe that reason is and should be the slave to the passions, because reason alone, reason the conqueror of the passions, can never be "a motive to any action of the will."[19] Could it be that closet elitists such as Bourdieu condemn the lowly arts that raise emotions because for them absolute and total control over the emotions is their goal?

Said rightly wants to understand the structure of feeling that will be, he believes, a better guide to what it is to inhabit and build a civil society. Most commentators on the aesthetic talk about the experience of art as if they are God, looking down from on high at insects copulating in the dirt on earth. Said has the assurance that allows him to risk the censorious label of being naïve and plunging in to try to understand activities not transparent to the understanding.

The rock group Romeo Void made one absolutely great single called "Myself to Myself." In it, Debora Iyall sings, "I used to try to change, / To tone down my responses / To disassemble the mechanism, / But love kept leaking out." But, she continues, now she has changed, and she is "giving up a false attitude of life."[20] She is learning to deal with her responses, and perhaps she is learning how to understand the functioning of the mechanism that connects feeling and affect to life. Said's chapter is an attempt to explore the mechanism that connects "myself to myself" and myself to others through music via response and feeling.

How to understand or even find that feeling? Not, perhaps, by looking to things inside but outside ourselves—in things such as the artworks that we know, if we are honest with ourselves, that arouse feeling in us. Proust is a good guide to this territory, and it is Proust who provides Said with his starting point and all the theory he needs. In a passage from Swann's Way, which Said does not quote but must have had in mind, is Proust's classic statement about the workings of "involuntary memory," which is the prelude to the moment in which the narrator describes the effect of the madeleine on the narrator: "The past is hidden somewhere outside the realm, beyond the reach of the intellect, in some material object . . . which we do not suspect. And as for the object, it depends on chance whether we come upon it or not before we ourselves must die."[21] The key word here, for me, is "outside." Perhaps Proust led Said to the decision to look outside the human and to figure out how humans get attached to things, but no matter, for it is a brilliant and necessary move. It is necessary, because what Merlin Donald calls "external storage" is probably a basic step in human development and because the interaction of humans and things that are not human (though they may be fashioned by humans to human needs the way tools are) is a key to under-standing human flourishing.[22] Of course, it is not just contemporary evolu-tionary psychologists who understand the role that mediation has to play in human history. Mediation (*Vermittlung*) is considered by Hegel as a central characteristic of human reason: "The cunning of reason is in the mediating activity which, by causing objects to act upon and react to each other in ac-cordance with their own nature, carries reason's intentions without any di-rect involvement in the process."[23] It is the *indirection* of art's activity that de-fies analysis and causes most analysis to founder. Said seems to be making music a special and unique instance in human behavior, but in fact he is not. He clearly wants to see music as an activity that performs social work. But his Proustian approach gives him the purchase he has on art's action. As he says, "The transgressive element in music is its nomadic ability to attach itself to, and become a part of, social formations" (70). His focus is absolutely on the object and the recipient's interaction with the object. But the object offers all those who interact with it no resting spot, no image of completeness, no hope for the coincidence of art and morality or art and the world. This is not human-ism's old fetishism of the art object. By displacing attention from the object to the interaction, Said raises the possibility of what I think is a new and deeper fetishism.

So he sets for himself the question of how can a thing that is not human and that is, as he says repeatedly, mute be so eloquent to humans? If what is most important about music, as he argues (89, 91, 97), is the interaction of music and humans, no mere musicological analysis will be adequate to the task of explaining the wider human impact of music. Some musicologists were not pleased with Said's book when it appeared. Perhaps they were unhappy that he was poaching on their territory. Perhaps they thought he was chastising them for their failures to make musicology anything but a profession locked in on itself, like a seacoast harbor whose boats cannot move out because the town is socked in by fog, but this time a fog of its own making. I do not think so. Said was concerned with matters that are of more general human concern and thus of critical concern. Benjamin writes, in his essay on Goethe's *Elective Affinities*, that some scholarly analyses of literature — and this would work for music as well — can give us the equivalent of chemical analyses and a break-down of the component elements of a work of art, but the critic's job is to give us the truth; this calls for alchemy on the critic's part, not mere chemistry.[24]

The job of the critic must be to attend to the new chemistry that happens between the work, the recipient, the producer, and the performer. This loop of overlapping relations and interdependencies will not take place in the shape of a hierarchical tree but of an electric current. No element in the loop is sov-ereign and independent, so we should not misconstrue the solitude of which

Said speaks. There is something in humans that is incomplete and open to things and uncannily capable of projecting itself on things and thereby getting "attached" to them in ways that begin humbly and simply and often end up complex and many layered; Said's relation to the piano work of Brahms bears much evidence of this possibility. It works like this: It is as if the work of Brahms were an uncharged battery that gets charged by the energy Said puts into it. Perhaps all works of art function like this in the interaction with human beings, who charge them with power. Artworks may function like rechargeable batteries, whose charge can run down to zero and then be stoked up again. This is the way artworks become "history-laden."

Every work of art is necessarily incomplete. All those grand works of music and literature from the nineteenth century were promoted to us, Said suggests, as if they were complete worlds unto themselves. With no God to authorize the Bible, we would have to accept Dickens, Wagner, and Joyce as gods, wouldn't we? But all these works offered to us were "illusions of aesthetic unity" (75), says Said, not real unity. They were fundamentally incomplete, but this incompleteness is not a deficiency. Artworks beckoned to humans to come and bond with them, not to make them whole but just to add to them, to join in their working.

Music in its glorious muteness is especially beckoning. As Frith writes, "Music does not have a content—it can't be translated—but this does not mean that it is not 'an object of understanding.' Or, to put it another way, the gap in music between the nature of the experience (sounds) and the terms of its interpretation (adjectives [remember all of Said's adjectives]) may be more obvious than in any other art form, but this does not mean that the pleasure of music must not lie in the ways we can—and must—fill the gap." Yet, as Frith says, making a point in common with Said, "The critical issue is not meaning and interpretation—musical appreciation as a kind of decoding—but experience and collusion: the 'aesthetic' describes a kind of self-consciousness, a coming together of the sensual, the emotional, and the social as performance."[25]

To understand this social performance, we are thrown back, paradoxically as it might seem and so Said feels it to be, on ourselves as lone individuals. To dwell on the paradoxical nature of resorting to the individual—the last place where a good critic of the social status quo would hope to have to be forced to seek refuge—might be misleading. It is the case that our access to all things outside our individual selves has to be mediated, and so we have no immediate access to the social world. Not only does it have to be mediated. Mediation is the very name of the game as far back as cave paintings, as Donald shows. The one realm to which we can have unmediated access is our affects. The empirical philosophy of England during the first half of the twentieth century, drawing on a long tradition, tried to argue that we had immediate sense impressions of the external world, but this is not a popular position today, and rightly so. We do, however, have direct awareness of mental episodes in our own lives, "including the limited but very real privileged access" to those episodes of our own lives.[26] I do not mean that we have access to our thoughts and emotions as if they were transparent to us. They are not. What we can know is that we have been emotionally engaged. We may not know what hit us, but we can know that we have been hit.

This is why, I would argue, Said's philological accounts of his states of affective engagement with music are most instructive for anyone trying to understand the nature of aesthetic experience. Said helps us to see how those mental episodes are brought on by jumps, starts, changes, and various other emotional abnormalities, such as Proust's involuntary memory, that trigger episodes and that can bundle themselves into a coordinated process that gives us an experience. Such activity is not the semblance of an experience, as if art were somehow always parasitic on life, but is experience itself. One drawback, of course, is that, since what one can be certain of is only the occurrence of affect, one cannot articulate it in words. Said crashes against this wall again and again, and this is the right wall to crash against if you want to understand the nature of the aesthetic experience. One cannot articulate it in words in the sense of connecting a discrete set of items into a whole, but one might and must, if one can, reelaborate it in new objects of art and criticism.

Said talks a fair amount about will when he describes what it is about the classical sonata form after Beethoven that seems like a Procrustean bed. He does not discuss will so much in the other parts of the chapter, partly, I suspect, because he believes (and I think he is right) that the will is not at all dominant in the aesthetic experience. Emerson may provide a useful gloss here on what Said says. Emerson, in "The Method of Nature," argues that "all knowledge is assimilation to the object of knowledge." Said wants to understand how the "precarious singularity" (75) of an individual attaches itself to the object outside it—music. Proust attends to the connection of the intellect to something beyond the reach of the intellect "in some material object." The mechanism in need of understanding is the way that we assimilate either by mind or by some combination of body and mind to the object of knowledge. Proust suggests that "it depends on chance" whether we will come to understand the workings of this mechanism. Emerson's poet will come to knowledge by inspiration sparked by "a sort of bright casualty." Force will not yield knowledge. In the experience of engagement, "his will in it" will consist "only in the surrender of will."[27]

You will be hard pressed to answer "yes" to the question "Are we having fun yet?" when in the midst of the aesthetic experiences Nussbaum recommends to you for your good moral health. Nussbaum is the Martha Stewart of the humanities, giving us prescriptions for "Better Living through Literature." No walks on the wild side. Your travels through art do not jeopardize your equanimity and balance. Reading literature is a form of moral workout, callisthenics as you count to ten as if reciting the Ten Commandments. Not so with Said as your guide. He is willing to take you up into the Heart of Darkness, even if he does not do so in the course of the travels narrated in "Melody, Solitude, and Affirmation." Traveling with Said features a bumpy ride partly because he takes his pleasure so seriously. Ideologues "measure musical seriousness by reference to reality."[28] The Rolling Stones shocked because they insisted that the reality principle and the pleasure principle were not in opposition to one another but ought to be and were the same. Said "gives in"—the Puritan might say—to his pleasures, insists on the reality of his pleasure in music, and acts as if all the occasions of his past experience of the particular musical object were relevant to his conveying to us what the nature of musical experience might be.

The process Said describes does not, indeed, look like one under the control of reason. Indeed, the process is one of coming to terms with one's passions. Commenting on Proust, Benjamin says that "a sort of productive disorder is the canon of the *memoire involontaire*."[29] A first reading of the Said chapter might give one the impression of disorder because of the way he submits his will to the promptings of memory. Because "emotions never occur singly, . . . as Descartes observed, no emotions ever occur in pure form, but they always come in a mixture, many different and often contrary emotions being experienced at the same time."[30] Musical emotions "differ from ordinary emotions . . . in going straight to the depth of the emotions. Darwin then can be seen to be right, that musical emotions *are* vague, with respect to their objects, yet also deep. They are vague or general in having no particular apparent object to give matter to the formal object yet are highly specific in their deep object."[31] As Baier writes, reflecting on Descartes and Hume on the passions, musical emotions have deep objects. It is those deep objects, I think, that Said dredges up for us in this chapter. Working under what seems the not-so-stern control of Proust's "involuntary memory," Said finds himself thrown back, just as Proust was, "in the antipodal regions of my past memories."[32] What makes them passions and not mere sensations is that they are anchored in time.

Said takes a risky course, I think. He shows us how he experienced art, not lashed to the mast the way most moderns and moralists have done, but on his own two feet, on the deck of a boat pitching in the sea in the midst of a productive disorder. He adds to the work of art by culling up memories. He assimilates to the work of art. He wills repetition. He does not merely recollect. "What is recollected . . . is repeated backwards, whereas repetition properly so-called is recollected forwards." [33] It is the forward propulsion of Said's movement that differentiates him decisively from the humanism of the Marthas Nussbaum and Stewart. The artwork is incomplete. It can never in itself be the definitive object of our striving, and ought never be the final term of our longings as social creatures. The thing it can never be is a permanent abode or exemplar. There is no "concrete universal."

The critic who worked hardest to revive the work of the Jena Romantics was Benjamin. In various of his essays and most especially in "The Work of Art in the Age of Mechanical Reproduction," he began to explore how it is that emotions work on us in the state of what he called "distraction." Said ends his chapter by giving us a powerful sense of the alternative we must choose between "control" and "elaboration." Benjamin offers us what I think is a parallel dichotomy between "concentration" and "distraction." Here is what he says: "Distraction and concentration form polar opposites which may be stated as follows: A man who concentrates before a work of art is absorbed by it. He enters into this work of art the way legend tells of the Chinese painter when he viewed his finished painting. In contrast, the distracted man absorbs the work of art." [34] Benjamin's allegorist, to cite *The Arcades Project*, "has given up the attempt to elucidate things through research into their properties and relations. He dislodges things from their contexts and, at the outset, leaves it to his profundity to illuminate their meaning . . . no possible reflection suffices to foresee what meaning his profundity may lay claim to for each one of them." [35] Said risks sounding like a twentieth-century Walter Pater—an aesthete more concerned with his impressions than getting a point across—to be true to his experience and to show us the way in which he was in attendance when his profundity allowed him to absorb Brahms's Theme with Variations for Piano. He puts aside for the moment Adorno, whom he admires so much, both with regard to the value of Wagner and with regard to how one ought to participate in the aesthetic experience. Adorno was disturbed because listening to Wagner induced the auditor to abdicate sovereignty.[36] Said is willing to look into just those experiences where the auditor loses control.

The account Said gives of his musical experience is very unlike the sort of thing Adorno prescribes. It is very different from Foucault, too. Said's picture is congruent with a structuralism that holds that there is no authentic core reality that we can penetrate in order to get beyond the structures in which we come to experience things. Everything we get is structured, but all we end up with is not just structures. Earlier in *Musical Elaborations*, Said writes that he finds Foucault's work valuable but "flawed" (50), because he finds its vision of the totally structured society implausible. In essence, in *Musical Elaborations*, Said contests the idea of the death of the author and the death of the subject, dead in the maw of an all-powerful system, by rejecting the death of the reader, or the recipient of the artwork—in this case, the musical artwork. All is structured, yet there is a place where Said sees room for the individual.

Delmore Schwartz wrote a book entitled In Dreams Begin Responsibilities. Said has argued, in effect, that in responses, in our individual responses to works of art, begins responsibility. We are not all merely relays in the system. As he wrote in After the Last Sky, the story of our responsibilities "cannot be told smoothly," because the "past, like the present, offers only occurrences and coincidences." Chapter 3 of Musical Elaborations has risked seeming to be only the recitation of a string of coincidences, but it is not. His characteristic mode in this work is not a narrative or an argument with tight logical control "but rather broken narratives." As in all his work concerned with questions of identity, individual and social, the real problem is "the problem of the inside": "the problem of the inside is that it is inside." [37] How does an individuality, much more precarious and unstable than Adorno wants to accept, attach itself to things? "Constructed and deconstructed, ephemera are what we negotiate," says Said, speaking of the situation of the Palestinians, but speaking in a way that is responsive to the difficulties of negotiating a space for singularity in a world of empires crumbling and abuilding.

Said does not leave us helpless, slack, and supine like Ulysses' crew, who are turned into animals when they let passion overcome reason. He makes it very clear that there is hope for what he calls a "consolidation" to be brought about by the effective coming together of the variety of recollections sprung loose by involuntary memory, and that this consolidation can enable us to hear the "music of the music" of Brahms and of Umm Kalthoum. Such consolidations mark a whole episode as an experience, one that might itself be the sort of thing that would arise unprompted in our lives in the future and give us a sense of the better life to be elaborated on in the future, a future Said does not hesitate to face.

JIM MEROD

The sublime lyrical abstractions of Edward W. Said

For three decades or so, the complex harmonies of Edward Said's published meditations—writing that spans a remarkable range of subjects with no less remarkable intellectual control—have gathered a momentum (an elaborate conceptual entanglement) that now approximates a fully manifested symphonic edifice. Said's themes have probed literary problems and theoretical rarefactions, philosophical tangles and political quagmires. Said has searched out, and examined with analytic imagination, the cultural contexts of the institutional authority that enables (and frequently disables) creative and intellectual work. His angle of witness has grounded itself within a quasi-autobiographical self-consciousness that is unique among academic writers. This self-referential mooring has never been out of proportion to the lived circumstances of its occasions. It has not dramatized itself as a personal performance put forward in celebratory gestures, even when Said appeared in the media as an "expert" commenting on the deep structures of international strife. He has worn the role of the expert lightly, and with well-ruminated ambivalence, in deference to the vaster, more compassionate role of the "amateur."

Such a position of respectful analytic consciousness Said absorbed from the example of R. P. Blackmur's majestic critical writing. Blackmur was Said's teacher at Princeton. Where Blackmur's intellect went, others followed soon or later. Where Said's intellect has arrived now, others will continue to gather. At every point, the uniquely grounded intellectual stance in Said's work has been earned by extra-academic engagements that continue to immerse him in public events and political controversies where the density of the term *secular*, a frequent term in his texts, accumulates enhancements and debilities that oppositional intellect inevitably encounters.

No one writing about literary or cultural theory today has escaped Said's long reach. It is, in truth, the reach of an amateur, which is to say it is the informed, unimpeded labor of one who cares greatly about his work. The potentially sentimental surplus of that care, of course, rests with its reach beyond mere professional acumen, professional flourishes displayed caringly, carefully. If one cares genuinely and long about the consequences of intellectual work (about the outcome of one's mental love and labor), professional detachment inevitably opens onto the unpredictable give-and-take of men and women creating, contesting, and urgently enlarging boundaries for an unnameable variety of shared activities. Such an opening (up, out, or inward) carries its own stress with responsibilities of solicitude and personal dispatch.

The overt celebration of the sentimental is not Said's project in the least, although an undercurrent within his writing suggests a desire to exert a utopic theme, a hope for the usefulness of intellect to increase cultural contestation at the expense of outright skirmishes, bloodshed, brutality, and carnage. At moments, Said's opponents and detractors have corrupted his positions with predictable histrionic misrepresentations. A cautious reader of Said's texts comes away not only with admiration for their conceptual precision but with respect for their example of intellectual courage in the face of protocols, effective and largely unexamined, that enforce complicity with the way things are. In that regard, Said's main project as a critic has been to widen the scope of inquiry surrounding texts and reigning intellectual assumptions, to deepen the analysis of terms, texts, and positions (as well as of the contexts that support them), so that the activity of intellect at its most acute may count for something in a world in which intellect is often exploited, diverted, silenced, marginalized, miscomprehended, or simply mocked by the general encumbrance of idiocy in a culture advanced by cynical popular entertainment logic. The purpose of such a project, which Said has crafted for years, is not to display its own superior insight. It is to reveal what may be extended toward others for the sake of truly human uses—which is to say, for the sake of conscious, creative, and discriminating intelligence.

If Said's lifelong intellectual work has been a labor of love, excruciation, delicacy, deliberation, ascesis, pride, worry, commitment, and hope—and I think it exhibits such pressures all across its verbal landscape—it also has achieved tangible results in the world that few university intellectuals aspire to or accomplish. Its permanent value cannot be assessed yet, but it will surely carry among its attributes, and for an indeterminate time, the inextinguishable example of Said's principled refusal of certainties: dogmas, doctrines, and received premises that torment any mind aiming to approach Michel de Montaigne's vulnerable self-conscious dereliction. Or to embody its own. Such a mind, in that instance, rejects and, ultimately, refutes the seductive persuasion of certainties that impede its own meandering path.

Among the meditations that extend such a refusal, one that might escape full notice is the thin book that comprises Said's 1989 Wellek Lectures at the University of California, Irvine, *Musical Elaborations*.[1] A pianist of serious and long-standing commitment to the "Western classical" repertoire broadly conceived, Said comes to his musical commentary with a wealth of specific knowledge grounded in the dynamics of performance and in scholarship, recent and traditional. That knowledge situates both the technical apparatus and the cultural apparatus by which (as Said follows it out) music can be seen to play "a role in what Antonio Gramsci has called the conquest of civil society" (xx). Unwilling to capitulate to totalizations of any sort, Said's qualifications extend Gramsci's notion while complicating its useful suspicion that informs the one hundred or so pages of the three lectures delivered at the Critical Theory Institute in May 1989. This context of academic suspicion—and expectation awaiting fully rendered theoretical clarity in the form of reflections on classical music (its texts, its performers, its reception, and its complex cultural significance)—can be felt at each moment of elaboration in these lectures.

Said's point of departure is Richard Poirier's set of still prescient essays on the tangled logic of culture in the modern and postmodern eras, *The Performing Self*.[2] The idea that Said picks up from Poirier—that "performance is an exercise of power" (1)—provides a fulcrum for exploring investments of institutional, political, and personal alienation common to musicians, writers, and composers with a highly developed artistic syntax. Said builds on Poirier's sense of the disruptive energy at work in powerful creativity. In the world of classical musical performance, Said notes, one finds that the artist's "furiously self-consultive" (1) habit (which frequently moves beyond the doubt or blockage of its initial anxiety to an extreme desire, or need, for perpetual affirmation) can be found embodied in a stylized formal stage presentation, "rather like an athletic event in its demand for the admiringly rapt attention of its spectators" (2). One of the points at stake here is the division of labor between composers and performers. The demarcation that can be found in the world of classical music, segmenting Chopin the writer of gloriously poetic compositions from Chopin the performer of his own pieces (and so on, with Mozart and Beethoven, Pierre Boulez and Leonard Bernstein), can be located with similar consequences in the world of African American classical music. That body of texts and performances may be thought of, perhaps, as a subset of Western classical music—an enormous virtual edifice with extraordinary authority that demands to be transgressed and to be transgressive all at once. Said is precise here, as in his well-known essay, "Traveling Theory," [3] when he invokes "the transgressive element in music [, which] is its nomadic ability to attach itself to, and become a part of, social formations, to vary its articulations and rhetoric depending on the occasion as well as the audience, plus the power and the gender situations in which it takes place" (70). In sum, musical invention is not a self-contained occasion or event. The making of music in "classical" formats defined by the history of compositions from, say, J. S. Bach to Karlheinz Stockhausen and defined, as well, by a tradition with a shorter time span (roughly a century), from Buddy Bolden to Thelonious Monk to Charlie Mingus, from W. C. Handy to Horace Silver to Tom Harrell, eventuates in cultural energy and human expression well beyond its own inclusive confines.

A useful illusion, revived to perennial creative effects, is the sense of artistic or intellectual boundaries constructed around the musical event and its creation. That illusion, a pretense with several unembarrassed disguises, funds the inventive moment by enhancing the feeling of experimental intimacy. Such disguises operate no less forcefully for Glenn Gould than for Monk. In fact, a conspicuous parallel exists in the improvisational processes of their creativity as pianists. But the larger issue taken up in Said's "elaborations" on music (with its vast weight of meaning, tradition, invention, and performative power) is the adumbration shared between two bodies of music—one reductively known as "classical" and the other, no less reductively, designated as "jazz"—that still enlarge possibilities, first, of pleasure as a solitary act of immediacy and reflection, and, second (not at all incidentally), of cultural disturbance and personal disruption, outcroppings of the visceral force of organized sound, thematic or otherwise, melodically beautiful or otherwise, harmonically stressed, and so on. However qualified or muted one finds this to be, the provocative material components and dramatic rhetorics of these two most self-consciously reticulate bodies of music unfold on their listeners within contexts of enactment that still hold the possibility of surprise, agonized consciousness, and intellectual perturbation.

If the transgressive elements, to use Said's term, in the tradition associated with Gould and in the tradition associated with Monk have common features, that is a consequence of the specific portability and amorphous appropriation in the deep logic of contemporary institutional reality. Fredric Jameson's analyses of the transmogrifying circulations of symbolic exchange illuminate a nomadic movement (and its constant potential for reinvigoration) that music lends to physical space—malls, Web sites, athletic spectacles, cars, advertisements—as anonymous authority: the blank lucidity of an absent intensity secreted everywhere. The places and occasions are limitless. But this does not begin to designate the scope of "the problematic of music's autonomy" that Said engages, following Adorno's reflections on what can be thought of as the gathering energy of late capitalistic commensurability, an expanding habit in the perfection of twentieth-century culture industries to subvert each previously "autonomous" domain by devaluing its significance and worth (48). All cultural moments or events now come to their "significance" in terms of worth defined by exchange value and that alone. Despite the glow of appreciation rendered by critical interpretation—Said on Gould or Arturo Toscanini; Whitney Balliett on Monk or Duke Ellington—and, because of the legitimacy conferred on exchange value in its full abstractness, needing the symbolic blood of cultural capital to gain authority denied or extracted by massive capital exchanges (disruptable as scarcity repressed, surplus value inflated or misjudged), music as an aspiring transgressive energy now and for some time has succumbed to a global negative dialectic: emotional hyperventilation, imaginative gadgetry, and intellectual (as well as lyrical) evaporation. The recuperative dialectic is somewhere else.

This does not mean that music does not count for something real and persuasive. One turns to music as an affirmation of life, of songful creativity, and of the earth's expressive mysteries. What I point to as an *adumbration* common to the public world of jazz and that of the "other" classical tradition of Western music can be found in one manifestation that Said glimpses in passing. It can be found in troubling forms of self-congratulation scattered all over the commercial music industry as a somber drugstore philosophical density. Here is Said's insight into Gould's ambivalent and somewhat crudely rendered intellectual ambition:

> Gould's ideas are worth looking into not so much only because they are of inherent validity . . . but because they also show us Gould grappling publicly with his predicament as a performing pianist who discursively notes everything that he can comment on as pianist and as critic along the way. As such, then, Gould's observations furnish the most intense example of the performance occasion being forcibly pulled out of the tired routine and unthinking consensus that ordinarily support the concert performance as a relatively lifeless social form. But what I am also saying is that Gould's restless forays into writing, radio, television, and film enhanced, enlivened, and illuminated his playing itself, giving it a self-conscious aesthetic and cultural presence whose aim, while not

always clear, was to enable performance to engage or to affiliate with the world itself, without compromising the essentially reinterpretive, reproductive quality of the process. (28–29)

Said's formulation of the "tired routine" within "a relatively lifeless social form" is stunning. It casts light on the current state of jazz as well as on the elite scene of classical musical performance. Jazz, so long demoted in official academic and critical circles, was a massively more alive and culturally buoyant art form than its apparently superior rivals for the entire duration of the century now coming to a close. Like the droll strategies of marketing and production that have made Luciano Pavarotti a multimillionaire, similar tactics of symbolic inflation pressure the world of jazz today. Such strategies promise stardom, large bank accounts, and unearned authority to second-rate talents. The concert hall seldom lights many emotional fires. The upscale cabaret is similarly dim. One looks for blazing performances or revelations of mature inwardness, probing displays of art with glorious sonic textures: music madly uttered. Said's point holds true, perhaps, more fully in regard to performances in the concert hall, where the exercise of profoundly well-rehearsed talent creates "highly concentrated, rarified, and extreme occasions" (11). Performers who transcend this interactive (ethical as well as artistic) decompression by lifting themselves and their listeners to full alertness promote the concrete possibilities for a sublime influx of surprise. In this respect, artists and their best critical partners share important spiritual stakes. The experience of such sublime moments is without names. It resides in a somewhat stunned, wholly receptive awareness, which is like the hesitation within a stuttered phrase. That hesitation is an opening to otherness in the midst of something bold and new. Such a pause from the ordinary flow of existence disables linguistic tags and categories. This is one of the purposes of music: to go beyond naming.

There is an illuminating moment at the beginning of Said's third lecture. During an Alfred Brendel recital performance of transposed variations drawn from Brahms's String Sextet in B-flat at Carnegie Hall, Said encounters a sense of double consciousness. On one side, Brendel's playing; on the other, Said's mental search for the text being performed. To some extent, this divided attention puts the music on hold. Said disengages the performance and enters into momentary rumination. This search for a piece of information attempts to contextualize the music under way and, thus, to lend the performance added specific weight. It enacts what in many ways is an ordinary experience of being within the movement of an event, yet outside of it. Especially for a pianist such as Said, the tug on attention is inevitably in two directions: to hear and to put the hearing in a larger context of recognition. This divided moment of attention reflects the nature of daily consciousness, in general, and the more precise focus of critical consciousness, in specific.

Said's pause at that point is not like the stumped awareness that eventuates in an influx of surprise, the heightened alertness I just alluded to. The more dramatic and initially more disorienting hesitation, in that instance, occurs as a radically expanded openness to otherness, to an event or to a significant moment that arrests attention in such a way that the one who undergoes its momentary blockage is not likely to see or hear things quite the same way again. What I am indicating here is an act of witnessing that approaches the Wordsworthian sublime: attention fulfilled (or filled up, taken over). This is an experience that moves away from the self-who-hears to a self, somewhat stunned and engaged by remarkable information (pleasure, ecstasy), at the brink of a cognitive chasm. The experience both alters and traverses perception. It stages the witness at a point of observation that seems to stymie and, in some forms of sublime arrest, to swallow the self. The movement of the experience, however, is beyond the self, toward a de-temporalized, displaced consciousness that is defined by a confused sense of meaningfulness and perplexity. That sense both suspends and enlarges immediacy. The experience, of course, is enigmatic. Alertness is expanded. The seductive, possessive object of attention fills the time and place of witness. The self-looking, the self-hearing, searches for stable ground, ordinary rationality, to reconnoiter its mind-boggling new experience. Emotional crisis and severe personal trauma exploit the same mental features. In retreat from such a daunting occurrence, one searches for translations. Few are ever available at the moment of retreat. Nevertheless, the experience lingers in awareness. Unprepared for this assault on ordinary interpretive habits, the mind sometimes retreats, in advance, before an experience of temptation, blockage, and the expanded (stumped) reverberation of intelligence occurs in the first place. That premature retreat in part explains the flight of uninitiated listeners confronted with powerful music such as Arnold Schoenberg's *Verklärte Nacht* and Ellington's "Reminiscing in Tempo."

The majestic performances of Gould, published as wholly edited articulations of Bach's *Goldberg Variations*, soar beyond the usual exercises of artistic hommage to the misremembered dead. These recordings constitute one instance of sublime exertion, an outcome of nearly inhuman artistic inspiration. Gould could not have crafted these performances without an awesome, sustained act of personal will. Heard straight through (another act of will), they constitute an invitation to expanded attention. One does not delve at ease here. Gould provides a paradigmatic instance. Much of his vaunted eccentricity can be reckoned in terms of his hunger to merge himself, in every possible way within his power, with bodies of music that essentially possessed the means by which his self-definition could be achieved. That culminated, of course, as a self without equals: a self always in the act of reinvention and self-discovery, a self under siege—a self integral only in those moments when it was most under siege in the act of musical exploration.

One of the paradoxes of that project is the extent to which it resides on technological fulfillment. Gould's recordings of the *Goldberg Variations* offer a splendid example. What we are given here is a product of the magic of analogue editing, tape spliced and transferred as a virtual performance impossible without prosthetic assistance. The illusory quality of a "whole" event, a "single performance," is not important, finally, since we now live in the age of digital reproduction, in which the concept of an "origin" is essentially irrelevant. One imagines that even Walter Benjamin would be pleased with Gould's avant-garde sense of the performer's artifactual aura. For each who hears Gould's daring spellbound wonder—which absorbs Bach's texts as if Bach were still here to enjoy their audacity, as if Bach never existed, since these texts are far beyond the reach of human complexity ordinarily conceived—for each who hears Gould's manufactured performance, a palimpsest, in fact, Gould's virtuosity is a reminder of energy meant to erupt from time to time in the ascetic confines of concert halls. Such performances, alive on stage or represented by the illusory integrity of recorded wholeness (spliced and patched), revive the imagined possibility of a public scene in which the merging of shared awe and pleasure might overcome, however briefly, the muteness of contemporary aesthetic witness. One cannot admire a performance such as Gould's execution of the Bach pieces, therefore, and not utter a personal syllable of complicitous voyeuristic appreciation.

Gould in the Columbia recording studio and Monk at his best on stage at the Blackhawk in San Francisco enact the dramatic choreography of well-paced prize fights. Said's analogy is apt. The enactment of an "essentially reinterpretive, reproductive" (29) challenge to drag the written score and the polite formal scene of spectatorship from slumber, to make them flare with audacity, as if the genius to perform (and to write music) were iterative commands, iconoclastic, furious, and indomitable, places us in the arena of extreme exertions akin to sportive combat. Only those performers whose passion lives in dialogue with the counterpoint of the bizarre (creative thought unwelcome on arrival) can hope to surmount the occasion that gives it life. This is a transgression worth seeking.

Gould's career offers an instance of an artist whose "favorite state was 'ecstasy,' his favorite music was music ideally not written for specific instruments and hence 'essentially incorporeal.'" Said notes that Gould's "highest words of praise were *repose, detachment, isolation*" (29). The career of Monk, no less eccentric, no less consequential for its impact on a generation of musicians and informed followers who continue to sort through the glories and contradictions of his legacy, offers another instance of a search for ecstasy, repose, detachment, and isolation. In truth, Monk may have achieved those states more fully, and more hermetically, than did Gould. Comparisons are useless, but the parallel inspiration to wrap the personal self in the artistic cocoon of the performative self is striking both for similarities and divergences that make the two pianists interesting studies, jointly and separately.

Monk was, by far, less garrulous. He was in no way a writer of reflections, aperçus, or sustained commentary of any sort. Monk tended toward effusive rambling on occasions, later in life, when his despondency relented. Earlier, as a young man, he tended to express himself nonmusically in frequent games of pickup basketball in the Sugar Hill section of Manhattan, where he spent nearly the whole of his life. He also talked at great length, privately, to his girlfriend Nellie Smith who, as his wife, guarded his emotional and creative solitude. Numerous younger musicians, such as Sonny Rollins and Bud Powell, visited the Monk residence often. Monk was a composer of difficult music, and his harmonic and melodic conceptions instructed his apprenticed visitors. They were fascinated by his musical ideas, startling then with the appearance of undiminishable uniqueness, intact even now, fifty years after they were composed. Monk's domestic seminars were essentially wordless executions of his songs, whole and parsed out phrase by phrase, one bar at a time. The big bear of a man sucked on his cigarettes, rumbled across the keys of his upright piano, grunted a few comments, and directed his brilliant, eager pupils to follow his directions. The scene of instruction was conducted with Zen pedagogy. Words gave way to sounds. Ideas were tonal inflections, temporal blots. Monk struck the piano keys. "This way, see? That sound, huh?" These mumbled, understated lessons were defined by rhythmic pace and pianistic accent. Unexpected open "spaces" of seemingly misplaced sonic clusters — disjunctive, deformed, disturbing — became primary texts for study. Not so much the notes scrawled on rumpled sheet music as the surprising misdirections of time and expressive emphasis: That was the lesson. All of this, of course, was appealing for the young musicians gathered in the small Monk dining room. The clarity of Monk's music enacted a profound coherence that carried then, as now, the force of calm insistence. Monk's music was pure in a way that no one had ever heard before. It still is pure in ways that have withstood countless interpretations, recorded and public performances, and (most corrosive of all) academic inspection. His songs have been probed, rehearsed, and executed thousands of times — nearly codified, in fact. But a distinct feature of Monk's musical universe rests with its evasiveness. One can attempt to formulate the Monk sound, concept, or feel, but the attempt fails: No codification is possible. Literally. Monk's angular lyric gracefulness swings with unexpected (unnotated) accents of inner propulsion that can be ridden emotionally and carried out performatively (as pianist Kenny Barron and drummer Ben Riley, along with bassist Buster Williams, demonstrate on remarkable recordings and in person). Monk alone understood the bizarre syncopation at work in his time sense. It is perhaps a constantly shifting eruption of a comic principle, something very much like an irreducible intuition of countersyncopation or a dervishlike tormenting of the principle of syncopation at the very core of the concept of swing (with all of its modalities of pace and accent). Simply enough, the habit of Monk's thought is outside attempts to fully grasp it. Those attempts have been frequent and continue bravely to search for Monk's mysterious creative center. His music somehow escapes capture. One hears what Monk's compositions assert. One hears what Monk's piano playing is up to on his recordings. Certainly one recognizes the bizarre, compelling, and surprising accents (time sense, tonal clusters, and so forth), but the comedic uplift at the heart of Monk's musical secret is not duplicable.

No surprise, thus, that Monk did not construct organized verbal musings. We have nothing approaching written statements, self-reflections in the guise of an apologia, a manifesto, or a final set of observations, aesthetic or otherwise. This verbal habit just did not cut across Monk's entrenched habits of practice and compositional revision. Easily recruited into family games and chatter, often playful, funny, devilish, puckish, urbane, and analytically sophisticated in pithy verbal bursts, Monk was not a philosopher manqué but a witty if laconic conversationalist whose irony expressed itself in the conspicuous seriousness of his endlessly complex musical comic sense. The idea of Monk holding forth about economics or psychology or politics is, in itself, amusing, not because Monk did not have thoughts about those realms but because he found deep and expansive means of registering the nuances of his inwardness—his repose and ecstasy—in compositions such as "Crepuscule with Nellie," "'Round Midnight," "Ask Me Now," and "Ruby, My Dear." Each of these defines nonverbal intelligence of a remarkably immediate and self-regenerating sort. I mean by this to point toward Monk's musical control, an orchestrated structural completeness that suffuses his compositions (a source of their difficulty) and that informs his playing as well. Monk registered ninety-one compositions. Orrin Keepnews, his finest commentator, has noted that only thirty or so occupied the bulk of his attention as a performer. Across the expanse of those pieces, Monk found compositional means to assert structural gambits that create beauty and intrigue while withholding the means of aesthetic closure. This is in part why his songs assert curious subtexts, songs within the song itself. Monk's writing depends on simultaneous structural assertiveness and uncertainty. His most accomplished inheritors, such as pianist Tommy Flanagan and saxophonist Steve Lacy, preserve the undecidability at the core of a Monk song even as their executions are exercises in enchantment. Both Flanagan and Lacy interpret Monk's compositions. They enter into the space of his imaginative orbit, as it were, and avoid the foolish mistake of trying to recapture what Monk himself executed in performance. The point here is that Monk's way of setting up the possibility for a strong musician to enchant is based on an intricately crafted set of enigmas, or the poised appearance of enigmas, in the harmonic voicing and interpretive choices his material offers. Saxophonist Benny Golson, a composer of enormous strength and longevity, insists that Monk's compositions are "ditties." I suspect that Golson is calling attention to the fragmentary and disrupted (out-of-joint) quality of Monk's writing. The staging of songs in which every note has a considered rightness of placement while expressing a sense of detachment, disunity, dissonance, angularity, and, finally (for awhile at least), "wrongness" lends itself to misrecognition. That, of course, was Monk's fate for most of his career. Increasingly, the power of Monk's structural precision reveals itself. Monk's writing is an art of unambiguous but seemingly errant control.

Said has isolated "the notion of control, which is the motif of much of Gould's life" (29). Control in this sense is somewhat at odds with the sense of ecstasy and detachment Gould sought in a variety of forms. The tension there is precisely what is useful about the rigor that informed Gould's practice habits and performance executions. If we hear a faint autobiographical allusion in Said's awareness of the prevalence of control as a dominant trope in Gould's voluble yet self-enclosed artistic personality, it may be constructed on the understandable identification that Said brings to a reading of Gould's art. Said the pianist is not the essential identity in common with Gould so much as Said the writer, critic, and scholar, whose construction of a de-totalizing, disruptive theoretical complexity has avoided the traps of system building and of undialectical critique in order to create expressive means adequate to the lived circumstance of his own projects.

Said's lectures on music reveal a writer in the trajectory of his own performance—rigorous, informed, probing, and in control of his terms of critical elucidation. This is characteristic of Said's intellectual poise. A preferred inclination of Said's critical grasp is the writing of essays that are genuine meditations that roam the divagations of impulse and intellect here and there beckoning a writer and therein offering possibilities for curiosity to find enchantment or discovery. It seems to me that Said, among only four or five critical writers of his generation, has minimized the baggage of predictable utterance, predetermined understanding, and theoretical closure. His work ceaselessly comes across revelations, small and large, of intellectual discovery: things found in the process of reading, thinking, writing, and sorting among the crisscrossing entanglements of personal inspection.

The critical essay is, and has been, Said's art form. It benefits, no doubt, from the artistry that informs his playing of Chopin and Bach. One wonders what effect familiarity with Monk's powerfully ironic deepening of the great blues tradition in American music might have had on a critical intelligence so prone to nuances of literary and musical enjoyment, and to the delight of verbal exploration. One imagines what its fulfillment might concoct, since Said's writing displays a playful mind in the service of difficult truths that can only be approached or approximated in an act of controlled intellectual abandon. His essays are exercises in the strict sense, which means they are necessarily playful and assert their intelligence as experiments — provisional, poetic, declamatory, but urgently hypothetical. Said means less to exert an ultimate statement or final well-considered intellectual position (summative, autonomous, or heroic) than to pose the logistics of hypothesis making as a reasonable, necessary, humane, and, finally, creative operation of passionate intelligence.

Said's long-standing readers will certainly choose among dozens of essays that continue to haunt the critical imagination. Looking through their wide-ranging themes, a statement that partly captures the habit of mind so generously evident in Said's work at every point occurs near the end of his essay, "On Originality." Said worries here, as elsewhere, the logic of reception that inhabits the deep structures of literary influence. The enjoyment of this theme resides in part with the excuse it offers for erudition to move through bold instincts and hidden alleys in its learning. It is an innocent pastime. If ever the term *innocent*, weighted with concerns that amount to full-scale doubt in Said's thinking, stands equal to harassing qualifications, in this instance, I think, it does. Innocent or productive with muffled design, the statement he offers is telling: "Traditionally the temporal convention in literary study has been retrospective. We look at writing as already completed. . . . But how much more challenging is a theoretic for study that takes writing as being produced for something formed *in the writing*: this was Mallarmé's discovery."[4]

This logic of writing "produced for something formed" in writing itself is a discovery of any committed composer and performer, as well. Said's reflections on Gould in the context of Adorno — Adorno in the framework of musical advances that subsume (and defeat) much of Adorno's dyspeptic view of musical experiences and uses — express the mediation between discovery and assertion, the play of thought and its aleatoric or more scripted exercises. That interiority of writing *for itself*, an external event in its execution, informs the composition of music and of literary or critical writing. This elusive theme reappears in a self-referential form near the close of Said's Wellek lectures. It offers a view of the pianist who writes critical essays and who, simultaneously, is a critic who plays music:

> In my experience of music[,] the composer's *air de la chanson* I hold onto and whose embellishments over time I enjoy represents a personal obsession of the individual hearer or interpreter, with no more status than those pathetic family photographs described by Berger as "fragile images, often carried next to the heart or placed by the side of the bed . . . used to refer to that which historical time has no right to destroy." Perhaps. But I am intellectually impressed by the richness of what I have called the alternative formation in music, in which the nonlinear, nondevelopmental uses of theme or melody dissipate and delay a disciplined organization of musical time that is principally combative as well as dominative. Glenn Gould, I think, understood the potential interest in this essentially contrapuntal mode—that is, you think of and treat one musical line in conjunction with several others that derive from and relate to it, and you do so through imitation, repetition, or ornamentation—as an antidote to the more overtly administrative and executive authority contained in, say, a Mozart or Beethoven classical sonata form. (101–2)

The distinction here is instructive. So is the allusion to John Berger's recuperation of lost human voices. Gould's inclination toward variations on thematic material preserved the openness of his own virtuosity unhampered by constraints in which the pianist might succumb, or feel forced to give way, to the priority of a composer's intention or to the weight of traditional readings. Gould's will to assert his own dazzling pianistic capacity could certainly survive a composition's framework of notation, accent, pace, expressive shading, tonal and harmonic coloration, and its memorialized heritage of interpretation. His career documents that challenge overcome time and again. In fact, one of Said's most articulate accounts of Gould's improbable success as an estranged and estranging performer moves through the forms, varieties, and dynamics of "ownership" that "the pianist's prerogative to dominate over all other fields of music" (7) accomplished to stunning results. This was no obvious set of appropriations—musical conquest as a style of thievery (like Miles Davis literally stealing publication rights from Cleanhead Vinson and others; and Irving Mills, Duke Ellington's manager, putting his name on more than fifty Ellington compositions, often with the composer's blessing, between 1929 and 1947—a sustained act of "ownership" and "prerogative" perhaps unrivaled in the history of music copyright). To this it must be added that Gould was nothing if not an exacting revisionary musical intelligence. The expanse of received song structures was, of course, Gould's native artistic domain. Said is right to note that Gould essentially remade himself as an artist from roughly 1964 onward, rejecting live performance for the technical representational control of the studio and recordings that allowed far greater documentary permanence for his astounding physical and interpretive talents. The final eighteen years of his life exhibit an eccentricity very much like that of saxophonist John Coltrane, whose obsessive work habits kept him constantly, eighteen hours at a time, practicing to extend his range, fluency, technique, execution, and knowledge of exotic song traditions.

The point here is to see that another invitation to "make musical sense" exists in the wide variability of the contrapuntal mode that is attractive to Said. This optional mode is improvisatory in nature, less constricted than conventional musical structures seem to demand or want. One remembers, in this regard, trumpeter Red Rodney's exclamation one late night in 1991: "It's only music," he protested, "we'll play it anyway we like." Rodney was, as he insisted until the end of his too short life, "a bebop player" and that elicited from him unsentimental respect for the melodic complexity of the songbook composed jointly by Charlie Parker, Thelonious Monk, Bud Powell, and Dizzy Gillespie.[5] Rodney understood the expository demands of harmonic frameworks that defended themselves from what Adorno thought of as "regressive" accommodations to standard Western patterns of hearing. On that point — the regressiveness of aural perception in a technologically mediated culture — I am in agreement with Adorno. The demise has enlarged since the moment, nearly two-thirds of a century ago, when an awareness of general cultural loss dawned on him. The contrapuntal "alternative formation" championed by Said carries a pedagogical power now in short supply. Postmodern habits of attention are laughably eroded. The frivolity of noticing audio dumbness (an exact phrase in this instance) does not help. What possibilities are imaginable in reversing the many ways in which sound contributes to the massive erosion of the poetic sense broadly defined? Very few, if any. Said's emphasis poses the apparently modest energy of contrapuntal elaboration (Gould's or, only slightly less audacious, Vladimir Horowitz's or Earl Wild's) as an attainment of "nonlinear, nondevelopmental uses of theme or melody [that] dissipate and delay a disciplined organization of musical time that is principally combative as well as dominative." As such, the contrapuntal mode might be read as an elegant supplement, in advance, as well as a sub-rosa substantiation of playfulness at the heart of the jazz tradition. The contrapuntal mode and the inventive (elaborative) energy that Said illuminates could be thought of as working in alliance with the tradition of Monk and Ellington to the extent that both are identified as improvisatory in some inexpungible, practical way. In this, however, jazz becomes essentially a jam session routine: a familiar entry to "blowing sessions," in which the difficult, "combative as well as dominative," logic of harmonic expectations (including, of course, the codes of jam session protocols in part defined by the progression of mostly predetermined key changes) is underemphasized or depreciated wholly.

That is not an accurate identification. No less than the "other" classical tradition, the one that follows disruptively from the legacies of Ellington and Monk enforces powerful strategies of scripted musical maneuvering: textual elaborations not solely given up to, or defined by, improvisation. And so we see, on one hand, that Said is not making a cryptic case for jazz as an ally of his preferred alternative mode here; on the other hand, we see that the relationship between the open-ended "play element" in jazz and the personally or performatively dominative (as opposed to a textually dominative) practice of Gould's late career carries a difficult but not at all exaggerated complicity of bravura, outlook, and energy. A difference to note here, within that perhaps surprising affinity, is the stretch one needs to make to imagine Monk's or Ellington's music as texts organized in such a way, covert or otherwise, that they operate with combative or dominative "musical time." Indeed, from the points of view of powerfully gifted performers such as Gould and Coltrane, all temporal structures appear to be restraints. The Promethean artistic impulse of such awe-inspiring facility and imagination is to break out of structures of every sort, to create music as an immediately self-determined energy free of preconceived modalities. At this level of instinct and execution, the object of desire is to transform the performative self (in truth, the actual spiritual and physical self) into a pure organ of receptivity. Emotional need and conscious self-justification account for but are not able to explain or exonerate sacrifices involved in their dissolute lives, which maniacally pursued the influx and outflow of musical ideas: impulse with remarkable technical exertion. Such an impulse articulates lyrical authority as if from an unnameable "somewhere" that supplies unearthly inspiration to a nameless "nowhere." In this transfer from somewhere to nowhere, inspiration is personal power realized in the artistic sainthood of de-individuated creation.

Like Gould, Coltrane lived in that imaginative, private height. Like Coltrane, Gould sought personal divination in the vapor of unfettered musical paroxysms. The hilarious surplus of such a contradictory urge (the inscrutable hocus-pocus of its practices) resides with the unquenched thirst of all ambitions that follow the trajectory of art's inherent rules for conquest. Conquest in the world of musical invention is inevitably provisional until the normative rationality of idealized critical hyperscrutiny runs its course. Art, in each of its realms, reinforces the formal, bounded, disciplinary, yet malleable confines of expressive structures. It follows, then, that one cannot "hear" Gould's willful elaborations (compressions, shortcuts, distentions, and angularities) on Bach's frequently unmarked tempi without appreciation for

Bach's rather extraordinary faith in the servicing of his written texts—his solicitation of the improvisatory. The tradition of execution that defines, imperfectly, Bach's musical repertoire establishes no fixed boundaries, only more invitations to experiment. One understands, therefore, Gould's artistic and spiritual achievement against the backdrop of previous attempts to cope with Bach's difficult art. The whole of that archive cannot be held in view because it cannot be known. And yet how little memory or fantasy it takes to project Gould's monumental summation that engages the entire tradition of attempts literally to preserve (embody) Bach's divine notations. Their constraint provides an obstacle. The performer's incomplete knowledge of what went before him opens more room for his musical search. Therefore, everything is at stake when Gould enters the Columbia studio, his gloved hands held against his body for warmth, Neumann and RCA tube microphones placed all across the floor of the large, high-ceilinged room to catch his piano directly and indirectly (as an ambient sonic ghost added to the edited mix). Everything that can prove his own enduring artistic difference is at stake when Gould, week after sleepless week, gives himself to the frantic piecing together of so many thousands of recorded fragments.

Gould's achievement is wrenched from nothingness itself. The something of discovery, which is a performer's delight and thrill, is now left with us as another script—this one recorded, infinitely repeatable. One can time Gould's musical thinking, especially in the darting flight of his most demonstrative allegro and presto passages. His fingers leave mementos of his graceful nervous height. His quickness of thought and execution can be matched by others, perhaps; the unlikely rhythm of Gould's touch (and pace and will) cannot. It erupts in medias res as a natural force, a hurricane intended to sweep over us once and many more times. Gould's timing and the underlying disappearance of the real self inside the playing are the manifest outcomes of an excuse, a permission to exercise this text right here, right now, without any intervening doubt that the owner of the text is the one who is playing it. It is a necessary illusion in a fatal game. The scripted variations offered up for Gould's recorded surgery, then, hold a powerful notation scheme. Bach left them for others to exercise but also to debate. They are set before the combative performer contentiously. Gould's acceptance of their challenge to pianistic and performative sense was essentially inevitable. The combative monomaniac was thereby confronted by a no less "combative" text. But the one who triumphs is the one who most permanently dissolves into the executed text.

There is in all of this a residue of Gould's prestidigitation. A sort of magic lingers after the hours of practice, the invocation of divine good luck, with recorded performances left behind. The hearing and rehearing its listeners give these recordings celebrate a winsome magic because no artistic domination ever prevails. The playing is a moment only. The text is no less momentary despite its archival perseverance. The recording is a moment of time. No more. These recognitions are dauntingly obvious and yet the illusions needed to compose and to perform at such elevations of lyrical majesty demand a more concrete sense of victory, and longevity, to sustain them. Music, far more than literature or philosophy, dissolves in the ether of its own immediacy. Recorded music re-creates an event. Gould's edited manipulations with Bach's scores cannot preserve the vulnerability of his executions.

For the most part, the categorical definitiveness of formal criticism—eliciting theoretical and practical strategies to avoid closure (choose your favorites: Kenneth Burke's rhetorical jigsaw games, Blackmur's suggestive puzzles, Paul de Man's shrewd map of rhetorical undoing, Gayatri Spivak's conceptual density)—misses completely the turbulent self-assertion and self-erasure of musical accomplishments. Literary criticism has effectively walked away from music altogether. This may be yet one more indication of a regression in hearing, part of a lamentable segmentation between artistic realms, as well. Not long ago, poets, painters, and musicians hung out together, each learning from the others. That scene is thinner now.

The purpose of Said's musings on music is clear. "Music is of fundamental interest," he writes, "because it represents the rarity, uniqueness, and absolute individuality of art, as well as its intermittent, fragmentary, highly conditional, and circumstantial existence" (75). So much is held within that teasing, final phrase. Not surprisingly, the three Wellek lectures underscore the personal meaning, for Said, of the musical experience. His affirmation throughout rings true. It is a moving affirmation in which the encroachment of idiomatic domains of private feeling on well-known lyrical monuments exacts a subtlety of pleasure difficult to render, but rendered quietly and whole for all of that.

Seldom is that quietness and wholeness of personality illuminated so well in Said's writing as in the final pages of *Musical Elaborations.* I am struck by the calm momentum of their intellectual repose. Said's text at this point gathers up a sunlit vista that suggests, as we follow its figurations, the recollection of an afternoon nap in which the partial slumber of consciousness hears children's voices. In that figure, I find an image of the emotional deepening in the company of powerful, important music that Said advances within a culture in need of solicitations to explore what José Ortega y Gasset once called *ensimismamiento.* Such discourse, and such taking up of responsibility for one's own awareness, Said approaches cautiously. He notes, for example, in Brahms's String Sextet in B-flat, op. 18, written in 1859–1860, "a sort of unstatable, or inexpressible, aspect of his music, the music of his music, which I think anyone who listens to, plays, or thinks about music carries within oneself"

(93). Said's phrase, "the music of his music," is a perfect iteration of the elusive topic—music itself in its complete consort—that haunts these lectures. It carries a sense of surrender that, traditionally, is not thought to pertain to analysis and critical attention. The surrender I have in mind is the giving up of awareness to the vulnerabilities of attention that suffuse art and consciousness. Both are vulnerable to nearly infinite dilemmas of uncertainty, guesswork, flawed perception, and all the inner tugs of preference and enchantment that confuse our way through life. The "giving up of awareness," as I witness it here in Said's personally documented, performatively supplemented lectures (the text is bereft of his playing), is a precondition for the critical mind if it is to trust its own perceptions and relax without importing into the event of critical listening anything extraneous, adventitious, or constricting. The taking on of responsibility for the inevitable eccentricity of critical self-consciousness is wholly dependent on one's surrender to impediments that are built into the act of attention and to those that culture, education, and the warmth or chill of discernment put into play. One recalls here William Gass, reflecting on Ludwig Wittgenstein. In the presence of his halting discourse, so hesitant with "the cruel recognition of failure," Gass finds in Wittgenstein "the total naked absorption of the mind in its problem." [6]

Said's thoughts, in this regard, respect what musicians themselves say. The most talented, experienced, and accomplished musicians report (when they open themselves to such ruminations) a sense of meaning-filled height and power on their best days. Their sense is enigmatic but welcome. It is a generosity of talent expressed generously. It is the relaxed, unconstricted musical outflow of those who have successfully plowed through the torments of self-doubt, despair, and the inability to believe that any performance can ever arrive at a successful conclusion. Whatever height artistic capacity can enter into as a fleeting occurrence is earned by demonic struggle with the whole subterranean darkness of self-consciousness. The relationship of music and musician here is not dialectical. It is transumptive, a passing of one into the other. If that term is workable, it designates a relationship of abnormal spiritual value. It may be thought of as a coin that catches the glint of sunlight on both sides at once.

I am not seeking to obscure the stakes of Said's project: music in its whole consort, the deepening of awareness. I am interested in the spirit of discovery there. The joy (what I called earlier the hilarity) of the formal overcoming that characterizes transformative musical expressions—Bach's *Goldberg Variations*, an instance perhaps, and his cantatas; Mozart's oeuvre (his debunkers to the contrary); Ellington's collaborations with Billy Strayhorn; and Coltrane's encounters with Monk—is not an emotion derived at the expense of musical structures. Joy, in the forms that Said's text accounts for it, joy as an inborn complement to the brooding expression of Beethoven's dark fugue that initiates his C-sharp minor string quartet, op. 131, is indivisible from the performance of great music. Music on the scale of these examples, rooted (without fail) in its moment and occasion, becomes a placeless, blameless joke whose joyful motion, as Antônio Carlos Jobim suggests, is the sun, a lake, sunlight on the lake, and all one's dreams of magical gibberish. If deep musical insight constructs a means of joking seriously without fully imaginable purposes, it opens a territory that is puzzling for traditional critical inspection since such diverse but inherent insight, coded in musical and essentially emotional terms, is at the outer expressive limits of language. We are well aware that music is another language (or set of languages), but critical discourse about that reality is very difficult. Few things in the ordinary movements of life are so hard to talk about accurately, meaningfully, and with nonreductive illumination. My remarks are meant to take all this into consideration as an issue needing far more understanding, and greater comprehension of the intrinsic joy in the composition and creation of music, than we find in learned analysis at present. My sense in all of this is that the most extraordinary bodies of music (Bach's, Ellington's, Beethoven's, Monk's, and others') literally speak with forms of awareness that expand the boundaries, and the vocabularies, of rational linguistic utterance. I think, also, that the expanding of emotional and expressive meaning (which Susanne Langer spent the best part of her philosophical lifetime engaged with) depends on precisely the sort of imagination and delineation under way in Said's lectures in Irvine.

I think that we find here a distinct realm of "textuality," as yet very little illumined, available for reflection and analysis. One might ponder these texts, "intertexts," in fact, which can be found everywhere extraordinary musical performances emerge. A thorough exploration of Sarah Vaughan's recorded work with the provocative pianist Jimmy Rowles, for example, provides material to challenge the most astute critical capacity. This may require, of course, a refinement of our current critical vocabularies, primed to deconstruct institutional, overtly social and cultural, as well as ideological "texts." If, nonetheless, the careful inspection of musical intertexts approaches the ironic complementarities of a potentially circular allegorical insight implied by the excess symbolic possibilities of this most self-referential of all the arts (sounds giving way to more sounds open to the commentary of further musical interpretation, sounds more eloquent than any verbal critique or analysis), the joke is ours: a truly universal human hilarity that encompasses but also nullifies such categorical shorthand as the "multicultural" designation. Pick your favorite terminological bulwark that serves standard thematic critique. The shift of irony from its semantic ground to a vaster musical world, in which time is a far more relentless and ineradicable fact of the text under scrutiny, leaves us somewhat adrift without practices that authorize critical activity. Thus, Béla Bartók's *Hungarian Dances* no less than Ellington's "Harlem Airshaft" can be seen to draw, in divergent ways, from folkloric elements. Charles Ives and Dizzy Gillespie, also, found means to merge European harmonic structures, indigenous New England or New Orleans lyric fragments, and non–North American (in the case of Gillespie, Cuban and North African) rhythmic or tonal frameworks. The list grows long; analysis grows weary with discoveries and entanglements. But something arresting in the music, interpretable within allegories than can be found as thematic cultural identities intertwined, goes well beyond the logic of such merged, mixed, or combative identities. And that something else, of course, is now what is most at stake in Ives's monumental compositions and in Gillespie's endlessly celebratory excursions across musical traditions that had no necessary or likely affiliation of any kind until his playful curiosity (from roughly 1945 to 1960) set about the work of creating uncategorizable musical mischief. Once we come to these illuminating allegories, how should they be read? Should they be explored in the spirit of their own conceptual oppositions, supplementations, and inner dialogues, their endless parabasis?

A study in the correlative ironies of music and literary allegory may find, perhaps, the principle of hypochondriasis that Burke asserted as a means of resolving thorny personal dilemmas, ugly frustrations. Hypochondriasis, he tells us, is a reigning tactic in Walt Whitman's poetic outlook. It is the trick whereby you internalize what ails you or threatens to defeat you. As a variation of the old farm wisdom, to join those folks and accept those circumstances that cannot be thwarted, it makes pragmatic counsel. Once we extend the principle by a small degree, we might adopt Burke's adjacent suggestion: "Whatever poetry [or art] may be, criticism had best be comic." [7] Amateurs, facing the sublime experience and much else that music can accomplish, find here in Burke precisely the sort of room to think back the ground of its humanity, which, at moments, may seem abstract, obscure, or illegible in the evanescence of essentially unsummarizable tonal formations. Music may be thought of as a form of speaking with many very elusive forms of speech. Musical attentiveness and hypochondriasis, thus, make useful partners.

The dialectics of such companionship, at any historical moment, should not be lost to the counterhegemonic tactics of an earlier era. Burke, Raymond Williams, Toni Morrison, Gabriel García Márquez, and the massively inclusive worlds of Ellington and Akira Kurosawa all provide the imaginative and spiritual reach necessary to explore, and articulate, a project such as the one Said's lectures have opened up here.[8] Literary and musical intelligence, as well as filmmaking and critical analysis, employ highly refined intellectual and technical skills for the purpose of promoting something far more useful than disputation and debate. In each of their several more or less rarefied domains of erudition and expertise, the business of accomplishing concrete results depends on the work of amateurs, insofar as that work is understood as the usable excess of intelligence that motivates accomplishment—production—in the first place. The amateur, I imagine, is someone who foolishly or otherwise believes in the good of things that are final and complete in their own right. In sum, no creative work with the degree of power we find among the examples chosen here is likely to get done without an extrabusiness sense of viable excitement to supplement all logics of accommodation and commensurability. In each of these creative domains, there is a need to explicate texts as well as contexts of invention and production. It may be that critical intellectuals, along with art's pragmatic business partners, have wandered further from the human pulse and comic insight of the art in play in our contemporary world than previously was routine in other, also somewhat befuddled, cultural eras. If so, then the work of critical intellect is still to elucidate the tricks and tactics, the interpretable meanings and strategies, of the formal and informal outcomes (however amorphous or indeterminate that may be) circling through and all about the work of art. Music here is our central, but not at all a singular, instance.

My perhaps unflagging faith in the usefulness of critical thought and writing—despite the institutional lack of faith at present in the intellectual values and human pursuits outlined here alongside the manic humor needed to sustain them—is aligned with a well-considered hope that has informed Said's projects from an early moment in their maturing stubbornness. How could it be otherwise, since the texts and performances Said accounts for, here witnessed as profound silence mastered, create the illusion of intelligence adequate to the universe itself? My argument is that the nearly overwhelming power of great art fully encountered initiates a deepening, sometimes a darkening or a sobering, sometimes a heightening, of personal power that is an ally of the engaged critical self. The terms of engagement can vary, but the balance of well-proportioned judgment needed for critical imagination and analysis to move outside the poised domain of acceptability finds there motivation otherwise denied without the courage of artistic instruction. My argument has been that Bach and Monk contain the energies of insight and ironic intellectual (and emotional) differentiation sufficient to inaugurate the private dialectics of personal overcoming useful in the making of critical strength eccentric enough to engage useful intellectual interests.

To this end, Said's lectures at Irvine open up a realm of intertextuality that participates in a world of ideas where the arts might be seen and felt to encounter one another, to comment provocatively about their own condition (and thus the general condition) by means of sounds, words, and images that gather further life from the audacity of critical imagination. Said's cogent statement in his Reith Lectures, four years after the ones at Irvine, shed light here. Intellectuals, he asserts, are "precisely those figures whose public performances can neither be predicted nor compelled into some slogan, orthodox party line, or fixed dogma."[9] In his reflections on the cultural consequences of music as it is created as a vocation, as it is a harbinger of frequently unstatable human truths, Said brings us to think about what is familiar (and affirming) as well as what is estranged or estranging in our musical experiences. One may take courage from that. Said suggests something more ambiguous: "Music," he writes, "becomes an art not primarily or exclusively about authorial power and social authority, but a mode for thinking through or thinking with the integral variety of human cultural practices, generously, noncoercively, and, yes, in a utopian cast, if by utopian we mean worldly, possible, attainable, knowable" (105). For Said, what appears of use is getting on with the play of mind and art that brings people together for clarifying purposes of eventual goodwill. In a cynical time, any utopian prospect is scoffed at, and that is why Said hedges elegantly in asserting the "knowable" and "possible" grounds of such energy. No project makes sense unless it takes up facts and actions, events and practices, in concrete steps. And this is why the examples of Gould, Monk, and others serve the concrete function of showing not just how music circulates through social space with the economic and cultural practices that condition them but also how it operates against easy reductions that diminish the possibility that something genuinely disruptive may be born from the well-prepared instincts of imagination. This promise, the repeated eruption of excited musical discovery right here and now, is the source of a specific (sobering) hilarity at work in Gould's career. It was a career that offers perennial lessons. Gould's career, and Coltrane's, rehearse the costs of manic intensity. Coltrane passed away at thirty-nine; Gould at fifty.

Gould gave himself up, without reservation, in pursuit of his own performative authority. Such authority appears, perhaps, for Said, as a tyrannical partner. It is not. Said's preference, like Gould's, is for all the room he wants (or needs) to exert ideas, insights, fragments, long developments, intuitions, and trial exercises. In that, Said and Gould share a habituated practice.

Another preference embraces a different emphasis. Let me invoke it figuratively at first. Late afternoon light, in May or June, sometimes dissolves with a brooding, hopeful glow. Its tenor depends on the latitude where one sees it and on the weather, too. Sometimes in such delicate light, one finds an image, barely perceptible. It is a secondary quality of light, before twilight appears, no more substantial than a glitter of green on deeper greens. The image I have in mind here is like the flesh of consciousness itself—something ethereal, palpable, and exteriorized all at once. This quick, perhaps imaginary flicker emerges from the landscape. That does not, of course, make much sense, but it is a friendly illusion, and it has the use of putting a certain cast of mind into a familiar mood of self-recovery. No less mysterious and enchanting, we hear in Beethoven's final string quartets an embodiment of emotional subtlety very much like this. These quartets speak and sometimes whisper with uncanny human feeling. At moments (as in the opening allegro chords of the E-flat quartet, op. 127), they groan from an altogether incorporeal location, distant, pensive, and outside our own recognition of place. They carry foreboding inspiration. Deliberately, among their varied voices and tempi, Beethoven's late string quartets explore a shattered, stubborn inner landscape. The drama of their invaginated unfolding expresses pain, loss, or premonitory bliss. Repeatedly, in motifs that test the capacity of musical time to exert such halting movement, their intertwined strings seem propelled by a will not to let time stop. Time beneath their collected momentum seems held in check, arrested, part of a lyric spectacle in which melodic lines that are merged (dissonantly, beseechingly) in conversation become, thereby, heavier than any mind would wish to bear. The emotional signature of these quartets (opps. 127, 130, 131, 132, and 135) lives in a world of its own. It encompasses enormous musical authority. The drama under way throughout their reflective, sometimes somber progress is not easily spoken of accurately or adequately even though a century or so of commentary has tried to do just that. That drama is extremely private, at moments unspeakable: profound despair resolved, voided. Life's meaningfulness placed against the whole edifice of the world. Something like that. Nothing less.

One cannot hear these pieces, as they form their dense and fractured chatter in haunted counterpoint, and not be summoned to them. In their presence, one relents. Against their brooding energy, the mind seeks to internalize their elusive force. Against their gracefulness, there is only one defense: to listen as one might listen closely to a very wise, old person. There is a fundamental humility at the core of artistic truthfulness. As such, Beethoven's last string quartets dominate consciousness and its critical reverberations as very few artistic accomplishments can. They embody and thereby go beyond the joy and torment of individual artistry. Dante's Comedy provides a worthy supplement and equal.

I am certain that Said's commitment to the essentially ineffable influx of musical provocation is stronger than his testimony admits to in his Irvine lectures. An understandable hesitation, a discretely cultivated self-consciousness, suffuses his text. He was, on the occasion of the Wellek Lectures, speaking to a genuinely sophisticated academic audience. Perhaps, as Said finds in

Gould's contradictory artistry, a similar truth prevails in his own. "From his writing," Said asserts, "it seems quite clear that Gould saw nothing at all exceptional about playing the piano well. What he wanted was an escape from everything that determined or conditioned his reality as a human being" (29). One thinks here of Blackmur's observation that those "extremes with which Henry James was obsessed had largely to do with the personal human relations and almost nothing at all to do with public relations except as they conditioned, marred, or made private relations." [10] Insight as clear as this sometimes carries autobiographical depths. So it may be with Said's observation. One suspects that Said has not fully taken on the knowledge of how exceptional his critical writing is, how insistent with self-made force, how brave with unflinching, somewhat guarded intelligence. As we see with Gould's late-night practice sessions, or those conducted throughout days and nights of his long sleepless stretches, the triumph of the possible (however improbable) is often an accepted capacity for those with extraordinary command.

Just there, in casual "worldly" places and informal activities in which Said's temptation to intellectual romance now and then finds room, the provisional transgressive intellect of his amassed critical symphony casts cold light and imaginative warmth for those who follow. Such analytic force, against the grain of his time, has sustained a remarkable critical self unfailingly (restlessly) performing with discernment refined enough to engage the best minds of its era, resilient enough to sometimes thwart them. Said has always challenged himself to write "in order that the enabling conditions of [literary, musical and professional] performance and their connection with the sociocultural sphere can be seen as a coherent part of the whole experience" (12). That tantalizing phrase, "the whole experience," pertains to the public experience of musical performance integrated, somehow, with the private experience of a listener and a performer. With both perhaps, but what that coherence might be needs elaborations yet to come. Few, other than Said, could approach that project engagingly. Such imagined integration strikes a welcome chord on the calm music of Said's intellectual achievement. This unity of an expansive "whole experience" may be part of Said's private sense, something he lives out in the multiples of his considerable musical acumen. Certainly it is a figure now in the weave of his critical tapestry.

Edward Said has given us an enduring model of the arduous made useful, an inward mastery shared generously. His world is, as it has been for the whole of his increasingly encumbered career, a world of reflection. In that venture, Said has followed the miseries and redeeming truths of his experience. He is a man who lives productively in divergent worlds on several continents. His adopted community is the university, an uncomfortable familiar territory that looks out over the contradictions of a planet where, for Said, home is many places. As with Wallace Stevens's incarnation of George Santayana, the nowhere which is Rome and Beirut and New York becomes an abiding, scrupulous somewhere that the mind goes to and returns from as it meanders through its inspirations. And so Said's imagination of musical performance and critical attention, inhabitable as a private exercise of worship for all that is joyful and enduring, owns the privilege of its sympathies. The measure of this privilege is the strength of its life's projects brought to purposeful interactions. In this, Said has succeeded more than most would find the strength to dream of. Those tasks, his, given over to us, contest the scope and discourse of our individual and collective bonds.

Uses of aesthetics: after orientalism

I

Let me begin with a recent event—an exchange between two Nobel Prize–winning novelists: Kenzaburo Ôe of Japan and Claude Simon of France. It began when Ôe refused to attend a conference in France in 1995 as a protest against nuclear testing by France. In response, Claude Simon wrote a letter to Ôe, which was published in Le Monde on 21 September 1995. Neither Ôe's antagonism nor Simon's defense was particularly new in their respective positions. Simon recalled his experiences during the German occupation of World War II and insisted that nuclear weapons and tests were necessary for France to prevent future invasions. What was remarkable, however, was that he invoked Japan's past—its invasion of Asia—to refute Ôe. Furthermore, making this argument, Simon totally omitted reference to France's own past, to its colonization of many regions of the world before World War II, and especially to the fact that the nuclear testing took place near a particular island of the South Pacific that is a vestige of its colonial past. But even more noteworthy was a twist in his reasoning: At the same time as he reproached Japan for its past invasion of Asia, Simon did not neglect to add that he was moved by Japanese calligraphy.

It is possible to say that Simon is exemplary of the broad intellectual tendency in France today that has concluded all of its revolutionary gestures and fuss in praise of the modern Western value it represents. Simon does not want to listen to intellectual and ethical criticism from a country such as Japan, and he does not even think that it is something Japan can offer. If the Japanese can offer anything at all to France, it can only, and should only, be something aesthetic. Which does not mean, however, that Simon looks down on Japan, just that he would rather talk about his love and respect for Japanese culture. But in this passionate love and respect there is a certain bracketing of the concerns of pedestrian Japanese, who live their real lives and struggle with intellectual and ethical problems inherent in modernity. Inasmuch as these Japanese lives and concerns do not stimulate his sense of wonder, he would rather ignore them.

The Japan that Claude Simon and other "Japanophiliac" French love and respect is a Japan whose culture has enthralled them with things such as Ukiyo-e and Zen, and not the real existing Japan that threatens France with its economic power, namely, Japan as the other. He loves aesthetic Japan and the Japan that is represented in the French mind, and he hopes that that Japan will faithfully remain. He does not want to see westernized Japanese or listen to Japanese speak with what he believes is the Western epistemology. In certain senses, this is not only Simon's stance but an attitude shared by many French intellectuals and other Westerners who are interested in Japan insofar as they express their love and respect for Japanese culture. I would call this stance toward another culture "aestheticentrism."

In the United States today, very few, if any, intellectuals take this kind of stance toward the non-West, undoubtedly because of Edward Said's *Orientalism*. But considering that this powerful book, though translated into German and French, has not gotten as much attention in those countries as in the United States, I have to acknowledge that a book, no matter how powerful, cannot change a situation all by itself. What helped make *Orientalism* so widely accepted in the United States were lessons learned from the 1960s experiences of the Civil Rights and antiwar movements. While intellectuals in America can perhaps be categorized as pre- or post-Said, the European intellectual paradigm can only be seen as pre-Said or pre-*Orientalism*. Why?

One of the points Said made clear in the book is that "Orientalism" sees people of the non-West as convenient objects of analysis for the social sciences but ignores their intellectual and ethical existence. This undoubtedly designates non-Westerners as intellectually and ethically inferior. But what is more gnarled about this stance is that it goes hand in hand with an aesthetic worship of the very inferior other. This worship, in turn, produces an uneradicable self-deceit: Those with an Orientalist attitude come to believe that they, unlike others, treat non-Westerners more than equally—they treat them with "respect."[1]

What I would like to make clear is, first, that this attitude is not necessarily traditional but rather is rooted in modern science and aesthetics, which together produce the ambivalent worship; second, that if the first is true, this stance cannot be limited to the West but must have permeated non-Western zones, as well. Looking down on the other as an object of scientific analysis and looking up to the other as an aesthetic idol are less contradictory than complicit. The stance of social science to see the other as a mere object of analysis is based on modern natural science, which approaches objects by stripping away all the elements that have been integral parts, for example, magico-religious attributes, among others. The embodiment of this stance can be seen in the eighteenth-century Enlightenment. Then, in the romanticism of the late eighteenth century, the attitude changed: An aesthetic stance toward the other—the ambivalent worship toward those who are deemed intellectually and ethically inferior—came into existence.[2] Europeans began to discover "sacred savages" externally and "sacred medieval people" internally. Therefore, these scientific and aesthetic stances are never contradictory; the aesthetic stance could not have existed prior to the scientific.

I want to clarify the conditions of the aesthetic stance theoretically. It was Kant who proposed the clearest and most distinct account of the aesthetic stance that appeared in the late eighteenth century. Following the traditional categories, he divided our relation to objects into three domains: (1) cognitive concerns of true or false; (2) ethical concerns of good or bad; and (3) concerns of taste, either pleasant or unpleasant. One of the points that distinguishes Kant from his predecessors is that he simply clarified the three domains where different attitudes intervene, but unhierarchically, without giving them any order. What does it mean? All of us respond to a certain object in at least three domains at once. Confronting an object, we receive it cognitively (as true or false), ethically (as good or bad), and according to taste (as pleasant or unpleasant). In other words, these domains always appear to us as intermingled, yet often contradictory, sets. For this reason, it so happens that a certain object can be pleasant even if it is illusory or evil, and true even if it is unpleasant or boring.

What Kant constituted as a condition for the judgment of taste was the stance of seeing a certain object with "disinterestedness," namely, to see it by bracketing cognitive and ethical concerns. Bracketing becomes necessary because it is impossible to discard any of these categories. And this is not limited to the judgment of taste. The same is true in scientific recognition, where concerns of ethics and taste must be bracketed. For instance, it is not recommended that a surgeon see his patient aesthetically or ethically while diagnosing or operating. On the other hand, when making ethical judgments—

judgments of faith—the concerns of true or false and pleasant or unpleasant should be bracketed. This bracketing is inherent in modernity; scientific recognition was constituted by bracketing the previous stance toward nature: as religious signification or as a result of magical motivation. Bracketing other domains is not the same as eradicating them. Modern aesthetics after Kant also depends on the conscious method of bracketing.

According to Kant, beauty does not exist simply in sensual pleasure, but neither does it exist in simple indifference. Beauty is achieved by the conscious method of positively abandoning a direct "interest" in the object. In such cases, the more difficult the bracketing of interest, the more pleasurable the subject's effort to bracket. It is in this sense that the Kantian aesthetic is said to be subjective. Kant existed in a transitional moment from classicism to romanticism. The norm of the classicistic aesthetic was established: Beauty was considered to be in the form of the object itself; in other words, whether it was beautiful or not was judged as objective form. For Kant, on the other hand, beauty comes into existence only by way of the subjective act: for instance, to imaginarily reconstruct symmetry (or finality) while observing a building that subtly lacks symmetry. It can be said, in such a situation, that the more difficult it is to bracket the interest, the more intense is the pleasure of doing it.

It is in the theory of the sublime that we see the crux of Kant's aesthetic thinking. The sublime is nothing other than the pleasure that results from the subject's effort in going beyond the unpleasant object. According to Kant, the sublime exists not in the object itself but in the infinity of the reason that goes beyond the limitation of sensibility. To express this in reverse, the sublime is "self-alienation" in the act of discovering an infinity of reason in the object that is contradictory to the self.[3] However, the sublime is not a manifestation of religious awe. An object that overpowers a human—lightning, for instance—is deemed sublime only insofar as its cause is scientifically evident and the spectator is protected from its brutal force. If not, lightning remains an object of religious awe or supernatural attributes, like a divine message. For this reason, the sublime as an aesthetic judgment is connected to the recognition of modern science.

At this point, it becomes necessary to consider a realm that Kant did not scrutinize—a place where all differences are unconditionally bracketed: the monetary economy. This is where manifold use values and the practical labor that produces them are reduced to exchange value, or, in Marx's terms, "social and abstract labor." In the beginning of *Capital*, Marx wrote: "The commodity is, first of all, an external object, a thing which through its qualities satisfies human needs of whatever kind. The nature of these needs, whether they arise, for example, from the stomach, or the imagination, makes no difference. Nor does it matter here how the thing satisfies man's need, whether directly as a means of subsistence, i.e., an object of consumption, or indirectly as a means of production."[4] In other words, it is in the world of the commodity economy where we find an attitude that is totally indifferent to the difference of things—the use value—and concerned only with one thing: interest.

Albert O. Hirschman has pointed out that in eighteenth-century thought, "interest" was introduced as a passion against passion; what suppresses passion is neither reason nor interdiction but passion that pursues interest.[5] It follows that in the context of the commodity economy, Kantian "disinterestedness" is the act of rediscovering the difference of things by bracketing the interest. For the romantics, then, Kantian disinterestedness functioned mainly to bracket economic interest, which was manifest as "art for art's sake." But what is more crucial in this context is that Kantian bracketing, or, namely, purification of all domains, was inseparable from the capitalist economy that nullifies differences of all domains. In fact, it was by bracketing the elements of interest/usefulness/happiness that Kant attained the purified ethical domain. He did not hierarchize the three domains precisely because the commodity economy reduces everything, equally, into interest. In The Critique of Judgement, Kant attempted to bracket interest, but what made this thought possible was the commodity economy itself. Hence, ever since art came to be art, it has been connected to commodification.[6]

To repeat, with Kant it became clear that what makes art art is the subjective act of bracketing other concerns. This stance is not classicistic or romantic. In rejecting classicism, Kant did not tend toward romanticism. He dealt with the modern problematic of art lying beneath both, and this problematic is not yet obsolete. Clement Greenberg considered Kant to be the first modernist critic. Following Kant, he defined "flatness" as what makes painting painting in contradistinction to architecture or sculpture.[7] But the impetus of purification in modern art inexorably results in its self-destruction. Greenberg saw this in Mondrian's attempt to make painting architectonic. This is nothing but a self-decomposition or an unbracketing from within that occurs at the moment when a pure domain, constituted by the manipulation of bracketing, is mistaken to be autonomous in and of itself.

It is possible to say, therefore, that Kant's reflection involves a modernist statement but also its immanent critique. For instance, Marcel Duchamp exhibited a urinal with the title "Fountain" and urged us to see it by bracketing our daily concerns. In this case, the signal "This is an artwork in an exhibition" demanded that we bracket it. An object seen in this context is no longer an object with use value but a material thing that constitutes the form of art. Duchamp showed that what makes art art lies only in the signal "This is an artwork." To me this means "Let's bracket it." Duchamp showed us that anything can be an art object, not just the objects that are customarily exhibited in museums and galleries. But this manipulation works only insofar as the convention—that being exhibited in museums and galleries guarantees the "art-ness" of the objects—is mutually understood.

Using the example of "Fountain" and its constituting frame of "art-ness," one can access various problematics embedded in Kant's reflections. First of all, what Duchamp presented was an object that, in the ordinary context, is associated with dirtiness. In the context of art, we are compelled to bracket this feeling. But, importantly, Kant maintained that the act of bracketing displeasure gives pleasure on another level, that is, metaphysical pleasure. In romanticism, this bracketing was pushed to the point of perversion. For instance, an evil that calls for ethical opposition can offer pleasure in the subjective project of bracketing the ethical concern. For this reason, aestheticism rather needs evil or abjection. Kant certainly did not appreciate the extremism. But he revealed to us that it is by bracketing that the domains of truth/good/beauty can be established and, furthermore, that the bracketing must be removed when necessary. That is to say, he refused to grant superiority to any one of these categories over any other; instead, he requested that we perform the most difficult task, that is, to bracket and unbracket flexibly, whenever required.

The aesthetic stance, or aestheticism, gets pleasure not from its object but by bracketing various reactions to the object. An aesthete praises a certain object not because the object is comfortable but rather because it is uncomfortable and possibly something to be shunned in daily life. An aesthete kneels before something not because he has really submitted to it but because he derives pleasure out of bracketing the displeasure of obeying an object that he can dominate if he wants to. We can liken it to a masochist who gets pleasure out of obeisance only in a relationship wherein his superiority to the master is confirmed and he can play within a set of rules that does not violate his ultimate security. It corresponds to what Kant saw in the sublime. Masochism in this sense is a modern phenomenon par excellence.

It was true that Ukiyo-e shocked French impressionists in the late nineteenth century and that Japanese crafts became widely influential and even laid the foundation for the advent of art nouveau. But Japonism was not necessarily an exception. Later, African art influenced cubism in a similar way. In both cases, the appreciation was only aesthetic, coupled with the intention to absorb it into their own art. Such appropriation was possible only under the condition that the artists' cultures were or could be colonized anytime. Aesthetes nevertheless think that kneeling before the beauty of the other is the same as respecting the other from an equal position.

This phenomenon began with romanticism. In Germany, it surfaced after Kant, while in England and France, it had begun even earlier. It was triggered by the advent of mechanical reproduction, which had appeared earlier in England. After all, romanticists began to praise handmade crafts from the past at the moment they were made obsolete by mechanical reproduction. Walter Benjamin maintained that the aura of artwork disappeared in the age of mechanical reproduction. But the truth is the opposite: It was mechanical reproduction that prompted an aura to emanate from artworks of the past. And this can be amplified further: It is the mechanization of production that endows handmade products with auras and changes them into art. In a strict sense, however, being handmade is not an absolute condition for having an aura and thereby being art. Mechanically reproduced objects, too, can have an aura. The point is that an aura does not exist in the object. As Kant showed, art does not exist in the form of the object but in considering the object as art, or seeing it with disinterestedness. Andy Warhol's maneuver was to force us to change our stance (the bracketing) toward the kind of object (of reproduction) in which it is difficult to abandon our daily interest.

Thus, the aesthetic positionality came into existence along with the Industrial Revolution. It first appeared as an appreciation of handicraft—the means of production that industrialization made economically obsolete—and the lives of craftsmen that became equally obsolete. It was in this climate, in England, that John Ruskin represented the aesthetic movement. Significantly, the aestheticism that appreciates handicraft is inseparable from aesthetic worship (aestheticentrism) toward colonial cultures that are dominated and destroyed by the worshipper's culture; this is in the same sense that anthropology, which studies external aboriginals and non-Western societies, and folklore, which attempts to return to an internal premodernity, go hand in hand. The aesthetic stance is established by bracketing other elements, but one should always be ready to remove the brackets. As a simple example, it is like the distinction between a movie and reality: In the movie theater, we can admire gangsters as heroes, while outside we have to beware them. However, the characteristic of the aestheticentrists is that they forget to remove the brackets. They confuse the reality of the other with what is achieved by bracketing. Or they confuse their respect for beauty with respect for the other. Thus, for aestheticentrists, colonialism is conveniently obscured.

Colonialism and imperialism are accused of being sadistic forms of invasion and domination. But the most typical subversion of colonialism is its aestheticentrist way of appreciating and respecting the other. I believe this is what Said meant by the term *Orientalism*. Orientalism could never be characterized as an attitude that neglects the other but as that which exists within the aesthetic exceptionalization of the other. Had expansionism not had the twisted admiration to savor, that is, had it been simply the will to rule and to know, we would not have accumulated such a colossal Orientalist corpus. Aestheticentrism refuses to acknowledge that the other who does not offer any stimulative surprise of a "stranger" lives a life "out there." Aestheticentrists always appear as anticolonialists. In the same way, they always appear as anti-industrial capitalists, although their aesthetic stance was produced by the advent of industrial capital. Furthermore, aestheticentrism is at the core of fascism: Appearing to be anticapitalist, it attempts to aesthetically sublimate the contradictions of the capitalist economy.

Duchamp's example leads us to another aspect of bracketing and unbracketing. The African American novelist James Baldwin did not feel like reading Shakespeare's *Othello* because of its discriminatory stance toward blacks. However, while living in Paris, where English is not generally understood, he became aware of himself as a black writer, and as one who writes in English, which finally enabled him to accept Shakespeare.[8] In this case, it might be said that by bracketing the discrimination of blacks in *Othello*, Baldwin came to see Shakespeare's tragedy as art. But the real problematic originates less in Baldwin's stance than in that of white, English-speaking audiences, who see *Othello* merely as art. It is not that they attempt to bracket the discrimination that enraged Baldwin but that they omit this from the beginning. They would maintain that those who degrade Shakespeare for such a minor flaw do not understand art. Ultimately, this is the same position that allows the belief that works exhibited in museums and galleries are art. My point is that they should unbracket the race issue in Shakespeare, at least once.

Similar dynamics of unbracketing exist in the recent achievements of feminist critiques and queer theory. They reveal what heterosexual male readers have always bracketed and been unaware of. In other words, they unbracket what has been suppressed under heterosexual domination. But their unbracketing is not necessarily a denial of works as art. For instance, if, in a text, a woman is described mainly as an aesthetic representation of desire, the unbracketing of the sexual representation is not a simple denial of the work. If the text is strong enough, it will accommodate different interpretations. And when we commit ourselves to rereading the text from alternative positions, we would again bracket that particular critique. Yet the new reading, of course, is not, and should not be, an erasure of the critique.

2

What I have said so far might seem as if I am accusing France or the great Western powers, but what I really want to address is that the same thing can be said of Japan. Escaping the colonization of the West in the political domain, Japan accepted it with no resistance in other dimensions; then, by the early twentieth century, it became an imperialist par excellence vis-à-vis other

Asian nations. But this is not an idiosyncratic case. We see the same pattern in the United States, Israel, China, India, and even Vietnam after its independence. Nationalism—an idea that had positive meaning under colonization or the threat of colonization—became imperialism because of its latent characteristics of nationalism itself, rather than the peculiarities of this or that state. Under Napoleon's occupation, Johann Gottlieb Fichte said, "But, in regard to space, we believe that it is first of all the Germans who are called upon to begin the new era as pioneers and models for the rest of mankind."[9] Any nation-state has the right to say the same, and every one has.

It was around the time of the Sino-Japanese War of 1894 that Japan turned from nationalism to imperialism. Historians have scrutinized the political discourses surrounding the war, but the fact that aesthetic discourses were the motivating moment has been ignored. Inasmuch as nationalism is rooted in affection (in the Kantian context) and concerned with beauty, we have to scrutinize it in the aesthetic dimension. Enter Okakura Tenshin and Yanagi Soetsu—two Japanese thinkers who used aesthetics politically. As if exemplifying the above accounts of aestheticism, Okakura appreciated crafts as art, and by applying the same measure to all Asian nations, he confirmed the oneness of Asia within an art historical context. Furthermore, he wrote his *Ideals of the East* in English and published it in India; appealing to the superiority of East over West, his book advocates the liberation of Asia from Western imperialism and its foundation, industrial capitalism.

The following should be considered with respect to Okakura. First, it was American scholar Ernest Fenollosa who introduced him to the Western notion of art and the possibility of applying it to Japanese native art (although Okakura later shunned him). Second, it was only because arts and crafts were the only Japanese products that were appreciated and exported—flourishing as Japonism in France—that Okakura could stress the superiority of Japanese art and attempt to represent Japan by it.[10] That is to say, this was purely an issue of commodity production. Okakura's agenda could not have worked had it not been for the preexisting boom and desire for folk art in the West. Furthermore, many of Okakura's ideas were prefigured by Western aestheticism: His counterposing of Eastern handicraft versus Western industrial capitalism was modeled after Ruskin and William Morris; in fact, the English woman with the Indian name who published Okakura's books called him the "Morris of the East" in her preface to *Ideals of the East*. Okakura, too, must have been familiar with Western trends.

All in all, the so-called universal principle of the East—which Okakura claimed to have found in Buddhist philosophy—was only discovered retrospectively and was contextualized along with the spread of industrial capital. Appreciating and protecting the preindustrial form of production became possible only after industrial capital established its hegemony. It is hard to determine how this retrospective revaluation occurred: whether it was an elegy to a declining form, or a psychological compensation for the guilt of destroying the preindustrial form of production, or a tacit display of one's own superiority. These factors are all interconnected, and none is more definitive than any other. In *The Book of Tea*, Okakura wrote:

> He [the average Westerner] was wont to regard Japan as barbarous while she indulged in the gentle arts of peace: he calls her civilised since she began to commit wholesale slaughter on Manchurian battlefields. Much comment has been given lately to the Code of Samurai—the Art of Death which makes our soldiers exult in self-sacrifice; but scarcely any attention has been drawn to Taoism, which represents so much of our Art of Life. Fain would we remain barbarians, if our claim to civilisation were to be based on the gruesome glory of war. Fain would we await the time when due respect shall be paid to our art and ideals.[11]

It was only after Japan defeated Russia with military might in the Russo-Japanese War that Okakura could say this. After the war, Okakura abandoned the movement of liberating Asian colonies and confined himself to aesthetic research at the Museum of Fine Arts in Boston. His books began to be read in Japan in the 1930s, at the time when Japan began to move toward the "Great East-Asian Co-Prosperity Sphere." And it was from this moment on that the oneness of Asia, which he had discovered through his aesthetic thinking, came to function as an ideology that added the flourish to Japan's domination of Asia.

At this point, I would like to call attention to two events. It is known that Okakura, with Fenollosa, uncovered the statue of Kannon (the Goddess of Mercy) as art. Previously, it had been hidden in a section of Horyuji Temple called Yumedono for centuries. The whole history of Asia is stylistically condensed in this sculpture. Affected as he was by this discovery, Okakura began to call Japan a "museum of Asia." In the following passage, we can see how the discovery was made:

> It was around the 17th year of Meiji [1885] that I, along with Fenollosa and Kano Tessai, requested that the monks open the gate of Yumedono. But they claimed that if it were opened there would be thunder and lightning. According to them, in the first year of Meiji, when the doctrine of mixing Shinto and Buddhism was all the rage, people became frightened as they began to open the gate and stopped half-way because of the sudden spread of dark clouds and the roar of thunder. The monks' resistance was hard to overcome because they thought this had been an obvious

sign. Then we began to open the gate anyway, claiming that we would take care of the thunder. The monks all fled.[12]

It was not only the monks but also people in general who had feared opening the gate. That is to say, the statue had been the object of religious awe rather than artistic worship. Okakura's act demonstrates that the disinterestedness that allows us to acknowledge artistic beauty can be achieved only by the same sort of change of stance (bracketing) that takes place in the natural sciences. In the West, it was after romanticism that ornaments and ecclesiastical implements began to be seen as art. It was also at this moment that religion itself came to be grasped aesthetically.[13] In the same sense, when Okakura stressed the importance of religion (Buddhism) time and again, he interpreted it from the modern, aesthetic view. What Okakura took to be religious belief was something that, without hesitation, destroys the religious faith and customs of native people. When this change of stance is promoted within a nation, it is called modernization, and once it is applied abroad, it is called colonialism. As he traveled around other Asian nations collecting artifacts, Okakura most likely approached them with the same attitude he took in Horyuji. When he advocated antimodernism and anti-industrial capitalism, while praising native cultural products, his position was that of a modernist and a colonialist.

One cannot blame Okakura for bracketing the real, living people while praising their art, but he can be blamed for never unbracketing. Furthermore, Okakura was indifferent to Koreans, Japan's neighbors, while promoting the independence of Asian people. About Korea, the victim that was forced to submit its land as the stage of the Sino-Japanese War and then forced to merge with Japan after the Russo-Japanese War, he said little, except that Korea was "naturally" ruled by Japan.

Considering these points, Yanagi Soetsu, who appeared after Tenshin, might seem to have an exceptional attitude. Yanagi was active in the Taisho era, after Tenshin's death, not only at the time when humanism and democracy seemed to be flourishing domestically but also when Japan was gradually heading toward overt imperialism, which was symbolized in the annexation of Korea in 1910. The ambiguity of the time was directly related to the ambiguity of Yanagi's position. He first studied William Blake, and from this it is easy to see the influence of the English Arts and Crafts movement of Ruskin and Morris. But what is important about his work is less his commitment to the Arts and Crafts movement in Japan than his discovery of Korean folk art. At that time, Korea was influenced by Confucianism, which neglected handicraft, and it was extremely difficult to see crafts as art, as being detached from their daily usage. Therefore, it might not be too much to say that it was Yanagi who discovered, or rather invented, Korean folk art, and, in precisely the same sense, that it was Fenollosa who invented Japanese art.

At a glance, Yanagi's stance toward Korea seems flawless. Among Japanese intellectuals, even including Marxists, he was an exception. He was not only a connoisseur of Korean art but, contrary to the prevailing opinion, he also considered Koreans to be completely different and independent from Japanese and opposed the Japanese policy of annexing Korea. During a lecture given in May 1920 in Seoul, he declared:

> Whether or not a nation can assimilate another nation is one of the most crucial questions of twentieth-century reality. Aside from the oppression of annexation, even the idea that assimilation is possible by means of a peaceful policy can never be affirmed, either by those who are familiar with world history or by those who just live in today's world as human beings. And who can believe that a country such as Japan, full of internal contradictions and an extreme example of imperfection, could enlighten others for a new civilization?
>
> What we should always keep in mind is that Korea is a country that has produced a great sense of beauty and a place where people live with great art.[14]

Clearly, it was only by recognizing Korea as "a country that has produced a great sense of beauty and a place where people live with great art" that Yanagi could stress the greatness and independence of the Korean people as a nation; it was not by acknowledging them just as a different other. If it had been so, Yanagi's epistemological ground would not have been so different from Okakura's, who thought it was inevitable that Korea would become a Japanese colony. Okakura praised India and China because they were countries that produced a great sense of beauty, but for him there was no great beauty in Korea. Later in the 1930s, Yanagi used the same logic, when he opposed Japan's policy of enforcing linguistic and cultural assimilation by describing the people of Okinawa as having a "great sense of beauty."

It is possible to say that by way of aestheticism, Yanagi tried to encourage those peoples who were under colonial domination to gain their own cultural identities and pride. However, we people do not necessarily live for and by beauty per se. Yanagi saw folk art in terms of commodity production and its quality as something to be judged seriously. But I have to pose a question to him and aesthetes like him: Could Koreans really resist the domination of Japanese industrial capitalism with folk art as their sole commodity product?

Yanagi was clearly against the idea of Koreans achieving independence by violent means, because violence would only be an imitation of the Japanese method—which, he claimed, was destined to fail. Thus, Yanagi's logic is essentially the same as Okakura's. Okakura could praise the sense of beauty in other Asian cultures only because his discourse was tacitly based on Japan's violent victory over Russia, made possible by its industrial capital. It was only natural that Korea's independence movement would become violent and inclined toward heavy industrial production—there was no other way. If it did not remain aesthetic, who could blame it?

According to Yanagi, the main characteristic of Korean folk art was its sense of sorrow and sadness. But this perception was simply a selfish sentiment of sympathy—on the part of a colonial ruler—toward a nation that was to be colonized and destroyed by his own nation. In fact, Yanagi's book, *Korea and Its Art*, was severely criticized by Korean intellectuals after its publication in 1974, long before my own criticism was published. For Mui Ing, it was wrong to define Korean art as one of sorrow and sadness, that rather it is an art of optimism. And according to Kim Hyon, many people pointed out that "Yanagi's theory of art is a version of a colonialist view of history." [15]

Certainly, Yanagi, an exception among Japanese, loved Koreans, had sympathy for their national destiny, and persisted in protesting the Japanese occupation. But he is inevitably criticized today because his conceptualization was limited to aestheticentrism. To the Koreans who read his book, his message sounds more like "What we truly expect from you Koreans is that you give us the same sense of wonder that your celadon porcelain of Koguryo once inspired in us rather than your economic growth that threatens us."

Said never denied British authors (even Kipling) even as he criticized them with respect to imperialism and colonialism. I mention Okakura and Yanagi not simply to denounce them. My point is not to deny the aesthetic stance any more than I deny the scientific one, for each is a faculty indispensable to the bracketing of various concerns, as Kant said. The mistake of aestheticentrism is that it forgets to unbracket. In fact, this lapse is common in science as well as in fundamentalist moralism. They both bracket other concerns, but never unbracket.

Said painstakingly analyzed how Europeans constructed the representation of the Orient. In a sense, his work makes the Orient seem like the Kantian "thing-in-itself"—in other words, unrepresentable. This does not, however, prohibit objectifying the societies of the Orient. Nor does it imply that only the Orient has the right to speak for itself. It seems to me that Said pointed to the opposite. That is to say, he fought not only against the domination of the West but also against the domination of the Arabic tradition. His lessons present that there are others, namely, individuals, who cannot be mere objects of analysis or beauty, and that it is necessary to fight against any power— whether Western or Oriental—that suppresses individuals.

RASHID I. KHALIDI

Edward W. Said and the American public sphere: speaking truth to power

Edward Said's work has had such a profound impact on so broad a range of fields that it is easy to lose sight of one important distinction: the difference between the realms of literature and culture, where Said has had his main effect, and the quite distinct realm of the question of Palestine. Of course, there are similarities in the ways in which Said has affected our understanding of both the realms of literature and culture and the question of Palestine. Over nearly three decades, his seminal scholarly publications, formal public lectures, and classroom teaching have significantly changed the way in which Americans and others all over the world perceive the people of Palestine and the contours of the conflict between the Arabs and the Israelis. Said's publications, including The Question of Palestine, Covering Islam, After the Last Sky, Blaming the Victims, The Politics of Dispossession, and Peace and Its Discontents, have had a marked and sustained influence.[1] Most of these titles are still in print, which is evidence of their continuing timeliness and relevance. However, where the question of Palestine is concerned, another factor must be considered beyond scholarship, lectures, and teaching: Said's extraordinary impact as a public intellectual on public political discourse in the United States.

Said's impact is all the more significant because both this public political discourse and the media that feeds on it and nourishes it were, and in large measure still are, fundamentally sympathetic to the Israelis, and by extension are hostile to the Palestinians. Indeed, in assessing American attitudes since the Arab-Israeli war of 1967, it is immediately apparent that Said's voice on television, on radio, and in articles in a range of magazines and periodicals has provided the main—and sometimes the only—antidote to the consensus of idiocy that generally prevails whenever Palestine is discussed in the mainstream media. While the ubiquitous image of the Palestinian terrorist has not been effaced (and indeed has been reinforced in some ways by a number of horrendous attacks against Israeli civilians in recent years), and while the idea that the very word *Palestine* is subversive is still strong,[2] Said has undoubtedly done more than any other individual to establish the idea of the basic humanity of the Palestinian people in the minds of the American public.

By comparison with the scholarly output of a figure who has been influential in so many academic fields—among them comparative literature, postcolonial studies, anthropology, and cultural studies—Said's impact on American public attitudes toward the question of Palestine may seem relatively unimportant. Surely, some may argue, it is his major books, either those on literature and culture, or those on Palestine, that we should be looking at, not the *Nightline* appearances, the lectures to college audiences, or the opinion pieces in the *New York Times*, the *Nation*, or *al-Hayat*. In fact, Said has probably influenced greater numbers and a far wider range of people by means of the print and broadcast media than by his books. Through media channels, he has incidentally exposed many who have been impressed with his work on literature and culture to dissenting ideas on Palestine, ideas that many probably would not have otherwise encountered.

The media offer a different sort of audience, and one that cannot be influenced as deeply or as permanently as the audience of Said's books or his formal academic lectures. Nevertheless, the realm of the media represents a crucial arena of public culture and political struggle. Few intellectuals possess the qualities and capabilities necessary for dealing successfully with the media (or for using it for their own purposes even as they retain their popularity with the media), while preserving their integrity or the integrity of their message. Fewer still are willing to come down from the rarefied Olympian heights of the academy to the crass level of television, radio, and the daily press, with all their much discussed flaws.

Such a public presence has a price, of course, especially given the voracious appetite of the media when a story breaks. It has a price as well, particularly in times of crisis, in terms of the plethora of insistent demands that are generated as a result of media appearances: Groups all over the country ask for information and elucidation and extend lecture invitations. When these moments come, and they have come frequently over the past three decades where the question of Palestine is concerned, there is almost no limit to the intrusiveness and persistence of television and radio producers, journalists, and interviewers, many of whom know nothing whatsoever about the topics being discussed or about the individuals with whom they are talking. The multibillion dollar American news and entertainment industry has apparently lost the ability to maintain and use a Rolodex, and the turnover in its ranks is so rapid that it is extremely rare for the same reporter to cover the Middle Eastern beat from one crisis to the next.

These phenomena are perhaps related to the nature of the communications industry in this phase of the history of capitalism, when the competition for market share between more and more branches of fewer and fewer conglomerates—CNN, CNN Headline News, MSNBC, NBC, and all the others—has grown considerably more intense, when news has become increasingly indistinguishable from other forms of entertainment, and when many in the news business are blissfully innocent of any knowledge of, or interest in, world affairs. This situation is most pronounced with regard to television news, which, as it has developed in the United States in recent decades, is surely losing whatever capability it may have once had to convey complex information in depth and with historical context (this, incidentally, is much less true of TV news in other countries, especially Britain, France, and Italy). Coverage of foreign affairs by the American media suffers the most from this degenerative process: Indeed, since 1990, TV network news stories that are broadcast from foreign bureaus have declined by 59 percent.[3] The situation at major newspapers, which have closed many of their foreign bureaus in recent years, is not much better. As a result, for some stories, virtually the only remaining easily accessible source in the United States for information on international affairs is the depthless drivel of CNN and its clones, which endlessly repeat the same snippets of information without background, detail, or content, but always accompanied by riveting images, albeit the same ones, hour after hour, from one channel to another.

Whatever the reason for this situation—the spread of *People* magazine-style celebrity coverage in the guise of news; the inexorable pressure to provide visuals, however meaningless; the need to provide "breaking news," with or without context or content; or the decline in historical and geographical knowledge among American youth—beyond all of these factors there is an all-consuming nature to the American media, a disbelief that anything can be as important as a few seconds on the small screen, and a level of banality and bland ignorance that is sometimes breathtaking, even for those hardened to it by many years of bitter experience in dealing with the media. For these and other reasons, engaging the media is often a most uncongenial task, and always a tiring one, for those who have to do it regularly and who care about the topics they are asked to comment on.

In this situation, Said could easily have done what many others have done and escaped the unwelcome attention, not to speak of the thanklessness of the task of trying to impart his views to others less informed. He could thereby have preserved his privacy (and his personal security, for media appearances on the subject of Palestine often have provoked hate-filled and even dangerous responses)[4] and spent the time thereby saved on the far more congenial tasks of writing and lecturing for smaller audiences on less topical matters. But he has courageously refused to do so, at great cost in terms of his time, energy, and peace of mind, because he understood the importance of this public arena of struggle. He also understood the importance of allowing a voice such as his to be heard above the babble of the conventional political and media consensus in blind support of the destructive vagaries of American policy in the Middle East and of the Israeli political agenda at any given moment. As Said has said of the role of the individual in the face of the power of the media, "I think individuals are the ones who make the difference."[5]

Said has been successful in conveying a difficult and unpopular message regarding Palestine, in part because of his transparent personal integrity, his obvious erudition, his sense of humor, and his engaging and open personality. All of these characteristics are readily apparent in person, in lectures, and in the classroom, but they are also manifest on radio and television. Said's ability to express himself in an articulate and concise way are supported by his commanding, authoritative presence on camera. It is this presence that appeals to audiences and encourages open-minded thinking on the question of Palestine.

As the public advocate of an unpopular cause, Said is an outstanding example of the role of the public intellectual, which he defined in *Representations of the Intellectual*. The intellectual, Said argues,

> is an individual endowed with a faculty for representing, embodying, articulating a message, a view, an attitude, philosophy or opinion to, as well as for, a public . . . someone whose place it is publicly to raise embarrassing questions, to confront dogma and orthodoxy (rather than to produce them), . . . someone who cannot easily be co-opted by governments or corporations, and whose *raison d'être* is to represent all those peoples and issues that are routinely forgotten or swept under the rug.[6]

In representing views to and for a public, or in putting forward questions that are embarrassing and difficult, or in giving voice to those who are without one, Said has certainly lived up to this description.

Said's *Representations of the Intellectual* is based on his Reith Lectures, which the BBC broadcast in 1993. It is virtually inconceivable that an American media network would sponsor anything like the Reith Lectures, let alone invite a figure such as Edward Said to deliver them. The very idea of more than three or four minutes of continuous, intelligent speech on any topic uninterrupted by advertisements on American television or radio is nearly revolutionary: Six lectures of thirty uninterrupted minutes, each being delivered by one person over a six-week period, is beyond the capabilities even of PBS and NPR, the closest examples of the type of media institutions existing in Europe and elsewhere, and represented by the BBC.

In spite of the absence of such a forum in this country, Said has generally succeeded in using the media, most of which are irredeemably addicted to the superficial image and the sound bite, to put across quite complex ideas regarding the question of Palestine, ideas that were often initially both unfamiliar and objectionable to a large portion of his audience. In doing so, he has cut across the grain of conventional public discourse in two ways—in precisely the manner he suggests the intellectual must do in *Representations of the Intellectual*.

First, Said has consistently criticized the consensual complicity with American policy on the Middle East that is habitually shown by both representatives of the media and the so-called experts whom the media bring in generally to validate a point of view, or a conventional polarity,[7] that they have already determined in advance. Instead of the kind of rigorous critique of those in power that is regularly offered by the media and academic and other "experts" when the foreign policy of another state is at issue, most of these paragons repeat the line of the current administration in almost Stalinist fashion where U.S. foreign policy is concerned.[8] Said has always attacked this cozy complicity and has suggested critical ways of looking at U.S. policy in the Middle East. His impact on the way in which this policy is now regarded by broad sectors of public opinion in this country is remarkable and rivals that of only a very few other American public intellectuals, such as Noam Chomsky and Gore Vidal.

A blatant example of this media complicity with U.S. policy involves the treatment of the Middle East "peace process." The peace process is virtually a media sacred cow, with few journalists or commentators willing to state the obvious—that this "process" has been an utter failure in bringing peace to the Palestinians and the Israelis, or even in building confidence between them, and it has left the Palestinians considerably worse off than they were when the process began in Madrid in 1991.[9] Said was an exception to this media complicity from the earliest stages of the Oslo process, and his trenchant predictions have been proven correct by the events of the past few years. These predictions have been belatedly acknowledged as accurate by many with a serious interest in the Middle East (although others have reacted churlishly to Said's preciseness).[10]

The second way in which Edward Said has cut across the grain of conventional public discourse on Palestine has been to frame Middle Eastern issues in terms of Palestine first and foremost, rather than in terms of Israel, Zionism, and Jewish history, as is commonly the case. American coverage of Arab-Israeli issues, and indeed of much else that happens in the Middle East, is generally not only based on an Israeli perspective but is often undertaken by reporters who are based in Israel, many of them Israelis or Americans who have emigrated to Israel. Given the obsessive interest so many millions of Americans have in Israel, and their close attachment to it, and given the pervasive influence these Americans have, it is not hard to understand why the media conventionally frame Middle Eastern issues in terms of Israel and its interests.

Said has insisted that the Palestinians have the right to represent themselves, to speak for themselves, and that they are entitled to narrate their own history, which he has argued has a value and a specificity of its own.[11] He has recently chided Palestinian historians for not taking more of a role in writing their own history (earlier, in his 1987 introduction to Blaming the Victims, he pointed to "significant Palestinian-sponsored efforts to take research into the Western metropolis itself").[12] Equally important, Said has argued that this history and narrative are independent of those of the Israelis, in spite of all the connections—most laden with ironic tragedy—between the two narratives and the two peoples. In the American media, these connections, and the obsessive concern of so many in the United States with Israel, have generally meant that a Palestinian voice has not had what Said has called "permission to narrate," and if such permission was granted, it was only on condition that there be a balancing Israeli countervoice.

Most frequently, therefore, when a Palestinian voice has been allowed to be heard in the media, it has been "balanced" by either an Israeli or a pro-Israeli voice. This was the case not only regarding Israeli-Palestinian matters, where there might be some justification for such a procedure (although quite frequently on NPR and in other media, such matters are covered exclusively from Jerusalem, by Israelis, and from an Israeli perspective), but also regarding purely Palestinian internal matters or other matters involving the Palestinians and other Arabs, the United States, or other countries. Needless to say, it is generally not deemed necessary to have a balancing Palestinian voice to legitimate coverage of Israeli internal affairs or of Israeli-American or Israeli-European relations.

However bad American media coverage of Palestinian matters may seem today, it is not as abysmal as it once was, in particular since the watershed events of the Israeli invasion of Lebanon and the ensuing siege of Beirut during the summer of 1982, and the Palestinian intifada, which began in December 1987. The consequence of both events was a more critical view of Israel in the media—or, rather, the first hint of a critical view of Israel. In at least some segments of the media, despite being perceived and portrayed as a small, helpless victim, Israel came to be seen as a powerful oppressor, transformed from David to Goliath, as it were. Needless to say, only the extraordinary sacrifices and the hideous suffering of the Palestinians and other Arabs at times of great tribulation—such as the siege of Beirut, the *intifada*, and the Israeli bombing of southern Lebanon in April 1996—have forced the media to focus on something other than the customary Israeli object.

One recent example of this sudden change in the focus of the American media involved the intensive coverage of the bloody clashes triggered by Israel's opening of an archaeological tunnel in the middle of the Muslim quarter of Jerusalem, close to the Haram al-Sharif, in September 1996. There was similar coverage of clashes in Hebron and other West Bank towns in the spring and summer of 1997, following the commencement of the building of yet another new Israeli settlement in occupied Arab East Jerusalem, on Jabal Abu Ghneim (Har Homa). On both occasions, vivid television coverage showed the extent of Palestinian dismay at Israeli actions in Jerusalem and the overwhelming power that could be marshaled by the Israelis to suppress the Palestinians. This example reminds us once again that such dramatic action footage, conveying the horrifying and indelible images of F-15s attacking apartment buildings, or of artillery bombarding Lebanese villages, or of Israeli soldiers beating children and shooting demonstrators (or, for that matter, of suicide-bus bombs exploding in crowded streets in Israeli cities), has had an overwhelming power and valence of its own, which no amount of spin control or media management can contain.[13]

During crises such as the opening of the tunnel in Jerusalem or the Israeli settlement in East Jerusalem, we have seen how, in a matter of hours, the potency of such images suddenly renders meaningless the vacuous "peace-process-speak" that, over the past few years, has emanated like an endless stream of pabulum from Washington, only to be endlessly and reverently recycled by the media. At such critical moments, the ugly face of this unequal conflict has broken through the layers of cosmetics so carefully applied by the guardians of Israel's image. And at such moments, Said's insistence on the legitimacy of the Palestinian perspective on television and radio and in publications such as the *Nation*, the *London Review of Books*, and the *Progressive* has had a powerful impact on the public. He has influenced many who have no ties to Israel, some of whom had unconsciously adopted the worldview of those who do. He has also affected others who are deeply tied to Israel emotionally but who have nevertheless been sensitive to the universal arguments he makes.

The universal nature of these arguments relates to another important aspect of Said's interventions in the American public debate on the question of Palestine: his linking of Palestinian issues to larger, more general problems, such as decolonization, the resistance to imperialism, the need for democracy, and the dangers of narrow, chauvinistic nationalism. In Said's view, among the reasons for the failure of the Palestinian cause to win the kind of support it deserves in the West in general and in the United States in particular has been the failure of the Palestinians themselves, and of many of their supporters, to maintain their original insistence on its universal nature:

> That was the genius of the Palestinian revolution, as we used to call it, when . . . the PLO was perceived by its supporters as leading a battle for liberation: Arabs and others were drawn to join an inspiring movement for freedom and justice, across national divisions, boundaries, and language. Palestine concerned everyone so long as liberation was the goal. The present PLO leadership ended all that.[14]

As time has gone on, the Palestine Liberation Organization (PLO) has enclosed the Palestinians ever more tightly in an exclusivist nationalist cocoon and has forfeited much of the sympathy they once rightly had and might have retained.

Of course, some changes are inevitable in the course of any anticolonial and nationalist struggle, where seizure of state power is the ultimate objective, with all the sordid compromises that go along with that objective. Other problems have to do with the decay of the Palestinian national movement, the aging of its leadership (many of whose most able figures have fallen victims to Israeli and Arab assassins over the past three decades),[15] its corruption, and its loss of strategic vision and of moral purpose. Over the past few years, much of Said's writing in the English- and Arabic-language media has been devoted to castigating such Palestinian failures. He was one of the few Palestinian voices to do so publicly and has been personally taken to task for this by none other than Yasir Arafat.[16] The fact that all of these changes for the worse do not appear to be inevitable is shown by the South African case, where a loss of moral and strategic purpose has so far been avoided. Some South African observers have noted that Said began his first public criticisms of the failings of the PLO leadership after his visit to South Africa and his meeting with President Nelson Mandela in May 1991.[17]

Said has always argued, with Frantz Fanon, that the objective of liberation cannot simply be to "replace the French policeman with an Algerian policeman."[18] His prescient critique of the policies followed by the PLO over the past few years is largely founded on this basic argument. Although Said's critique has been reflected in the American and European media, his articles in the Arabic-language press have had the greatest impact. These articles have been collected in books that are widely available inside Palestine itself and are considered to be so subversive that the Palestinian Authority once ordered their seizure.[19] Thus, in the latest irony among so many in Palestinian history, the "native"/Palestinian policeman has taken up, almost without interruption, the functions of his "white"/Israeli predecessor, confiscating "subversive" literature written by a leading Palestinian intellectual! Sadly, this pitiful mimicry of the Israeli security Moloch has not been confined to a few cases of censorship or to minor human rights abuses but has already caused at least nineteen detainees' deaths as a result of torture, widespread detention without trial, and other arbitrary police actions.

Let me now move on to Said's role in the American public sphere: his influence on Palestinian politics. As a member of the Palestinian National Council (from which he resigned in 1991), through his involvement in various Palestinian and Arab forums, and through his scholarly work, Said is considered by other Palestinians and Arabs the leading Palestinian public intellectual. He has had this impact in part because of his prominence as a renowned scholar and intellectual in the United States but also because of his stature as the leading Palestinian commentator in the American media. There are other reasons for Said's influence on Palestinian politics, namely his ability to bring to Palestinian political deliberations a profound understanding of American society and culture, and an acute awareness of how to speak to the American public.

Said has devoted a great deal of energy and time to what might be called a task of public education in the Arab world. As far back as 1979, he helped organize a seminar series on American foreign policy at the Institute for Palestine Studies in Beirut for Palestinian intellectuals, students, and political cadres, to which a number of American public figures were invited. As part of this series, Said gave a talk that resulted in a monograph, published in Arabic and English, which was widely read at the time: *The Palestine Question and the American Context*.[20] More recently, he has continued these efforts with the collection *Peace and Its Discontents*, which is comprised of articles that he originally wrote "from start to finish with an Arab audience in mind"[21] and includes many lengthy passages and several entire articles that are devoted to explaining the American political process, setting U.S. foreign policy in its domestic context, and otherwise enlightening an Arab audience about the United States.[22]

Said's understanding of how to address an international audience, and an American audience in particular, had an effect on Palestinian political and diplomatic initiatives as early as Arafat's visit to the United Nations in 1974. In 1988, Said played a large role in drafting the Palestinian Declaration of Independence. In his publications and lectures, and in public and private Palestinian political forums, Said has argued forcefully that the Palestinian national movement must make its case cogently in the international arena, particularly in the American component of this arena. He perceived very early on that changing the balance of forces that is very unfavorable to the Palestinians would involve their making a serious effort to wage the battle for opinion in the American arena, as did the South Africans, the Vietnamese, and the Algerians in France.

In recent years, however, as Said himself has outlined in The Politics of Dispossession, most of what he advocated to the Palestinian leadership fell on deaf ears, as Arafat and his colleagues in the PLO leadership, nearly all of them ill-informed about the United States, its society, culture, and politics, preferred to follow their own course.[23] This course was, in large measure, responsible for leading the PLO to the brink of disappearance by the spring of 1991. At that point, after the Gulf War debacle, the PLO leadership saved themselves and their organization by accepting U.S. Secretary of State James Baker's invitation to join negotiations on terms dictated by the United States and Israel, a course about which Said had grave misgivings. These negotiations led ultimately to the Oslo Accord, which was a godsend to members of the PLO leadership, who at that point were outcasts scattered throughout the Arab world, and to the political apparatus they controlled. By accepting the terms of the accord, the PLO leadership returned to Palestine, where, after over six years of negotiations, they have so far obtained restricted control of a string of Palestinian islands in the Israeli-occupied Gaza Strip and West Bank (less than 3 percent of the West Bank is under even nominal Palestinian control). In hindsight, it is clear that this accord has not led to the liberation of Palestine or to much, if any, improvement in the lot of the Palestinian people, although those who negotiated the terms of the accord have enjoyed considerable benefits from it. Indeed, since Oslo, between 1993 and 1997, there has been a 38 percent decrease in the GDP per capita for the over two million residents of the West Bank and Gaza Strip, indicating a significant deterioration of the economic well-being of the majority.

Said's critique of the mistakes, oversights, and lack of rigor in the approach of the Palestinian leadership to the negotiations with Israel and their dealings with the United States over the past few years has been scathing:

> Is it acceptable to formulate and sign an agreement with Israel without seeking any expert legal opinions? . . . Arafat and his principal aides . . . do not speak or really understand English, which is the language in which the Oslo document is written. Nor did they seek advice about the language. If you want to sign an agreement with Israel, then you must know that the other party to this agreement will take what you sign seriously. . . . I really do not know the explanation for this kind of performance—lack of competence or complicity, or both.[24]

This critique has had more of an impact in the Middle East, and among Palestinians in particular, than it has had in the United States. One reason for this is that in recent years, Said has regularly published commentaries on political topics in the Arabic press, first in the magazine *al-Majalla*, and more recently in the newspaper *al-Hayat*. The latter is published in London and has a large circulation in the Arab world, Europe, and North America. Two collections of these articles have now been published in Arabic (Palestinian *mukhabarat*, or secret police, recently attempted to ban these books but then desisted). Whether through this medium, or as a result of their original publication, Said's views have had a growing impact on Arab public opinion. This has been most notable over the past year, when the flaws, deceptions, and fallacies embodied in the Oslo Accord and the subsequent Israeli-Palestinian agreements have become clearer to Palestinians and other Arabs.

There are several reasons why, in recent years, Said's critiques of Arafat and of American and Israeli policy have had the greatest effect on Arab readers. First, while Palestinians have begun to figure out that what has happened to them has the makings of a historical catastrophe, Americans are ignorant — or, more precisely, are kept in ignorance — of the actual provisions of these agreements. By and large, they do not know that, seven years after Madrid, not only has the thirty-year-old Israeli occupation of Palestinian territories not ended, but it has been maintained over more than 97 percent of the West Bank and perhaps 40 percent of the cramped Gaza Strip; they do not know that Israel still retains effective control over security, movement, trade, and virtually everything else of importance throughout the West Bank and the Gaza Strip; and they have undoubtedly not seen a map of these territories after the accord took effect.

The map of the territorial dispositions established by the Oslo Accord and the agreements that followed shows the tiny dots of Palestinian control, the splotches under Palestinian administration but subject to Israeli military control, and the vast swathes over which Israel is to retain absolute control until the end of the so-called interim period in 1999. The official map itself, looking like some hideous skin disease, with its tan and yellow blotches and spots indicating small areas of Palestinian control in a sea of white denoting continued Israeli occupation, is such a devastating indictment of the accord — from a Palestinian perspective, and indeed from that of anyone who would like to believe that these agreements can lead to a real, lasting peace — that it is no surprise that it is not more widely circulated.

Although the U.S. government, ably assisted by the media, keeps the American public in a state of ignorance about the true nature of these accords, many in the United States have expressed dissatisfaction with the "peace process." As I have already suggested, the deaths of over sixty Palestinians and fifteen Israelis at the end of September 1996 in fighting over the archaeological tunnel opened in Jerusalem by Benjamin Netanyahu's government was a rude awakening. The incident drew attention to the appallingly disadvantageous situation in which five years of negotiations have left the Palestinian people. However, in spite of numerous incidents since then, the fate of the Palestinian people remains undetermined and ignorance as to their situation continues. Although Said's critiques of the Oslo Accord and of Arafat's leadership are beginning to be echoed in the mainstream American media, by and large, his ideas are still regarded in both the West and the Arab world as daringly radical.

Why does such resistance continue? Even though his administration had absolutely nothing to do with negotiating the Oslo Accord, in September 1993, and again in September 1995, President Clinton opportunistically seized on the "peace process" for politically crucial White House photo opportunities. The peace process was thereafter vigorously featured as one of the major achievements of the Clinton administration in his 1996 reelection campaign. It is obvious that Said and other critics are fighting an uphill battle. In addition to the big battalions that defend most Israeli actions, such critics now face the formidable power of the machinery that sustains the bipartisan establishment consensus in American foreign policy. Needless to say, the mainstream media are a central part of this machinery, with their uncritical reiteration of formulas produced by the State Department and the White House, irrespective of the manifest inanity of these formulas.

Thus, any critic of the impracticality, or the inequity, not to say the intolerability, of the arrangements imposed on the Palestinians in the name of this peace process is almost automatically ruled outside the boundaries of civilized discourse, as an enemy of peace, and perhaps even worse—as a sympathizer with Islamic or other hideous terrorism. This may seem to be an exaggeration, but it should be remembered that the definition of these boundaries is almost entirely in the hands of people—producers, agents, op-ed page editors, and others in the executive reaches of the media—who have no familiarity with the issues at stake in the Middle East, or elsewhere for that matter. Their outlook is governed by a commonsensical conventionality, a very American pragmatism, and an exquisite sensitivity to pressure exerted by the institutions they work for, as well as by special interest groups, concerned citizens, and sponsors.

It takes little imagination to understand where most of this pressure comes from as far as the Middle East is concerned, especially when the inertial weight of American foreign policy is added to that of the substantial interests of Israel. And in an administration such as Clinton's, where foreign policy is rarely more than an adjunct to the election-driven domestic political agenda (including operating abroad as a shill for the major corporations and other economic interests whose political contributions are essential for keeping the expensive election machinery running), those are both heavy weights, indeed.

Thus, if we find what appears to be a deadening silence in the American media where criticism of the peace process is concerned, it should not be so hard to understand why this is the case. For all the reasons I have suggested, this consensus is likely to last, at least for some time to come. Nevertheless, it would be a mistake to underestimate the possible impact of the critical and principled voices of Said and a few others like him. These voices have already influenced American (and Arab) thinking on the question of Palestine, and they will surely continue to be heard commenting on the latest episode in the odyssey of the Palestinian people as they struggle to obtain their inalienable national rights—still denied them—of self-determination and statehood.

As the cruel falseness of the promise of peace offered to both Palestinians and Israelis by this process—as it is currently structured—becomes more apparent, and as the cracks become ever larger in the ramshackle edifice constructed in Palestine as a consequence of this process over the past few years, more and more people will perhaps listen to these voices. Certainly Israelis feel less secure today than they did in 1991, when this process began, and Palestinians are demonstrably worse off economically and in terms of freedom of movement, while occupation, settlement, exile, and the other travails of the Palestinian condition continue unabated.

In carrying out the often unpopular and lonely duty of pointing out these truths, Said will remain faithful to the vocation of the intellectual:

> The role of the intellectual is to say the truth to power, to address the central authority in every society without hypocrisy, and to choose the method, the style, the critique best suited for these purposes. This is so because the intellectual produces a kind of performance that continues for years, whose main goal is . . . to give utterance not to mere fashion and passing fads but to real ideas and values.[25]

BARBARA HARLOW

Sappers in the stacks: colonial archives, land mines, and truth commissions

[Kip] had approached the villa on that night of the storm not out of curiosity about the music but because of a danger to the piano player. The retreating army often left pencil mines within musical instruments. Returning owners opened up pianos and lost their hands. People would revive the swing on a grandfather clock, and a glass bomb would blow out half a wall and whoever was nearby.

He followed the noise of the piano, rushing up the hill with Hardy, climbed over the stone wall and entered the villa. As long as there was no pause it meant the player would not lean forward and pull out the thin metal band to set the metronome going. Most pencil bombs were hidden in these — the easiest place to solder the thin layer of wire upright. Bombs were attached to the spines of books, they were drilled into fruit trees so an apple falling onto a lower branch would detonate the tree, just as a hand gripping that branch would. He was unable to look at a room or a field without seeing the possibilities of weapons there. — Michael Ondaatje, The English Patient

But in most cases it is possible, I believe, to ascertain whether in fact a massacre was committed, or an official cover-up produced. The first imperative is to find out what occurred and then why, not as isolated events but as part of an unfolding history whose broad contours include one's own nation as an actor. — Edward W. Said, Representations of the Intellectual

Pencil bombs hidden in metronomes, bombs attached to the spines of books, official cover-ups. . . . How, then, might the contemporary critic go about pursuing the "imperative" to inquire into the historical continuities and discontinuities that connect nineteenth-century colonial narratives with late-twentieth-century cultural and political agendas? The overall trajectory of such an inquiry might, for instance, begin — and end — with examples of truth commissions as hallmarks of the contemporary attempt to settle accounts and to come to terms with a past of colonialism, decolonization, and neocolonialism (focusing perhaps on South Africa, and with comparative considerations of other contexts, as well — Argentina, Brazil, Uruguay, Chile, El Salvador, Rwanda, the former Yugoslavia — and the perilous prospects for such commissions in Northern Ireland and Palestine as alternative examples). The nineteenth-century narrative, however, provides its own examples of controversial precedents to these contemporary commissions of truth: Florence Nightingale's administrations in the Crimean War (1853–1856), Wilfred Scawen Blunt's support for the Egyptian nationalist Ahmad 'Urabi Pasha (1882), the expedition to relieve General Charles George Gordon at Khartoum (1884–1885), the Anglo-Boer War (1899–1902), and the Congo Reform Association at the turn of the century. Such crises of colonialism were, in turn, relocated by the world wars of the twentieth century and the history of international organizations that were established in their aftermath — for example, the League of Nations and the United Nations (UN) Security Council — but the earlier crises serve even now to highlight some of the documentary and literary historical transitions that have brought the global order to its current pass. Arguments for the right to national self-determination and the humanitarian emphasis on "human rights" are integral to that narrative, but the literary critical contribution to the reconstruction of such a history is a field that is both grounded in the archives and littered with land mines. What happens in the attempt to draw out some of the implications of that contested history for literary studies at the turn of still another century, for "sappers in the stacks," or for those intellectuals caught "speaking truth to power"?[1]

In the poem "Five Thoughts Concerning the Question: What Happens After Mandela Goes?" Jeremy Cronin reflects on transitions, historical and political, the conundrums of pasts, passing on, carrying on. Cronin is currently deputy general secretary of the South African Communist Party (SACP). He spent seven years in prison for his work in the African National Congress (ANC) and as a participant in the struggle against South Africa's apartheid government. The collection of poems, *Inside*, published following his release, was written within and from out of that experience. This more recent poem, however, addresses another issue — namely, the very difficulties of redefining "struggle" in the "new South Africa." It was written in 1996, when South Africa was coming to terms with its past through the meetings convened by the Truth and Reconciliation Commission (TRC), and Mandela had announced that he would not seek reelection in 1999 when he had finished his five-year term as the first president of a postapartheid South Africa. There was, inevitably, to be another "transition." Cronin's "Five Thoughts" are followed by "Poem for Mandela":

> It's impossible to make small-talk with an icon
> Which is why, to find my tongue,
> I stare down at those crunched-up
> One-time boxer's knuckles.

> In their flattened pudginess I find
> Something partly reassuring,
> Something slightly troubling,
> Something, at least, not transcendent.[2]

If not "miraculous," what are the historical legacies left to the late twentieth century? How are they to be retrieved, and where are they to be located once they have been recovered? What are the geographies that they map, the chronologies that they trace? Who are the participants and what roles can be assigned them? Where are the safe places and who are the expert witnesses in such an inquiry? The overriding imperative of settling accounts and coming to terms with the past is a challenge that radically disturbs the cultural and political processes of the turn of this century. It is a past defined by the history of colonialism, decolonization, and neocolonialism, and littered with the detritus of those very histories. And it is written brazenly across the literary traditions of the Euramerican canon.

1. In the Colonial Archives

The nineteenth century has been hailed—and is still recalled—as the era of the "civilizing mission," but that mission was not without its own crises. The twentieth century, in turn, was one marked and marred by world wars, the demands for national self-determination on the part of "small nations," and the consolidation of "human rights" as the grounds for cultural and political realignments. From the League of Nations (1919) to the UN (1945), the global configurations were being—and continue to be—renegotiated. What was once called a civilizing mission now goes under other euphemisms, including perhaps "humanitarian interventionism"—or peacekeeping (and, at times, peacemaking). But the terrain remains no less treacherous. The commissions of truth are perilous, and the archives littered with land mines. Like the sapper Kip in Ondaatje's novel, it is—or should be—impossible now for the literary critic to venture into the stacks "without seeing the possibilities of weapons there," the undetonated mines left not just in the "spines of books" but in and between their very lines. The *Oxford English Dictionary* defines *sapper* as "one who saps; spec. a soldier employed in working at saps, the building and repairing of fortifications, the execution of field-works, and the like." Rudyard Kipling is less sanguine in his description of the profession in his poem "Sappers," subtitled "Royal Engineers": "We lay down their sidings an' help 'em entrain, / An' we sweep up their mess through the bloomin' campaign." [3]

It should, however, as Edward W. Said maintains, also "be possible to ascertain whether in fact a massacre was committed, or an official cover-up produced," to "speak truth to power." [4] What is it, then, that occurred in the second half of the nineteenth century in the Crimea, in Egypt, in Khartoum, in South Africa, and in the Congo, to take a set of examples whose historical narrative continues as today's journalistic headlines?

The Crimea: From the War Office to the Hospital Ward

"The Eastern question": Was it the issue of the holy places in Jerusalem and the conflicting claims to them on the part of the Greek and Latin Churches? Or was it the concern for the Christian minority of the Ottoman Empire? Or was it a response to Russia's aggressive expansionist policies? Czar Nicholas I had launched his military campaign against the Sublime Porte, the government of the Ottoman Empire, in 1853, but it was another year before England, in support of the Turkish sultan, declared war against Russia on 28 March 1854 to settle "the Eastern question." In an alliance undertaken with France, British soldiers, led by Lord Somerset Raglan, embarked in the spring of 1854 for Constantinople—beginning still another, and even more catastrophic, of England's "imperial wars." The Allied troops landed in the Crimea in September 1854. By the time peace was declared in April 1856, more than 20,000 British soldiers were dead—2700 killed in battle, 1800 from wounds incurred in the fighting, and 17,600 from disease—and England's War Office had become the subject of numerous inquiries, official and unofficial, that eventually led to its radical reform. Whereas the "great game" defined the question of how the British should defend India, "the Eastern question" asked what was to be done with Turkey. In each case, however, the great Russian bear to the north loomed ominously over the designs and plans of the imperial policymakers.

The Crimean War, however, is remembered not just for the unpreparedness and continued incompetence of its London overseers but also for its dramatic battles, the brutal hardships of the winter of 1854–1855, its contentious war correspondents, and the ministrations to the sick and dying soldiers provided by the "lady of the lamp." In acknowledgment of those battles, Queen Victoria announced on 30 November 1854 the creation of the Victoria Cross, writing to the Duke of Newcastle that she was "sure that nothing will gratify and encourage our noble troops more than the knowledge that this is to be done." The medal's design was to be marked with the word Crimea and complemented with clasps that identified the names of those battles in which the recipient had participated. The Battle of the Alma had taken place on 20 September 1854 and was followed by the extended Siege of Sevastopol. According to Her Majesty, "Se[v]astopol, should it fall, or any other name of a battle which Providence may permit our brave troops to gain, can be inscribed on other clasps hereafter to be added." [5] The Battle of Inkerman, in November 1854, already had its clasp. Alfred Lord Tennyson and a host of other poets remembered the Battle of Balaklava, which took place on 25 October 1854, for the "Charge of the Light Brigade," the disastrous charge for which no military commander was ready to take full responsibility. Of the 607 soldiers who went into action that day, only 198 returned.

The notorious "charge of the Light Brigade" was but one of the military mishaps reported by Sir William Howard Russell, war correspondent for the (London) Times, whose relentless dispatches exposed to the English public at home the suffering of their soldiery in the Crimea, and which some have credited with bringing about the collapse of the Aberdeen cabinet and initiating the demands for an investigation into the British war machinery more generally.[6] Commenting on the cholera epidemic, the climate, and his colleagues, as well as describing scenes of battle, Russell initiated the tradition of the intrepid war reporter and a new kind of journalism. Meanwhile, from London, Karl Marx delivered more than one hundred letters and editorials to readers of the New York Tribune on the other side of the Atlantic, critiquing in particular the political practices of empire — British, Russian, French, and Turkish alike — and anticipating the opportunities these made for a revolutionary alternative "from below." [7] Photographers, too, such as Roger Fenton and James Robertson, returned images of war using newly developed technology. Unlike Mathew Brady's pictures of the American Civil War, which revealed the devastation and destruction of the battlefield, Fenton and Robertson dutifully observed the strict instructions from the War Office: No dead bodies. Their photographs not only found their way into collections of Queen Victoria and Louis Napoleon, as well as into the family albums of soldiers who had fought on the plains of the Crimea, but provided, as well, the basis for many of the engravings printed throughout the war by the Illustrated London News.

Florence Nightingale was responsible for instituting military and medical reforms that resulted from the Crimean catastrophe, rehabilitating the professional role of the nurse, and providing new opportunities for women in medicine. Nightingale arrived in Scutari on 3 November 1854, just after the

Battle of the Alma, to discover that soldiers were dying not so much from battle wounds as from illness—cholera, dysentery, and malnutrition—while stores and supplies remained locked in the bureaucratic morass. While the image of Nightingale is that of the "lady of the lamp," succoring suffering soldiers, her accomplishments were as much administrative as ministrant.[8] She reorganized hospitals, released supplies, and fought politicians and medical officers who resented her interferences. As Lytton Strachey remembered her, "This remarkable woman was in truth performing the function of an administrative chief"[9]—a function she continued when she returned to England, working unstintingly for hospital, medical, and sanitary reforms until her death.

The Crimean War may not have settled "the Eastern question," but the Crimea, a small, otherwise insignificant peninsula not two hundred miles wide extending into the Black Sea, became the grounds for radically altering the premises and makeup of the British War Office, the popular representations of the battlefield, and the organization of hospital wards. Today, the Crimea figures as a no less contested space in a new "great game," the current global competition that is being waged and staged over Central Asia following the collapse of the Soviet Union.

The 'Urabi Uprising: "Egypt for the Egyptians" or a British Egypt?

"Egypt is ready still, nay desirous, to come to terms with England, to be fast friends with her, to protect her interests and keep her road to India, to be her ally. But she must keep within the limits of her jurisdiction."[10] In these terms, 'Urabi Pasha appealed to England's Prime Minister William Ewart Gladstone on 2 July 1882, just days before the bombardment of Alexandria on 11 July 1882. 'Urabi, who hailed from an Egyptian fellah, or peasant, background to become a colonel in the Egyptian Army, had led an army mutiny—or, as it was also argued, a nationalist movement—against Khedive Tawfiq and his English supporters on 9 September of the preceding year and, since January 1882, had been acting as Egypt's minister of war. What was to become of England's jurisdiction? In June, the London government had ordered General Garnet Wolseley and the English fleet to the area and threatened military action against the nationalist opposition. That threat was carried out in the 11 July bombardment of Alexandria, followed by the seizure of Ismailia on 29 July, and then consummated in the devastating destruction of Egyptian forces at Tel al-Kebir on 13 September. 'Urabi and his associates were arrested and tried, and 'Urabi was sentenced to exile in Ceylon. And with that, the British formally occupied Egypt.

For 'Urabi and his followers, the Suez Canal had become part of the pilgrimage route to Mecca and Medina; for England, however, it had assumed significance for allowing a shortened passage to India. In both cases, however, the canal had burdened Egypt and the Egyptians with a colossal debt. Since Muhammad 'Ali's reign as viceroy of Egypt from 1805 to 1848, and through the reigns of his successors, Ibrahim (1848), 'Abbas (1848–1854), Sa'id (1854–1863), and Isma'il (1863–1879), Egypt's commitments to European interests in Egypt had been costly, including the financing of the canal's building and the expenses of the ceremonies that celebrated its opening. Those costs were exacted through ever increasing taxations, but the Egyptian economy continued to deteriorate, and, in 1876, the French and the English took over the canal in the name of Dual Control, the khedive's government. With the Dual Control, the "relationship of ruler and ruled was placed under the official notice of Europe."[11] Various investments were at stake in ensuring the stability and dependency of Egypt. Economically, European financial and commercial groups competed and cooperated with indigenous merchant and landowning classes toward increased participation in trading advantages, while the rural population and the impoverished inhabitants of the cities suffered under the mounting pressures of fiscal extraction. Politically, England and France were concerned with maintaining their alliance against both Russia and the Ottoman Empire for control of the Mediterranean and the routes to the East.

'Urabi's uprising claimed to represent the interests of Egypt and the Egyptians in these contests: Egypt for the Egyptians. What, then, was to become of England's jurisdiction following the threat to the even then precarious status quo? Already in 1877, Gladstone had raised the question in his article, "Aggression on Egypt and Freedom in the East," arguing that "enlargements of the Empire are for us an evil fraught with serious, though possibly not immediate danger."[12] But there were other members of his government and public policy and opinion makers who insisted that direct intervention in Egyptian affairs, if not territorial occupation, was incumbent on an empire that needed to maintain both its suzerainty and its access to territory, trade, and expansion. If the occupationists seem to have won the day in the immediate aftermath of the 'Urabi uprising, the debate nevertheless continued. Should England restore order and withdraw quickly to its previous role of a "moral influence" or remain in Egypt to ensure reform following the restoration of order? How long, that is, would or should the occupation last? (In fact, British occupation continued until 1956 and the Suez Canal War, in which France, England, and Israel sought to contest Gamal Abdel Nasser's nationalization of the waterway.)

But if England was to assume control of Egypt, 'Urabi and his followers had first to be dealt with. Arrested in the fall of 1882, their trial took place shortly thereafter. There were those in both England and Egypt who clamored for

'Urabi's immediate and summary execution. Others argued just as adamantly for the imperative of a fair trial and due process. It was perhaps not just the man but his example that needed to be disposed of. Lord Cromer (Sir Evelyn Baring) urged that the effects of such insubordination as 'Urabi's be canceled. Cromer asked in his memoirs "at what point the sacred right of revolution begins or ends, . . . at what stage a disturber of the peace passes from a common rioter . . . to the rank of a leader of a political movement?" For Cromer, the 'Urabi uprising marked neither such a point nor such a stage, and, he would maintain, the English had had practical experience in contending with "mutinies." Cromer, following his own assignment in the India Service, had only recently taken over the consul generalship of Egypt in September 1883. His admirers and detractors alike emphasized his administrative prowess and discipline in carrying out his politically mandated work—whether in India or Egypt. According to Sir Alfred Milner, his colleague in the service, for example, "It would be difficult to overestimate what the work of England in Egypt owes to the sagacity, fortitude, and patience of the British Minister."[13] Wilfrid Scawen Blunt, by contrast, had earned the reputation, as he himself proudly admitted, of a "nonconformist conscience." A champion of 'Urabi and his cause of self-government for the Egyptians, Blunt challenged the attempt to criminalize the work of the national leader and organized legal counsel through Mark Napier and A. M. Broadley to represent 'Urabi throughout his trial. As it happened, 'Urabi was not executed but exiled to Ceylon—where Blunt later met with him on the occasion of his visit to India in the interests of establishing an institute of Muslim higher education there, even as he championed the mission to rescue General Charles George Gordon at Khartoum in 1885. Denied thereafter entry into British Egypt, Blunt's subsequent engagements as a "nonconformist conscience" included a period in Galway Jail in consequence of his support of Irish claims for Home Rule and self-government.[14]

Meanwhile, the British did occupy Egypt, requiring further development of the attributes of the "Anglo-Egyptian official." As Cromer pointed out, "The efficient working of the administrative machine depends . . . mainly on choosing the right man for the right place."[15] Many of those same officials, however, saw the "right place" for the "right men" as at "office, club and dinner." But the larger place, Egypt, representing for Benjamin Disraeli the "key to India," for others "the Gate of the East," had, for the time being, become British Egypt.

Today, Egypt's interests may be said to be divided anew among its affiliations in the Islamic League, the Organization of African Unity, and the Arab League, and against its duties to such Western financiers as the United States, the European Union, the World Bank, and the International Monetary Fund.

Gordon at Khartoum: From Cavil to Catastrophe

"At Last!" was the title of the Punch cartoon of 7 February 1885, which jubilantly anticipated the arrival of a relief expedition that had been sent to General Gordon and his forces in the besieged city of Khartoum. A week later (14 February 1885), a bereaved Britannia, her sword thrust into the ground, bemoaned in the same magazine, "Too Late!" The caption of this Punch cartoon read further: "Khartoum taken by the Mahdi. General Gordon's fate uncertain." General Gordon had, in fact, been beheaded and his head presented with all due ceremony to his opponent, Muhammed Ahmad, the "Mahdi" who led the popular Sudanese insurrection against the Anglo-Egyptian occupation of that territory.

"Chinese Gordon," as he had come to be known, was famous for his role in England's earlier colonial exploits in China, first at the capture of Peking (October 1860) and later during the Taiping Rebellion (May 1862). But he is remembered most for his renowned defense of Khartoum in 1884–1885. All England, it seemed, awaited word of his fate in the early months of that year, from his sister Mary, in whom he confided both his belief in the will of God (or D.V. as he invoked it in his letters to her) and his distrust in the intentions and policies of the English government, to Victoria herself, who, on 17 February 1885, sent condolences to Mary following the news of Gordon's demise. "To think of your dear, noble, heroic Brother," she penned, "who served his Country and his Queen so truly, not having been rescued." [16] Even before China, however, Gordon had served in the Crimea, at the siege of Sevastopol, and in Turkey. He had participated in the exploration of the African continent, fought the Arab slave trade there, and done archaeological research in Palestine. To Lord Cromer, who administered English interests in Egypt, Gordon was "above all things a soldier, and, moreover, a very bellicose soldier." By contrast, for Blunt, a distinguished critic of England's colonial policies and practices in Egypt, India, and Ireland, and an ardent supporter of the Egyptian nationalist Ahmed 'Urabi, Gordon was a "man of many contradictions and a singularly complex character," well "above the rank of the common soldier of fortune." [17] No less than had been the case during England's involvement in the Crimean War (1854–1856), or following the Indian Mutiny (1857–1858), and much as would happen in the course of the Anglo-Boer War (1899–1902) and throughout the Congo controversy at the turn of the century, public opinion and political positions were divided over the integrity of England's imperial project as it foundered on the failed rescue of Gordon.

In late 1883, however, Gordon was about to enter King Leopold's service in the Congo, when, abruptly, he was called on by his own country to embark on a mission to the Sudan. Whether Gordon was the most appropriate choice for such a task was much debated, no less than were the parameters of the mission itself. There was an uprising under way in the Sudan, led by the Mahdi; British interests were at stake; and English and Egyptian lives were at risk. An earlier mission in 1883, led by Colonel William Hicks, had met with devastating disaster and death. What was Gordon to do? According to Cromer, Gordon was supposed to evacuate who he could from Khartoum and withdraw. But how did Gordon understand his orders? And just what were those orders? Evacuation of the city? Defense of the city? The establishment of an orderly government there? Or, as some critics imputed to Gordon, was he himself set on nothing less than the determination to "smash the Mahdi"?[18]

If there were questions about sending Gordon to Khartoum, there was even more consternated debate over the decision to rescue him, to send a relief expedition to his aid. For Gordon, it was the second such expedition; his mission, he maintained, had been the first to send assistance to the city and its inhabitants. In any case, in August 1884, General Wolseley was given the orders to pursue such an endeavor of relief . . . "at last." But Wolseley and his troops arrived "too late." Khartoum fell to the Mahdist forces in early February 1885, and the Mahdi received the head of Gordon as evidence of his success and England's catastrophic failure to pursue its imperial policy through the congested corridors of political cavil and public outcry.

The fall of Khartoum has been subsequently recounted in various ways, among them, in John Buchan's novel *Gordon at Khartoum*, in Sir Arthur Conan Doyle's reprise, *The Tragedy of the Korosko*, and in Basil Dearden's 1966 epic film version, *Khartoum*, which starred Laurence Olivier as the Mahdi and Charlton Heston as Gordon.[19] The delivery of Gordon's head became, in turn, an icon in the hall of heroes of empire—and his statues memorialize the stand he took and the political cavil and colonial catastrophe that it enlivened. The Mahdi himself outlived Gordon by only a few months, but it was more than a decade before England retrieved its place of prominence in the Sudan, when General Horatio Herbert Kitchener's army defeated the Mahdist forces at Omdurman in 1898. From Omdurman, Kitchener, in pursuit of his own illustrious colonial career, traveled south, to join the Anglo-Boer War in South Africa. Today, the Sudan and the larger "horn of Africa" remain contested among the parties to international interest, humanitarian interventions, and local conflicts.

The Anglo-Boer War: Accusations and Apologias

Fought for nearly three years, from 1899 to 1902, the Anglo-Boer War is perhaps the last of the major imperial wars (following, for example, the Crimean War, the Afghan Wars, the Ashanti War, and the Zulu Wars.)[20] As the nineteenth century turned into the twentieth, global powers prepared, instead, for world war. In the meantime, the Anglo-Boer War—variously known as the Boer War and the South African War—cost more than £200 million, and the lives of some 22,000 British, 25,000 Boers, and 12,000 Africans. While prosecuted in the name of the British empire in southern Africa, the war effort served no less the interests of international capital and monopoly trade. The war provided as well the extended occasion for a discussion of the controversial concomitants of imperialism, domestic support, foreign interventions, and the settlement of scores, both topographic and demographic. From parliamentary speeches, to poetic renditions, political cartoons, and popular reviews in journals and music halls, the archive of debate was voluminous and involved such literary luminaries as Kipling, Conan Doyle, and Olive Schreiner, and such popularizers as Sir H. Rider Haggard and G. A. Henty.

The professional careers—financial, diplomatic, and military—of men such as Cecil (John) Rhodes, Sir Milner, and Major General Kitchener that had developed across the stretches of British imperium were further consolidated in the course and consequences of the war. William Thomas Stead, for example, the influential editor of the *Review of Reviews* and publisher of Rhodes's *Last Will and Testament* (1902), described the magnate as a "very Colossus, [one who] stood astride a continent which was all too small a pedestal for the imperial dimensions of the man." Rhodes himself, in his 1894 speech on "The Native Question," described his position as being "responsible for about two millions of human beings." Kitchener, on the other hand, had only recently arrived in South Africa, newly triumphant following his defeat of the Sudanese Mahdist forces in Omdurman in 1898. Milner, in turn, provided the diplomatic backup for his imperial colleagues. Their critics, however, were no less distinguished and included in their ranks the South African feminist writer Schreiner and the political economist J. A. Hobson. For Schreiner— who knew Rhodes well—the "political situation" in South Africa in 1896 was this: that the "kafir's back and the poor men's enhanced outlay on the necessities of life pay the Monopolist's bribe." Three years later, she presented *An English–South African's View of the Situation*, in which she "fell to considering, who gains by war?" and concluded that it was not England, nor Africa, nor the great woman (Victoria), and certainly not the "brave English soldier." Hobson was just as adamant in his challenge to the policies of the "new Imperialism": "Aggressive Imperialism," he wrote, "which costs the taxpayer so dear, which is of so little value to the manufacturer and trader, which is fraught with such grave incalculable peril to the citizen, is a source of great gain to the investor who cannot find at home the profitable use he seeks for his capital, and insists that his Government should help him to profitable and secure investments abroad."[21]

The British war effort in southern Africa required support at home as well, both for the economic outlay and for the soldiery that was required. Simi-

lar contests had long characterized the propagation of the imperial project—
from debates over the East India Company's role in the Indian subcontinent,
to the proprieties and improprieties of the Crimean War, and including the
reports of atrocities in the Belgian Congo and the vexed mission to rescue
General Gordon at Khartoum. The policy debates, expressions of public opinion, and the popular protest that marked these imperial crises provide important evidence and documentation of the complex of issues that accompanied
the continuation of empire and its discontinuous departures and oppositional
practices. The very personnel of empire building and its maintenance functioned as well—even alternatively—as prototypes of the "public intellectual."
The discussion was vituperative in the autumn of 1899, with the buildup to
and outbreak of the war. "Shall We Let Hell Loose in South Africa?" was the
banner to the *Review of Reviews'* "Topic of the Month" in September of that
year. The article questioned priorities: Where did the question of the Trans-
vaal stand relative to the Dreyfus trial in France or the overcrowded condition
of London's poor? In other words, how would politicians secure popular support for an imperial war? "Impressions and Opinions," in the December 1899
issue of the *Anglo-Saxon Review*, compared the South African crisis with those
of the Crimea and the 1857 mutiny in India, and reminded the policy makers
of the disastrous consequences of their previous miscalculations and mistake of underrating the power of the enemy. Stephen Wheeler compared the
situation to the Sikh War of 1845–1846, specifying the "bewilderment of the
public mind, the dubious wisdom of people in power, the equivocal victory of
troops attacked or attacking at a disadvantage." Empire, then, had a history,
which posed a threat as much as it might have held promise—and held *out*
promises. Arthur Waugh, author of the essay "The Poetry of the South African Campaign," published a year later in the *Anglo-Saxon Review*, identified—
and castigated—what had become a literary history as well. Pointing to the
role of poetry in time of war, he laments the lost "opportunities of the present
campaign." Where Tennyson had ennobled the Crimean War with "Maud,"
Kipling, the critic complained, had commercialized the South African campaign with "The Absent-Minded Beggar," a poem that had become popular
from the street corner to the music hall and had indeed served to collect the
pennies needed to support the families of the soldiers fighting the Boer:

> Each of 'em doing his country's work
> (and what have you got to spare?)
> Pass the hat for your credit's sake,
> and pay—pay—pay! [22]

But what had become of "the beggar's country's work"? And for whose
country was he fighting an imperial war? To the hero of Kipling's story, an

Indian in colonial service in South Africa, it was a "Sahibs' War": "Do not herd me with these black Kaffirs. I am a Sikh—a trooper of the State," he says, and continues, "It is for Hind that the Sahibs are fighting this war. Ye cannot in one place rule and in another bear service. Either ye must everywhere rule or everywhere obey. God does not make the nations ringstraked. True—true—true!"[23] Breaker Morant, of the Australian Bushveld Carbineers assigned to South Africa, saw it differently still, "scapegoated" as he was by the empire he fought for. Morant and several of his fellow Australians were court-martialed for shooting prisoners—under orders, they claimed at their trial, from above, from Kitchener himself. Morant was hung for his deeds, but Lieutenant George Witton was released. His account, *Scapegoats of the Empire*, is a narrative of the progressive loss of faith in the imperial mission expressed in the story's opening paragraph: "When war was declared between the British and Boers, I, like many of my fellow-countrymen, became imbued with a warlike spirit, and when reverses had occurred among the British troops, and volunteers for the front were called for in Australia, I could not rest content until I had offered the assistance one man could give to our beloved Queen and the great nation to which I belong."[24] But if the Australians had entered the fray on behalf of empire, there were Irish volunteers, such as John MacBride of the Irish Republican Brotherhood, who saw the Anglo-Boer War as a challenge to Britain's imperial sway. On his return from the front, he met Maud Gonne, whom he eventually married. But Gonne, in *A Servant of the Queen*, remembered the tales MacBride first told:

> It was so late that it was not worth while for MacBride to go to his lodgings, so he shared Griffiths's bed. Next morning, seated at my writing table wrote the lecture, supplementing the sparse notes from MacBride's memory. I sat in an armchair, smoking cigarettes and listening. It was great to hear of Irishmen actually fighting England. The capture of General Buller's guns near the Tugeela was thrilling; the capture of English officers delighted me; the English have imprisoned so many Irishmen that it was good at last to have it the other way around.
>
> "I hope you treated your prisoners decently to give them a good example and show how much more civilised we are than they?"[25]

The issue of the treatment of prisoners was central to public discussion of the war and crucial in mobilizing domestic opposition to its prosecution. Emily Hobhouse, for example, found herself forbidden readmittance to South Africa following her earlier *Report on the Camps of Women and Children in the Cape and Orange River Colonies* and other appeals on behalf of the South Africa Conciliation Committee and the Ladies' Commission on the Concentration Camps. "Will you try," she pleaded to the addressees of her report, "to make the British public understand the position and force it to ask itself what is going to be done with these people? . . . If only the English would try to exercise a little imagination—picture the whole miserable scene." Hobhouse's pamphleteering and public speaking were effective in enlisting outrage and indignation in England about the atrocities committed in the name of war in South Africa. She was so effective that Millicent Fawcett, best known for her suffragist activism, was sent with a women's delegation to counter the charges that Hobhouse had leveled. For Fawcett, the assignment was an "interruption" of her work for the enfranchisement of women, but she, too, had to acknowledge the abuses to the civilian population, to the Boer women and children, carried out by her countrymen. Not that the Boer women were without their own share in the struggle, Fawcett argued nonetheless, indicating that the very goods with which they had been charitably supplied served in the strife: "We did hear, however, that the Boer women were very expert in using candles as a means of signalling to their friends on commando in the quiet hours of the night." But, she went on, "I for one could not blame them if they did; if we had been in their position, should we not have done the same thing?" Conan Doyle, meanwhile, had come to the defense of the British military offensive—including executions, train hijackings and hostage taking, farm burnings, and the use of expansive and explosive (dumdum) bullets (outlawed at the Hague in 1899). The War in South Africa: Its Cause and Conduct claimed to be a full-length representation of the British case: "In view of the persistent slanders to which our politicians and our soldiers have been equally exposed, it becomes a duty which we owe to our national honour to lay the facts before the world." Conan Doyle's research on this project was perhaps not without a certain resemblance to the detective work of his sleuth, Sherlock Holmes, in defense of "national honour" and the protection of a particular rule of law and order—and against the human rights reporting of Hobhouse and other members of her committees.[26]

When the war ended in 1902, the question still remained as to whether South Africa would be joined by a "closer union"—or bound together through federated allegiances. Today, still, South Africa's position in Africa is critical: negotiating the truce between Laurent Kabila and Mobutu Sese Seko in Zaire, legislating immigration policies in southern Africa, and maintaining a historical alliance with such anathematized leaders as Cuba's Fidel Castro.

The Congo: Abominations and Denunciations

In Heart of Darkness, Joseph Conrad's Marlow, aboard the Nellie, tells his audience—the Company Director, the lawyer, and the accountant—"All Europe contributed to the making of Kurtz."[27] The Berlin West Africa Conference (1884–1885), which had convened the nations of Europe, together with the United States, to distribute parcels of Africa among the participating countries, had excluded the Congo. This country was given to Belgian King Leopold II as his own personal prize and was recognized as the Congo Free State, which had its beginnings in Leopold's Association Internationale du Congo (AIC), established in 1876. In 1884, the United States was the first to recognize the AIC as a state, followed by Germany and Britain, and continuing with the acknowledgments of France, Russia, Portugal, and Belgium, which were made official at the end of the Berlin West Africa Conference in February 1885. The Congo Free State was formally proclaimed in July of that year. Leopold made his case for suzerainty in a rhetorical announcement declaring improvement, delivery, and development of the country's resources, and humanitarian assistance to be provided to the natives—all of which would ensue from his rule. He also announced the abolishment of slavery and the slave trade. But Leopold's rhetoric and the atrocities it concealed were yet to be exposed. Such exposure, however, was itself an arduous process, involving committed individuals and the movements they represented across several continents. It engaged the work of men such as political activists Sir Roger Casement and E. D. Morel, and was complemented by the writings of literati such as Mark Twain and Conan Doyle. Conrad, his own travels and observations in the Congo notwithstanding, and for all of Marlow's dislike for the "lie," was less forthcoming in support of the work. As Conrad wrote to Casement:

> It is an extraordinary thing that the conscience of Europe, which seventy years ago has put down the slave trade on humanitarian grounds, tolerates the Congo State today. It is as if the moral clock had been put back many hours. And yet nowadays if I were to overwork my horse so as to destroy its happiness or physical well-being, I should be hauled before a magistrate. . . . In the old days, England had in her keeping the conscience of Europe. The initiative came from her. But I suppose we are busy with other things—too much involved in great affairs to take up the cudgels for humanity, decency and justice.[28]

Conrad, apologizing, for his part, that he was "only a wretched novelist," declined the request from Casement to assist in the public protests against Leopold.

Despite early, if sporadic, reports from missionaries and traders, the various accounts of the inhumanity of Leopold's sway over the Congo and its indigenous inhabitants were largely dismissed in European political circles and dispelled by Leopold's own protestations to the benevolence of his African regime and its select representatives. In 1903, following concern about Leopold's monopolization of commerce in the region and the obstructions to the "free trade" of other European enterprises, Casement was commissioned by the British Foreign Office to carry out a fact-finding trip up the Congo River. Casement, who came from an Irish Protestant family in Antrim, had acquired significant experience in West Africa in the employ of a Liverpool trading firm with interests there. He submitted his *Congo Report* to the British Parliament that same year. The report he presented was perhaps more than even his contractors had anticipated, containing as it did appalling narratives and eyewitness accounts of abuse and atrocity rampant in the Congo Free State. Not just an obstruction to the interests of "free trade," Leopold's rule was an abomination to humanitarian ideals. Casement's immediate audience, however, was not ready to hear the story that he had to tell. The British Foreign Office was torn between the need to placate Leopold (a relative of Victoria) and assure his support for their own European designs, on the one hand, and to respond to the demands of Liverpool merchants, on the other. Humanitarian objectives were almost incidental to their immediate agenda, despite the overwhelming evidence of the abuse of humanity in Casement's *Congo Report*.

In 1904, then, Casement and Morel formed the Congo Reform Association. Morel, a Frenchman residing in England, had long been involved in the efforts to right the wrongs being perpetrated in the Congo Free State and had worked in significant part with H. R. Fox Bourne and the Aborigines' Rights Protection Society. Morel's account of *King Leopold's Rule in Africa* is a passionate denunciation of the state of affairs in the Congo at the time and expresses, as well, the reformers' frustration at the persistent recalcitrance of politicians and public opinion alike to recognize the "horrors" being committed there. "How much longer," Morel wrote, "would the civilised world tolerate these things?" He went on to reveal that it was "only by accident [that] we ever hear of those deeds of darkness." It was necessary, he determined, to organize a movement that would systematically appeal to and mobilize public indignation and political action. *The History of the Congo Reform Movement*, a work Morel began in 1910, tells the story of that movement, its strategies of information gathering, its modes of presentation, and its tactics of appeal that were undertaken to challenge Leopold's hold over the territory and the peoples of the Congo Free State, a hold that Conan Doyle decried in 1905 as nothing less than the "crime of the Congo." Such a crime, argued Conan Doyle, should be not just exposed but punished at an international tribunal that would additionally award reparations to the victims of the Belgian king's brutality and concupiscence. Leopold, though, would not submit without a retort of his own—and a massive countercampaign, from Europe to the United States, of disinformation and rhetorical defamations of his denouncers—a retort that Twain caricatured in his essay "King Leopold's

Soliloquy." "They spy and spy and run into print with every foolish trifle," Twain's Leopold complains. But Leopold's complaints and countercampaign notwithstanding, the Congo Free State was abolished in 1908, when it became the Belgian Congo. Casement, for his part, went on to denounce similar abuses as those he had uncovered in the Congo on the rubber plantations in South America in *The Putumayo Report*. In 1916, Casement was tried and hung for treason after being caught running guns to the Irish republican movement on the eve of the Easter Rising. According to Casement, "In those lonely Congo forests where I found Leopold, I found also myself, the incorrigible Irishman." [29]

The Belgian Congo became in part Zaire and is now called the Democratic Republic of the Congo, following Kabila's overthrow of Mobutu in the spring of 1997. How Mobutu came to power is still another story in the stacks.

2. Land Mines and Truth Commissions

Examples, then, were set in the nineteenth century that have had consequences in the twentieth century. If an erstwhile "civilizing mission" finds a new euphemism in "humanitarian intervention," the West/East divide is redrawn as North/South, even as developing countries are regrouped as emerging markets and academic area studies are repositioned in the economic interests of regional trading blocs. The agendas of national liberation become the work of nongovernmental organization as debates over armed struggle meet at the table of peace processes, and practices of interrogation must contend instead with the civilities of negotiation. And totalitarianism takes on the altered states and alternative parameters of "globalitarianism."

According to Said, the nineteenth century was a "period when the ideas of a universal norm of international behavior meant in effect the right of European power and European representations of other people to hold sway, so nugatory and secondary did the nonwhite peoples of the world seem." In the late twentieth century, however, Said continues, "most, if not all, countries in the world are signatories to a Universal Declaration of Human Rights, adopted and proclaimed in 1948, reaffirmed by every new member state of the UN. There are equally solemn conventions on the rules of war, on treatment of prisoners, on the rights of workers, women, children, immigrants and refugees. None of these documents says anything about *disqualified* or less equal races or peoples." [30]

In February 1965, in the last speech that he delivered before his assassination a week later, Malcolm X argued that "all the nations that signed the charter of the UN came up with the Declaration of Human Rights and anyone who classifies his grievances under the label of 'human rights' violations, those grievances can be brought into the United Nations and be discussed by people all over the world. For as long as you call it 'civil rights' your only allies can be the people in the next community, many of whom are responsible for your grievance. But when you call it 'human rights' it becomes international. And then you can take them before the world. And anybody anywhere on this earth can become your ally."[31] But that was more than three decades ago. Today, as the century turns. . . . Human rights reporting, itself a genre in the contemporary world of writing and rights, entails both documentation and intervention. What, however, of solidarity and the examples of the likes of Nightingale, Blunt, Hobhouse, Casement, and Morel? A recording of facts and events, of abuses of individual lives and national histories, as well as an effort to correct an "official record" that has systematically obscured those abuses, the writing of human rights draws by necessity on conventions of narrative, autobiography, and biography, of dramatic representation, and of discursive practices. Indeed, the thirty articles of the Universal Declaration of Human Rights, which was proclaimed by the General Assembly of the United Nations in December 1948, translated the standard literary paradigm of individual versus society and the narrative practices of emplotment and closure by mapping an identification of the individual within a specifically international construction of rights and responsibilities. The Universal Declaration, that is, can be read as recharting, for example, the trajectory and peripeties of the classic bildungsroman. While the Universal Declaration has, since its adoption, been as much abused as used by governments throughout the world, peoples and their representatives continue to appeal to its principles. Those written appeals, the reports of human rights monitors, the documentation of international organizations such as Amnesty International, Human Rights Watch, and others, and the narratives of individuals recounting efforts to reconstruct a human history form the basis for a discussion of the relationships between writing and human rights, and of the place of a new body of literature, the active intersection of the cultural and the political, in a changing, contemporary international order. This "post-bi-polar" world order is constantly being revised through the work taken on at UN conferences, where topics have included the environment (Rio de Janeiro, 1992), humans rights (Vienna, 1993), population and development (Cairo, 1994), women (Beijing, 1995), and the habitat (Istanbul, 1996).

But human rights is a questionable discourse. Do human rights standards, for example, apply to all cultures? What are the differences between solidarity and human rights reporting? Can anybody anymore anywhere on this earth really become one's ally? Said has defined *universality* as "taking a risk in order to go beyond the easy certainties provided us by our background, language, nationality, which so often shield us from the reality of others."[32] What are those risks? What are the chances taken when inquiring into the past, as with truth commissions? What are the peripeties of getting there, when land mines still litter the surrounding fields and routes?

In "Even the Dead," another poem by Jeremy Cronin, the precipitous questions of truth and reconciliation, the combined charge of South Africa's TRC, are raised. What is there to forgive, and what is it necessary to forget? Can there be amnesty without amnesia? Cronin read the poem in Cape Town as the TRC was hearing testimony and receiving the reverberations of criticism. Amnesty was wanted, but amnesia provided the panacea. And altogether too many other amnesias afflicted the reorganizing of the world map:

> Amnesia appoints another commission, the Lethe Commission, Limbo Commission,
> Nirvana Commission, Justice van deFerred Commission
>
> Amnesia prevails when we claim we have returned to the family of nations
>> forgetting to ask:
>> who is we?
>> forgetting to wonder:
>> WHAT family?
>
> Amnesia classifies Third World Countries as "developing" (structurally adjusted amnesia)
>
> CNN is globalised amnesia
>
> The Gulf War—lobotomised amnesia
>
> Santa Barbara, the Bold and the Beautiful, Restless Years—the milk of amnesia
>
> Amnesia embraces the global reality of 23 million per annum dead of hunger and hunger related disease
>
> That's a daily average equivalent, in fatalities, of one Hiroshima
>
>> Buried each day
>> Under the cloud of amnesia . . .[33]

"Beware," Cronin's poem goes on, "amnesia has no cut-off date." Perhaps "truth commissions" pose another kind of "structural adjustment"—strategies (complex, conflicted, compromised as they might be) for rewriting the historical legacies left to the late twentieth century. Crucial to their work—whether in Latin America, the former Yugoslavia, Rwanda, or South Africa—are the determinations of just how to retrieve those legacies, where to place them, and who will have access to these archives, the new additions to the modern library, the expanded stacks? What will be the new geographies, and what the revised chronologies? Who are the participants and what are the roles assigned to them?

In his analysis of "government responses to human rights reporting" as itself constitutive of a generic discourse, Stanley Cohen examines the parlaying of claims and counterclaims, and the convoluted strategies of denial that inform the exchange of parties to the maintenance of human rights narratives. For Cohen, these colloquies identify decisive alterations of time and place:

> The notion of witnessing and telling the truth that informs the production of human rights information belongs to a simpler era. The task is now more complicated than our traditional methods of reporting allow. On the one hand, the increased international awareness of human rights, the spread of new information technologies, and the globalization of the mass media mean that the sovereign state is being "watched" like never before. On the other hand, the profusion of so many images, the blurring of the lines between fiction and facts (reconstructions, factoids, and documentary dramas), and the relativist excesses of postmodernism and multiculturalism make the representation of old-fashioned human rights information more difficult than ever.[34]

What, then, might be the role of human rights in peace negotiations? In other words, what is the relationship between human rights fact finders and peace negotiators? As another, anonymous, critic writes: "The pursuit of criminals is one thing. Making peace is another." Or, in still other words, as Mike Tomlinson puts it, there is still the problem of "how wars end and what to do with the peace."[35]

There remains the problematic terrain on which it all is to take place, and that territory is mined. What has happened to the ground one walks on? Where does one trace a plot? Land mines have been variously recalled as remnants, reminders, and realities. Yo-yos in the stacks, the detritus of such macronarratives as the transition from colonialism to decolonization, from the "civilizing mission" to "humanitarian interventionism," from the League of Nations to the UN, and the rubble of micronarratives as well, from the Congo Reform Association to the assassination of Patrice Lumumba and the first UN peacekeeping mission, to genocide in Rwanda and war crimes tribunals, from the Anglo-Boer War to the TRC. Land mines represent the pitfalls of medicine, mutilation, military, and memory. They are a "weapon of mass destruction in slow motion," the "explosive remnants of war," that turn "clearing the fields" into "solving the land mines crisis." [36] But the "world is losing ground against the spread of mines" in that a "land mine is a specialized piece of ordnance designed to explode in response to pressure or proximity of a person, on a time-delayed basis. A mine is designed not to need an operator who chooses to detonate it; it is designed to require no initiation to set off apart from a footstep or other movement by the target." And "mine clearance still consists principally of a person with a stick, probing the ground a few centimeters at a time." [37] According to still another commentator, land mines are a "crisis," an "EPIDEMIC"; they are "pollutants," and one must consider the "sheer magnitude of the devastation already wrought by land mines and the extended time period over which that devastation will continue." [38] Land mines provide the grounds for arrested/handicapped/mutilated development narratives — and the need for their structural readjustment. Sapping in the stacks.

"Deadly Legacy" is what a Superman comic book calls land mines. Coproduced in 1996 as a joint venture involving the United Nations Children's Fund, or UNICEF, as this program is commonly called, the Mine Action Centre, the Department of Defense, and private industry to teach mine awareness to the children of Bosnia, *Deadly Legacy* is available in English, Latinic, and Cyrillic versions, and stresses the critical requirement of literacy:

> Superman: Joey, we'll do our best to find Lisa before that happens! Keep your eyes peeled.
> Joey: I wish Wolf [the dog] could've read that sign . . .
> Superman: I know how you feel. It's terrible to see any creature in pain!. But even though Wolf can't read—you can. Even where there isn't a posted sign, smart kids like you can "read" the other signs that tell you to steer clear! Old checkpoints, bases, and abandoned buildings with military markings may look like fun things to explore—but they're usually rigged to protect what's inside! Watch out for former trench lines, firing lines, and other places with lots of military debris—those are automatic tip-offs that the area is dangerous!

Deadly Legacy concludes with Superman's admonishing anticipation: "Maybe someday the mines will be removed—maybe even gone altogether—but until that day, the children need to stay smart and strong. But they can still be heroes without superpowers. The only superpower they need is the power of knowledge!"

In "Articles of Faith," Michael Ignatieff writes that there is a critical difference that distinguishes between "narratives that tell what happened and narratives that attempt to explain why things happened and who is responsible," and he maintains that "critics of truth commissions argue as if the past were a sacred text which has been stolen and vandalised by evil men and which can be recovered and returned to a well-lit glass case in some grand public rotunda." [39] But what do truth commissions do when they "commit the truth"? Bill Rolston considers the ramifications in the instance of Northern Ireland: What would it mean to "turn the page without closing the book"? What would happen to the mines in the spines of that book? For Rolston, "whether or not a truth commission occurs in a society in transition from a previously repressive regime depends on the balance of political forces at the point of that transition." In other words, what matters is whether or not "the negotiating position in relation to past human rights abuses is . . . worked out in advance." [40] Because the stacks can be a perilous place, indeed, and sappers are still needed . . . to "ascertain whether in fact a massacre was committed, or an official cover-up produced."

Counternarratives, recoveries, refusals

It was left to the African, Caribbean, and Asian writer to imagine the alternative and start writing back. Edward Said is foremost among those who pushed this quest forward beyond nationalism and post-colonial statehood, crossing boundaries to interpret the world and the text "based on counterpoint" as he would say, "many voices producing a history." — Iqbal Ahmad, The Pen and the Sword: Conversations with David Barsamian

My paternal grandfather had for a time worked as a tour guide, and when he was a boy my father sold crowns of thorns to tourists near the Sepulcher. . . . Still, a few yards away from the Sepulcher, underneath a declivity in the city wall, we stumbled on Zalatimo's, the renowned pastry shop whose speciality mtabaqa, a flat pancake folding in hazelnuts and sugar, was a great family favorite. A wizened old baker was in there stoking the oven, but he looked as though he was only barely surviving. — Edward W. Said, "Palestine, Then and Now: An Exile's Journey through Israel and the Occupied Territories"

So Edward Said writes movingly of Said Sr., the Jerusalem relic vendor, who turned into an ace modernizer: He was the man who, through his Egyptian business, introduced filing and the typewriter into Arabic culture. He saw identity principally as a question of backbone and was chronically upset by his son's inability to stand up straight, in the ramrod style approved by the Boy Scouts. When young Edward's vertebral slackness got too pronounced for him, he was packed off to America, aged fifteen. He had never seen snow and was compelled to invent a new personality at a puritanical New

England boarding school. A few years later, he escaped to Princeton, and then in 1963 to New York's Columbia University as an instructor of English literature, where he has remained until now and from where, in relative safety, he continues to operate.[1]

This brief background provides an unusual humus for identity. Self-conscious of his bourgeois upbringing, Said attended St. George School in Jerusalem and the best Cairene prep schools, including the American School, where his schoolmates were the likes of diplomats, ironically enough from the United States. Later, at Victoria College, he studied with Zeid el-Rifai, later Prime Minister of Jordan, the future King Hussein of Jordan, Adnan Khasoggi, and the actor Omar Sharif, then known as Michel Chalhoub. He received piano lessons from Ignace Tiegerman and had tea at the Mena House Hotel at the Gezira Club in the middle of the Nile (what he later described as "colonial habits: tea in the garden").[2] Nevertheless, Said spent his life standing up for a people and a cause—a cause that requires a certain distance, a space, an implicit separation of the self from background and community: "What I like about New York City is its anonymity."[3] And while it is true that Said grew up riding horses, speaking several languages, re-creating himself in the old colonial fashion—the episode is eloquently narrated in "Cairo Recalled"—he chose to do fieldwork. He may, in fact, be called a wild anthropologist in that he, like Gayatri Chakravorty Spivak, has done fieldwork not in the disciplinary sense, but, pushed by class alliance and power line, he has acquired his authority from such devices as quoting from fieldwork data and telling stories that testify to his presence at the scenes of action. His direct experience with the West made him successful, almost indistinguishable from wild anthropologists. "I must confess to a certain pleasure in listening in," Said writes,

> uninvited, to their [Orientalists] various pronouncements and inter-Orientalist discussions, and an equal pleasure in making known my findings to both Europeans and non-Europeans. I have no doubt that this was made possible because I traversed the imperial East-West divide, entered into the life of the West, and yet retained some organic connection with the place I originally came from. This was very much a procedure of crossing, rather than maintaining barriers; I believe *Orientalism* shows it.[4]

In meeting with the West on Western turf, in defining, interpreting, as well as circumscribing his experience, Said sets himself apart from other postcolonial intellectuals who are still interested in proving that they are either ethnic subjects and therefore the true marginals or that they are as good as colonials. As a matter of fact, Said may be said to resemble the character Jasmine, in

Bharati Mukherjee's novel Jasmine, who, living through many reincarnations, says, "There are no harmless, compassionate ways to remake our self." [5] And while Jasmine must murder who she is so she can be reborn in the images of dreams, Said claims that he is Palestinian American. He made known this identity in an interview he gave in 1976, when he spoke of the "two quite separate lives" he leads. "On the one hand," he notes, "I'm a literary scholar, critic, and teacher. I lead a pretty uncontroversial life at a big university. . . . Yet I lead another life, which most other literary people know nothing about. . . . My whole background in the Middle East, my frequent and sometimes protracted visits there, my political involvement: all this exists in a totally different box from the one out of which I pop as a literary critic, professor, etc." [6] It was that other, less-known aspect of his life that provided the impetus for his world celebrity.

The fact, however, remains that Said, in spite of his breaking up the boundaries both physically and ideologically, is still profoundly an *outsider* and his work truly the product of exile from his homeland (Palestine). Said's Palestine is not that of the national poet Mahmud Darwish and perhaps even less that of Samih al-Qasim. What he retains from it is less its legendary past or its uncertain political future than its tormented present, that of the beginning of its annexation and appropriation by the Zionist movement after 1948. The photo-essay *After the Last Sky* portrays the transient nature of the Palestinian existence and testifies to the Palestinian predicament. As Elizabeth Hayford writes in 1986, "While the photographs rivet the reader's attention, Said puts their pain and dislocation into words." [7]

My purpose here is not to sing along with Darwish the pain of that hollow condition called *al-manfa* (exile and estrangement), which amounts to an epic effort in his poetry to transform the lyrics of loss into the indefinitely postponed drama of a thwarted coming home, but to investigate Said's role as an intellectual whose authority operates both inside academia and in American society at large. He is, in fact, the only cultural critic—with the possible exception of one or two feminists—not only to address large audiences from positions of institutional independence and serious cultural engagement but also to inhabit a space of multiple allegiances. [8] Although considerable attention has been directed to the superficial aspects of the "Said phenomenon," little has been said about its true nature.

In this spirit, I want to map out a counternarrative based on three different sets of questions. First, there is the difficult task of the currently changing— and challenging—space Said is constantly called on to occupy: How are we to view his intervention in the world, an intervention he regards as an intellectual mission dedicated to the proposition that the world is not a stage on which to dash about and moralize by yourself but a place to be lived in and shared with others? Second, what of Said's perception of texts as events and his endorsement of oppositions as linear, narrative time and space? "The inherent mode," for Said's "contrapuntal method" is, as he insists, "not temporal but spacial" (Culture and Imperialism, 18). What of the "adversary" role of the intellectual within his discipline and its institutional supports, which are indicative of a critical consciousness that is caught in a cultural double bind, while refusing to confine itself in any way possible? Third, how has Said's work on theory informed his politics or vice versa? What are we to do with the constant pummeling Said has received both at the center and at the periphery? Finally, how far is Said indebted to Michel Foucault, a social critic and philosopher he both admired and disposed of? In proposing to discuss some of the joint interrogations posed here, I do not want to deny these categories their specific historicities and particular meanings within different theoretical and political contexts. What I am attempting to formulate are the complex strategies of cultural identification and discursive address that function in the name of the critic as both mujtah'id (one who perseveres) and mufass'ir (one who explains) and have made him the subject of a range of social, political, and literary investigations.

I

At the center, Said is acknowledged, but not without criticism. Of all Said's works, none has elicited more comment than Orientalism, "much of it positive and instructive," Said remarks, "yet a fair amount of it hostile and in some cases (understandably) abusive." Dennis Porter, for example, rejects it as being an ahistorical and inconsistent narrative. For Porter, the differences that tie together "national" narratives of empire and the conflicting arrangements of representation to which they give rise are more complicated than Said purports to know. In a scathingly critical review, Bernard Lewis, whose work is subjected to a minute critique in the book, blames Said for "poisoning" and "polluting" Orientalism's true history and meaning. Attributing the origin of this pollution to the Muslim world, Lewis declares Orientalism to be an ideological and illegitimate intrusion of politics into the world of scholarship. James Clifford goes so far as to argue that Said's work emerges as a subversion of his own authority, an authority he is constantly nurturing from within the Occident, where he performs all the maneuvers necessary for his survival. Robert Young asserts that, for Said, conflict can only "arise [within the dominant discourse] from the intervention of the outsider critic, a romantic alienated being battling like Byron's Manfred against the totality of the universe." For Jacques Berque, Said "has done quite a disservice to his countrymen in allowing them to believe in a Western intelligence coalition against them." Berque, who excoriates Orientalism for nostalgia, sensuality, and exoticism while assuring himself profitable consultancies, frequent TV appearances, interviews, and book contracts, comes under sharp criticism from Abdelkebir Khatibi for his Orientalism. The passage is telling. "This phony heir to Orientalism in the Maghreb is experimenting, with his era and field of study ('his Arabs'), in a mechanical and ravenous way."[9] For Khatibi, Berque, an emir from the West, has appropriated the Maghreb from his strategic location (Le Collège de France) thanks to pseudoscholarship (a mixture of anthropology, sociology, theory, and misreadings of certain Islamic texts, and creamy translations of authoritative texts, including Al-Qur'an). To paraphrase the Canadian pianist Glenn Gould, a little learning is a dangerous thing, and a lot of it is positively disastrous.

The son of a hakem (colonial officer), Berque was born in 1910 in Frenda, Algeria. After graduating from the Sorbonne in the 1930s, he became a civilian controller. During his tenure of fieldwork in the Atlas region, he observed, filed, and studied the Seksura tribe's social structures in Imintaout. In intruding on a people confined to their mountains, speaking for them, and telling his readers in what way they are "typically Oriental"—pointing out their exotic, monogamous, Sufist, agrarian, shy, shrewd, simpleminded ways—Berque places his research in the long history, broached by Jacques Derrida's Of Grammatology, of the West's attempts to appropriate Oriental culture for its own various ends. The result of his inquiry culminates in Structures sociales du Haut-Atlas, his admission ticket to the Collège. Khatibi's argument is that Berque's rapport de force with the natives was not an isolated instance. It stands for the pattern of domination of the Maghreb by France and the discourse that it enabled. Berque is the legitimate heir to the colonial ideology that Said tried to break open. His theory of anthropology is one such example of the "modern" technology of power, and, Said would argue, so is the whole system of colonial knowledge gathering, whether ethnography, compilations of lexicons and grammars, or physical surveys. It is designed to strengthen colonial rule by redefining the meaning of traditional culture for Algerians themselves.

But the Berque case alone does not impart to Maxime Rodinson a curious sense of critique. For he thinks that Said is not a "pure Arab" the way Darwish is, for example, and that he writes out of egocentricity and a guilty conscience, since he stood up for the cause (the Arab predicament) only late in life. "He feels an acute sense of guilt," Rodinson notes, and he goes on to suggest that the only way out of the impasse for Said is to be heavily involved in the affairs of the homeland. For Rodinson, there can be only one explanation for why Said writes with such intensity: to make up for his absence from the arena. Furthermore, according to Rodinson, Said's knowledge of the East is totally flawed.

He dedicates an entire superficial volume to what he calls "Oriental-ism" without ever having studied subjects known as Orientalist, which he criticizes vehemently, without even having had any close contact with them.

For the sake of brevity, I will only mention here what can be called his ethnocentricity. He is an Eastern Arab. Without prejudice as to his lack of knowledge of Arab history, literature, and civilization, which he experiences only through popularizing works characterized by nationalistic-type apologetics, his interest in the Arab world is no more than secondary.[10]

As if you could not be born in Pakistan or Palestine and still become an authority and lay claim to serious and authentic scholarship on Zionism, for example, when it is fairly easy for a Jew to play the role of the expert on matters pertaining to Islam, terrorism, Arab culture! It seems to me that Rodinson's critique of Said represents a narrow and chauvinistic view of Jewish culture that does not take stock of the interesting role played by the likes of Said, non-Jewish intellectuals who have written on Judaism, Zionism, terrorism, and other matters relevant to the Orient.[11] The effect is clear: Said becomes alien to his own culture. That he should pay Berque and Rodinson handsome tribute for their "methodological self-consciousness" (*Orientalism*, 326) is beyond comprehension. "What one finds in their work is always, first of all, a direct sensitivity to the material before them, and then a continual self-examination of their methodology and practice, a constant attempt to keep their work responsive to the material and not to a doctrinal preconception" (*Orientalism*, 327).

The crux of the claim against Said and his disciples is advanced, I think injudiciously, in the following quotation: "As they move out from traditional literature into political economy, sociology, history, and anthropology, do the postcolonial theorists master these fields or just poke about? Are they serious students of colonial history and culture or do they just pepper their writings with references to Gramsci and hegemony?"[12] Therefore, Russell Jacoby concludes, Said fails to understand imperial history and historiography. He thinks Said generalizes historical representation or scheme, which can be articulated with the experience or reality that it is opposed to and that remains for him unsolved. Said takes the totalization of the historicism he is opposed to too much at its own word: The problem is as much how it can be closed as how it can be opened. The fact is that Jacoby's claims about *Orientalism* are ludicrous. How can he, on the one hand, insist on the nebulousness of Said's ideas and, on the other, confidently assert that they are distillable into specific ideas of anti-Westernism? He scarcely allows for the possibility that people can read Said and disagree with him on certain fundamental issues the way Bart Moore-Gilbert does, for example, in his brilliant essay "Edward Said: Orientalism and Beyond." Jacoby makes no provision for counterinterpretations of Said's thesis, nor does he consider it a possibility that his work might (as Adorno once suggested) contradict itself or that there are other ways of reading Said besides Jacoby's own literalist canons. There are also troubling continuities and analogies in John MacKenzie's *Orientalism: History, Theory and the Arts*, most of them too obvious to point out. The epistemology of his arguments about Said is seriously deficient, since it all too easily collapses art, history, and politics into each other, and seems by extension to validate excision and avoidance as tools of analytic research.[13]

In his review of *Culture and Imperialism*, which reveals one of the great advances in modern cultural theory, namely that cultures and civilizations are hybrid and heterogeneous as well as interdependent and interrelated, Ernest Gellner, another spokesman for the guild of Orientalists, accuses Said of "inventing a bogy called Orientalism" and attributing to it a far too pervasive cultural influence. His attack is twofold. First, Gellner blames Said for not locating his chosen cultural polemic accurately enough within a grander, epochal framework—the "transition from agrarian to industrial society," which has long been Gellner's own preferred trope. Second, he argues that because it lacks this degree of theoretical articulation, the anti-Orientalist crusade has too often sunk into a banal vindication of its victims. If most Western scholarship and writing about the East is Orientalist conspiracy, then hope lies exclusively on the other side, in the camp of those put down, crassly categorized, or adored for the wrong reasons. But the trouble with this anti-imperialist "camp" is the hopelessness of so much of it—its vile dictators, censorship, clerical mania, and traditionalism that are incompatible with any sort of modernization (Western-led or not).[14]

Gellner is quite right on the first point: Said is no theorist and rarely situates his cultural forays within a wider historical perspective. It is true that progress was bound to take off in one region of the world rather than another. Unevenness could have been avoided only with guidance from outer space by something like the miracle stones in Arthur Clarke's *2001*. Progress might have erupted out of China, in which case some Atlantic equivalent of Edward Said might by now be denouncing Occidentalism and the near universal contempt displayed by the academic lackeys of Peking for the bulbous-nosed and straight-eyed. About Gellner's second point, I am less sure. Out of unevenness came nationalism, including the sort Said defends, and I would have thought that, in the long run, the victims would be likely to tell a better and more accurate story about what happened to them and about their own social and cultural histories. That Said should pay handsome tribute to Third World cultural critics such as C. L. R. James, George Antonius, Ranajit Guha, and S. H. Alatas is understandable, but he "clearly prefers the first pair to the second," Moore-Gilbert writes. He quotes Said as saying: "This is because James and Antonius are more directly connected to broader political struggles, whereas the second pair are seen as primarily preoccupied with methodological problems in academic fields of study."[15]

Marshaling the facts of Said's Western critique, one cannot help but notice that at the center of these remarkably confident statements is a somewhat recalcitrant reality that Gellner and critics like him deftly incorporate yet also dismiss: that Western scholarship is beyond any reproach. This is not to say that they have explored Said with a miraculous, zany lightness of touch. On the contrary, they have called him names, have denounced his ideas, and have condemned what he has written. To them, Said is a "professor of terror," "an anti-Semite," "an accomplice to murder," "a liar," "a deranged demagogue." The tirade is not only mean-spirited and perverse but disquieting. Their condemnation of him brings to mind Gustave Flaubert's defense of Louis Bouilhet, who was awarded the Belles-Lettres et Arts de Rouen medal of honor in 1862:

> The life of the man of letters is . . . a painful business for those who have a higher regard for Art than for vaunting their own names or swelling their fortunes. Innumerable obstacles impede this career in which one is assailed by calumny and slandered by stupidity as one is obliged to trample one's way over those Lilliputian vanities that writhe in the dust! Even after all the anguish of giving birth and the disappointments of the ideal, once the task is completed, nothing is achieved. Then one is subject to indifference, to rejection, to disdain, to insult, to the promiscuity of banal applause or to the sarcasm of the malicious; obliged to avoid the plots of the jealous and to stay forever silent in the face of triumphant mediocrity. And yet there are men who, by force of talent and energy, soon grasp the prize for which so many are striving.[16]

Flaubert thought of the speech as an impeccable piece of ironic mischief, worth writing for its mimicry of the official high style, which he so detested, and for the oblique expression of his deepest feelings about the situation of the artist. There is a prize for those who, like Gellner but unlike Flaubert, not only pass formal sentences on Said but also fail to show how the insurgent existence of *Orientalism* is due, more than anything else, to its relentless transgression of boundaries drawn by disciplines of knowledge and imperial governance. In unsettling traditional oppositions between the Orient and the Occident, reading literary texts as historical and theoretical events and crosshatching scholarly and political writings, *Orientalism* forced open the authoritative modes of knowing the Other.

The indeterminacy in the authority of Western knowledge brought about by *Orientalism* has provoked us to rethink the modern West from the perspective of the Other, to go beyond Orientalism itself in examining the implications of its demonstration that the East/West opposition is an externalization of an internal division in the modern West. Even if Said's work performs this task inadequately, the proliferation of writing back with a vengeance would be unimaginable without it.[17] "There has been a revolution," Said claimed in 1995, sixteen years after the publication of *Orientalism*, "in the consciousness of women, minorities and marginals so powerful as to affect mainstream thinking world-wide. Although I had some sense of it when I was working on *Orientalism* in the 1970s, it is now so dramatically apparent as to demand the attention of everyone seriously concerned with the scholarly and theoretical study of culture." In addition, Said may be the only cultural critic living today who has acquired both the resources to survive and the "cultural capital," in Pierre Bourdieu's formula, to thrive as a writer in revolt. Selective appropriation, incorporation, and rearticulation of Western ideologies, cultures, and institutions alongside an Arab *tur'ath* (heritage) have been some of the strategies he deploys and employs. He has succeeded because he possesses the high-quality skills required to engage in critical practices and, more important, the self-confidence, discipline, and *ijtih'ad* (perseverance) necessary for success without an undue reliance on the mainstream for approval and acceptance.

> My way of doing this has been to show that the development and maintenance of every culture require the existence of another different and competing *alter ego*. The construction of identity—for identity, whether of Orient or Occident, France or Britain, while obviously a repository of distinct collective experiences, *is* finally a construction—involves establishing opposites and "others" whose actuality is always subject to the continuous interpretation and reinterpretation of their differences from "us."[18]

At the periphery, even though Said's work assumes a wide relevance and has already generated a considerable amount of debate in several circles, it still raises questions to which critics such as Sadaq Jalal al-'Azm, N. al-Bītār, Aziz al-'Āzmih, Anwar Abdel Malek, Mohammed Arkoun, Homi Bhabha, Zakia Pathak, Aijaz Ahmad, and others have addressed themselves. They argue that if Said duplicates the Foucauldian notions of field and archive, and uses the poststructuralist method of reinterpreting texts within their historical contexts, he must also surrender to its ideology. Although marred by virulence, this debate has had at least one salutary effect: Middle Eastern and Islamic-affairs specialists—a breed not much interested in the hermeneutic questions underlying their endeavor—have been jolted into soul-searching. Most notably, they find themselves asking the basic questions posed by *Orientalism*: "How does one *represent* other cultures? What is *another* culture? Is the notion of a distinct culture (or race, or religion, or civilization) a useful one?" (*Orientalism*, 325). Furthermore, "Can one divide human reality, as indeed human reality seems to be genuinely divided, into clearly different cultures, histories, traditions, societies, even races, and survive the consequences humanly?" (*Orientalism*, 45).

Said has underlined the terms *represent* and *another* for the obvious reason that his is a critique of Western (especially British, French, and American) writings about Islam. It is indeed among such Western observers of Islam that the debate about Orientalism has been taking place. But what do Third World observers of Islam think of Orientalism? Their contribution, coming as it does from the inside, may add some valuable insights into what has become a repetitive cycle of (exclusively Western) polemics. It is a measure of the importance attached to Said's thesis that al-Azm and al-Bītār—the most prominent critics of the group—have given it the most exhaustive treatment. Both readily agree with Said that knowledge (l-mi'rifa quwwa) is intertwined with power. Both grant that Orientalism as an intellectual enterprise has close ties with colonial domination in the Middle East. And yet, unexpectedly perhaps, they are ill at east with the argument. No paragraph in *Orientalism* infuriates them more than the one where Said maintains that "Orientalism flourishes today. . . . Indeed there is some reason for alarm in the fact that its influence has spread to the 'Orient' itself: the pages of books and journals in Arabic . . . are filled with second-order analyses by Arabs of the 'Arab mind,' 'Islam' and other myths" (*Orientalism*, 322). Arab scholars see this as an attack on themselves, for it becomes imminently clear as they read further that, for Said, any cultural critique from within Arab society is merely a brand of "Arab Orientalism," a pejorative term in Arab conservative parlance. "If he says that these are second-order analyses . . . shouldn't he explain to us in what way they are so bad?" Al-Bitar asks ironically. "Is it because they try to liberate (the Arab) from the dregs and vestiges of the past?"[19] In effect, what Said objects to is a considerable body of writings produced in Arabic, especially over the last three decades, that tries to come to terms with the Arab past, and more specifically with the impact—not total, nor even direct, but still important—that this past has on the Arab present. (I shall come back to this point in section two.)

Bhabha distinguishes between Said's latent or *batin* Orientalism—"an unconscious positivity"—and a manifest or *zahir* Orientalism—"stated knowledges about the Orient," while implying that *Orientalism*'s shortcomings are mainly due to

> Said's inadequate engagement with alterity and ambivalence in the articulation of these two economies which threaten to split the very object of Orientalist discourse as a knowledge and the subject positioned therein. He contains this threat by introducing a binarism within the argument which, in initially setting up an opposition between these two discursive scenes, finally allows them to be correlated as a congruent system of representation that is unified through a political-ideological *intention* which, in his words, enables Europe to advance securely and unmetaphorically upon the Orient.[20]

For the colonizer, representing the colonized Other—the word has acquired a sheen of modishness that has become extremely objectionable—is by no means clear. According to Bhabha, Said falls victim to a single originating intention. He summarizes his argument thus: "There is always, in Said, the suggestion that colonial power is possessed entirely by the colonizer which is a historical and theoretical simplification." The act of razoring out Said may be quixotic, but it is not accurate. In his founding text, *Orientalism*, Said has characterized the intransigence of Orientalist tropes and typologies—their ability to sink into consciousness as credible stand-ins for reality itself—as "radical realism" (*Orientalism*, 223). Said explains that the book is a study of the ways in which the power, scholarship, and imagination of a two-hundred-year-old tradition in Europe and America viewed the Middle East, the Arabs, and Islam. He intends it to be explicitly antiessentialist in its arguments and radically skeptical about all categorical designations such as Orient and Occident: "What interests me as a scholar is not the gross political verity but the detail, as indeed what interests us in someone like Lane or Flaubert or Renan is not the indisputable truth that Occidentals are superior to Orientals, but the profoundly worked over and modulated evidence of his detailed work within the very wide space opened up by that truth" (*Orientalism*, 15). Equally important to Said's work are his deep sense of personal and collective loss and his quest for positive and universal alternatives to sectarian ideologies, structures, and claims. In his oeuvre, these tropes are connected by knowledge and power, and he establishes the link between them. He makes these connections always in ways that offer a more interesting and humane choice—a counternarrative, a spirit in opposition, a culture of resistance, the promise of a secular liberation.[21]

Said's analysis of Orientalist discourse implicates not only the internal politics of the colonized but also the ways in which European linguistic conventions and epistemologies underpinned the conception, management, and control of colonial relationships. In "East Isn't East," he points out that the guild of Orientalists has a specific history of complicity with imperial power. He observes that, in *Orientalism*, what he calls for is a new way of conceiving the separations and conflicts that stimulated generations of hostility, war, and imperial control between East and West.[22] Bhabha is at pains to show Said's counterpoint, a kind of testimonial to subaltern studies, and his preoccupation with memory and with the narrative of the oppressed, but he is also fastidious in describing Said's commitment never to let a dominant myth or viewpoint become history without its alternative. Hence his failure to master the whole question of political agency, narrativization of experience, and the struggle for cultural hybridity, which is at the center of Said's undertaking instead of regarding it as so much exotica—amusing, perhaps, but eminently dispensable. "All I *have* to do," a black folk saying has it, "is stay black and die."

Bhabha's verbosity scarcely conceals the underpinnings of his position and his extraordinary capacity for getting nearly everything wrong. A case in point is his reading of the "colonial plot" in *The Location of Culture*, where his ensuing conclusion is trapped by the cultural binarism that he wants to critique. Insisting that the modern cultures of Western nations must be entirely *relocated* from a postcolonial perspective, one usurped by the project of a new cultural politics of difference, Bhabha proposes an emergent body of critical knowledge issuing predominantly from the ranks of the subaltern and the displaced. The book aims to map out *within* a psychoanalytic/deconstructive framework the very "conceptual imperative" and "political consistency" necessary for such a project. In an immensely troubling fashion, he examines the way in which this ambivalence at the heart of colonial and neocolonial discourses both structures and problematizes legitimating claims to authority and singular or determinate meaning. Although refined and adjusted throughout the book, this argument is shaky, to say the least. Bhabha suggests an understanding of the colonial stereotype as a "complex and contradictory mode of representation, as anxious as it is assertive," based on an oppositional model analogous to psychoanalytic theories of the split structure of the mind. As such, he redefines this concept as a suture, or seam, by way of conveying the contradictory nature of an authority that to guarantee its representational function, is dependent on the continual fixing of discriminatory identifications along with a fetishized process of "fantasy/denial."[23] Here, Bhabha is not only simplifying social and political matters but sacrificing history at the expense of poststructuralist forays as well.

Bhabha, who somehow obtained ascendancy over the discipline of postcoloniality, has been a critic of considerable authority in the debate over hybridity, mimicry, and ambivalence, concepts borrowed from French "high" theory. The ramifications of this style are advanced by Arif Dirlik, Bhabha's most disobliging critic, who writes:

> [Bhabha's] work . . . is responsible for more than the vocabulary of post-colonialism, as he has proven himself to be something of a master of political mystification and theoretical obfuscation, of a reduction of social and political problems to psychological ones, and of the substitution of post-structuralist linguistic manipulation for historical and social explanation—all of which show up in much post-colonial writing, but rarely with the same theatricality (and incomprehensibleness) that he brings to it.[24]

The problem of dependency on Western theoretical productions is not simply a matter of cultural sellout on Bhabha's part. These problems exist everywhere in postcolonial writing, and they can easily be addressed. Nor do I mean to take anything away from Bhabha's achievements as an acclaimed postcolonial critic. His footnotes bear rich testimony to the insights he has derived from his nonsubaltern critics' knowledge and creativity. The dominance of Europe as the subject of all histories is a part of a much more profound theoretical condition under which historical knowledge is produced in the Third World—what Foucault perceptively calls the Reign of Terror. He announced that there is nothing really worth explaining in its coming, since everything in Western culture, seen properly, is a reign of terror. This condition ordinarily expresses itself in a paradoxical manner. Third World critics acknowledge their debt to Western authorities; Western critics do not feel any need to reciprocate. They produce their work in relative ignorance of Third World scholarship, and this neglect does not seem to affect the quality of their work. This practice is a luxury "we" cannot afford without running the risk of appearing old-fashioned or outdated. Bhabha adds to this symptom of subalternity.[25]

Nowhere is Bhabha, or his humanistic closure, more severely criticized than in Abdul JanMohamed's pungent attack, evidenced by the following jaw-jutting comment: "In this kind of imperial context, what does it mean to imply as Bhabha does that the native, whose entire economy and culture are destroyed, is somehow in 'possession' of 'colonial power?'" He asks and then answers with equal aplomb:

> Bhabha's unexamined conflation allows him to circumvent entirely the dense history of the material conflict between Europeans and natives and to focus on colonial discourse as if it existed in a vacuum. . . . By dismissing "intentionalist" readings of such discourse as "idealist" quests, Bhabha is able to privilege its "ambivalence" and, thereby, to imply that its

"authority" is genuinely and innocently confused, unable to choose between two equally valid meanings and representations.

Bhabha's view "severely brackets the political context of culture and history,"
JanMohamed says carefully. "This typical facet of humanistic closure requires
the critic systematically to avoid an analysis of the domination, exploitation,
and disenfranchisement that are inevitably involved in the construction of
any cultural artifact or relationship." [26] For JanMohamed, Bhabha's critical
stance provides a rather odd example of this closure in his assumption of the
"ambivalence" of colonial discourse, which conflates colonizer and colonized
into a single subject. These are penetrating remarks, not merely for what they
imply about a domesticated Bhabha but for the ways in which they appear to
consolidate the view that today he is exemplary of the Third World intellectual
who continues to depend largely on First World criticism.

Bhabha may, in fact, find solace from his misreading of Said in Moore-
Gilbert's essay "Edward Said: Orientalism and Beyond." The core of Moore-
Gilbert's reading lies in the immediacy with which he brings out the irreducible tension between latent and manifest Orientalism. "In Said's scheme,"
he asserts, " 'latent' signifies the 'deep structure' of Orientalism, the political
positionings and will to power which supposedly remain constant in the discourse, whereas 'manifest' signifies the 'surface detail' — the individual discipline, cultural work, scholar or even national tradition." Moore-Gilbert can
be read not only for the most recondite and deep knowledge but also for the
minute scrupulosity of its exactness, its wit, and its dash. He continues to
evoke this process of latent, as opposed to manifest, Orientalism in another
passage that stakes out for Orientalism its quite unusual angle of attack: "The
conflicts involved in Said's attempt to theorize the relationship between
'latent' and 'manifest' Orientalism are signalled at the most basic level in his
divided view of how Orientalist texts are to be read. Insofar as he focuses
on 'manifest' Orientalism, he elaborates a reading strategy characterized by
close readings of the individual text, to highlight the ways in which particular
writers diverge from the patterns established by 'latent' Orientalism." [27] This
essay works wonderfully as *explication de texte* in an entirely classical sense. But
just as important — and this gives the often cheeky venturesomeness of *Postcolonial Theory* its breadth and passion — Moore-Gilbert cares about human enlightenment and emancipation. Underlying his essay is the steady unfolding
grand narrative of the struggle to achieve justice, freedom, and knowledge.
That he discerns it so unfailingly in the broad features, as well as in the hints,
ellipses, and figures of the books he reads, testifies to what an extraordinary
student he is of the unending contest between life and literature.

Ahmad's shrill attack in *In Theory: Classes, Nations, Literatures* — a book charged with considerable polemical heat but little insight—deserves all the patience one can muster. Uncomfortable with Said's stance with respect to Marxism, this work repeats many of the earlier criticisms of Said. But unlike other critics who note and explore the contradictions in Orientalism, particularly with respect to humanism and Foucault, to outline perspectives that remain in sympathy with the book, Ahmad reiterates these criticisms to orchestrate a savage attack that accuses Said of mobilizing all sorts of eclectic procedures to establish "that Europeans were ontologically incapable of producing any true knowledge about non-Europe."[28] As for the effect of In Theory, Ahmad attributes it to the aspirations of the middle-class immigrants and "ethnic" intellectuals in the West who allegedly find Said's perspective useful in their upward mobility. His theory's critique of Said is caricatural, to say the least.

For Ahmad, Said's thesis is riddled with "inflat[ed] differences of individual formation and attitude into meaningless global typologies." He tells us that Said's reading of Kim, his essays "Third World Intellectuals and Metropolitan Culture," "Figures, Configurations, Transformations," and to a large extent Orientalism itself are defective. They show, he writes, the "most arrant idealism . . . and facilitate a very peculiar kind of ahistorical levelling." This is a curious reading, coming from a die-hard Marxist. One would expect Ahmad to see the politics of identity that is at the heart of the imperial cultural enterprise that Said analyzes in both Orientalism and Culture and Imperialism. The politics of identity had needed to assume, indeed to believe, that what was reproduced (stereotyped features, ideas, phrases) about Orientals was always done according to one and the same fixed pattern set by the Europeans. For Said, if a French, English, or American scholar intends on identifying the main characteristics of, for instance, the Chinese mind, he or she should also determine how the Chinese mind is different from the Western mind.[29]

In other words, Said is articulating centuries-long heartfelt human responses to being oppressed and exploited, disfigured and misrepresented by powerful European and now American imperial countries. For Said, the difference between the occupying French in La Nouvelle-Calédonie and the Israeli Army in Palestine is minor, since the occupying forces' common denominator is domination of lesser races and cultures: the Canaques, the Palestinians. This fact seems to escape Ahmad, who reduces Said's argument to the assumption that Western discourse, including diplomatic and academic as well as fictional texts, has projected an image for the Orient that has, for all intents and purposes, become its reality. Armed with this assumption or conviction, Ahmad proceeds to dismantle Said's argument as an instance of yet another colonialism that does not know itself and is therefore even more powerful and insidious in its effect. This is preposterous, since for Said, to speak of someone as Oriental, as Orientalists did, was not just to designate that person as someone whose language, geography and history were the stuff of learned treatises; it was often meant as a derogatory expression signifying a lesser breed of human being. This is not to deny that for artists like Nerval and Segalen the word "Orient" was wonderfully, ingeniously connected to exoticism, glamour, mystery and promise. But it was also a sweeping historical generalization.[30]

To pretend, as Ahmad does, that Orientalism is too complex, various, and ambivalent to exist in a form for any postcolonial to criticize is to show his tactic of misreading a significant amount of historical experience. For in writing a book such as *Orientalism*, Said not only rereads the canonical cultural works, not to degrade them but to reinvestigate some of their assumptions, going beyond the stifling hold on them of some version of the master-slave binary dialectic, but also gives voice, and this is perhaps more important, to the wretched of the earth (Orientals and others) to talk back to a West they no longer see as one homogeneous bloc. Consequently, there is some poetic justice in the perceptive criticism that Moore-Gilbert levels against Ahmad. He maintains that despite his polemic against Said, Ahmad is unable to escape the influence of Said's thinking. "The force of *In Theory*'s critique," he observes, "derives in large measure from attention to Said's privileged position within an institutional framework."[31]

Let me now return to what Zakia Pathak, Sawati Sengupta, and Sharmila Purkaystha have called "The Prisonhouse of Orientalism." Their hindsight not only stimulates in them a sense of what Freud called la *dénégation* at what they could or ought to have done but did not; it also gives them a wider perspective from which to comprehend what they did. I quote from their essay: "The history that *Orientalism* helps recover from the white text is thus monologic; it does not help us to recuperate the other narratives of Imperialism."[32] To counterargue this misleading claim, and for evidence of the ways in which postcolonial discourse itself provided the means to generate a counterdiscourse, one needs to point to Wilson Harris's essay "Interior of the Novel: Amerindian/European/African Relations." This predates by two decades Said's recently developed approach to texts such as Joseph Conrad's *Heart of Darkness*. Like Harris, Said seeks to consider it and other texts like it in "a new dimension . . . within which the losses and the gains on both sides are beginning to cross-fertilize the imagination of our times."[33] Pathak, Sengupta, and Purkaystha fail to note how crucial for Said's conception of counterpoint is the desire, as in Harris, to circumvent the "politics of blame" identified with cultural nationalism—what Said terms in a telling image, worth quoting: "Contrapuntal analysis should be modelled not (as earlier notions of comparative literature were) on a symphony but rather on an atonal ensemble" (*Culture and Imperialism*, 386). His interest, therefore, lies in a reconstructed "humanism" as a way out of binary oppositions, "a certain 'void' or misgiving attending every assimilation of contraries," in Harris's celebrated phrase.[34] Like Derrida's figure of the hymen or the *entre*, Said's "void" is also a place that allows cultures to come together. Additionally, for evidence of the ways in which postcolonial discourse itself provides the means to generate a counterdiscourse, Pathak may find some consolation in Sara Suleri's *Rhetoric of English India*, Mary Louise Pratt's *Imperial Eyes*, as well as in the work of Spivak, Fatima Mernissi, and Ania Loomba.

What Said seems to share, however, with most First World and Third World critics, both hostile and sympathetic, is that, on the one hand, in writing *Orientalism*, he rethought what for centuries had been believed to be an unbridgeable chasm separating East from West, and, on the other hand, he stressed the conviction that in the Third World, modernism has been nothing but a shallow pretense with its local games and pastiches. For the Third World today is still limited at best to instrumental borrowing, or at worst to gadget borrowing, what V. S. Naipaul has ably called "playing the ape," that is, the natives being capable only of mimicking the white man, who forever keeps them in check.[35] Yet the mimicry that Naipaul speaks about begs the question of the values of modernity that are inexorably linked to the instruments of technology. It does not relate to the problem of what is to be done when some of these values clash with one's *tur'ath* (heritage) but tries to "reconcile" them by vague formulas. Much like the great public intellectuals of the sixties—Frantz Fanon, Amilcar Cabral, and James—Said not only refutes Naipaul's thesis of neocolonialism but also argues that the so-called revolutionary regimes are nothing but a sham, that they have failed to bring about structural change, and that the direction the Third World in general and the Arab world in particular should take is that of a *nahdha* (cultural revolution), and with it make a complete break with the past.

2

I shall now return to the trope of the past, which so ubiquitously characterizes the speaking subject of subaltern history. Along with Nietzsche, Freud, Foucault, Derrida, and Gilles Deleuze, Said recognizes the *problématique* of an originating moment in the history of an individual, race, or civilization, where an idea or a set of ideas may be said to have emerged. But in the end, it leads to nostalgia and all its attendant falsifications. Foucault's unfolding of the trope of origins, for example, needs to be quoted so that we may appreciate its particular quality, which Said has described as a "poetics of thought."

Why does Nietzsche challenge the pursuit of the origin (*Ursprung*), at least on those occasions when he is truly a genealogist? First, because it is an attempt to capture the exact essence of things, their purest possibilities, and their carefully protected identities, because this search assumes the existence of immobile forms that precede the external world of accident and succession. This search is directed to "that which was already there," the image of a primordial truth fully adequate to its nature; it necessitates the removal of every mask to ultimately disclose an original identity. . . .

History . . . teaches us how to laugh at the solemnities of the origin. . . . The origin always precedes the Fall . . . it is associated with the gods, and its story is always sung as a theogony. But historical beginnings are lowly: not in the sense of modest or discrete like the steps of a dove, but derisive and ironic, capable of undoing every infatuation.[36]

Foucault's point is that the search for origins is essentialist and militates against a proper sense of historicity. For the colonized people, such a search for their origins is doubly foreclosed, "derisive and ironic," because the process of colonization meant precisely wiping out their history, traditions, language, and culture. As an instance of this foreclosure, Said glances at the Middle East as the locus for biblical origins: "All pilgrimages to the Orient passed through, or had to pass through, the biblical lands; most of them in fact were attempts either to relive or to liberate from the large, incredibly fecund Orient some portion of Judeo-Christian-[Muslim]/Greco-Roman-[Arab] actuality" (*Orientalism*, 168). The consequence of these investments, as Said has repeatedly emphasized, has been the denial of human rights, the legal right of residence, the status of nationhood, and the historical identity accruing to the Palestinian people. The Palestinian problem is a dramatic case of the ways in which beginnings are constantly being made afresh.[37]

Before Said, Fanon, his *maître à penser*, recognized that in the triangular dialogue between the settler, the native, and the native intellectual, there is "a prominent confrontation on the phantasmic plane." Versions of origins are offered and resisted in a continuing dialectic. Fanon likes the self-justifying ideological operation of colonialism to the mother "who unceasingly restrains her fundamentally perverse offspring from managing to commit suicide and from giving free rein to its evil instincts. . . . The colonial mother protects her child from itself, from its ego, and from its physiology, its biology, and its own unhappiness which is its essence."[38] In this Oedipal tyranny, the search for identity by the colonized people continually returns to the terms of opposition set by the colonial mother. In effect, the search for origins becomes, for the subordinate, a longing for an impossible purity and a yearning for the fullness of meaning that is not only uncritical but also politically suspect, in that it can unwillingly serve the reactionary forces of communalism evidenced by the erection of more and more little enclaves and more and more hostility about people outside those enclaves all over the world.

Nowhere is this danger greater than in colonial Algeria, where schools either did not exist at all under French occupation or, if they did, were the domain of the privileged. According to Alain Ruscio, the minority of Algerian Arabs who were schooled memorized such passages as "our ancestors, the ancestors of the French, are the Gauls" and learned the principal roads, rivers, and valleys of France—the mother country. Those who succeeded according to French standards were later described as *évolués*. Many of the intellectuals—like Shakespeare's Caliban, whose profit from learning the English language was that he now knew how to curse—went on to become leaders in the independence movement. At the same time, however, France's *oeuvre civilisatrice* in Algeria produced what Malek Haddad has described as "the most perfidious case of depersonalization in history, a case of cultural asphyxia." Algeria, of course, is not alone in being subjected to this kind of intellectual terrorism. The adoption in 1996 of a text containing thirty-six articles by the Algerian Assembly installing Arabic as the official language of the people was an attempt to reclaim a *tur'ath*, a language, a history, a culture, a "mémoire tatouée," in Khatibi's phrase. The full realization of Arabic at the administrative level was completed in July of the same year and should be carried out at the university level by 2000. As Martin Heidegger puts it, if "language is the center of being," then for Algeria, the implementation of Arabic as the native language means more than just the restoration of a past.[39]

Another example is India, where English literature was a major component in the ideology of nation building that was consolidated under British colonial rule in the nineteenth century. The universal humanism put forward by institutionalized literary studies was useful in the task of hegemonizing native elite culture. It offered, as Ania Loomba shrewdly puts it, "a program of building a new man who would feel himself to be a citizen of the world while the very face of the world was being constructed in the mirror of the dominant culture of the West." Conversely, it may be proposed that the enterprise of teaching English literature in India can be read as one of the texts of imperial governance, as brilliantly elucidated in Gauri Viswanathan's *Masks of Conquest: Literary Study and British Rule in India* which reminds us that the argument about English literature, about its canon, and about its curriculum is necessarily as much an argument about things unseen and unsaid, about its submerged and excluded voices, and about the powers outside the realm of literature as it is about the displayed objects.[40]

In England, literary education was a participant in the creation of a paternalistic, elitist culture designed to contain the challenges variously posed to the status quo by the working class, women, and marginals. But in India, and elsewhere, it not only helped colonial rule but shaped, to a large extent, what Fanon calls the "native bourgeoisie," those who took over the reigns of power after the white man's exit but who have done hardly anything to better the situation. They still display characteristics common to their counterparts in the *Métropole:* They are insular and insulated, incestuous, smug, and contemptuous of the masses. They protect and nurture their own interests, while professing egalitarianism and practicing their pernicious bourgeois system that is based on an overreliance on Western ideas and prescriptions, which have eroded the Third World ethos and pretty much ruined it. "The triumphant natives," Said observes of Third World liberation struggles, "soon enough found that they needed the West and that the idea of *total* independence was a nationalist fiction designed mainly for what Fanon calls the 'nationalist bourgeoisie,' who in turn often ran the new countries with a callous, exploitative tyranny reminiscent of the departed masters" (*Culture and Imperialism*, 19). In fact, the native bourgeoisie has yet to recover from its colonial hangover. Democracy and the nation-state have failed because the people whom the poor have elected rule—not represent—them. If all that were wrong with the native bourgeoisie were a particularly bad hangover from colonialism, there might well be room for optimism. But the crisis goes deeper than expected. Take their growing consumerism or incapacity to govern, and the case will be clear enough. (The two open sores—Algeria and Nigeria—among many are good examples of what I have in mind.)

Interesting in this context is Said's *Beginnings: Intention and Method*, in which he engages head-on in the project of decolonization by divesting himself of the illusion of origins and foreign thinking, a project that involves an extensive play with theoretical possibilities: "Those traditional conceptions of primacy such as source and origin, the principles of continuity and development, and those metaphors for originating authority such as author, discipline, and the will to truth are all the more or less cancelled by Foucault."[41] In Said's reading of Foucault, the correlatives of the Western search for origins are several sets of ideas that need to be unpacked here. Origins, authority, author, the Law of the Father: The quest for the moment of origin (in history, in collective consciousness) by its own inner logic moves insistently toward fixing a document that is made authoritative by scholarship and sealed by their commentaries, which argue and debate but continue to affirm the authority of the initial discovery. Thus, authority and all its connotations of authoritativeness, the chief one being the system that sets up the author as model, are confirmed.

Origins are also implicated in narrative and representation, in the novel-istic model of successive continuity, which gives formal reassurance of a be-ginning, middle, and end. This chain of begetting and fatherhood, mixing memory and desire, constitutes a patrimony that, in relation to the ideologi-cal operation of colonialism, becomes a celebration of the law of the empire, disguised so successfully as to be invisible. "This is all the more true in the case of the Arab world," Said writes, "which for several centuries had been dominated by Ottoman or European colonialism. National independence for countries like Egypt and Morocco, say, meant that young people at last could be educated fully in the traditions, histories, languages, and cultures of their own particular Arab countries."[42] In my own case, for instance, I was edu-cated entirely in French colonial schools in Tunisia and France, where all study focused on the history of French society, literature, and values. Much the same was true in the main French colonies, where it was assumed that native elites would be taught the rudiments of intellectual culture in the idioms and methods designed, in effect, to keep those native elites subservi-ent to colonial rule, the superiority of European learning, and so forth. Until I was about sixteen, I knew a great deal more about Albert Camus's L'Etranger and André Gide than I did about Ibn Khaldun's Muqaddi'mah or the Tunisian poet Abu-al-Kacem a'Chabbi, and to me—irony of ironies—colonial consuls such as Jules Ferry and missionaries such as Charles de Foucauld were more familiar than emira al-Qahina and emir Abdel-Kader.

Authority, knowledge, the law of empire, and colonialism would seem to be the ideological correlatives of the Western sign, the interlocking by which Western man fabricates his "self" into a coherent identity, positing himself as beginning and end of all knowledge and grandly naming it humanism. As Foucault formulates it, "Continuous history is the indispensable correlative of the founding function of the subject."[43] This Foucauldian position against the dominant humanist tradition has still to be evaluated in the perspective of our time, but what can be said at once without fear of contradiction is that it becomes particularly liberating for Said. He is no longer part of the endless speculations about a lost, pure, precolonial origin. Said makes this fact abun-dantly clear in his introduction to Orientalism: His purpose is not to recover a reality behind the European distortions and misrepresentations but instead to focus steadily on the production of the Orient as a textual construct: "It is clear, I hope, that my concern with authority does not entail analysis of what lies hidden in the Orientalist text, but analysis rather of the text's surface, its exteriority to what it describes" (Orientalism, 20). In repudiating al-batin, or "what lies hidden in the Orientalist text," Said is working toward dismantling the entire machinery of origins, in the sense that this machinery dictates a specific way of apprehending truth in terms of depths and surfaces. Within this cognitive metaphor that clothes all our thinking, the past is perceived as *a-zahir*, or a surface. On the face of this performance of *batin/zahir*, I would like to risk the assertion that surely the texts, always already there, need another community of interpreters sympathetic to the integrity of authors. For Said, the Orient deserves an analysis with an emancipatory vision that assumes the unconscious arrogance of discovering its depth and inner meaning.

Some of these influential theoretical positions regarding origins have thus provided Said with a point of entry into the ongoing critique of colonialism. The Third World intellectual must grasp the entire cause-and-effect corollary of origins and the different intricacies produced in it. It remains to be seen where Said's claim to liberation leads: Can Said free himself and us entirely from the paradoxes of the Western philosophical tradition? If all roads lead to false origins, where does inquiry begin without being implicated in them? These are some of the questions I will attempt to address next. There can be no argument about the fact that Said does liberate himself totally, not only from origins but also, and perhaps more important, from Western tradition as represented by Foucault, Deleuze, Derrida, and others, in that he breaks away from all forays to claim what he calls "an independent critical consciousness" (*Orientalism*, 326). But it is the second question that poses some difficulty: Said certainly sees the modern critic as more of a "wanderer," a nomad, just as he sees knowledge in general as being "less formally embodied," whether in a subject, a teacher, or a narrative.[44] But is that enough to renounce the question of origins?

Clearly, one cannot help noticing Said's debt to Foucault, a debt that is most evident in his use of Foucauldian concepts such as discourse, field, and, most of all, archive. The points of difference between Said and Foucault, however, deserve particular attention. The contrast between Foucault's antihumanism, which goes with his exclusively theoretical activism, and Said's self-styled humanism, which opts for an interventionist critical practice, derives from the theorist's respective historical position, location, constituency, and audience. That Said should choose to live in New York is no accident; as a cultural critic, he maintains for himself a perpetual distance from official discourses as well as from family quarrels of the Western philosophical tradition, even though he at times speaks out, as in the culture wars debate.[45] Actually, not only Said but also Paul Rabinow, David Couzens Hoy, Ian Hacking, and other critics of a politically left persuasion, especially in Britain, have found in Foucault a way out of the Derridian *mise-en-abîme* that does not simply lead back to liberal humanism and traditional literary scholarship but also claims a certain *engagement à la* Jean-Paul Sartre. Foucault's concept of all discourse as a field of contest for power has obvious attractions for those who, like Said, feel that criticism should have something instrumentally pertinent to say about such matters as imperialism, colonialism, the class struggle, nationalism, and so forth.

Yet the very inclusiveness of Foucault's theory makes it hardly more promising as a basis for action than Derrida's critique of logocentrism or even deconstruction, about which Said writes, "It has always seemed to me that the supreme irony of what Derrida has called logocentrism is that its critique, deconstruction, is as insistent, as monotonous, and as inadvertently systematizing as logocentrism itself." The question then becomes: If there were nothing but the struggle for power, what good reason would there be to persuade people that they should give up some of their power for the greater good? Foucault, Said regretfully concludes, "takes a curiously passive and sterile view not so much of the use of power, but of how and why power is gained, used and held on to. . . . What one misses in Foucault is something resembling Gramsci's analysis of hegemony, historical blocks, ensembles of relationship done from the perspective of an engaged political worker for whom the fascinated description of exercised power is never a substitute for trying to change power relationships within society." [46] Later, Said rejects Foucault, mainly because he "seems actually to represent an irresistible colonizing movement that paradoxically fortifies the prestige of both the lonely individual scholar and the system that contains him." He turns instead to Fanon, because he moves "from confinement to liberation." Although both Foucault and Fanon are influenced by Freud, Nietzsche, and Sartre, Said feels that only "Fanon presents that formidable arsenal into anti-authoritarian service" (Culture and Imperialism, 278).

For Said, Fanon is also valuable because of his insight into the persistence of colonial interests even in a decolonized world. But the lesson from Fanon he finds most compelling is the " 'pitfalls of nationalist consciousness' " — the notion "that unless national consciousness at its moment of success was somehow changed into a social consciousness, the future would hold not liberation but an extension of imperialism" (Culture and Imperialism, 267). Fanon teaches the postcolonial intellectual, in effect, to be wary of the native bourgeoisie and their loud cries of total national liberation, since such cries prove ultimately to be nothing more than a sort of nativism disguised in "nationalist fictions" that are designed to replace one form of tyranny with another. To overthrow such tyrannies and deconstruct such fictions, the intellectual in the decolonized world must strive for "the conversion, the transformation, of nationalist consciousness into political and social consciousness." [47] With his experience as writer and intellectual in protest against oppression of any kind, Said may be said to have lived up to Fanon's principle of the critic as *conscience évoluée* in solidarity with those who suffer at the hands of the oppressor. Insofar, then, as the armed struggle and resistance to oppression pro-

duce or confirm particular and concrete kinds of political actions, Said sees
Fanon's work as providing a far better means than Foucault's to understand
neocolonial culture as a material network of connections between knowledge
and power.

3

What must be noted immediately is how well, how enviably well, Said knows
these actualities, their secrets, and their pitfalls: that human injustice is not
only not natural but constructed, and occasionally even invented, outright.
This fact will be evident to anyone who has read his account of the manifold
devious connections between the history of "serious" Western scholarship
on the Orient and the uses to which it has been regularly put by government
agencies, military strategists, and ideologues of various persuasions keen to
exploit its handy repertoire of "Arab" cultural and character stereotypes. If
further proof were needed, then the Gulf War undoubtedly provided it, with
examples ranging from thinly veiled racist overtones, to Bush's anti-Saddam
Hussein crusade, to the usual array of media experts vying to explain how best
to deal with these tricky individuals, to the fine frenzy of xenophobic sentiment witnessed in the right-wing popular tabloids. Few events in recent history have managed to create such an upsurge of irrational fears and phobias
in the service of a Western neo-imperialist drive to reinforce the old ethnocentric values and certitudes.

Confronted with such evidence, one can hardly deny the moral justice of
Said's case and the risk that must be courted by any commentator who sets
out to analyze the Gulf War and its aftermath in terms of "enlightened" critical reason versus the forces of ignorance, prejudice, or unexamined popular
belief. For such arguments can always be suspected of trading on the version
of the typecast "us-and-them" attitude, a stance of superior knowledge or
moral wisdom that all too readily perpetuates the cycle of oppression. Thus,
in Said's words,

> There is a pattern of such contemptuous attitudes towards the Arab
> world, from the days of the British expeditionary force sent to Egypt in
> 1882 to put down the Orabi rebellion to the 1956 attack on Egypt under-
> taken by Anthony Eden in collusion with Israel and France—Eden's at-
> titude, delivered in the accents of petty and vengeful stubbornness,
> strangely prefigures Bush's personalized hatred for Saddam Hussein. . . .
> Bush has treated Saddam as his personal Moby Dick, to be punished and
> destroyed. . . .
> For decades in America there has been a cultural war against the Arabs

and Islam; the most appalling racist caricatures of Arabs and Muslims have conveyed that they are all either terrorists or shaiks, and that the region is a large arid slum, fit only for profit or war. The very notion that there might be a history, a culture, a society—indeed many societies—to be thought of as interlocutor or as partner has never held the stage for more than a moment or two. A flow of trivial books by journalists has flooded the market, and has gained currency for a handful of dehumanizing stereotypes.[48]

This attitude is given a further pathological twist when the "subaltern" or the "subordinate" culture shows signs of producing its own secular or modernizing trends, its own high-grade technology, and other such modes of "rational" adaptation to the pressures of global change. The West then finds its interests threatened by a kind of parodic self-image whose challenge can only be met by overt militarist aggression or through the various techniques of demonization deployed against pawns such as Anwar Sadat, Hosni Mubarak, and King Hussein, among several. Hence, what Said describes as "an attenuated example of those [Arabs] who in the past have incurred the wrath of a stern white man, a kind of Puritan superego whose errand into the wilderness knows few boundaries," a situation in which "Saddam has become Hitler, the butcher of Baghdad, the madman who is to be brought low," is proven true. The result is all too familiar: a sharp turnabout in strategic thinking, whereby the ex-ally or protector of U.S. interests in the region becomes a menace to regional stability and a target of massive retaliatory action. What is played here, as Said remarks, is a version of the Frankenstein scenario, with the creators looking on in appalled fascination at their own distorted self-image. "There has seemed to be a kind of pleasure in the prospect of the Arabs as represented by Saddam at last getting their comeuppance. Scores would be settled with Palestinians, Arab nationalism, Islamic civilization. Most of these old enemies of the 'West,' it should be noted, had the further cheek to be anti-Israel."[49] And any notion that the image is not so distorted must be warded off with the maximum degree of strenuous disavowal.

There is no denying the force of such arguments, especially when read against the background of Said's impassioned yet meticulous scholarship. Said's purpose, after all, is not just to devise an alternative rhetoric, discourse, or language game to set against the forms of racist prejudice that have so far governed Western perceptions of the Orient. Rather, it is to show the false, mendacious character of what passes for expert Occidental wisdom about Arab history, politics, and cultural values and to do so from a standpoint informed by a more profound and extensive knowledge of the documentary sources and more critical unillusioned grasp of the ideological issues involved. Such a work clearly does rest content with producing a mere counter-narrative that happens to fit some exciting left-liberal agenda of cultural debate.

No doubt Said's argument owes something of its persuasive force to his command of large-scale narrative structures. His marshaling of detailed evidence into a powerful indictment of Western attitudes and policies would not make the point effectively if treated in a more dispersed or piecemeal form. Moore-Gilbert writes, "For Said, . . . Western domination of the non-Western world is not some arbitrary phenomenon but a conscious and purposive process governed by the will and intention of individuals as well as by institutional imperatives." [50] Additionally, Said's works derive much of their authority from the rhetoric of moral anger, the stance of speaking on behalf of an oppressed and misrepresented culture, which he uses to great effect against the voices of cynical U.S. and/or European realpolitik. One can readily concede the arguments about the Gulf War to neopragmatists such as Richard Rorty and Stanley Fish and still hold on to the crucial premise: that there is a difference between truth and falsehood in such matters, and that honest scholarship is the alternative best equipped to maintain a due sense of that distinction. Otherwise, there simply would be no way to choose between the various compelling narratives or rhetorical strategies, aside from their degree of suave appeal in this or that cultural context.

At the most basic level, what Said exposes are those symptoms of prejudicial thinking—manifest, obsessional motifs, manipulative rhetoric, undocumented blanket assertions, and so forth—which signal the presence of an overriding drive to construct an image of the "Orient" in line with Western beliefs and policy interests. Beyond that, he locates a whole repertoire of stereotyped attributes, a system of exclusive binary oppositions where the "West" connotes values of reason, enlightenment, progress, and civilized conduct, while the "Orient" is shown in a negative or inverse relationship to those same values. Again, the Gulf War provides an example of the way that these deep-rooted cultural prejudices could be mobilized in the service of a moral crusade with insistent racist overtones: "The whole premise of the way the war was prepared and is being fought is colonial: the assumption is that a small Third World country doesn't have the right to resist America, which is white and superior. I submit that such notions are amoral, anachronistic, and supremely mischievous, since they not only make wars possible, but also prevent diplomacy and politics from playing the role they should." [51] This is a bold position that brings to mind a comment once made by Cyril Connolly, who said, "Let us reflect whether there be any living writer whose silence we would consider a literary disaster." [52] Said's silence would certainly be one.

In spite of the accruing violence against him, however, Said has remained closely connected with and urgently committed to his constituency and to the vocation of the humanist, as demonstrated by his refusal to be lured by power, money, and patronage. "At bottom," he writes, in *Representations of the Intellectual*, "the intellectual, in my sense of the word, is neither a pacifier nor a consensus-builder, but someone whose whole being is staked on a critical sense, a sense of being unwilling to accept easy formulas, or ready-made clichés, or the smooth, ever-so-accommodating confirmations of what the powerful or conventional have to say, and what they do. Not just passively unwilling, but actively willing to say so in public."[53] He has nobly lived up to these criteria during his long activity as the critic as displaced talent. Said writes, moreover, in the explosive, unstable, and, as anthropologists like to point out, culturally disruptive world—a world in which the United Nations has become the West's mercy mission to the flotsam of failed states the white man left behind, where old hatreds have been spurred on by nationalism and tribalism, where the United States has become the unchallenged Uncle Sam of the world that operates at its will. "The imperial stage is now the scene of a Pax Americana," Tom Mitchell comments, "one that teaches the world to sing in the perfect harmony of international corporate culture, while dispatching its smart bombs to surgically cleanse trouble spots."[54]

Said's *ijtih'ad* and *tafss'ir* (explanation), almost his leading characteristics, are configurations the modern reader finds hard to sketch but that, in the future, would constitute the indispensable grids to which we and our culture become legible. Not that there is anything nightmarish about this world of Said's, in the crude sense in which other critics have drawn it. Said breathes into his world the vitality of poetic prose, cultural politics mixed with deep philosophical reflections on masterpieces such as *Kim*, *Heart of Darkness*, and *Aida*. He understands their dichotomies and is particularly effective on what he terms the "sheer link" between a work of art, for instance Jane Austen's *Mansfield Park*, and its context, where the passing reference to the distant slave plantation on Antigua becomes the trope for the representation of Mansfield Park itself in all its intimacy and grace. He draws attention not so much to *how* to read as to *what* is read and *where* it is written about and represented.[55]

In fine, Said is a "rare commodity" these days—a resolutely principled, political intellectual. His affirmations of emancipation and enlightenment have not been compromised by the end of "actually existing socialism" because their sources lie elsewhere: in the struggles of diverse peoples for democracy and justice. His comparative historical analyses of political culture and cultural politics are globalized rather than totalized. The achievement of his proposition is expressed, above all, in its distance from narrowly national visions of the political processes that promise social and economic transformation. Open-ended, clear, and modest about the limits of his own roles as critic, commentator, and interpreter, Said has developed further the inter-cultural and international approach signaled long ago in his influential essay "Traveling Theory":

> Like people and schools of criticism, ideas and theories travel—from person to person, from situation to situation, from one period to an-other. Cultural and intellectual life are usually nourished and often sus-tained by this circulation of ideas, and whether it takes the form of ac-knowledged or unconscious influence, creative borrowing, or wholesale appropriation, the movement of ideas and theories from one place to another is both a fact of life and a usefully enabling condition of intellec-tual activity.[56]

This novel standpoint stresses the circulation and dissemination of cultural artifacts, oppositional ideas, and people. The border, the frontier, and the diaspora are its central tropes.

Said describes *Culture and Imperialism* as "an exile's book": "For objective rea-sons that I had no control over, I grew up as an Arab with a Western educa-tion. Ever since I can remember, I have felt that I belonged to both worlds, without being completely *of* one or the other. . . . Yet when I say 'exile' I do not mean something sad or deprived. On the contrary belonging, as it were, to both sides of the imperial divide enables you to understand them more easily" (*Culture and Imperialism*, xxvii). Living on the borderline contributes to a refined politics of (dis)location that, in Said's hands, becomes capable of supplementing the familiar Euromodernist interest in time, with an equiva-lent understanding of space and spaciality: the geography and cartography of identities and movements, and systems of domination and countercultures of resistance. More so than in Said's previous works, *Culture and Imperialism* is driven by the new political conscience generated within the overdeveloped world by the dissident sensibilities of peoples of color, women's movements, and ecological and anti-imperialist voices. Operating within a constellation of political identities that joyfully exceeds the closed, moribund world of class politics, these movements and voices converge to talk back with a vengeance in one voice.

The panic over "political correctness," which replies to these new utopian hopes, is currently setting the terms for discussion of the future of the uni-versity as a humane institution and a vital symbol of the value of civilization. Said's exemplary work gives the lie to the idea that the great canon of the West is imperiled by a tide of left-wing McCarthyism. However, while we are told that authentic scholarship is being debased by the tribunes of multicul-turalism, there is danger that *Culture and Imperialism* may be trivialized like *Black Athena* or *The Invention of Tradition* and read primarily as an elliptical and misguided intervention into the culture wars on American campuses. Those battles have far greater strategic significance than the jokey tone in which they are mimicked.

But it would be a great shame if the breadth and imagination of such a book were reduced to the status of riposte to the Right. For one thing, Said is a long way from advocating anything like a wholesale transformation of literary scholarship. He makes ritual obeisance to anticolonial figures such as Toni Morrison and Chinua Achebe but is, at the same time, keen to reassure his readers that, regardless of the political aspirations of his work, he still appreciates the literary merit of the nineteenth-century texts he rereads and relocates amid the distinctive "structure of attitude and reference" that characterizes imperial power. Said rests his case as follows: "I have this strange attachment . . . to what I consider in a kind of dumb way 'great art.'" Pressed by Michael Sprinker to elucidate his point further, he answers flabbily: "There is an intrinsic interest in [canonical works], a kind of richness in them." [57] The idea of aesthetics, like the concept of "race," survives the narrative intact. He provocatively occupies the uncomfortable space between imperial domination and its negation by anticolonial forces. This he does not to dismiss the great art of the West but, it would seem, to redeem it by locating it properly. Hence his reading of *Mansfield Park*, for example—"a novel I praise," Said reminds us, "as much as I do all Jane Austen's work." [58]

Said seeks not to excuse the racism of Rudyard Kipling, Conrad, and Gide, or the colonialism of E. M. Forster and Camus, but to shift analysis so that such unsavory attributes do not become a source of fuel for the moralistic pseudopolitical responses he rightly castigates as the "politics of blame." For Said has always intended his readers to be instructed by the various comprehensive examples of the practice he provides. And if Austen is the first such extended instance, Camus is another one. Here, Said's interpretation does seem to be highly informative, even if at times he falls short in his reading of the Algerian novelist. He fails to see the contradictions in a writer who was racked all his life by conflicting allegiances: to his mother and yet to his "new" friends; to his *pied-noir* roots and yet to the Arabs; to his pacifist instincts and yet to his macho hunger for action; to his wife and children, and yet to his need for sexual reassurance and his love for Maria Casarès; to his ideals and yet to his distorted truth. [59]

One of the most attractive aspects of Said's reading of Camus is his plain discomfort with the way(s) in which Western critics (Michael Walzer and Conor Cruise O'Brien, to mention a few of the better-known names), have read and/or interpreted the *pied-noir* novelist and his uneasy relationship with Algeria and the *indigènes* who do not get to tell the stories they have. In fact, they are scarcely perceived as capable of having stories; their stories are not so much refused as ruled out, unimaginable as pieces of recognized history. At times, Said is tentative and seems to be groping for an alternative theory (of reading) or at least a general mode for articulating the relationship; at others, he is impatient, even dismissive of those who "read Camus outside of the colonial context, with no indication of the rather contested history of which he was a part." Said recalls Roland Barthes's description of Camus's style in *Le Degré zéro de l'écriture* as *écriture blanche*, but he would be better off evoking Barthes's "Can we ever . . . read [a writer] in all innocence? Can we ever want to?" Said, like Barthes, knows that authors and texts do not exist in isolation and that "the morality of fiction," in Nadine Gordimer's words—its inherent need to loot quotidian reality—is frequently questioned by readers and critics alike.[60] However, what is important about Said's "contrapuntal" reading of works of literature—a reading in which ordinarily separate histories are allowed to play against each other, to produce not harmony but a complicated polyphony—is not its occasional bluntness but the range of insight and argument it makes possible. There is no exaggeration in such a claim, and by analogy we recognize other missed or displaced configurations, too.

I do not think it is entirely unsporting of me to note that when Said crosses the English Channel and writes a scrupulous and painful chapter on Camus's fiction and its relation to Algerian independence, he looks like a lawyer whose evidence is shaky. To have Said speak for himself: "Camus's narratives have a negative vitality in which the tragic human seriousness of the colonial effort achieves its last great clarification before ruin overtakes it" (*Culture and Imperialism*, 176). There is a lot of work for the reader to do here, and different readers will do different work. In trying to formulate an alternative reading, Said loses sight of the drama of impossible choices that Camus found himself wrestling with and that his characters express so well: Rambert in *La Peste* is forced to choose between his private love and the social demands of plague-stricken Oran; Daru, the French Algerian schoolteacher and reluctant jailer of the Arab prisoner in *L'Exil et le royaume*, offers his charge two possible itineraries, one road pointing to freedom, the other leading to incarceration and a murder trial at the hands of his colonial masters (bizarrely, the prisoner chooses the latter); and, perhaps most memorably of all, the Renegade, shuttling between the single-mindedness and Eurocentrism of the Catholic seminary and the cult of the African fetish, finishes up mutilated and brutalized.[61]

From the outset, Said reminds us of Camus's history as a *colon*, a *pied-noir*, that he was born and grew up in the town of Annaba, as the Arabs call it, or Bône as the French designate it, and that his novels are really expressions of the colonial predicament. He then goes on to advance several lines of commentary that might help us to understand Camus. For example, he suggests that we should read the episode in *L'Etranger* wherein Meursault kills the Arab, to whom Camus gives no name and no history, as an ideological fiction and that the whole idea at the end of the novel wherein Meursault is put on trial is a lie since no Frenchman was ever tried for killing an Arab in colonial Algeria. Yet despite his responsible reading, Said proves inadequate in understanding Camus's portrayal of the trial, in that it cannot be taken as a realistic account of the legal process in a French colonial court room any more than his hero's apocalyptic experience during his ten-minute walk on the beach after a French luncheon in a setting of banal domesticity. Camus offers a recognizable account of the trial not as a trial but as a parody of the French judicial system. He goes into considerable detail in depicting its conventions and procedures, from the behavior of the participants, to the cordial atmosphere in the courtroom where habitués greet each other as in a club, to the formality and mechanical regularity of the procedure, to the inflation of language perpetrated by both the prosecutor and the defense attorney, to the sarcasms of the presiding judge, to the browbeating of the witnesses and the misleading truthfulness of their testimonies, all of which culminates in Marie's tearful protest: "They forced her to say the opposite of what she was thinking." Camus builds a fortress of the French legal system with its own values. What invalidates the trial is its ease, its contempt for the court, its lack of remorse on behalf of the killer, its rhetorical glibness, its blindness to ambiguities, and its exclusion of any feeling for the real victim, since the only people who mattered to Camus were Europeans. Arabs were there to die. No more. Or as Julia Kristeva puts it, "It doesn't matter that Meursault killed an Arab—it could have been anyone." [62] A curious reading, to say the least! One further objects that Kristeva's analysis of the novel proceeds without regard for archival evidence, so that speculation is paraded as historical fact.

The same attitude is reflected in La Peste. The shopkeeper, whose reaction to a news item concerning a young office worker who has killed an Arab on a beach, proposes a solution of sweeping simplicity: "If they put all that rabble in jail . . . decent folks could breathe more freely." [63] Authority and discipline are not ends in themselves. Rather, they are the necessary stuff of which colonialism is made. The note is perfectly struck in a description of the Arabs that comes near the middle of Le Premier homme, wherein Cormery père fought in the Moroccan campaign in 1905 and witnessed barbaric killing. Two of his fellow soldiers were murdered and horribly mutilated by the natives, prompting the father to protest at the injustice of his coming out of an orphanage and poverty, straight into a military uniform and horrific violence. His outcry culminates in the explosion of his anger: " 'Filthy race! What a race! All of them.' " The same language of racial abuse rings out later in the chapter, this time half a century later during the Algerian revolution. In the wake of an armed resistance attack, a worker in the street calls out, "This filthy race." [64]

Notwithstanding the story of racism, the story of the plague, interestingly enough, is always interpreted as a parade or an allegory of the German occupation of France. In 1944, Camus acknowledged that the humiliations suffered by the French at the hands of the Germans meant that they must have incurred a loss of prestige in the eyes of the Algerian population. He nevertheless assumed that French rule should and would continue. To this end, he said, it would be very shortsighted if the French were to use force to reassert their authority over Algerian Arabs: "Our colonies will genuinely support us only when we convince them that their interests and ours are identical, and that we are not applying double standards: one giving justice to the people of France and one sustaining injustice towards the Empire." [65] The implicit suggestion that force was unnecessary presupposed that the natives would willingly follow French models and instructions, in practice through a policy of assimilation.

Said elaborates a more convincing strategy. "My reading of Camus," he writes, "and certainly of his later stories, starts with the fact that he, in the late 1950s, was very much opposed to independence for Algeria. He in fact compared the FLN [Front de Libération Nationale] to [Gamal] Abdel Nasser in Egypt, after Suez, after 1956. . . . He denounced Muslim imperialism. So far from being an imperial observer of the human condition, Camus was a colonial witness. The irritating part of it is that he is never read that way." [66] Here the point Said is making is sound, yet it lacks the depth and insight he offers in, for example, his reading of *Mansfield Park* or *Heart of Darkness*. Said nowhere mentions the fact that there are too many myths about Camus, whose life was short, deceitful, often squalid, and ultimately pointless: Even its physical delights merely made death a crueler joke. One of the most persistent of these myths, first propagated in Britain by Cyril Connolly's introduction to the 1946 translation of *L'Etranger*, is that he "played a notable part in the French Resistance Movement." [67] The much photographed figure with Humphrey Bogart features and wearing a trench coat certainly looks like Hollywood's idea of an underground hero. In fact, Camus derailed no more trains than Sartre. What he did do, from the winter of 1943–1944 onward, was to help the Resistance circuit Combat with its clandestine newspaper of the same name, which had been started three years earlier by Henri Frenay. But even after Camus joined, he only gradually assumed a leading editorial role.

A second myth is that his novel *La Peste* is simply an allegory of the Nazi occupation of France. This is a canard. To the novel's first readers, it seemed obvious. The plague was the enemy; those who fought it were members of the Resistance. But even at the time, the metaphor seemed faulty. Sartre points out quite sensibly that disease is everyone's impersonal enemy, whereas the Occupation was a complex phenomenon, involving temptation, collaboration, indifference, treachery, and moral choice.[68] Only a strict Buddhist, unwilling to kill even bacteria, would have faced in the plague city the ethical conundrums that beset Resistance workers who knew or suspected that if they killed a Nazi, the authorities would take savage revenge on civilian hostages. It is obvious, then, that Camus, who knew a great deal about guilt, was aware of the situation but chose to ignore it. So those of us who were reading La Peste as a straightforward allegory were being both too clever and too simpleminded—which goes not only for Sartre and O'Brien but also for Said, who writes: "La Peste [is] about the deaths of Arabs, deaths that highlight and silently inform the French characters' difficulties of conscience and reflection" (Culture and Imperialism, 181). Yet the novel contains no discussion whatsoever of the political conditions in Algeria or of the misery that ripped apart Oran, where La Peste is set. Camus always disdained the city of Oran, "an ordinary town, nothing more. . . . The town itself is undeniably ugly"; and if Algiers never ceased to be "the pristine city," Oran was "the black town" in Camus's novel. The severe cholera epidemic of 1849, which caused widespread loss and ruin in Oran, set the stage for its destructive history.[69] Unlike Algiers, Oran turned its back to the sea, a reality Camus could not accept. He was unable to think beyond the mental horizons of his French background, which looked onto the blue-purple Mediterranean Sea.

A third myth, still current, is that Camus was an existentialist. This is partly an offshoot of his being so often coupled with Sartre. The blurb on the cover of Joseph Laredo's rather too creamy translation of L'Etranger even alleges that Sartre was coeditor with Camus of the postwar Combat.[70] But the more time passes, the easier it becomes to see their essential differences. Even Le Mythe de Sisyphe, Camus's only work of anything like "pure" philosophy, published in 1942, which expresses his reaction to the "absurdity" of a bleak, indifferent universe, was no existential "leap" into scurrying political activity; it was an exhortation "not to be cured, but to live with one's ailments"—the articulate man's version of "the lumpen 'mustn't grumble.' "[71] Perhaps somewhere behind it was an echo of his work-worn mother, whom he chose over justice. Even so judicious a critic as O'Brien, writing in 1970, saw it fit to comment, "The defense of his mother required support for the French army's pacification of Algeria."[72] But it was not so simple. Camus's own position was inherently split. He was the pupille de la nation as a war orphan, saw the French presence as a historical given, and was not inclined to question it in any fundamental sense. In prewar Algeria, Camus had long championed the Arab underdog. He played what is called in Arabic lis 'aan al-mustamiriin—the porteparole of the oppressed. Yet while his first loyalties lay with the working-class French Algerians, whose lifestyle he frequently idealized as something spontaneous and historically innocent, he campaigned passively as a journalist in

1939 on behalf of the destitute of Kabylia; hence the series of eleven articles, "Misères de la Kabylie." He also strongly believed in a partitioned Algeria and had backed Mendès-France and Ferhat Abbas while the *colons* were calling for his blood. As his novel *La Chute* makes clear, he realized the inescapable contradictions of his plight.[73] The car crash that killed him in 1960 came too soon for him to see the sequel to Algerian independence, but history, he already knew, is not prodigal of happy endings.

Said hints at all these counterarguments but refuses to go into them: "Camus's plain style and unadorned reporting of social situations," he writes, "conceal rivetingly complex contradictions, contradictions unresolvable by rendering, as critics have done, his feelings of loyalty to French Algeria as a parable of the human condition"; he then goes on to show how Camus's limitations as a writer who championed the cause of justice are "unacceptably paralyzing" (*Culture and Imperialism*, 185). Of course, the whole essence of Camus's position on the Algeria question was that there was no real reason why a choice between the safety of his mother and justice should be necessary. Justice and the French presence in Algeria were, he consistently argued, perfectly compatible.

Yet another myth is that Camus was what is now quaintly called a "cold war intellectual." In 1951, the heyday of the Left Bank neutralism and fellow-traveling, when revolution still seemed to many a desirable goal and the Russian Revolution seemed a hopeful beginning, Camus published *L'Homme révolté*, an uneven survey of the advocates of revolt. It reaches a conclusion not unlike that of George Savile, the first Marquis of Halifax, the seventeenth-century "Trimmer": "When the People contend for their Liberty, they seldom get anything by their Victory but new Masters." This, naturally, drew thunderbolts of Sartrean abuse, making permanent the breach between the two writers. As Sartre puts it in what Olivier Todd calls his Sorbonnard tone: "You may have been poor once, but no longer; you are bourgeois like Jeanson and like me." Unlike Arthur Koestler, Camus was not performing a public *autocritique* of his past as a communist but tried to put utopian politics in its place. "Politics," he insists, "is not a religion; if it becomes one it becomes an inquisition." Only those who believe in the primacy of politics and dismiss other priorities as "reactionary" could possibly regard *L'Homme révolté* as a cold war tract. This has not prevented allegations that Camus was being subsidized by NATO or the CIA.[74]

One final myth bears a family resemblance to the cold warrior taunt. In 1957, at the height of the Algerian war, Camus was awarded the Nobel Prize for Literature "for his important literary production, which with clear-sighted earnestness illuminates the problems of the human conscience." In his Nobel address, Camus ignored Algeria, the war, the Resistance movement, and all the determining influences that marked his childhood and youth in Algiers. Instead, he spoke of high European art and the way he saw and understood what he called the "humble and universal truth" of the writer "impassioned for justice," while the country of his birth was going through unending misery. "Truth is mysterious, elusive, always to be conquered," he added.[75] The phrase strikes one as odd; it is, in fact, another lie. For how can a writer of his stature, especially at that time, claim to tell the truth and yet declare, "As far as Algeria is concerned, national independence is a purely emotional formula."[76] For Camus, there had never been an Algerian people with a native history, culture, and traditions, except, of course, for the *pieds-noirs* who

> had been coming here for more than a century, had ploughed and made furrows, deeper and deeper in some places, in others more and more wavy until a light earth covered them and the region reverted to wild vegetation, and they had procreated and disappeared. And the same for their sons. Then their sons and grandsons found themselves on this land as it was when their forefathers arrived, *with no past, or moral, or lesson, or religion, but happy to be so and to be so in the light.*[77]

So far from being an impartial observer of the human condition, Camus was a colonial witness and a committed antipartisan of the FLN. He refused to give up the idea of an Algeria that was special to France, *l'Algérie française*. In fact, unlike France's other colonies, Algeria was proclaimed by the Second Republic (1848–1851) as a whole and then incorporated into France legally and constitutionally. It was identical (at least in theory) to Calvados, Tarn-et-Garonne, and Bouches-du-Rhône. Henceforth, all that distinguished Algeria, now *fille de France*, from the so-called *hexagone* (the roughly six-sided mass of European France) was precisely a hollow, a space, the enormous vacancy of the sea separating it from *Maman-Fouance: outre-mer, outre-mère*.[78] Algeria continued to be perceived, spoken of, and acted on, both locally and in Paris, since it became involved in a subordinate filial relationship with the *Métropole* under which the old androgynous *mère-patrie*, or what Derrida has perceptively called "La métropole, Ville-Capitale-Mère-patrie," clearly lived on in the unconscious of "French" and "Algerians" alike.[79] At this point, it would be difficult not to recall Said's perceptive formula: "overlapping territories, intertwined histories" (*Culture and Imperialism*, 5). It could not be any other way. For Camus, Algeria was "un pays sans leçon," and only the presence of the French could provide the lesson.[80] Additionally, if Camus's commitment to the idea of French Algeria was the product of an unusually well-intentioned disposition, it also supposed the moral validity of French colonization.

Camus's trip to Sweden to receive the Nobel Prize was as much an occasion for controversy as celebration. A few days after the pomp and ceremony of the presentation, Camus addressed a group of young students and was unexpectedly harangued by an Algerian student, who berated the laureate for his silence on the question of the colonial war that was then raging in his native Algeria. The writer's visceral response to the tirade is now a central part of Camusian mythology: "No cause, however right, will ever dissociate me from my mother, who is the greatest cause I know. . . . I believe in justice, but I will defend my mother before justice." [81] For some, the outburst spelled filial loyalty, for others, tribal obduracy in the face of manifest social injustice and military repression. In the minefield of French and Algerian public opinion surrounding the war, the words were more a provocation than a statement of vision and reconciliation. What the episode demonstrates is a very public and painful testing of Camus's allegiance. Significantly, he couches the choice he exercises in the seemingly incompatible terms *la mère*/justice, thereby marking an uneasy confusion of public and private concerns.

Patrick McCarthy's introduction to *L'Etranger*, which escaped Said, shows his intellectual and emotional involvement, remarkable in someone who was only nineteen when Camus died, which comes out most clearly in his discussion of Algeria. When Camus was growing up there, the extrovert attractions of sun and sea added piquancy for two reasons: his tuberculosis, which cut him off from careers in football and teaching, and gave him an outsider's envy and energy; and, as can also be sensed today in a country such as Israel, the colonist's vigor and underlying fear. "Usurpers in this land, the Europeans had become its legitimate owners. So they faced the deserts and the droughts. Yet they remained less authentic than the Arab who became an object of fascination and jealousy." [82] The words are McCarthy's, but the sentiments pervade the depths of *L'Etranger*.

The novel's antihero, Meursault, shoots an Arab for no apparent reason except for telling readers about a racial category he fears is a threat to his identity. After hearing that his mother has died, he turns, as McCarthy suggests, into at least one other character, possibly two: from ignorance and indifference, he shifts to an awkward awareness of having "destroyed the harmony of the day" and then to the role of "the imprisoned innocent" — neither nearly so convincing as the Meursault we first meet. McCarthy quibbles in comparing Meursault with his homonym "Mersault" in *La Mort heureuse*. "Meursault" suggests a leap to death whereas "Mersault" hints at a leap into the sea, which Camus delights in. The "happy death" is that of Meursault, despite the fact that he, too, has committed murder in cold blood. If there were no benevolent deity — if the answer to appeals for justice, as at the end of *Le Malentendu*, were a flat final "Non" — then Meursault's indifference would become completely natural. The best one could hope to be was Sisyphus, with his joyless stoicism; the worst was this stony-eyed, numb-hearted, unapologetic killer.

Meursault's unruffled existence depends on his avoidance of public and self-scrutiny, and on his evasion of responsibility. The director of the old-age home and Salamanco act as accomplices in helping him perpetuate the status quo. In their first interview, the director tells him: "You needn't justify yourself, my dear boy. I've read your mother's file. You couldn't provide for all her needs. She needed a round-the-clock nurse. Your salary is modest. And, all in all, she was happier here." This is at worst another lie, at best a pious exaggeration, since we know that Madame Meursault was still a vigorous woman who, on her evening walks with Pérez, could tackle the four-kilometer round trip from the home to the village. As witnesses at the trial, however, both the director and Salamanco, despite their goodwill, give damaging testimony. One function of the trial, then, is to break down this complicity in the illusion of innocence that Meursault had effortlessly obtained from others and in turn extended to them, as when he agreed with Raymond's self-exonerating assessment of his brutality to his mistress, "She's the one who did me wrong. It was not my fault." [83] In Camus, the ambiguity of innocence and guilt is not so easily resolved, no matter how genuinely Said means and experiences the sense of revision, insinuated into the lines of his otherwise excellent reading.

The problem of *translation* at work is obvious here. Its weakness lies not in the elaborate counternarrative Said provides but in a misprision or slip in his thinking: namely Camus's *background*. The details of his early upbringing in Algiers in a poor European family—his mother was a domestic, his father died as a result of wounds received in the Battle of the Marne—are well known, especially with the posthumous publication in 1994 of Camus's fictionalized autobiography, *Le Premier homme*.[84] But as Todd has shrewdly demonstrated in re-creating the *mentalité* and outlook of the *petits colons*, who were taught to see France as having civilized an anarchic indigenous population, Camus was blinded by his own insights about his native Algeria. The centenary of the French presence in Algeria in 1930 provides a telling illustration of the triumphalist colonial mentality, with Louis Bertrand of the Académie Française musing: "I wonder whether for us, twentieth-century French people, there is any more glorious century than that of our conquest of Algeria"; in the same vein, the Bishop of Oran invited Europeans and Algerians alike "to come together as one under the flag of Christ's beloved France." [85] To counterbalance the imperial *grandeur*, the *exposition coloniale* organized in Paris was opposed by Léon Blum as well as by the surrealists. Significantly, these contrasting French attitudes, alternatively celebrating and shunning the colony, anticipate the cleavage in French life brought about by the Algerian revolution a quarter of a century later.

The effect of Said's private revelations is to renew interest in Camus's imaginary world, which includes Sisyphus and Prometheus, and muddles the humanist legacy they represent, namely Don Juan. But the figure of Don Juan is also part of Camus's abiding fascination with Spanishness, what Todd aptly terms "Spain, that second home, mythical, in the blood." In what for the *petit colon*-turned-celebrity was the difficult search for cultural identity—indeed the battle to belong to Spain, the country of origin of his maternal ancestors—comes to stand mythologically as a place of adoption next to his native Algeria. The mood of defection is further underscored at another level in *Carnets*, as Camus opts for the Spanish side of his family, represented by his mother: "All my life, through the person France has made of me, I have tried tirelessly to return to what Spain left in my blood, which I believe to be the truth."[86] Writing to Kateb Yacine, the Algerian poet, Camus pleads for dialogue and for the recognition of what he saw—with a stubborn naïveté— as a shared *tur'ath*: "You and I were born in the same place. Whatever quarrels there may be, that makes us alike." But at the same time, he opposes the self-guilt of the Kabyle Christian poet Jean Amrouche, who, at the eleventh hour of the colonial narrative, can see no place left in the Maghreb for French Algerians. In Amrouche's case, the self-loathing is acute: "Men like me are monsters, *history's mistakes*," and again, "Colonial France is racist, greedy, oppressive, inhuman, destructive."[87] Camus countered this charge, appealing *beyond* history, and apparently in all sincerity, to the poetry of a shared landscape and destiny. Additionally, he was scathing about the injustice of stereotyping, lambasting the French press for giving the impression that Algeria contained a million *colons* with a whip in one hand and a cigar in the other. Indeed, his defense of the *petits blancs* remained as obdurate as the group he was describing, while for that section of French society that most opposed them, the "soft" Left, he reserved the condescending macho label of *la gauche femelle*.[88] But his cause was never that of the racist *pieds noirs*—he had campaigned all his life for universal suffrage. The messianic promises of the revolution (not only in Algeria but also elsewhere in the Third World) were simply false. Women were forced to wear the veil again; there was corruption, injustice, dictatorship, and social regression; and, for thirty years, no free elections were held. The present civil war—the aftermath—has already cost at least one hundred thousand lives. The figure that emerges from Said's revision is one often bruised by collisions and tests of loyalty. In contextualizing Camus for us, Said re-creates the *mentalité* of the age, even if he does not succeed in showing Camus's concealed side, which I certainly would not have surmised without his instigation.

4

Nevertheless, the prestige of Said and the sheer influence of his thought on English literature and culture marks both a new phase and one of the high points of the postcolonial movement. Anyone who has studied literature and/or culture cannot, when confronted by his method, fail to recognize how the originality and force of his achievement, stemming from individual talent, are combined with an attentive, painstaking, and close working-out of the argument—with that craftsmanship of the artisan as *mujtah'id* and/or *mufassir* in which postcolonialists take pride. He is a tutelary figure for dozens of artists who constitute, in a free-form way, a postcolonial emergent arts scene. *Culture and Imperialism* crowns a long and prolific writing career. It is an astonishingly learned, versatile study, which sweeps from Austen to Conrad, from James to Fanon, from English literature to Verdian Opera, from brash journalism to political activism. Its chapters are less phases of an unfolding case than lavish textual tapestries, dense works in which Nietzsche, Raymond Williams, Naipaul, and Salmon Rushdie are packed cheek by jowl.

From aesthetics to *Season of Migration to the North*, from Foucauldian recovery to Fanonist resistance, the Empire motif is turned like a crystal to the light to display its various facets. If its economies of negotiation, circulation, and exchange can shed light on the fixity of the dividing lines between domination and resistance, it also delves into the politics of postmodernism or contemporary nationalism as well as a number of related matters, all couched in a suave, impressively documented, dense style. Some of the essay's connections between past and present subjugation, as certain parts of the conclusion might suggest, have a modish ring, and parts of its treatment of hybridity (a topic well nigh de rigueur in writing these days) concede rather a little to exoticism. But *Culture and Imperialism* is a major work of literary scholarship, daunting in scope and subtle in perception, whose parts seem to profit from never quite adding up to the whole toward which they gesture.

Under Said's influence, literary criticism flirted halfheartedly with structuralism, emerged from a brief affair with Marxism into the grip of Williams, moved straight through Vico, Antonio Gramsci, and Foucault to culture studies, dived into anthropology, and teetered on the brink of postmodernism. Said himself emerged as the architect of a new field, namely postcolonial literature, a revisionist current of commonwealth literature, which scandalized traditionalists with its new relish for readings, analysis, and interpretation. He became a pioneer in "new" readings of canonical texts, while loathing insularity and parochialism as well as disdaining "flat-minded" approaches, an avant-gardist who had been hopping from one cultural cutting edge to another for more than three decades. One may well say that what has been unchanging about Said is his open-endedness. This is no doubt partly a matter of temperament and conviction but also perhaps a matter of his colonial origins. The move from Egypt to the United States was one between clashing cultural frames, whose partial, perspectival nature he was thus more likely to spot than, say, an American, reared within a wall-to-wall working-class milieu. Said was pitched between conceptual frames as well as countries, alert to the rough edges of any single doctrinal system, as heterodox in theory as he was hybrid in culture. It is no accident that he started with a doctoral dissertation entitled "Joseph Conrad and the Fiction of Autobiography," hardly the most congenial of topics, but of obvious appeal to a student of intercultural relations. As he puts it, "I felt, first coming across Conrad when I was a teenager, that in a certain sense I was reading, not so much my own story, but a story written out of bits of my life and put together in a haunting and fantastically obsessive way. He has a particular kind of vision which increases in intensity every time I read him, so that now it's almost unbearable for me to read him." [89]

His suspicion of full-fledged systems (Northrop Frye, Derrida, and Fish) is also, ironically enough, characteristically English. The most obviously alluring creed for Said, some sort of Marxism, was one with a notoriously vexed relation to the conditions of the colonized, so that he was bound to come at it left-handedly. He never reneged on revolutionary Marxism, since he was never much of a Marxist in the first place.[90] In postcolonial conditions, culture is a vital medium of power, and culture had never exactly been Marxism's strongest point. If culture is integral to colonial power, however, it is equally central to advanced capitalism, so that Said was able to transport his "culturalism" from the colonial periphery to the metropolitan center. The colonial background that set him askew to classical capitalism—he sprang from the liberal Arab upper class and inherited its habits of thought along with its assumptions of privilege—was also, paradoxically, what lent power to his elbow as a commentator on a media-ridden, postimperial West, for which culture has become increasingly a significant political issue and which is now undergoing in its own way the kind of identity crisis it once induced in its colonials. With pure chance, Said's move to America coincided with the dreadfully corrupt King Farouk's waddle off to Europe and Abdel Nasser and his free officers' takeover. Nothing is more native to the colonies than getting out of them.

Displacement tossed the problems of culture and identity into the metropolitan heartland, which Said, as an intellectual as well as an exile, was peculiarly well-placed to dissect—so in this sense, too, the margins shifted with him to the center. His in-betweenness meant a heightened awareness of questions about his own as well as other cultures and peoples. Nowhere is this feeling more poignant than in Said's recollection of the relationship that tied him to his music teacher, Tiegerman, a Polish Jew who emigrated to Egypt during the 1930s, carrying with him a whole transplanted tradition of pianism and pedagogy. Said speaks of their friendship in nostalgic terms: "Its bases had shifted to an absent Cairo of splendid people, charming clothes, magnificent parties, all of which had disappeared." He also evokes Tiegerman's other gifted student, "a stunningly fluent and accomplished young married woman, a mother of four, who played with her head completely enclosed in the pious veil of a devout Muslim. Neither Tiegerman nor I could understand this amphibious woman, who with a part of her body could dash through the *Appassionata* and with another venerated God by hiding her face." He concludes: "Like Tiegerman, she was an untransplantable emanation of Cairo's genius; unlike him, her particular branch of the city's history has endured and even triumphed. For a brief moment then, the conjunction of ultra-European and ultra-Islamic Arab cultures brought forth a highlighted image that typified the Cairo of my early years." [91]

Reading the world in terms of culture is a familiar habit of the colonial subject, but it is also an occupational hazard of the metropolitan literary intellectual, and Said happens to be both. He has, however, blossomed into a different species of critic altogether—an aesthete, you may say, as *Representations of the Intellectual* and *Musical Elaborations* amply testify. Far more than Foucault or even Williams, and more persistently than any Third World intellectual, Said has been that *other* fine instance of the *strategic* intellectual, theorist as mediator and interventionist, political activist, and commentator, bringing the more arcane l-mi'rifa (knowledge) to bear on questions of televisual imagery and culture. Nimble, mercurial, and tirelessly up-to-date, he has nipped from one burgeoning topical issue to another, turning up wherever the action is, like a cross between a father figure and Mr. Fixit. In some thirty years of ijtih'ad, Said has become an icon of the kind found in Fanon, James, and Williams in their heyday. His elective genre is the essay, that most supple, tactical of literary forms, and he fashions it with a rare blend of metaphorical flourish and polemical punch. In contrast with the *identikit* style of many of his acolytes, Said pitches his tone somewhere between heavy-duty theory and learned journalism, at once quick-witted and high-minded, erudite, and specialist. He is an original thinker as well as a brilliant *bricoleur*, an imaginative reinventor of his own ideas. Indeed, he shares with critics such as Williams a certain impatience with abstract notions, in which one can detect both the political activist and the residual Jamesian. His concrete, contextualizing style of thought marks yet another fortunate conjuncture between what seems psychologically native to him and what the age demands.

This intellectual range is reflected in his personal serenity of being, which seems to contain multitudes. But if he resembles Williams in his apparent equipoise, he combines it with the irenic and *engagé* together. "The intellectual must maintain a margin of independence and must be an instrument of resurrecting 'lost memory,' " he writes.[92] His role as a contemporary intellectual is to extract from the language of the community and of the homeland an idiom that is capable of articulating both the principles that Julien Benda spoke of some eighty years ago as well as the broad moral interests that define Gramsci's organic intellectual as affiliated not with a privileged but with a grassroots movement. And what is perhaps still important, the role of the intellectual, for Said, is that of *witnessing* against the misuses of history and the injustices of the time that befall the oppressed. As Milan Kundera once put it: "The writer has original ideas and an inimitable voice."[93] Certainly Said is a writer in Kundera's sense. I am not suggesting that he pushes his ideas at us, or that there is something inartistic or insufficiently ludic about his asking us to think so hard. I am suggesting only that he uses his works to focus on quite specific questions, rather than allowing his questions to arise, if at all, from a world imagined for its own multifarious sake.

AAMIR R. MUFTI

Auerbach in Istanbul: Edward Said, secular criticism, and the question of minority culture

Edward Said has never left any doubt as to the significance he attaches to what he calls secular criticism. It is by this term, not *postcolonial criticism*, that he identifies his critical practice as a whole. The meaning of this term is a theme that he has returned to repeatedly since first elaborating it at length in the introduction to *The World, the Text, and the Critic*. But this facet of the Saidian project has received nothing like the attention that, for instance, has been lavished upon the concept of Orientalism or the strategy of what he calls contrapuntal reading. Nor does it seem to have been productive for younger scholars in quite the same way as these two latter conceptual constellations. There may even appear to be something odd about the persistence of this concern in Said's work, at least within the context of the Anglo-American academy. Could all this conceptual and rhetorical energy and all this ethical seriousness really be directed at literary readings of the Bible or at works concerning the traditions of Judeo-Christian hermeneutics, as a few stray comments toward the end of *The World, the Text, and the Critic* might lead one to believe?

Interpreters have often shied away from this aspect of Saidian criticism, despite its undeniable importance in the corpus of his work. There are, of course, exceptions, the most notable from my point of view being Bruce Robbins. But in Robbins's work, too, one senses an extraordinary effort at interpretation and a dislodging of the term *secular* from its usual meanings. Secular, Robbins argues, stands in opposition not to religious concerns or beliefs per se, but to the nation and nationalism as belief system.[1] It is, I think, an ingenious suggestion, one that I would like to hold on to for the moment in order later to expand upon it and also perhaps to recontextualize and partially to displace it.

I would like to begin mapping out the meaning of secular criticism by arguing that a concern with minority culture and existence occupies a central place within it. This is not an accidental concern, such as one might expect from any progressive critical practice. It is, rather, a fundamental and constitutive concern, a condition of possibility of the critical practice itself. Furthermore, it is my view that careful attention to this subtext will help clear up some fundamental and widely held misconceptions about Saidian criticism, in particular concerning the concepts of culture, canon, and community that it deploys. The Saidian critical position implies not a contentless cosmopolitanism, but a secularism imbued with the experience of minority—a secularism for which *minority* is not simply the name of a crisis. Such a rethinking of the meaning of Saidian criticism is, of course, an enormous project. I can only hint here at one possible direction this rereading might take. I shall focus on the repeated appearance in Said's writings of Erich Auerbach, a figure I consider to be a locus both for the minority problematic I am speaking of and for the misunderstandings to which I have already alluded. Said's turn to Auerbach will serve as a starting point or *Ansatzpunkt*—in the sense in which Said, following Auerbach, himself uses that term—from which I shall approach and enter the field of secular criticism.[2] Along the way, I shall argue that Saidian criticism carries certain definite implications for debates about secularism in the postcolonial world, that it offers the means for overcoming many impasses generated by these debates, and that these latter cultural and political contexts provide some of the impulse for the critical notions themselves.

There are scattered references to Auerbach and his works throughout Said's major critical writings from *Beginnings* onward—to the tradition of German Romance scholarship of which he was a representative, to the breadth of philological knowledge that scholars such as he and Ernst Curtius brought to their work, to the importance of Vico for his conception of comparative scholarship, to Auerbach himself as a figure of exile. Like the notion of secular criticism—and for related reasons, as I shall try to show—the meaning and function of this figure for Said have also proved difficult to interpret. One possibility has been to read Said's interest in Auerbach as an instance of his interest in philology—his treatments of Ernest Renan, Louis Massignon, and Raymond Schwab being among the other instances. Tim Brennan, for example, has made an interesting case for what appears to him to be the paradoxical importance of the European philological tradition for Said's critical practice. Said's relationship to philology is indispensable, Brennan argues, for his success as "TV celebrity," adding that "philology is what has helped Said matter to political life in this country in a way that many Left theorists and academic Marxists do not."[3] Brennan has read Said's references to Auerbach within this larger argument.[4] I shall follow a somewhat different direction here and argue that Said's concern with Auerbach as philolog is inseparable from his interest in the latter as a figure of exile. Auerbach in Turkish exile appears at length in the essay on secular criticism and returns repeatedly in later works, including *Culture and Imperialism*.

The importance of Auerbach for Said was noted in earlier responses to his work as well. In his well-known review of *Orientalism*, for instance, James Clifford pointed to the famous passage from Hugo of St. Victor about the loss of home and strength of consciousness. Cited by Auerbach at the end of his late essay, "Philology and *Weltliteratur*" (1952), an essay Said himself cotranslated in 1969, the passage appears repeatedly in Said's writings (on four occasions, by my count):

> It is, therefore, a source of great virtue for the practised mind to learn, bit by bit, first to change about invisible and transitory things, so that afterwards it may be able to leave them behind altogether. The man who finds his homeland sweet is still a tender beginner; he to whom every soil is as his native one is already strong; but he is perfect to whom the entire world is as a foreign land. The tender soul has fixed his love on one spot in the world; the strong man has extended his love to all places; the perfect man has extinguished his.[5]

Said has used this passage in a number of related ways. In his essay on exile, it becomes a means for arguing that exile consists not in rejecting ties to the home, but rather in "working through" them: "What is true of all exile is not that home and love of home are lost, but that loss is inherent in the very existence of both" ("RE" 171). The ethical imperative of exile is to cultivate a "scrupulous" subjectivity, one that will not undermine a keen recognition of its own tentativeness and fragility by seeking "satisfaction from substitutes furnished by illusion or dogma" ("RE" 170, 171). Exile must therefore be seen "not as a privilege, but as an *alternative* to the mass institutions that dominate modern life" ("RE" 170). At the conclusion of *Culture and Imperialism*, the passage from Hugo stands as the credo of a politicized cosmopolitanism equally wary of an imperial universalism and the beleaguered solace of tribal identities.

Clifford offers a peculiar gloss on Said's citing of this passage in *Orientalism*. It appears to him to signal Said's endorsement of the "anthropological commonplace" about "participant-observer" immersion in distant cultures: "The anthropologist as outsider and participant-observer (existential short-

hand for the hermeneutical circle) is a familiar modern *topos*. Its wisdom—
and authority—is expressed with a disturbing beauty by Hugo of St. Victor." [6]
The casualness of this series of equations is startling: anthropological fieldwork as exile; Said as a closet anthropologist; participant-observation as an
instance of the hermeneutic circle; and, perhaps strangest of all, the twelfth-
century monk as a kind of precursor of Malinowski. But the upshot of all this
for Clifford is that Auerbach marks Said's continued adherence to "humanist
perspectives" and the failure of these perspectives to "harmonize with his use
of methods derived from Foucault" (PC 264). Clifford is wrong, as Brennan
has noted, to see *Orientalism* as merely an attempt "to extend Foucault's conception of a discourse into the area of cultural constructions of the exotic"—
Raymond Williams, Antonio Gramsci, and Auerbach himself being equally
potent sources (PC 264).[7] But my point is also that Auerbach becomes a sign
for Clifford (as for Brennan) of a liberal-traditional and *affirmative* conception
of culture and therefore of Said's elite cosmopolitanism.[8]

Auerbach also plays an important role in Aijaz Ahmad's infamous polemic
against Said. To begin with, he too, like Clifford before him, makes a great
deal of the Foucault-Auerbach opposition, even appearing disingenuously as
a sort of defender of the rigors of Foucauldian "Discourse Theory," as he puts
it, against the purported eclecticism of Said's work, in particular of *Orientalism*.[9] Where he does in fact diverge from Clifford is in making Auerbach
the site of a psychological melodrama for Said: "Said denounces with Foucauldian vitriol what he loves with Auerbachian passion, so that the reader
soon begins to detect a very *personal* kind of drama being enacted in Said's
procedure of alternately debunking and praising to the skies and again debunking the same book, as if he had been betrayed by the objects of his passion" (IT 168). This passage exemplifies the somewhat blustery view of literary and cultural criticism that informs Ahmad's entire book; for him it is all
a matter of praise or denunciation, *either* praise *or* denunciation.[10] And this
soap-opera vision of Said as a battleground for a never ending struggle between Foucault (standing in for "anti-humanism") and Auerbach (standing
in for "High Humanism," the canon, "Tory" orientations) forms the basis of
Ahmad's entire critique of Said (IT 164, 162, 162). But Ahmad goes further,
arguing that *Orientalism* is in every point of detail a riposte to *Mimesis*.

> The particular texture of *Orientalism*, its emphasis on the canonical text,
> its privileging of literature and philology in the constitution of 'Oriental-
> ist' knowledge and indeed the human sciences generally, its will to por-
> tray a 'West' which has been the same from the dawn of history up to
> the present, and its will to traverse all the main languages of Europe—
> all this, and more, in *Orientalism* derives from the ambition to write a

counter-history that could be posed against *Mimesis*, Auerbach's magisterial account of the seamless genesis of European realism and rationalism from Greek Antiquity to the modernist moment. (IT 163)

From my present perspective, it is this characterization of *Mimesis* as an "account of the seamless genesis of European realism and rationalism from Greek Antiquity to the modernist moment" that constitutes the most interesting failure of critical imagination in Ahmad's discussion of Said, for it reveals what he takes the intellectual and ethical meanings of Auerbach for Said to be.

First of all, *Mimesis* cannot appear to even the casual reader as a "continuous" or "seamless" account of anything. It is in at least one important sense a fragmentary work, literally, consisting of series of close readings of small fragments of texts with no overall argument or theoretical perspective. (I am not suggesting that the work lacks unity, merely an explicit frame or argument.) It begins, as Vassilis Lambropoulos has noted, in medias res, without any introductory statement of overall method and purpose. Furthermore, its entry into the analysis of the problem announced in the subtitle, *The Representation of Reality in Western Literature*, is "surreptitious" rather than systematic, as it is only several pages into the first chapter, "Odysseus' Scar," that it becomes apparent that the purpose is not to analyze the Homeric text as such, but rather to contrast two texts and modes of description, the Homeric and the biblical—the analytical and the interpretive—and that the former is to be approached not on its own terms but through the latter.[11] Auerbach himself also speaks, in his later book, *Literary Language and Its Public in Late Latin Antiquity and in the Middle Ages*, of the constitutive gaps in the structure of *Mimesis* and in fact refers to the later work as a "supplement" to the earlier one.[12] He mentions in particular one type of discontinuity, the jump roughly from A.D. 600 to 1100, a gap he blames on his Turkish exile, an interesting matter to which I shall return shortly. But my real point here is that Ahmad, like Clifford before him, has fundamentally misread the significance of Auerbach for Said, for whom *Mimesis*, far from being a triumphalist text, is inscribed through and through with pathos, dignity, and the ethical. I shall therefore now turn to Said's writing in an effort to interpret the meaning for him of Auerbach in exile.

What voices are colliding in the Saidian text? What happens to Auerbach in his appearance on this stage? What sense can we make of the fact that Said turns to this figure again and again? The first thing we should note in this connection is that even as early as *Orientalism*, we find Said counterposing Auerbach's critical practice to the procedures of Orientalist discourse. Both *Orientalism* and the comparative literary imagination share, Said argues, the tendency to interpret literature synthetically, "*as a whole.*"[13] And while they also both emphasize a certain estrangement from the object of scholarly inquiry, they diverge sharply as to the meaning and consequences of this distancing. Where Auerbach's notion of estrangement—as expressed in his use of the passage from Hugo of St. Victor—implies a generosity of spirit, an interpretive "magnanimity," as he had put it in his late essay on Vico, for the Orientalists, "their estrangement from Islam simply intensified their feelings of superiority about European culture" (O 260).[14] Furthermore, "if the synthesizing ambition in philology (as conceived by Auerbach or Curtius) was to lead to an enlargement of the scholar's awareness, of his sense of the brotherhood of man, of the universality of certain principles of human behavior, in Islamic Orientalism synthesis led to a sharpened sense of difference between Orient and Occident as reflected in Islam" (O 261). In the introduction to their 1969 translation of Auerbach's essay on philology, Said and his cotranslator had already emphasized that for Auerbach "philology treats contingent, historical truths," that it proceeds "dialectically, not statically."[15]

But Said's most sustained treatment of Auerbach to date is in the essay on secular criticism in *The World, the Text, and the Critic*, which serves as an introduction to that work. Auerbach becomes a central point of reference and resource in the elaboration of the key terms of the essay, *filiation* and *affiliation*, and it is through him that Said tries to recall and to recuperate for the present what he considers to have been "the destiny of critical consciousness in the recent past."[16] Said begins his discussion of Auerbach immediately with *Mimesis* and the occasion of its composition. Auerbach's own comments on this location come in the last passages of *Mimesis* itself, almost as an afterthought, in the brief methodological epilogue to the work. Commenting on the many gaps in content as necessary and unavoidable in a work of this scope, Auerbach adds:

> I may also mention that the book was written during the war and at Istanbul, where the libraries are not well equipped for European studies. International communications were impeded; I had to dispense with almost all periodicals, with almost all the more recent investigations, and in some cases with reliable critical editions of my texts. Hence it is possible and even probable that I overlooked things which I ought to have considered and that I occasionally assert something which modern research has disproved or modified. . . . On the other hand it is quite possible that the book owes its existence to just this lack of a rich and specialized library. If it had been possible for me to acquaint myself with all the work that has been done on so many subjects, I might never have reached the point of writing.[17]

Said notes "the drama of this little bit of modesty" pointing to the pathos and dignity of the passage, to the multiple ironies of Auerbach's situation (WT 6): that Auerbach, the German Jewish refugee from European fascism, writes from outside the European homeland what has perhaps become the definitive interpretation of European literary history, the dates of composition of *Mimesis*—1942 to 1945—roughly corresponding to the peak of the Holocaust; that this act of cultural survival, of survival through culture, of the reclaiming of culture, is performed at the height of the modern self-conflagration of the culture of the West; and finally, that the place of this exile, the place of refuge that enables and even requires Europe to be apprehended as a whole perhaps for the last time, is none other than Turkey, historically the site of Europe's other, the Terrible Turk.

> Throughout the classical period of European culture Turkey was the Orient, Islam its most redoubtable and aggressive representative. This was not all, though. The Orient and Islam also stood for the ultimate alienation from and opposition to Europe, the European tradition of Christian Latinity, as well as to the putative authority of ecclesia, humanistic learning, and cultural community. For centuries Turkey and Islam hung over Europe like a gigantic composite monster, seeming to threaten Europe with destruction. To have been an exile in Istanbul at that time of fascism in Europe was a deeply resonating and intense form of exile from Europe. (WT 6)

Abdul JanMohamed has discounted the importance Said accords to the place of Auerbach's exile on the grounds that there is no evidence in *Mimesis* that this location—Turkey, the Middle East, Islam—exerts any cultural "influence" on the content of the work.[18] Said's point, I think, is rather that the relevance of this location, or more precisely, this dislocation, lies in the light it throws on the relationship between the critical consciousness and its object of study—Western Literature.

For what really draws Said to this passage in Auerbach is the latter's own assertion that his non-Occidental exile was the *condition of possibility* of the work itself.

> At this point, then, Auerbach's epilogue to *Mimesis* suddenly becomes clear: "it is quite possible that the book owes its existence to just this lack of a rich and specialized library." In other words, the book owed its existence to the very fact of Oriental, non-Occidental exile and homelessness. And if this is so, then *Mimesis* itself is not, as it has so frequently been taken to be, only a massive reaffirmation of the Western cultural tradition, but also a work built upon a critical important alienation from

it, a work whose conditions and circumstances of existence are not immediately derived from the culture it describes with such extraordinary insight and brilliance but built rather on an agonizing distance from it. (WT 7–8)[19]

Said therefore reads Auerbach's exile, and the composition of *Mimesis* during that exile, as questioning received notions of "nation, home, community, and belonging" (WT 12). The point of Said's reading is that Auerbach's relationship to "the Western cultural tradition" is *already* one of exile, a condition tragically dramatized by the literal displacement to Istanbul—the preeminent site of non-Europe—an exile brought about by the rise of genocidal fascism in the European home itself.

In other words, Said reads Auerbach in a rigorous sense as a Jewish figure, as a member of a minority, of *the* minority par excellence, partly in the political sense in which Hannah Arendt uses that term. For Arendt, minority, as exemplified by the Jews of Europe, is a condition doubly determined: it is marked by specific forms of alienation vis à vis state and society. The Jews, she argues, remained as a group outside the class structure of society that emerged from the destruction of the *ancien régime*. And what made them "the *minorité par excellence*" in the years after the peace treaties of 1919–1920 was the fact that no state could be relied on to protect their rights. The predicament of the stateless in the twentieth century, Arendt argues, is not "the loss of specific rights, then, but the loss of a community willing and able to guarantee any rights whatsoever."[20] The right they are denied is the right to *have* rights. In other words, what the stateless are stripped of is human dignity, that quality of the subject that has been encoded since the eighteenth century in the language of the Rights of Man.

A remarkably compelling image of this dynamic of "dignity" in the literature of the modern West is Peter Schlemiel, the protagonist and narrator of Adelbert von Chamisso's 1814 novella of the same name. A man of humble means, Peter is convinced by another man to sell his shadow in exchange for a purse that contains boundless wealth. Although he is now rich, because he lacks a shadow Peter is turned instantly into a homeless pariah—taunted by children wherever he goes, avoiding sunny places, subject to the scorn of "those well-dressed burghers who themselves cast such a broad and imposing shadow."[21] This narrative from the early years of the modern era allows us to see that the right and the ability to, as it were, throw a "broad and imposing shadow" is distributed unequally among the members of modern state and society. Or, rather, that the universalism of the category of citizen is itself brought to crisis by this maldistribution of "dignity." And it is hardly surprising that Chamisso finds a figure for this distinctly modern form of haplessness in the Jewish schlemiel. For Arendt, the philosophical significance of the modern phenomenon of statelessness, as exemplified in the Jewish minorities of Europe at midcentury, is that it represents the denial to human beings of those basic attributes of humanness that come to us coded as dignity. The philosophical lesson that the death factories force us to learn is, therefore, the following: "The world found nothing sacred in the abstract nakedness of being human" (OT 299).

For Said, the resonance of Jewishness-minority for the modern critical temperament lies in this problematic of culture and dignity. The political dimension of this problematic for Arendt is that the Jew is a person who is perennially on the verge of becoming a stateless refugee. That for a Palestinian the resonance of such a political experience should be enormous and complex is not surprising, and I shall return to that question at the end of the present essay. But what interests Said more directly here is the history of Jewishness-minority as the recurring occasion for crisis and control in post-Enlightenment secularism, and the possibilities it opens up for the distinctly modern vocation of critique. The German Jewish critic in ("Oriental") exile becomes, for Said, the paradigmatic figure for modern criticism, an object lesson in what it means to have a critical consciousness: "The intellectual's *social identity* should involve something more than strengthening those aspects of the culture that require mere affirmation and orthodox compliancy from its members" (WT 24; emphasis added). It is, in other words, highly significant that it is Auerbach—and, in Said's more recent work, Adorno—who provides him the model for exile, and not, say, Joyce and his contemporaries, let alone Nabokov, Solzhenitsyn, or Brodsky.[22] The victims of fascism represent for Said the paradigmatic instance of the "social identity" called exile. Through the figure of the Jewish exile, Said makes direct links between the experience of minority existence in modernity and the problematic of exile in social, political, and cultural terms.

In a brief but remarkable essay on the ethos of comparative literary scholarship in the postwar U.S., Emily Apter has argued that the discipline Auerbach, Curtius, Leo Spitzer, and others founded (or reformulated) on their arrival in the U.S. was structured in fundamental ways around the experience of exile and displacement. The globalized strategies of reading proposed by "postcolonial" critics, she maintains, therefore do not constitute the kind of break with comparatist traditions that their so-called traditionalist opponents often characterize them to be.

One could say that new-wave postcolonial literacy bears certain distinct resemblances to its European antecedents imbued as it often is with echoes of melancholia, *Heimlosigkeit*, cultural ambivalence, conscious-

ness of linguistic loss, confusion induced by "worlding" or global transference, amnesia of origins, fractured subjectivity, border trauma, the
desire to belong to "narration" as a substitute "nation," the experience
of a politics of linguistic and cultural usurpation.[23]

The form of cultural "literacy" that Said calls secular criticism makes an ethical imperative of loss and displacement. It holds, with Adorno, that "it is part
of morality not to be at home in one's home."[24] It sees minority as a permanent condition of exile and requires that in our affiliative efforts at critical
community and comprehension we assume the posture of minority. The implications of such a critical project for, among other things, secularism in the
postcolonial world are enormous and have not even begun to be explored. The
significance of the exiled German Jewish author of *Mimesis* for such a project
therefore lies in the fact that "we have in Auerbach an instance both of filiation with his natal culture and, because of exile, *affiliation* with it through critical consciousness and scholarly work" (WT 16).

This problematic of the displacement of culture and authority, which Apter
and Said rightly emphasize in their interpretation of Auerbach, becomes
explicit in "Philology and *Weltliteratur*," Auerbach's late reflections on the
method and significance of comparative literary scholarship. Auerbach proposes a method for the contemporary philologist that is almost an anti-
method. The work of philology, he insists, is still the large synthesis, a comprehension of the whole—ultimately, of human experience or world history
as such. But such synthesis can proceed only by means that appear limited,
partial, and local: "in order to accomplish a major work of synthesis it is imperative to locate a point of departure [*Ansatzpunkt*], a handle, as it were, by
which the subject can be seized." This point of departure, itself concrete and
well circumscribed, must have a "radiating power" that brings a larger problematic within the philologist's purview. The whole, in other words, is to be
comprehended not on the basis of its most general or, strictly speaking, universal principle, but rather *contingently*, from one possible location within it
or a trajectory through it. For the choice of *Ansatzphänomen* is not subject to a
strict method. It emerges out of the particular experience and location of the
researcher, her "intuition," which itself is the sediment of the larger social
processes at whose intersection the individual is located ("PW" 13–14, 15, 11).
What is proposed here is a synthesis that nevertheless does not depend on
preexisting categories or at least is not a mere rearrangement of them. The
point of such synthesis is precisely not to reify the whole. It is this aspect of
the notion of *Ansatzpunkt* that Said turns to in elaborating his own concept
of beginnings, which he deems "eminently secular," as opposed to "origins,"
concern with which is the sign of a state of mind that is "theological."[25] In

other words, critics who read Said's turn to Auerbach as evidence of traditional and affirmative notions of culture and authority make the mistake of those readers who, in Said's own words, "will assume that [Spitzer and Auerbach] were rather old-fashioned versions of Brooks or Warren" (WT 149).[26] They fail to recognize that what Said evokes here is precisely the possibility of rupture in the purportedly continuous and seamless text of liberal culture.

What Said cites, therefore, is not so much the Auerbachian text, the text whose author-function bears the name of Auerbach, but rather Auerbach *as* text. It is a "worlding" of Auerbach and must not be confused with a confronting of text with context. Said's reading disrupts the economy of attribution and location within which the mutual relationships of text, context, and author are produced. That this "worlded" Auerbach should become in Said's work the source and the icon of a secular critical practice is therefore far from paradoxical. It is unquestionably true, as Robbins has noted, that the word *secular* has a long history of serving "as a figure for the authority of a putatively universal reason, or (narratively speaking) as the ideal end-point of progress in the intellectual domain."[27] Hence its association with elitism and its rejection, in the present atmosphere of the critique of Eurocentrism, by scholars as diverse as Ashis Nandy and Brennan.[28] But to speak of secularism in general in this manner is to treat all secularisms as formally equivalent, leading Robbins, for instance, in this important essay, to frame his defense of Saidian secularism within apologies for its supposed privilege and elitism. Such formalism does not equip us to perceive the distinctness of what I am here identifying as secularist arguments enunciated from *minority* positions. We need only pursue Robbins's own useful insight that Said most often opposes the term *secular* not to religion per se but to nationalism, in order to clarify what I mean. *Secular* implies for Said a critique of nationalism as an ideology of hearth and home, of collective *Gemütlichkeit;* a critique of the "assurance," "confidence," and "majority sense" that claims on behalf of national culture always imply; a critique of "the entire matrix of meanings we associate with 'home,' belonging and community" (WT 11). It contains the charge that the organicism of national belonging, its mobilization of the filiative metaphors of kinship and regeneration, obscures its exclusionary nature; it can be achieved only by rendering *certain* cultural practices, *certain* institutions, *certain* ethical positions representative of "the people" as such. Secular criticism seeks continually to make it perceptible that the experience of being at home can only be produced by rendering some other homeless.

Said's use of the word *secular* is therefore catachrestic, in the sense that Gayatri Spivak has given to the term—that is, it is a meaningful and productive *misuse.* It is an invitation to rethink, from within the postcolonial present, the narrative of progress that underlies the very notion of secularization. It carries the insight that nationalism does not represent a mere transcending of religious difference, as Benedict Anderson, among others, has argued, but rather its reorientation and reinscription along national lines.[29] Secular criticism is aimed at the mutual determinations of the religious and the national, at the unequal division of the field of national experience into domains marked by religious difference. Said's insistence on the critical imperative of the secular can appear elitist, and hence paradoxical, only if we fail to recognize this minority and exilic thrust in his work, if we forget the haunting figure of Auerbach in Turkish exile that he repeatedly evokes. It is in this sense that we must read Said when he himself speaks of exile not as "privilege," but as a permanent critique of "the mass institutions that dominate modern life." Saidian secular criticism points insistently to the dilemmas and the terrors, but also, above all, to the ethical possibilities, of minority existence in modernity.

This concern with minority-exile cannot be understood outside the tradition, now well over a century old, of the Arab Christian contribution to the elaboration of a secular Arab culture, in which Levantine Christians, in particular, have played a prominent role. In his classic study *Arabic Thought in the Liberal Age, 1789–1939*, Albert Hourani carefully distinguishes between the Islamic reformisms of the late nineteenth century and the varieties of secularism propagated by a wide range of Arab Christian thinkers and public figures, reading in the latter not just an echo of European precursors, but rather "the expression of an active political consciousness among the Arab Christians." For instance, when Farah Antun, the Syrian Christian thinker and polemicist, calls for a secular state—as an Ottoman subject in Egyptian exile, we might add—he is doing more, Hourani argues, than demanding religious tolerance: "He is calling for a community in which [Christians] can take an active part, for a sphere of political responsibility." Antun's is, according to Hourani, "an eastern Christian consciousness," anxious to distance itself from both "the western missionaries, and still more from the European Powers who use religion for political purposes." [30] We may find traces of such a minority consciousness in Said's quest for a secular criticism, a critical consciousness constantly alert to the terms of experience of majority culture, a consciousness both assertive and on the defensive, both vocal and alert to its own quiet vulnerabilities.

A great deal of this critical positioning becomes visible in Said's writings concerning what is variously called the Islamic revival, Islamism, or Islamic fundamentalism. His journalistic writings around the Rushdie affair are a case in point.[31] But there is a particularly revealing moment in the essay that is Said's contribution to *After the Last Sky*. The occasion is a photograph by Jean Mohr that shows a number of young Palestinian men in a classroom situation, sitting on two rows of desk-chairs, with a large book lying open in front of each student. They are wearing warm clothing for the winter and socks but no shoes. The caption reads: "Jerusalem, 1984, Koranic studies within the walls of the Mosque of Omar." In turning to the photograph Said has the following to say:

> To look at the perhaps plodding efforts of a group of Islamic school students in Jerusalem is therefore to feel some satisfaction at how their unexceptional attention to the Koran—I speak from an essentially non-religious viewpoint—furnishes a counterweight to all the sophisticated methods employed to wish them away. I do not by any means refer to the so-called Islamic resurgence, which is what every resistance to Israel is converted to these days (as if "the Shi'ite fundamentalists" of South Lebanon, or "the Arab terrorists" on the West Bank, did not have the same antioccupation drive as any other Maquis in history). What I do mean, however, is that the local attentions of Palestinians—to their work, families, teachers and friends—are in fact so many potential breaks in the seamless text, the unendingly unbroken narrative of U.S./Israeli power.[32]

Who is the addressee of this passage? The polemical drive here is directed, first of all, at the metropolitan public sphere, highlighting the neo-Orientalist turning of resistance into terrorism that characterizes the appearance of the Arab world within it. Said points to the impressive ability of the foreign policy establishment—think tanks, the State Department, the news media—to assimilate any act of self-assertion on the part of the victims of Israeli violence to the text of subversion and terror. But what is Said's relationship to "the so-called Islamic resurgence," which he mentions only to say that it is not what he refers to? Is Said denying the emergence, in Palestine and in Lebanon, of political formations and cultural identities that may properly be spoken of as Islamist? What is the meaning of this reference that disavows itself?

I suggest that we read in this text the presence of a second addressee, that we read it as directed simultaneously at the inhabitants of postcolonial space. This double movement, I would argue, characterizes Said's work as early as *Orientalism*, a fact Said touches on in the introduction to that work:

> For the general reader, this study deals with matters that always compel attention, all of them connected not only with Western conceptions and treatments of the Other but also with the singularly important role played by Western culture in what Vico called the world of nations. Lastly, for readers in the so-called Third World, this study proposes itself as a step towards an understanding not so much of Western politics and of

the non-Western world in those politics as of the strength of Western cultural discourse, a strength too often mistaken as merely decorative or "superstructural." My hope is to illustrate the formidable structure of cultural domination and, specifically for formerly colonized peoples, the dangers and temptations of employing this structure upon themselves or upon others. (O 24–25; emphasis added)

"Themselves" and "others" here obviously carry multiple references. But the dialectic of self and other in the contemporary "non-Western world" cannot be understood without reference to the determinations of majority and minority domains, as the postcolonial histories of any number of societies — including Ireland, India-Pakistan-Bangladesh, Egypt, Malaysia-Singapore, Lebanon, and more recently, South Africa — amply demonstrate.

One of the few places in his published works where Said himself explicitly makes this connection is in an interview with Jennifer Wicke and Michael Sprinker, when he begins to talk about the "fetishization" of national identity.

It must be possible to interpret . . . history in secular terms, under which religions are seen, you might say as a token of submerged feelings of identity, of tribal solidarity. . . . But religion has its limits in the secular world. Possibilities are extremely curtailed by the presence of other communities. . . . One identity is always going to infringe on others that also exist in the same or continuous spaces. For me the symbol of that, in the Arab world, is the problem that has been postponed from generation to generation: the problem of the national minorities.

Shortly thereafter, as if anticipating the charge of elitism, Said goes on:

Obviously I'm not suggesting that everybody has to become a literary critic; that's a silly idea. But one does have to give a certain attention to the rather dense fabric of secular life, which can't be herded under the rubric of national identity or can't be made entirely to respond to this phony idea of a paranoid frontier separating "us" from "them" — which is a repetition of the old sort of orientalist model where you say that all orientals are the same.[33]

This, then, is the connection in Said's critical practice between secular criticism and the critique of Orientalism: the critical and ethical imperative invoked here requires a scrupulous recognition of the "strength of Western cultural discourse," of the conflicting identities it produces, of the "dangers and temptations" that Orientalism in the broadest sense poses to our postcolonial modernity — temptations that are dangerous precisely because they are temptations and not merely external injunctions. A major impulse behind the critique of Orientalism is therefore the possibility, the danger, that Orientalist descriptions take hold and repeat themselves in the very societies that they take as their objects.

Thus, far from denying its existence, the comments on Mohr's photograph have Islamism as their second addressee, as the latest expression of majoritarian culture. In the image, all the students seem absorbed in their "plodding efforts" and "unexceptional attention to the Koran"—all, that is, save one. Along the right edge of the photograph, a man has turned his head to look to his left, directly at the photographer, resting his head on his hand and leaning slightly forward, as if trying to enter the frame. Mohr's photograph is a rich and complex text—a group of young Palestinian men engaged in the performance of Islamic identity, with one lone individual cautiously returning the gaze of the Western photographer who observes and records the scene. That the caption identifies the location of this scene as the Mosque of Omar, that is, as al-Haram al-Sharif/Temple Mount, is also highly significant.[34] For it points to the ease of appropriation of the secular symbolism and frameworks of nationalism and state by emergent forms of Islamist politics. It draws our attention to the terrifying doubling of neo-Orientalist discourse within the nation-space itself, the national struggle for sovereignty and self-determination now increasingly cast in religious terms as a struggle over the fate of places and meanings that predate the nation.

Said's text raises important questions about the intellectual "in exile," a subject-position from which this scene can be described as cause for "satisfaction." I have suggested that we give this subject-position, this location that here allows the critic to gloss religious-political piety as a species of the "local attentions" with which Palestinians combat their dispersed condition, the name minority. The secularism that is implicit in Said's comments must be clearly distinguished from a merely sociological one, one that seeks to explain the rise of Islamic political identity by placing it within a sociopolitical history—of the failures of secular nationalism, the continuance of colonial occupation, of the hurdles in the way of bourgeois modernization. Its priority is ethical engagement rather than historical explanation. It is also not the species of postcolonial secularism—irreverent, transgressive, and voluble— whose most visible international icon since 1989 has been Salman Rushdie. It seeks to place the historic turn towards Islamic identity in majority culture within a larger framework—the "local attentions" of all Palestinians to their lives—that allows the insertion of other, minority experiences into the realm of national experience, thus displacing fundamentalism's sense of itself as a counteruniversal.

We may begin clarifying what it means in Saidian terms to affiliate with, to adopt the critical posture of, minority by noting that when he is asked to explain the meaning of secular criticism, Said often uses language reminiscent of Bacon and sometimes even invokes the latter explicitly, as in the interview with Wicke and Sprinker: "The national identity becomes not only a fetish, but is also turned into a kind of idol, in the Baconian sense—an idol of the cave, and of the tribe."[35] What draws Said to Bacon in this context is the image of critical activity as the breaking of idols. But this critical posture must not be confused with a naïve trust in the traditions of Enlightenment as demystification. The relationship of Said's critical practice to Enlightenment is dialectical—as expressed in his account of the dialectic of filiation and affiliation in modern consciousness. This relationship is routinely misread in poststructuralist readings of his work as the sign of a lingering "humanism."[36] Said speaks of a "three-part pattern" in modern consciousness, in which the perception of the failure or impossibility of "natural" or filiative regeneration is followed by a "pressure" to produce alternative, affiliative human relationships, with this "compensatory" affiliative order then itself becoming the basis for a new "hierarchy," a new legitimation (WT 16, 16, 17, 19, 24). The challenge for the critic, broadly conceived—and here Said is really speaking of the intellectual vocation as such—is to avoid playing a merely affirmative role in this process, to avoid becoming its "midwife" (WT 24). What the secular critical consciousness seeks continually to make visible is this "cooperation between filiation and affiliation," this "transfer of legitimacy" from the former to the latter (WT 16, 24).[37] This is a form of critical engagement for which an obvious philosophical source is Adorno and Horkheimer's perception of the route by which Enlightenment becomes its opposite, mystification.[38] It insists upon the possibility of emancipation even as it expresses profound skepticism about the transparency of all such claims. Secular criticism does not imply the rejection of universalism per se. It implies a scrupulous recognition that all claims of a universal nature are particular claims. Furthermore, and most importantly, it means rescuing the marginalized perspective of the minority as one from which to rethink and remake universalist (ethical, political, cultural) claims, thus displacing its assignation as the site of the local. Said's critique of nationalism is not made in the interest of an elitist (and empty) cosmopolitanism. It is made in the interest, and *from the perspective*, of all those who would be minoritized in the name of a uniform "national" culture—"the homeless, in short" (WT 11). Therefore, to the extent that it implies a "cosmopolitanism"—that is, to the extent that it calls for a community of interpretation not based on the accidents of birth and always points, albeit asymptotically, toward the world as horizon—this is a cosmopolitanism of "stepchildren," and not of "the ruling kind," to use terms that Anita Desai has made meaningful in this context in *Baumgartner's Bombay*, her remarkable novel of Jewish exile and postcolonial affiliations.[39]

But if the community of criticism implied by Said is not formed under the intact and triumphalist sign of the universal, neither can it be conceived of as a sort of rainbow coalition of already existing (minority) identities. It requires the "secularization" of minority itself as a position within the social process to which may be imputed, in the Lukácsian sense, a consciousness of the social in medias res. For Said, minority is criticism, a fact that is obfuscated whenever and wherever actually existing minorities succumb to the "temptations" of "orientalism." For Said, therefore, the significance of minority for modern consciousness has nothing to do with the possibilities for separate existence of empirical minorities. His is a critique of minority separatism, the mode of political and cultural behavior that corresponds to the minority's desire to become a majority. The true meaning of minority for him lies in the vantage it allows on majority itself, the critique it makes possible of all forms of living based upon notions of being "at home" and "in place" (WT 8).

In the two decades since the Iranian Revolution, it has become an increasingly common perception—vague and general for the most part, but occasionally unnerving in its clarity—that the fate of the great secularization project of eighteenth-century Europe is being determined in the contemporary postcolonial world. It is a historical situation of enormous complexity—one producing, as Spivak has noted, distinctive forms of inversion and alienation, "asymmetrical reflections, as in a cracked mirror," and the dislodging of meanings from their "proper" domains.[40] The articulation between the process of global expansion of a regional (that is, European) bourgeoisie and the "sublation" of Christianity into secular ethics and politics is, she argues, a contingent one, but is routinely misread as the unfolding of (modern) society's "Law of Motion," the process of merely extending the fully formed European project of modernity to non-European spaces ("R" 239, 240). Marx and Engels already noted in the Manifesto that the European bourgeoisie is forced, by the nature of the production process in which it engages, to draw "all, even the most barbarian, nations into civilisation. . . . It compels all nations, on pain of extinction, to adopt the bourgeois mode of production; it compels them to introduce what it calls civilisation into their midst, i.e., to become bourgeois themselves." What they could not fully conceive of, but a conception of which is nevertheless compatible with the contingency that they ascribe to modern "civilisation," is the possibility that this attempt to create "a world after its own image" transforms the original itself.[41] As an ever increasing body of scholarship has demonstrated in recent years, the Western bourgeois subject is caught from its very inception between an impulse to reproduce sameness and a postulation of (colonial) difference. Sameness, articulated in the figure and the speech of the other, is displaced and made other than itself.[42] The failure to grasp this, whether in the name of the universalism of Western "values" and the end of history or in the defense of native "tradition," results in the erroneous presupposition that, as Spivak writes, "Reason itself is European" ("R" 240).

It is therefore not surprising that one of the salient dimensions of the contemporary crisis of postcolonial societies is expressed in debates about the purportedly European provenance of secularism.[43] One increasingly visible critical tendency has come to rely on what I shall call, dislodging Adorno's formulation from its own "proper" domain, the jargon of authenticity. In a famous argument about the meaning of secularism in modern Indian life, Nandy, for instance, has subsumed the Indian trajectory of this "idea" under the rubric of "imperialism of categories" ("PS" 71, 69). Secularism, contends Nandy, is an "import" from nineteenth-century Europe into Indian society and furthermore is the cultural banner of the dominant elite, so that to "accept the ideology of secularism is to accept the ideologies of progress and modernity as the new justifications of domination" ("PS" 71, 90). While it may appear at first that such a view is derived from the critique of Orientalism that Said has inaugurated, nothing could in fact be further from the truth, and it is a critical task of the utmost importance that we distinguish carefully between them.

Nandy critiques secularism in the name of Indian traditions of tolerance, for whose embodiment he often turns to the figure of Gandhi, conceiving of him naïvely as a sort of Archimedean point outside Indian modernity. He relies on a false dichotomy of religion as "faith" and as "ideology" and locates in the former a resistance to the modernizing juggernaut of the nation-state, which "always prefers to deal with religious ideologies rather than with faiths." By "faith" Nandy means "religion as a way of life, a tradition which is definitionally non-monolithic and operationally plural" ("PS" 70). Nandy's formulation is based, first of all, on a failure to recognize that the resources of "faith" itself in colonial and postcolonial modernity have come to be appropriated, shaped, and saturated by the political. The manner in which Islamic fundamentalist movements can mobilize, for their own political ends, social groupings whose religious life is judged in fundamentalist theology to be heterodox and even un-Islamic is a case in point. And the forces of Hindutva are quite capable of attracting to their kar sevas, or religio-political mobilizations, and of persuading to vote for the Bharatiya Janata Party individuals who at other times quite unself-consciously seek benediction at the shrine of the thirteenth-century Sufi saint Hazrat Nizamuddin.

Secondly, Nandy's elevation of "faith" over what he considers modern, ideological religion is based on a nostalgic notion of the syncretic nature of traditional Indian religious life, a syncretism that is then understood as the basis for indigenous forms of religious tolerance and coexistence. The first difficulty with syncretistic notions like Nandy's "faith" is that the practices that are described by the observer as syncretic are typically not conceived as such by their practitioners, as Gauri Viswanathan has noted.[44] The logics of cultural difference proper to them remain, by definition, invisible to the syncretism-invoking modern observer. Hence the circularity inherent in accounts of a syncretic premodern: all they say about the past is that it was not like the present. Furthermore, syncretism as a concept is by no means incompatible with secularism, including (and especially) the official variety. Facts —for example, that "200,000 Indians" declared themselves to be "Mohammedan Hindus in Gujarat in the census of 1911"—are not themselves transparent. If they can be marshaled by Nandy as part of his "anti-secularist manifesto," they can equally serve the opposite end: to shore up arguments about the popular basis for secularism itself. Jawaharlal Nehru, icon of Indian statesecularism and the bête noire of Nandy's argument, routinely turns to this image of the syncretism of popular life in order to condemn Muslim separatism as inherently elitist. "There is nothing in Indian history," Nehru writes, "to compare with the bitter religious feuds and persecutions that prevailed in Europe. So we did not have to go abroad for ideas of religious and cultural toleration; these were inherent in Indian life."[45] The only difference here is that while Nandy wants to protect, preserve, and extend this syncretism, as the basis for a form of tolerance that is religious and not secular, Nehru wants to see it transcended and sublated into a modern, rationalist secularism.[46] And, finally, whether or not it is historically accurate to describe premodern cultural life as syncretic, the problem of how to address religious and cultural difference under the conditions of modern life still remains. Within a nationstate composed of "equal" citizens, majority and minority are fundamental (and paradoxical) categories of political and cultural life. To propose the syncretic as a solution to the crisis of cultural difference under such conditions is both to ignore this basic fact and to take these categories for granted. From the perspective of cultural practices that are deemed minor, such a solution cannot but take the form of being subsumed within the majority domain. It is difficult to see how such a fate is preferable to the one promised by official, liberal secularism—being merely "tolerated." My main point here, however, is the following: no amount of talk of the plurality of "traditions" on Indian soil can erase the fact that these traditions have come to us in modernity differently located within the nation-space and, hence, differently and unequally authorized. The conceptual consequences of ignoring this are in fact on display in Nandy's own search for traditions of tolerance in Indian society. For despite gestures toward "everyday" forms of "Islam," what emerges from this search is an identification of national culture as Indic, an identification that, of course, has a long history in the conflict, now over a century and a half old, over the meaning of modern nation and community in South Asia ("PS" 86; see also 74).[47] Precisely because Nandy's critique of the secular nation-state is based on a gesture of disavowal—secularism as a Western ideology, to be countered by the recuperation of truly indigenous lived traditions—it ends up reproducing the metaphysical gesture at the heart of cultural nationalism itself: the translation of the problem of cultural discontinuity in the modern conjuncture into a narrative of the transmission of a cultural essence. The syncretistic critique of state-secularism inhabits the same conceptual terrain as this secularism itself.

To put it somewhat differently, Nandy's critique remains inescapably *majoritarian* in nature, seeing the crisis over secularism as a struggle entirely within the majority realm—between a tiny, Westernized, and modernizing elite, on the one hand, and the masses of "non-modern Indians (i.e., Indians who would have brought Professor Max Weber to tears)," on the other ("PS" 74). And it subsumes secularism entirely within the life of the state. While it is perceptive about the manner in which the postcolonial secular state manipulates religious identity for its own ends, it is incapable of seeing minority itself as a means of disrupting the majoritarian definitions of nation and state, as a site for the possible enunciation of secular claims on state and society. A mere denunciation of Nehruvian secularism is not a critical position within contemporary Indian society, for this merely replicates and affirms the self-representations of Hindutva as a popular rejection of an elitist secularism. This charge of elitism directed at secularism, which implies that Hindutva is a spontaneous resurgence of the subaltern, is bogus. At one level, all that the rise of (Islamic or Hindu) fundamentalism in South Asia means in social terms is that the ongoing bourgeois integration of society, together with the integration of the national economy into the global imperium, has reached a stage where it can no longer be conducted in terms of the culture of the bourgeoisie itself, but requires an appropriation of a petty bourgeois idiom for its cultural slogans. Nandy himself betrays a half consciousness of this fact when he says that he has "come to believe that the ideology and politics of secularism have more or less *exhausted their possibilities*," not that they have always been irrelevant to Indian modernity ("PS" 73; emphasis added). And he himself attributes this exhaustion of usefulness to the successes of bourgeois-liberal democracy itself, which has produced conditions such that "India's ultra-elites can no longer informally screen decision-makers the way they once used to" ("PS" 79). The danger inherent in the populism of Nandy's argument is that it reinforces and naturalizes, in the name of a numerical (that is, quantitative) majority of abstract citizens—as against the tiny minority that is the national elite—the privileges of a *cultural* (that is, qualitative) majority. In this sense as well, its procedures are no different from those of official secularism itself, which declares a formal equality of all citizens but at the same time normalizes certain cultural practices as representative of "the people" as such. The syncretistic critique of state-secularism is *internal* to the majoritarian terrain marked out by the state.

The (Saidian) critical imperative here is continuously to put "Hindu" and "Muslim" (and "Indian" and "Pakistani") in question, to make visible the dialectic of majority and minority within which they are produced, which constitutes the larger part of the movement of Indian modernity. The terms of Nehruvian secularism itself have to be turned against it with the demand that it "secularize" itself. A critique of state and society in contemporary South Asia that does not simply replicate the frozen categories of majority and minority must take as its basic premise the insight that the (Muslim) minority problematic continues to play itself out on a *subcontinental* scale, within and between three postcolonial nation-states. This fact is brought jarringly into focus at key historical moments, like the aftermath of the destruction of the mosque at Ayodhya, when in the rapid spread of the fires of communal violence a new map of the subcontinent seemed momentarily to have emerged, one in which the borders implemented over forty years earlier through the Partition of British India had been erased. Such a critique implies not proceeding as if Partition never took place, but rather rigorously examining what precisely it *means*. The arrival of Indian nationalism at the nation-state, which it viewed as its self-realization and the fulfillment of a historical destiny, required a partitioning of the society it had claimed to encompass and to represent. The problematic of Muslim identity in colonial India exceeded the categories within which nationalism sought to contain it. And this normalization of the categories of nationalist thought by the apparatus of a nation-state could not take place until this excess had been excised. Before "Muslim" could become "minority," the majority of the Muslims of India had to be turned into non-Indians. This paradox is always lingering in the background whenever secularism and its terms are invoked, whether in avowal or disavowal, in postcolonial India.

That Partition is not an accidental event in the life-history of Indian nationalism, that the division of the country is the only solution to the Muslim question with which it can live, has not been dealt with rigorously even by radical scholarship—for instance, Partha Chatterjee in his monumental work *Nationalist Thought and the Colonial World*. This radical scholarship, of which Chatterjee is a founding figure and for which his work continues to be a major resource, has sought to redefine the relationship of the intellectual to the truth-claims of nationalism as a critical rather than merely affirmative one. But in one important sense it continues to replicate the autobiographical assumptions of the postcolonial nation-state: it assumes an essential continuity of "Indian" polity from pre- to post-Partition times—an indefensible premise and point of departure. Chatterjee's work on nationalism represents nothing short of a revolution in our understanding of the forms of culture and politics that emerged in India in colonial times. It is an attempt to break with the projects of the nation-state and to make visible the disjunctures and displacements, the twists and turns, that the state naturalizes within a narrative of linear development as it writes "its own life-history."[48] The view of minority I am attempting to delineate here is possible only because of the successes of Chatterjee's work and takes these as its own condition of possibility. But it is also a partially critical engagement to the extent that Chatterjee's work reproduces the categorical structure that historically it has been the aim of the nation-state to normalize. The crisis over Muslim identity, which produced the division of the country amid a communal holocaust of unprecedented proportions, and which continues to resurface today in newer and more baffling forms, appears in Chatterjee's book as a marginal event in the life of nationalism, a placing of the "Muslim," person and problematic, at the margins of the nation.

The task of critical scholarship is to make possible a conceptual framework for a rethinking of "India" in which "Muslim" does not function as the name of minority. The obverse of this critical imperative is that Pakistan itself has to be scrupulously recognized, in the Saidian sense of that word, as an *Indian*—and not simply South Asian—polity and society. (This is a matter of more than mere terminology. Or, rather, it is entirely a question of terminology, and in this case at least, terminology is everything. For it is precisely in the language of geopolitics and regionalism that the nation-state seeks to normalize the Partition of 1947, translating the religio-communal conflict of colonial India into the "secular," and hence *acceptable*, antagonism of mutually hostile nation-states.) No attempt to think critically about and beyond the present impasse can bypass a genealogy of postcolonial citizenship. The abstract, "secular" citizen of postcolonial India has its *Entstehung*, its moment of emergence, in a violent redistribution of religious identities and populations.[49] Even as we are forced to use the antinomies normalized by the state— Hindu and Muslim, majority and minority, Indian and Pakistani, citizen and alien—our task is to make visible the work of this normalization, to reveal its unfinished nature.

In an important recent essay, "Religious Minorities and the Secular State," Chatterjee proposes that we rethink minority cultural rights as including the right to refuse to give reasons for one's difference. To declare oneself unreasonable in the face of the purportedly reasonable demands of the state is to refuse to enter "that deliberative or discursive space where the technologies of governmentality operate," thus staking a claim for the irreducibility of a cultural difference.[50] This right cannot be recognized as such by liberal theory, argues Chatterjee, because it undermines the universalism of the categories of liberal thought, or rather, introduces contradictions within them. Once such a right is granted—and Chatterjee here turns to Foucault and governmentality in order to move beyond the impasse of liberalism— what the cultural difference actually is could be negotiated entirely within the minority community itself. Chatterjee thus opens up the possibility of a distinct politics of minority, within which claims of representativeness could be fought out and tested. For the minority itself, this offers the advantage of (relative) cultural autonomy and the (probable) democratization of its own institutions. For the rest of society, Chatterjee hopes, such a formulation holds out the attraction that it opens up the question of minority rights to a *strategic* politics, thus freeing it from the frozen frames of the faltered liberal attempts at a solution.

Chatterjee's essay represents an important attempt to think beyond the present impasse. Particularly clarifying is its understanding of the politics of its own location; Chatterjee insists that the critical task is not "arguing from the position of the state" but rather exploring the conditions of a strategic politics "in which a minority group, or *one who is prepared to think from the position of a minority group*, can engage in India today"—a perception that is unavailable to Nandy's critique of secularism ("RM" 34; emphasis added). But in the figure of the *unreasonable* subject of the sovereign we may sense a replication of the relative positions of majority and minority that characterize the postcolonial status quo. For the minority subject's refusal to give reasons for his or her difference in no way alters the structure within which the minority is cast as the site of unreason and reason is subsumed entirely within the life of the state. It also leaves intact the *externality* of minority to the nation-state. Chatterjee's critique of the state's claim that it embodies a universal principle thus remains apologetic; the " 'minority group,' " he proposes we argue, "is an actually existing category of Indian citizenship" ("RM" 36). Give the minorities the *right* to a separate existence, he seems to be telling his potential critics, and it will give them a stake in the liberal state. But the larger problem in this essay is the same as the one in *Nationalist Thought and the Colonial World*, namely, that the contours of nation and state are taken for granted. The notion that what we are faced with is a problem internal to the Indian state continues to operate. The desire to defuse the charge—increasingly common and acceptable in Indian public life today—that Indian Muslims constitute a fifth column loyal to a so-called foreign power (namely, Pakistan) must not be allowed to produce a failure to think beyond the boundaries of the postcolonial state, a failure to rigorously question the foreignness of Pakistan (and, of course, Bangladesh). That the Muslim "problem" of the Indian state cannot be thought, let alone solved, without reference to Pakistani (and Bangladeshi) state and society remains in Chatterjee's article, literally, unthinkable.

The procedures of Saidian secularism are, as I have already noted, dialectical. In Saidian terms, to adopt the posture of minority—"to think from the position of a minority group" (in Chatterjee's words)—is first of all to renounce one's sense of comfort in one's own (national) home, that "quasi-religious authority of being comfortably at home among one's people" (WT 16). It is not simply to demand a separate existence for minorities—a demand not so incompatible with the classic liberal paradigm for tolerance as is sometimes assumed—but rather to engage in a permanent and immanent critique of the structures of identity and thought in which the relative positions of majority and minority are produced. It is, I believe, with such a view of minority in mind that Homi Bhabha has spoken of "minority discourse" as that which "acknowledges the status of national culture—and the people—as a contentious, performative space." [51] The critique of nationalism from the position of minority participates in the modes of critique that David Lloyd has ascribed to minority discourse in general: it undermines from within the narrative resolutions through which the representative self is produced.[52] To turn minority into the language and gesture of an affiliative community is to critique the filiative claims of majority; it is to interrupt the *narratives* of filiation through which the meanings of majority and minority are determined, fixed, and internalized. Said shares the perception, common to every radical critique of liberal society since Marx's early writings on the subject, that the crisis over the Jews constitutes an irreducible feature of Western modernity, that minority is a fundamental category of liberal secular society. Saidian secularism is based on a scrupulous recognition that not only does minority not disappear when we make it subject to a critique from the point of view of the universal, but it is precisely universalist categories that require its existence as the site of the local. Said demands that we critique this marginalized, threatened (and threatening) existence precisely by inhabiting it, that we make it the position from which to enunciate claims of an ethical, cultural, and political nature. Saidian secular criticism implies an "ethics of coexistence," as Bhabha has put it in a different context, whose basis lies in the sharing of social space with "others," a "subaltern secularism" for which "solidarity is not simply based on similarity but on the recognition of difference." [53] In other words, Said allows for the claims of secularism in the postcolonial world to be formulated in terms of the *contingent* demands of peace and justice, rather than as the imperative of a putatively universal Reason. In order to be authentically critical today, research and speculative thought must turn their attention to the urgent task of elaborating the bases of this formulation and the contours of this contingency, rather than succumbing to an undialectical rejection of Enlightenment as (colonial) domination.

As an outsider to the Palestinian-Israeli conflict, one is often led to wonder how the life of a Palestinian intellectual can be anything but an exercise in daily confrontation with the whole history and legacy of the Jewish question in European modernity. Said himself is of course exemplary in the detail of attention, the ironic imagination, and the Auerbachian critical "magnanimity" he has brought to the entangled histories of Palestinians and European Jews over the last century. In *The Question of Palestine*—a profound exercise in historical, cultural, and moral criticism that is too often read as a merely topical and polemical work—Said turns repeatedly to an exploration of what it means to be the victims of the paradigmatic victims of twentieth-century terror, what moral ground such an experience can come to occupy, and what it implies for the meaning of "Jew" and "Palestinian" in the latter decades of the twentieth century. The book's magnificent second chapter is an examination not so much of historical Zionism itself as of that entanglement—the colonial provenance of Zionism's emancipatory ideals; the baffling displacements and inversions of the roles of oppressor and victim, militarist and refugee; and the continuing and undiminished resonance of Jewish suffering for any project of social criticism.

Said traces what he calls the self-consciousness of Palestinian experience to the first Zionist settlements of the 1880s, thus refusing to base his case for Palestinian rights in a metaphysics of national essence and autonomous selfhood. Throughout this modern Palestinian experience, he argues, "is the strand formed by Zionism." The goal of the book, Said writes, is therefore to describe the process by which Palestinian experience has become "an important and concrete part of history."[54] So powerful are the moral consequences of the Holocaust that the mere existence of the Palestinians, which puts the narratives of Zionist settlement and redemption in question, becomes a sign of perversion, of terror, of anti-Semitism itself. The solution of the Jewish question—and here Said cites Arendt's famous conclusion in *The Origins of Totalitarianism*—"solved neither the problem of minorities nor the stateless. On the contrary, like virtually all other events of our century, the solution of the Jewish question merely produced a new category of refugees, the Arabs, thereby increasing the number of the stateless by another 700,000 to 800,000 people" (OT 290; quoted in QP xiii). For Arendt, the significance of the Palestinian-Israeli conflict in world-historical terms is that the "problem" of the quintessential European stateless has been "solved" by the creation of "a new category" of stateless person, this time non-European. The state of statelessness has merely been displaced from (and by) a European onto a Third World people. But Arendt goes even further in the sentence immediately following the passage cited by Said: "And what happened in Palestine within the smallest territory and in terms of hundreds of thousands was then repeated in India on a large scale involving many millions of people." While her primary focus throughout this chapter is, of course, on the plight of European minorities and stateless refugees in the first half of this century, Arendt reveals here a keen and prophetic sense of the manner in which the crisis of minority and statelessness has repeated itself in "all the newly established states on earth which were created in the image of the nation-state" (OT 290). Said, however, reverses the trajectory embodied in The Origins of Totalitarianism, for it is now imperialized Palestine that provides the starting point for an intellectual and ethical journey that leads back to the history of European anti-Semitism and its devastating consequences.

If in the decades leading up to World War II the Jews of Europe had been thrust into the foreground repeatedly as the site for crisis and control, and at the end of that era had become the ultimate modern symbol of the stateless and dispossessed, whose physical extermination marked the crashing of the Euro-centered world, in the era of decolonization it is the Palestinians whose terrifying fate it is to be beyond even oppression, to paraphrase Arendt's comments regarding the Jews. For the global culture of decolonization, it is the figure of the stateless Palestinian—wasting in prison without recourse, on the move ahead of yet another invasion, pleading at the border—that constitutes something like the reproach that the Jewish victim of fascism represents for Western liberal culture.[55] Fascism's Jewish victims confront liberalism with the terrifying possibility that genocide is not a sign of its incompleteness or failure, but part and parcel of its success, that the successful bourgeois integration of Western Europe—the sanitized Europe of the EU—required the extermination of its Jewish-minority cultures and populations. Similarly, the meaning of Palestinian experience for the culture of decolonization is not simply that it reminds us that decolonization is still ongoing and incomplete, that there are societies that are yet to acquire postcolonial sovereignty; rather, the figure of the disenfranchised Palestinian, repeatedly brutalized with international impunity, holds up a mirror to this sovereignty itself, revealing to us its limited, formal, and ultimately farcical nature.

It is often remarked in the West that there is something arbitrary about the resonance of the Palestinian experience for Third World intellectuals, given the proliferation of oppressed and disenfranchised peoples around the world. Apologists for Israeli terror routinely dismiss this resonance as evidence of a new anti-Semitism. The meaning of the Palestinian experience is indeed inseparable from the fact that the immediate oppressor is the Jewish state, and not a classic imperial power such as France or Britain. But the crisis here is precisely that this is liberalism at its best. In its support for the rights of the Jews of Europe—that is, in its most inclusive and universalist moment—liberalism trips on its own categories and can conceive of nothing but a colonial solution, a solution "by means of a colonized and then conquered territory," to quote Arendt's damning judgment (OT 290). At the very dawn of the era of decolonization, the crisis of Jewishness at the heart of post-Enlightenment European culture and society is finally laid to rest by the normalization of the Jews as a colonizing people. What the Israeli-Palestinian conflict makes visible is that the problematic of European modernity has *always* unfolded within a field of global, colonial dimensions. It is Said's accomplishment to have demonstrated that it is an entangled history that escapes the traditional —national and continental—molds in which official accounts seek to contain it. A comprehension of its immense ethical and intellectual implications requires, he writes, "an ironic double vision," a vision capable of simultaneously comprehending the enormity of the Jewish experience in Europe and the disaster visited upon a people in the Middle East (QP xiii).

This complex awareness is equally evident in the evocations of Auerbach in Said's writings. In "Philology and *Weltliteratur*," speaking from this side of the defeat of fascism and the normalization of European culture and society, Auerbach had asserted, as Lévi-Strauss would in *Tristes Tropiques* (1955), that the fate of culture in the new world to emerge from the war was "imposed uniformity." But this standardization of culture did not mean for him a world at peace with itself. The paradox of culture a century and a half after the age of Goethe was that while "national wills" were everywhere "stronger and louder than ever," each nevertheless promoted "the same standards and forms for modern life" ("PW" 2). Auerbach thus distinguished the concept of *Weltliteratur* he was proposing from the earlier notion derived from Goethe. While the present formulation was "no less human, no less humanistic, than its antecedent" had been ("PW" 7), it was distinct in one important respect: "There is no more talk now—as there had been—of a spiritual exchange between peoples, of the refinement of customs and of a reconciliation of races" ("PW" 6). In the light of twentieth-century events, it had become clear that although "small groups of highly cultivated men" had always enjoyed "an organized cultural exchange," such activity had "little effect on culture or on the reconciliation of peoples" ("PW" 6). In an era when the "antitheses" of national identity are "not being resolved except, paradoxically, through ordeals of sheer strength," the ethical ideal of *Weltliteratur* must come to be imbued with a sense of its own fragility and also "help to make us accept our fate with more equanimity so that we will not hate whoever opposes us—even when we are forced into a posture of antagonism" ("PW" 7). The vocation of philology was now tied to the crisis of Europe. Said's reading of Auerbach is alert to the final irony that this ethically complex sense of the fate of culture in the modern world is undermined by a sense of fear and loss at the displacement of Europe in the new world that emerged from the war. "When Auerbach . . . takes note of how many 'other' literary languages and literatures seemed to have emerged (as if from nowhere: he makes no mention of either colonialism or decolonization)," Said argues, "he expresses more anguish and fear than pleasure at the prospect of what he seems so reluctant to acknowledge. Romania is under threat." [56] Said records his own sadness at Auerbach's barely suppressed terror of the non-European world and its emergence onto the modern historical stage. This fear compromises the ethical ideal of *Weltliteratur* in its very formulation, even as it highlights the necessity with which any conception of world literature (or culture) must now confront the legacy of colonialism. Where Adorno once insisted that in the wake of Auschwitz speculative thought could no longer take the form of traditional philosophical system building, Said is relentless in pointing out the manner in which the concepts of culture, canon, and value must be inflected in the aftermath of the classical colonial empires. The question that Auerbach finally poses for Said is a version of the same underlying question that emerges from his consideration of historical Zionism: How is it possible that a conception of culture meant to embody the dignity of the victims of fascism could be at the same time ethnocentric and, in fact, fearful of the coming challenge to European cultural supremacy?

The presence of Auerbach in the Saidian text is far from the unproblematic citation of liberal cultural authority that it is so often thought to be. The full meaning of this figure emerges only out of a series of historical ironies and inversions. It marks the critic's exilic-minor relation to both metropolitan and indigenous-national culture, first of all. But, with haunting irony, it also points to the exiled state of the Palestinian people, their history now inextricably intertwined with that earlier European history of minoritization, dispersal, and persecution.

RALPH P. LOCKE

Exoticism and orientalism in music: problems for the worldly critic

Worldliness does not come and go. . . . Texts [including musical scores and performances] have ways of existing that even in their most rarefied form are always enmeshed in circumstance, time, place, and society. — Edward W. Said, The World, the Text, and the Critic

The issue is not freeing ourselves from representations. It's really about being enlightened witnesses *when we watch representations. Which means that we are able to be critically vigilant about both what is being told to us and how we respond to what is being told.* — bell hooks, Cultural Criticism and Transformation

To be persuasively autonomous . . . a structure must show some evidence of trying to define itself wholly through some implicit and intelligible principle of unity. . . . [But] Western *music has been* [rightly] *assumed in most periods to owe at least some of its significance to a larger cultural network of extra-musical ideas or stylistically related constructs.* — Rose Rosengard Subotnik, Deconstructive Variations

[As a schoolchild,] I used to wish the Arabian Tales were true: my imagination ran on un-*known influences, on magical powers, and talismans.* — John Henry Cardinal Newman, Apologia pro vita sua

I

Cultural products are "enmeshed" in their time and place, as the first epigraph—from Said's essay on worldliness in criticism—puts it. But the concept of enmeshment in the worldly, Said quickly goes on to warn, must not be taken as "a euphemism . . . for the impossibly vague notion that all things take place in time [and in a certain location]." Such an unnuanced formulation would result in a "reduction of a text to its circumstances"—a reduction that critics of a formalist bent would rightly reject as fallacious.[1] Worse (he implies), it would offer little insight into the *nature* of the relationship between a text and its circumstances (contexts). We need instead to be open to, even actively seek out, the ways in which a text's "circumstantiality"—its "status as an event having sensuous particularity as well as historical contingency"— is "incorporated in the text, an infrangible part of its capacity for conveying and producing meaning."[2] Such a quest forces us to consider larger social contexts that often go unremarked in standard critical and historical writings about literature and the arts. As Said puts it, "A text's being in the world . . . is a more complicated matter than the private process of reading" because it involves two separate and, in some cases, almost incommensurable entities—text and world—as well as the "interplay, the constitutive interaction" between them. Furthermore, the work of the critic (or I would add, the work of some other "interpreter," e.g., an insightful performer such as clarinetist Richard Stoltzman or actress Judi Dench) adds a third entity that then interacts with the first two.[3]

Said's call for a "worldly criticism" may thus be phrased as a series of three related questions:[4]

—How intricately does a text enmesh with—how deeply does it incorporate—the worldly?
—How does such enmeshment/worldliness vary with different works and "recipients" (readers, audiences)?
—How does it change with the passage of time as critics, listeners, recreative performers (in the case of existing works), and composers and other creative artists respond (in new works) to a work's original text and the overtones that it has acquired through decades of cultural interaction—overtones that have inevitably distorted, enriched, and/or impoverished the work?

Such questions are not easily answerable. Nonetheless, many critics nowadays are interested in exploring them. Yet they tend to focus on such cultural products as movies, television shows, popular fiction (including Harlequin romances), mass-market magazines, advertising campaigns, the lyrics of pop songs (and the dress and onstage antics of pop stars), or the ways in which the news media define and portray groups, current events, and social trends (e.g., "welfare cheaters," the Persian Gulf War, or responses to the spread of AIDS).[5] These cultural products, however diverse in other respects, have two properties in common that make them relatively amenable to social and cultural critique. First, they are constructed so as to serve as, among other things, representations: of places, physical objects, peoples, behaviors, events, and social situations. And second, they are universally taken as such by their intended recipients. These properties have prompted a clarion call from another cultural critic, bell hooks (in the second epigraph), urging us all to become more skeptical and analytical observers of the images and other representations constructed for and marketed to us by various streams of organized "culture"—especially Hollywood films and television news shows.[6]

Nonetheless, this same question of enmeshment in the worldly—which is relatively straightforward in regard to many, though of course not all, books, comic strips, photographs, films, and other instances of verbal and visual expression—turns intensely problematic when addressed to almost any music, but particularly instrumental music. The relationship between music (especially Western art music) and representation has long been indirect, when not outright contentious. Indeed, there is probably no more central or perpetually vexing question in the whole history of musical aesthetics than the relationship between music and the meanings and extramusical signification that it embodies/reflects/represents (or may be said to embody, etc.).[7] Much twentieth-century musical criticism, especially of the more academic variety, has skirted the problem entirely by abandoning criticism and becoming *analysis*, the term usually used for scholarly writing that focuses on a work's internal structure and other elements that are (or at least are often described as being) relatively independent of context and social function, and therefore by definition, highly "autonomous."

But as the third epigraph, by musicologist Rose Rosengard Subotnik, reminds us, this emphasis on autonomy and structure (even when the concept of structure is taken in a richly "replete" sense, as Subotnik calls it, rather than a pedantically narrow one) ignores other, no less crucial elements, such as sonority, stylistic background, societal function, extramusical associations, and the performer's creative input.[8] Indeed, the autonomy stance ignores/brackets—or at least tries to do so, as a matter of principle—everything that is implied rather than explicitly laid out in the printed notes of a score. Yet (we reasonably ask) of an infinite number of possible meanings and extramusical contexts, which ones might be most appropriately brought to bear on a musical text? Music is, after all, a form of expression that, by contrast to the visual and verbal, is far less obviously (less demonstrably) redolent of the larger world of people and things. (Said has described music's condition as "mute," though of course music does speak to the sympathetic listener, a process that Said himself explored in some detail in his *Musical*

Elaborations.[9] Furthermore, words, in particular, comprise the very medium in which we most often articulate meanings and contexts—and in which the critic or scholar (the third entity in Said's scheme) normally works. To be sure, music often allies itself in various ways with the visual and verbal— for instance, in vocal and dramatic works—and religious and social rituals, as well as other music-involving activities in various traditional cultures— from female lamenting in Finland, to ceremonial drumming in sub-Saharan Africa, to gamelan-accompanied shadow puppet plays on the island of Bali. Far from resolving the problem, however, this merely shifts it to a different level, which can be expressed as a fourth question, closely related to the first three:

—What meanings and inflections does the musical component bring to the combined cultural product as a whole?

It makes sense to try to "get a handle" on this problem of music's social meanings by choosing a repertoire in which extramusical meaning or reference is strikingly foregrounded.[10] This essay examines one relatively neglected repertoire of this sort: musical works from Europe and America that were/are patently inspired by and evocative of exotic places, including one or another area of the East or Orient.[11] (A new attempt at defining this repertoire will be proposed at the beginning of section 3.) Certain recent musical developments in various non-Western countries are also briefly noted—developments that could arguably be described as "reverse exoticisms" because of the ways they treat Western music, particularly American popular music. My primary focus, though, will be on music of the West, and even more, works that are, to some degree, autonomous or self-contained (rather than frankly social-functional): for example, piano pieces such as Claude Debussy's *La soirée dans Grenade* (from his *Estampes*, 1903), symphonic poems such as Nikolay Rimsky-Korsakov's *Sheherazade* (1888), or operas and other music theater works, such as Mozart's *Die Entführung aus dem Serail* (1782), Giacomo Puccini's *Madama Butterfly* (1901), or John Adams's oratorio-like *The Death of Klinghoffer* (1991).

That I draw most of my examples from Western art music, or "classical" music (as it is widely known),[12] derives from a desire to explore the special problems raised by musical works that present themselves as aesthetically elaborate and demanding (indeed, have succeeded at this, to judge by the devotion of many serious and attentive music lovers), yet are drenched in social meanings. And these meanings, though broadly shared at the time of the work's composition, may today seem distressingly regressive—as we shall see—and thus, problematic to many who love the musical works themselves.[13]

Put differently, I am attempting to help sketch some ways in which the *con-trapuntal* critic, to use Said's astute term, might approach works of Western art music. Said uses the word as a way of stressing the background contexts that might helpfully be adduced in studying a work of literature that is set in, or alludes to, a colonized locale. These contexts might, of course, include the often repressive colonial system and its military, social, and other branches, but also the growing native resistance to that system, a resistance that in most of the world's colonized countries, finally resulted in a process of de-colonization that reached a significant degree of completion around the mid-twentieth century.[14] As Said has frequently noted, one crucial facet or strand in a contrapuntal critical approach involves attending to the aesthetic features of the work (questions of genre, style, and so on).[15] That Said does not always *stress* the aesthetic approach derives primarily from his position that it has in recent decades been all-too-normative in literary and other artistic criticism, including music criticism, and deserves to be challenged now.[16]

The contrapuntal critic (as Jonathan Arac and others have emphasized) re-sembles yet differs from a more familiar type of cultural critic: the "opposi-tional" critic. What they have in common is a willingness to probe cultural products (novels, paintings, and the like) for their social or, more specifically, political/ideological subtexts. Still, on another point, namely aesthetic values, the two types diverge strikingly. Whereas the oppositionalist tends to dis-count a work's vocabulary, imaginative flights, uses of convention, and plea-surable or disturbing innovations, the contrapuntalist seeks to keep both the social and aesthetic levels in mind while developing a sensitivity to their cre-ative interplay, tensions, and mutual dislocations.[17]

Submitting musical works to any kind of social analysis, much less a care-fully contrapuntal one, is a tricky enterprise. The works to be sorted and at least briefly examined here, such as those mentioned four paragraphs back (works by Debussy, Rimsky-Korsakov, Mozart, Puccini, and Adams), have the advantage (for the contrapuntal critic) that they are self-evidently "about" some other place and people. We discern this from the works' titles and other clues, as will be discussed further in sections 3 and 4. But are the works really "about" what they claim to be about? This question will arise again and again in the present essay. Put differently:

— To what extent do such works offer representations at all, and particu-larly, representations of life in the real world — that is, representations of what Said, in *Orientalism*, has called the "brute reality" of human exis-tence in a colonized and/or non-Western country.[18]

Or perhaps we might phrase this somewhat more epistemologically or her-meneutically:

—How, and how concretely, do/can we *know* what is being represented in such a work?

After all, the supposed geographic and ethnic location in which a work of fiction plays out was not necessarily, even in its own day, taken as "true"—that is, as a reliable representation of that location—even by those who consumed it. This frank sense of exoticism's untruth is certainly clear in the last of our opening epigraphs, drawn from the oft-reprinted memoirs of John Henry Cardinal Newman (1801–90), the distinguished Victorian-era theologian and Catholic convert.[19] The stories that enchanted Newman in his childhood were those of the *Thousand and One Nights* (the so-called *Arabian Nights*, which he surely knew through one or another of the translations available to Europeans).[20] In the *Nights*, fictiveness is a crucial and overt premise of the telling; for example, a character in one tale might pause to tell another, sometimes quite lengthy story. Yet we cannot ignore the fact that the tales themselves are a product of the Middle East, the very exotic region that they describe— exotic to the schoolboy Newman, that is, as also to most other Europeans and Americans. They thus might well have struck European readers, at least at times, as inherently "truer" than pseudo-Arab tales concocted out of whole cloth by Théophile Gautier and other Western writers.

How do we deal with this? On the one hand, the *Nights* offer representations of a region that English or French people understood as being—or like Cardinal Newman, claimed to understand as being—frankly imaginary? The *Nights*, after all, announce their fictiveness not only through structural devices, as noted above, but also through narrative content: evil spirits, people rising from the dead, talking animals, and so on. On the other hand, the *Nights* had been composed (or at least had been elaborated, refined, collected) in a concrete, not at all fictional, geo-cultural region: the largely Islamic world extending from North Africa to Persia, a region that precisely during Newman's childhood years (the early nineteenth century) was in the process of being conquered and colonized by the European powers, especially England and France. Hence, even the supernatural aspects of the *Nights* could be written off as evidence of typically Middle Eastern superstitious beliefs; and the more directly human behaviors—the thievery, summary executions, sexual excess (as it appeared to Western eyes), and so on—could be taken as authentic ethnographic information about what life had been like in the Middle East in earlier centuries and, to an extent, remained.[21] That, too—the rootedness, or the believed rootedness, of the imaginary in the real—is a question that needs to be examined below.

The present essay explores, in a variety of ways, the exotic musical repertoire within Western art music and the various questions sketched earlier. An initial overview (section 2) notes how the repertoire's profile has changed over time. The middle portion (sections 3–4) attempts to define more closely the phenomenon of musical exoticism, and how it manifests itself through musical and extramusical "signs," not least in works set in the "Middle East," an area that—being located close to Europe, and having at various times battled with Europe for domination of the Mediterranean and Eastern Europe—has long served as the region of choice for exotic musical works (as also for the recreational yet not unserious reading matter of children and adults alike). The last portion (sections 5–6) offers thoughts on the relationship between exotic works and the reality of life and culture in the countries in which those works supposedly take place—including the reality of colonialist control by one or another Western power. In effect, then, the essay ends up returning to our first epigraph and, by implication, the six questions set out above, asking:

> —How worldly (to use Said's term) might our readings of a work such as Sheherazade plausibly or defensibly be?

2

Would-be opera star Susan Alexander, dressed as an exotic princess, and sitting on a pile of furs, gestures dramatically and sings, or rather screeches, "Ah! cruel, tu m'as trop entendue! Les Dieux m'en sont témoins." [22]

Composer Bernard Herrmann's parodistic opera scene in Orson Welles's Citizen Kane (1940) is one of that film's most memorable moments. Part of what makes it so striking is its cultural savvy, its comfortable expertise about what it is satirizing. The Western concert and operatic repertoire has long been rich in—or some might say, clogged with—works that construct imaginative visions of distant lands supposedly quite different from the West. Herrmann knew this, as (surely) did Welles and much of the audience that saw the final product in the theater. They knew it in their bones, without having to consult some reference book. (Indeed, the filmmakers' original plan had been simply to insert a scene from Jules Massenet's well-known opera Thaïs with its similarly bejeweled heroine, a courtesan in ancient Alexandria; copyright considerations prevented this.) Moreover, they recognized that these exotic operatic visions could be by turns vivid, tasteless, haunting, enamored of excess, and contemptuous of the given region and its inhabitants. Herrmann's scene succeeds in being all these things—and hilarious, besides.

Or at least so it was in 1940. But the internalized dictionary of cultural literacy that people in a given society, or in a specific segment of that society, carry around with them changes over time: certain "entries" get added, others get expanded or condensed, and still others drop out altogether. One entry that has nearly vanished for many people today is, precisely, the pampered "Oriental" princess that Welles and Herrmann satirized.[23] Nonetheless, as a whole, the "Orient" and other such invented exotic regions conjured up by generations of writers, scenic designers, and composers have survived rather well and continue to form part of our assumed but largely unacknowledged body of cultural knowledge. (Who the "us" is in such statements will be addressed shortly.)

These exotic regions remain familiar largely because a few prominent works, often using specific exotic "codes," still thrive in our musical life, and still speak to a wide range of listeners and opera fans today, at least as much as they did (though not necessarily in the same way that they did) in 1940, in the 1870s, or working our way back to Mozart, in the 1780s. To be sure, the phenomenon is not unique to exotic works: the concert hall and opera house repertoire as a whole consists primarily of "old" works (Bach, Mozart, Beethoven, Verdi, Brahms, Tchaikovsky, Debussy, some Stravinsky, and so on), a phenomenon found to a large extent also in art museums, but nearly unknown in certain other branches of literature and the performing arts.[24] Yet, whereas the broad cultural ripples of, say, Beethoven's Fifth Symphony are tricky to assess, certain equally hardy exotic works set among foreigners (or among other others, e.g., peasants, as will be noted in a bit, or Gershwin's denizens of Catfish Row) can be shown to have reinforced—and to reinforce today—in a wide sector of the populace a whole range of musical and musico-dramatic images and stereotypes of the given country or racial/ethnic group.

This impact is particularly evident in certain operas and other music theater works. Several of the best-loved items in the repertoire portray an exotic locale: *Carmen* (with its Spanish gypsy heroine, 1875), Giuseppe Verdi's *Aida* (ancient Egypt and Ethiopia, 1871), and Puccini's *Madama Butterfly* (Japan, 1901) and *Turandot* (China, 1926). From a century earlier, comes one of the foundational instances: Mozart's *Die Entführung aus dem Serail* (*The Abduction from the Harem*, 1782, set in Ottoman Turkey). Of these operas, *Carmen* continues to infiltrate Western culture most richly and at many different levels, its visual images and music alike popping up in distinctly middle- and low-brow venues, such as ice skating competitions, stand-up comedy routines, and children's television shows. (*Sesame Street* has long featured a cartoon segment in which a diva-like singing orange—yes, the citrus fruit—performs the Habanera.) And this is not to speak of riskier or more subversive reworkings of the opera's premises, scenario, and music by filmmakers of wildly different backgrounds and intents, including Peter Brook and Carlos Saura. *Madama Butterfly* has likewise found, and continues to find, echoes in new cultural products of varying density and pretention, including the play and movie *M. Butterfly*, the musical epic *Miss Saigon*, and popular songs and rock items ranging from Raymond Hubbell and John M. Golden's "Poor Butterfly" (1916), a sentimental foxtrot, to Malcolm McLaren's "Madam Butterfly" (1984), in which a modern-day Pinkerton raps his regret to an insouciant disco beat.[25] So the "us" that is saturated with musical images of the exotic can, at times, be quite a broad and inclusive one, not just the (supposedly) elite and exclusive "classical music" audience.[26]

The orchestral repertoire, too, remains heavily loaded with exotic works. Some of these were written directly for the concert hall, such as Rimsky-Korsakov's *Sheherazade* (based on the *Thousand and One Nights*). Others were originally composed as ballets, such as Stravinsky's *Firebird* (1910, set in a fairy-tale Central Asia; orchestras most often perform a suite comprising about half of the score) and Darius Milhaud's *La création du monde* (1923, set in sub-Saharan Africa, though the music, less African in inspiration than African American, features jazzily effective solos for clarinet and saxophone). And this is not to mention the significant number of dance works that do still hold the stage and contain substantial exotic moments, such as Tchaikovsky's *Nutcracker* (1892) with its Spanish, Arab, and Chinese dances.[27]

Nonetheless, the stranglehold of the old is by no means complete. In many and perhaps all of these genres, new exotic works continue to be created as well. Adams's aforementioned *Klinghoffer*, for example, puts various Palestinian terrorists and refugees on stage to state their case in word and music — not realistically, perhaps, but with a dignity rarely granted Middle Easterners in, say, Hollywood movies these days.[28] Likewise Middle Eastern in inspiration, yet strikingly different, is Sofia Gubaidulina's *Rubaiyat* (for baritone and chamber group, 1969), which invests seven classic Persian poems by Khagani Shirvani, Háfez, and Omar Khayyám (all sung in Russian translation) with music by turns scintillating and reflective.[29]

3

The exoticist repertoire within Western art music, when laid out in such neat categories, may sound simple and clear. Once one begins to think about individual pieces in it, though, one senses how problematic they are as cultural products, as supposed "representations" of a given place.

Indeed, I would propose that musical exoticism is, in a sense, a logical impossibility. What makes it impossible, as briefly noted above in regard to the remark by bell hooks, is that music is not primarily a representational art, in the manner of verbal descriptions or visual images. Still, music *has* been involved in representing alterity, or a verb I might prefer, in "evoking" it, in large part by allying itself with, precisely, the verbal and the visual.

Evoking seems to me the key. Existing definitions of musical exoticism—such as the ones found in most music dictionaries, encyclopedias, and critical writings—often give central place to issues of musical style. Jonathan Bellman calls this the "nuts-and-bolts level," giving it pride of place in his pithy and important introduction to the recent and first-ever book on musical exoticism: "Musical exoticism . . . may be defined as the borrowing or use of musical materials that evoke distant locales or alien frames of reference. . . . Characteristic and easily recognized musical gestures from the alien culture are assimilated into a more familiar style, giving it an exotic color and suggestiveness."[30] Thomas Betzwieser, in the authoritative encyclopedia *Die Musik in Geschichte und Gegenwart*, puts it even more plainly: "The chief characteristic [of exoticism, generally,] consists of the influence of foreign, especially non-European elements upon European art"; in the case of music, these elements are threefold: "The use of 'exotic' musical material" plus, in stage works, identifiably exotic plots and productions (sets, costumes).[31]

Focusing on concrete details of style and the authenticity/accuracy of the borrowings is undeniably significant and often utterly crucial; we shall return to this point at the end of the present section. But a too-exclusive emphasis on "nuts and bolts" can cause us to scant the broader and equally crucial principles of "evocation" and "suggestiveness" to which Bellman alludes above. We need, that is, to pay no less attention to what the music was intended to signify, and what it, indeed, meant to the listeners and audience members that first heard it. Furthermore, we need to have a working definition of musical exoticism that does not exclude works, such as certain of Gioachino Rossini's comic operas, that unquestionably evoke a place or people despite making little or no use of stylistic markers of "otherness."

I therefore propose the following new, and I think workable, definition of musical exoticism as a basis for our remaining deliberations:

> Musical exoticism is the process of evoking in or through music a place, people, or social milieu that is not entirely imaginary, and that differs profoundly from the "home" country or culture in attitudes, customs, and morals. More precisely, it is the process of evoking a place (etc.) that is *perceived* as different from home by the people making and receiving the exoticist cultural product.

This definition is, of course, woefully incomplete. It does not resolve or even raise the question of how music interacts with other (nonmusical) elements in a work in order to evoke. It also skirts the issue of how much the resulting music must sound like, or even seem to sound like, the music of the region or culture in question. In other words, it leaves unmentioned—though, please note, does not exclude—the very factor that previous definitions have taken to be the foundational (necessary and sufficient) indicator of musical exoticism. But it sets us on a path that I hope may eventually allow us to deal, at least in a preliminary fashion, with those questions and others.

I should add that the definition focuses on place rather than time as an indicator of the exotic. Arguments have been persuasively made for "antiquity as a site of Exoticism." [32] My definition certainly allows selected evocations of the ancient, including biblical, world to be considered exotic—for instance, Felix Mendelssohn's "War March of the Priests" (from *Athalie*), Massenet's *Hérodiade*, and Maurice Ravel's *Daphnis et Chloë*—but the findings of art historian Frederick Bohrer and others should warn us against a tendency to subsume, say, all operas set in ancient Rome—for example, George Frideric Handel's *Giulio Cesare*, Mozart's *Idomeneo*, or Richard Wagner's *Rienzi*—into the category of the exotic. Unlike the ancient Greeks or, even more so, Babylonians, Romans were most often viewed as the immediate forebears of "the West," praised for holding values and behaviors dear to modern-day readers and audiences.[33] To the extent that Julius Caesar was not perceived as "differing profoundly" (hence, not felt as essentially other), his Roman world, and most musical evocations of it (such as by Handel), were not in any significant sense exotic. Indeed, nobody to my knowledge has argued otherwise, has spoken of, say, "Mozart's exotic *Idomeneo*." In contrast, a search for an exotic alternative does very much seem to be part of the current fascination with certain aspects of the historical past, notably the Middle Ages, as seen in the wildlife success of CDs of Gregorian chants and the like, all marketed as entertainment at once escapist and restorative, the musical equivalent of a good back rub at an island getaway.

We could work out from this definition by extrapolating a somewhat elementary typology of different *varieties* of musical exoticism. One could, for example, distinguish between pieces by chronology and style (such as baroque or romantic), by "nation being evoked" (e.g., Spanish bolero, Hungarian czardas), or by "nation doing the evoking" (e.g., works composed in France for, primarily, French consumption, as opposed to ones composed in Italy or Russia).[34] Familiar typologies of these sorts have the advantage and disadvantage of subdividing musical exoticism into recognizable, more easily treatable categories.

I prefer to stress various dichotomies that are inherent, to greater or lesser degrees, in nearly any musical repertoire that observers (including, not least, listeners within the respective musical community) would recognize as carrying out an exoticizing project. The most crucial of these is the binary distinction between the "home" culture and places figured as "elsewhere," that is, the dichotomy between self and other. Within Western art music, of course, the normative pattern assigns to the West the role of exoticizer, the role of the exoticized falling to the East or some other contrasting region, such as sub-Saharan Africa. But we should not forget that exoticizing tendencies exist in many musical cultures. Some of these might amount, in the view of people in North America or Europe, to "reverse exoticisms." For example, in the rock music and rap of certain non-Western countries, the United States and its heavily African American inner cities have arguably become the other whose vitality, energy, and style (as "known" through, precisely, recordings and music videos) are envied, imitated, and elaborated in accord with local interests and traditions. How much do Algerians or Filipinos, for instance, know and understand the (largely African American) cultural context of the musical styles and genres that they are absorbing and adapting?[35] How much do they need to? Must these peoples' own search for expressive authenticity rely to some extent on a relative lack of knowledge about the original contexts of what they are imitating (and altering), just as ignorance of the realities of Spain has been something of a precondition for the popularity of *Carmen* in the rest of Europe?

No less interesting and, arguably, problematic are certain works that blend East and West inextricably because written by composers who have a foot in each of those worlds. Tan Dun, for one, was born in Hunan (People's Republic of China) in 1957, came to the United States in 1986, and continues to be active in both countries. His *Symphony 1997* was written to celebrate—or at least to mark publicly, in a hopeful spirit—the return of Hong Kong to China. It blends booming Chinese temple bells, folklike tunes for a chorus, a grandiose Western orchestra, and virtuosic writing for solo cello (a part written for and first performed by Yo-Yo Ma, the renowned American cellist whose parents were from China).

A second typological distinction, and binarism, has to do with nearness and distance. My definition above merely specifies that a work is exotic if it evokes a locale (people, social milieu) that is felt to be extremely *different* (in time or space/culture); perhaps surprisingly to some, the definition does not prescribe or presume—as previous definitions of musical exoticism tend to do—that the locale be geographically *distant*.[36] A work may be situated relatively close to the city or country in which the composer and intended listeners are located and yet qualify as exotic. Numerous French comic operas, for example, take place in some (often unspecified) rural French village, even though (or precisely because) the opera was composed for Paris, where peasants were thought to be vaguely simpleminded, good-hearted, and more or less amusing (i.e., diverting to see represented on stage). Model instances of this type of portrayal of (relatively nearby) rural life include the short but pathbreaking comic opera *Le devin du village* (The Village Soothsayer, 1752), with words and music by the philosopher Jean-Jacques Rousseau, and numerous operas from several decades thereafter, including Pierre-Alexandre Monsigny's *Rose et Colas* (1764). More recent examples might include Charles Gounod's gentle opera *Mireille* (1864, set in Provence) and—a nonoperatic case—the four sets of *Chants de l'Auvergne* (1923–30) that Joseph Canteloube arranged for voice and orchestra, selections from which have been recorded by singers as varied as Victoria de los Angeles and Barbra Streisand. Clearly related to the same tradition are instrumental movements marked musette (the French word for bagpipe), as in Bach's keyboard partitas or even Arnold Schoenberg's Piano Suite of 1921. But at least as often, the locale is quite far away indeed, as in Jean-Philippe Rameau's operatic extravaganza *Les indes galantes* (The Elegant Indies, 1735, revised 1736), as well as in, again, certain instrumental works, such as the concluding rondo *alla turca* (i.e., in Turkish style) from Mozart's Keyboard Sonata in A, K. 331.

A third crucial binary distinction implicit within my definition touches on the real and the fictive: an exotic locale must be "not completely imaginary." I insert this phrase for a reason, despite the fact that it is rarely specified in discussions of musical exoticism. The word *exoticism*, as its etymology suggests, could easily refer to a nonexistent realm, *ex-* meaning simply "out of" or "away from" (home, reality). But fully imaginary settings—at least in operas, musicals, symphonic poems, and the like—do not often seem to have stimulated composers or captured the attention of audiences. One has to strain to think of a successful opera or oratorio featuring talking animals, nonearthlings, or other fantasy creatures: the equivalent of, say, television's several *Star Trek* series or the vast literature of fable and fairy tale. Karl-Birger Blomdahl's science fiction opera *Aniara* comes to mind, as do a few other exceptional works, notably Wagner's *Ring* cycle, in which the gods turn out to be deeply human in their various motivations and impulses (ditto certain works about the Greek divinities by Francesco Cavalli or Jacques Offenbach), and Leoš Janáček's *The Cunning Little Vixen*, in which the same is true of the beasts of the forest. In any case, none of these works would probably strike most listeners and critics as invoking "the exotic."

In contrast, the concept very much occurs to us as soon as a work plays (however fantastically) on our knowledge (however erroneous) of some real, "other" place and its inhabitants. A crucial tension is thus evident in the phenomenon of musical exoticism: a tension between a real location and an imagined one. We (including composer, librettist, and performers) prefer to set up at least a screen of human believability—preferably anchored by concrete references to a place that we know (or think) really exists or existed— on which we can then project our wildest scenarios, however atypical of, or even impossible in, the real location in question. We set our exotic works—at least our successful, cherished ones—in places that we can locate on a map or globe or in a history book. Then the fantasy can begin, as it did for Cardinal Newman (and for millions of others) with Baghdad.

A fourth binary distinction has likewise already been briefly flagged in our discussion: musical versus extramusical signs or indicators. Sometimes the evocation of the exotic locale is carried out entirely through musical means (we might call this "implicit" evocation); sometimes through explicit verbal and, in opera, visual indicators; and often by the two in some combination. In instrumental music, the verbal indications are usually few in number, and usually brief, consisting at most of a specifying title and perhaps a supportive performance marking at the beginning. Sometimes these verbal indications easily defined (for contemporaries, at least) a whole realm of associations, as in Franz Liszt's nineteen *Hungarian Rhapsodies* (most of them composed in the 1840s and early 1850s). Similarly, several Antonio Lucio Vivaldi concertos (e.g., the Concerto in G Major for Strings and Continuo, RV 151) bear such subtitles as *alla rustica—in peasant style*. Any further details or richer associations are left by Vivaldi or Liszt to the listener's imagination. And, of course, to the performers', since a title or other verbal indication, such as *alla rustica* or (in Liszt's or other composers' "gypsy" works) *all'ongherese/alla zingarese*, can easily suggest not just a composed style, but a performed manner; a "rustic" or "peasant" manner might include such features as emphatic downbeat accents, implying a certain cheerful boorishness, just as a "gypsy" manner might include slashing bow strokes, implying a propensity for passion and violence. The character of the music may be further indicated by an actual performance direction, such as "allegro feroce"—"fast and wild"—or in rustic/pastoral works, "adagio piacevole"—"slow and peaceful." Vivaldi, as it happens, keeps his performance directions few and simple, in accord with baroque practice; most often they comprise little more than conventional indications of speed or basic mood.

Vocal music, by contrast, usually contains not one or two brief verbal indicators of a work's location, but three or more quite extensive ones. That is, in addition to carrying a suggestive title (Rossini's *L'italiana in Algeri*, Karol Szymanowski's *Songs of the Lovesick Muezzin*) and the usual range of performing indications, a vocal work offers the audience a sung text (frequently of real literary merit, as in many art songs). Moreover, opera and sometimes oratorio provide revealing names for certain characters, such as Mustafà Bey and Haly (i.e., Ali) in Rossini's *Italiana*. To all these verbal indicators, opera adds four specific and crucial visual ones: stage movement (e.g., dance and processional), mimetic gesture, sets, and costumes.

Let us not skip over the purely musical indicators of the exotic, however— those "exotic musical materials" that, as dictionary definitions rightly insist, are often an integral and defining component of exotic works. These stylistic devices can be found either alone or together with the verbal and visual indicators just described. In Western music of the past few centuries, numerous musico-stylistic features have been widely used to suggest an exotic locale:

—modes and harmonies different from the familiar major and minor, one category being pentatonic and other gapped scales;

—bare textures, such as unharmonized unisons or octaves, parallel fourths or fifths, and drones and static harmonies;

—distinctive repeated rhythmic or melodic patterns, sometimes deriving from dances of the "other" country or group;

—"asymmetrical" phrase structure, "rhapsodic" melodic motion, excessive repetition, sudden pauses or long notes, and other departures from normative types of continuity;

—unusual musical instruments, especially various kinds of percussion (bass drum, triangle, bells, and—for invoking Indonesia and the like—xylophone);

—unusual instrumental techniques, such as pizzicato, portamento, or double stops; and

—distinctive uses of vocal range and tesssitura (e.g., the sultry mezzo-soprano voice), and unusual styles of vocal production ("darkened" sound, throbbing vibrato, lack of vibrato, etc.).[37]

Some of these musical features are typical of, or were believed to be appropriate to, one or another region or people. Certain highly stereotyped drumbeat patterns (e.g., four equally spaced beats: loud soft soft soft) were/are thought to represent Native Americans, just as skittering around the major-pentatonic scale (e.g., on the black notes of the piano) could be reliably heard by the ignorant Western ear, and still often is today, as authentically Chinese or Japanese. In contrast, certain other features (such as the percussion instruments) can/could carry widely differing associations, depending on which other elements are combined with them. And, of course, the associations that such elements carry can fade or change with the passing of time, or vary with listeners of different origins and musical backgrounds.

4

The various works mentioned so far, it has now been several times asserted, "evoke" a distant or unfamiliar locale. But how do we, listening in the audience or at home, know that another place/people/group is at issue in such works at all? The problem is particularly acute in instrumental works. For the moment, therefore, it may help to stick with stage works or films.

There the matter would seem relatively simple: the exotic locale is most clearly announced in the visual and verbal adjuncts or "givens" just discussed, notably the basic plot being acted out, the characters' names, and the costumes, sets, props, and dances. But to what extent do, on the one hand, the libretto at a more detailed level (the sung soliloquies and conversations, the detailed stage directions) and, on the other, the music (in all its complexity and multifariousness) participate in this project of representing the other? What, to put the question more concretely, would happen were some enterprising director to shift the setting of an exotic opera—say, *Aida*—to another place and time (Nazi Germany and its battles on the Russian front?), making appropriate changes in costumes and sets, yet not altering a word or note of the verbal or musical text? Would the other (or in this case, would both others: Egypt and Ethiopia) then disappear from the work?[38] Those familiar with current fashions of stage direction in opera will recognize that I am not exaggerating, for the sake of argument, in imagining such a proposed relocation.[39]

The problem can be most easily understood, perhaps, by considering for the moment two well-known works set in East Asia.

—A recent televised production of Gilbert and Sullivan's *The Mikado*, from the English National Opera, removed the work from Japan to Edwardian England, a shift in time and locale that only served to make clear how little the work is concerned with Japan at all.[40] What was lost seemed mainly of superficial importance, whereas something arguably more basic to the work was reclaimed for a modern audience—for example, Gilbert's (and Sullivan's) wicked yet affectionate parodies of British bureaucracy, British legal maneuverings, and Western-style courtship rituals and gender stereotypes (such as the comically overbearing low-voiced Englishwoman, familiar from several other Gilbert and Sullivan shows).

—In contrast, Puccini's *Madama Butterfly* has been left unaltered by stage directors; that is, they have, to my knowledge, rarely if ever attempted to de-Japanize it. Their restraint derives, I would say, from a sensitive response to the work. To shift the scene of this opera to Chicago, Belfast, Havana, Algiers, or Puccini's Rome would be, I suspect, to resist or deny foundational features in the words and music—Said's "sensuous particularity"—and would possibly amount to creating a new, if potentially fascinating, parasite opera.[41]

And so, one wonders which of the operas or other musical works (including instrumental ones) mentioned thus far belong more to the first of these categories and which to the second. In which works, that is, does the exotic locale form, for the most part, a transparent veil meant to be "seen through"? And in which, by contrast, have the exotic locale and attitudes toward it entered into the substance of the work in permanent amalgam? For instance, *Carmen* may be understood as fitting into both categories. It is integrally tied up with musical signs of Spanishness, yet we can presumably also see Carmen herself as not just a Spanish gypsy, but more generally, a wily, resistant member of an(y) oppressed ethnic group.[42] Similarly, *Aida*, Camille Saint-Saëns's *Samson et Dalila*, and various Massenet operas (e.g., *Le roi de Lahore*, set in India) are filled with evocations of the ancient/clerical/hieratic that may have been intended to echo with Eastern associations as well as with Western meanings that might vary with the listener (e.g., Catholicism and its rich repertoire of liturgical chants and choral motets, but perhaps equally well—to a German or English person—with Protestantism, Lutheran hymnody, and Mendelssohnian oratorio).

The wondering gets more knotty still with purely instrumental works, such as Saint-Saëns's *Suite algérienne* and Fifth Piano Concerto (nicknamed the "Egyptian"), César Franck's *Les djinns* for piano and orchestra (based on a poem by Victor Hugo about an Islamic ceremony of exorcism), Debussy's *Ibéria*, Alfred Ketèlbey's pops-concert numbers *In a Chinese Temple Garden* and *In a Persian Market*, and numerous more recent works by Henry Cowell, Benjamin Britten, Colin McPhee, Alan Hovhaness, Arvo Pärt, John Corigliano, and others that evoke distant times and/or places.[43] Similarly, the problems of "representation" are quite severe in those ballet scores that long ago shed their associations with the stage and are now heard primarily in concert or on radio or compact disc; to the Stravinsky and Milhaud mentioned earlier, we might add Édouard Lalo's *Namouna*, Debussy's *Khamma*, and Ravel's *Ma mère l'oye*. The Ravel contains a movement entitled "Laideronnette, impératrice des pagodes" ("Little Ugly Girl, Empress of the Pagodas"); the girl's Chineseness (or Indochineseness?) is effectively conveyed by Ravel's music, but any sense of a distinctively Asian *laideur* (ugliness) may, for most of us, remain attached only to the movement's title, which we don't think much about (and which, in radio broadcasts, may not even be read out by the announcer and so, for certain listeners, might as well not exist).

What, in short, is the significance of the given exotic locale—and prevailing Western views thereof—to the varying works in this extensive repertoire? Or perhaps it is best to put it the other way around:

—What is the relationship between, on the one hand, these musical works (and the various elements that make them up) and, on the other, the many-sided reality of the region being depicted?

The remainder of the present section addresses this question. In the interests of convenience and (I hope) clarity, it will focus on what we call "the East," that is, the Middle East plus South and East Asia. Nonetheless, most of the arguments could be easily adapted to other regions, such as sub-Saharan Africa or pre-Columbian and colonial-era Central and South America.

The question is complicated by the nature of the two principal entities that it names: extramusical "reality" and the "elements" in the work itself. To begin with, the "reality" of the East is many-sided because it may involve not only (1) the actual life and culture of people(s) in the region (and the "brute realities" that they face, including the disruption of local economies and cultural traditions by Western colonizers), but also (2) the changing relationship between Western countries (and their private citizens, such as vacationing composers) and the region in question, and perhaps most of all, (3) a range of widely held ideas and images *about* the region — ideas and images once circulated in more or less factual (often illustrated) magazine articles (e.g., articles about Asian lands and peoples in *Harper's*, a magazine well-circulated among America's cultured and opera-going elites around 1900), or else in myths and tall tales, such as those in the aforementioned translations of the *Thousand and One Nights.*

Even more problematic is the second entity in the question: the musical and nonmusical (verbal, visual) representational "elements" that are found in works invoking the East or other exotic regions. The roles played by these elements (the most significant of which were listed in section 3) can be formulated in a relatively narrow, almost positivistic fashion:

> —To what extent do these operas signal otherness—Turkishness, Chineseness, and so on—through the composer's use of musical materials that either (1) depart in some basic but not ethnically recognizable way from Western stylistic norms, or else (2) make explicit use of characteristic musical practices of the region in question (drones and ostinato rhythms, distinctive modes and melodic patterns, even complete borrowed tunes)?

As noted earlier, music scholars and critics interested in exoticism, Orientalism, and the like have repeatedly articulated the problem in these terms. They have, though, found themselves frustrated by three undeniable limitations:

> —The general stylistic aberrations (category 1) are often applied indiscriminately by composers to vastly different geographical settings. What I call major-mode pentatonicism, for example, is the use of a five-note (rather than seven-note) scale, such as one achieves by playing only the black notes of the piano. Pentatonic writing of various kinds is found in numerous, disparate world musical cultures and so has tended to be invoked, with sometimes confusing results, in works depicting Algerians, Chinese, Scots, Native Americans, Slavs, and African Americans. It

remains tantalizingly unclear to what extent the pentatonicism in the works that Antonín Dvořák composed in America comes from Black spirituals, Native American chanting, or the folk traditions of his native Bohemia.

—Borrowed tunes and the like (category 2), to the degree that they are present at all, tend to lose their most distinctive features in the course of being uprooted and transplanted. What is left of the original materials is frequently combined with utterly Western procedures (e.g., rich, chromatic harmonizations; or developmental techniques such as "motivic work" and modulation to distant keys).

—Whole stretches of certain works purportedly describing or evoking a non-Western setting are written in an idiom that neither is stylistically aberrant (as in category 1) nor actively "borrows" foreign materials (as in category 2). The job of exotic coloration is thus left to a few, often relatively brief or patently lightweight sections of the work, such as the occasional choral number, ballet divertissement, or ceremonial march.

There is, nonetheless, more to be said about many of the styles and borrowings in question. As various of the essays in Bellman's collection The Exotic in Western Music demonstrate, some of these styles and borrowings prove, on careful examination, to be more distinctive than a first hearing with late-twentieth-century ears might suggest. For example, the pounding rhythms and descending minor-pentatonic melodic figures that Michael Pisani finds in his survey of "American Indian" pieces differ unmistakably from the curvaceous Orientalisms (complete with a chromatic "pass" from the fifth degree of the scale up to the sixth, or from the sixth down to the fifth) that Russian composers indulged in as a way of asserting their own distinctive national identity (i.e., through evocation of their own neighboring and, by the late nineteenth century, politically incorporated other: Central Asia).[44] Furthermore, some exotic "signifiers" are more characteristic of the region in question than skeptical observers might suspect.[45]

But as I asserted earlier (in my definition in section 3), our studies of "Eastern" or, more generally, exotic works would profit from giving attention to more than just those occasional passages that make use of specific markers of the exotic region in question. They should also note the ways in which the music and other components (verbal, etc.) in the given work are inscribed—deeply, broadly, almost from beginning to end—with a certain ideologically colored view of the East. This view is, of course, widely known by many as "Orientalism" and has been so known ever since Said's widely discussed book of that title (1978); it has taken root particularly in such fields as political science, literary criticism, and art history. The Orientalist worldview is inti-

mately intertwined with (it enabled, it was reinforced by) the various colonial and imperialist projects alluded to previously, projects that are not entirely dead even today, as became apparent in many aspects of the American
involvement in (and American broadcast news coverage of) the Persian Gulf
War of 1991. This worldview involves seeing non-Western regions—especially
the Middle East, though scholars other than Said have extended the term
to East Asia and elsewhere—in ways that suit(ed) Western needs: as inherently ("essentially") purer, or the opposite, viler; sultrier, or else more capable
of philosophical transcendence; lazier, or else more unthinkingly obedient.
(Even in this overly simple summary, I emphasize the diversity of possible
characterizations, as I consider it important not to treat Orientalism—despite
its systematic-looking suffix—as a monolithic and unvaried template, even
within a strictly Middle Eastern context, much less when extending it to other
regions.)[46]

By focusing on the larger attitude toward the East (or other "other" regions) in an exotic musical work, rather than on specific striking—because
atypical—passages, we free ourselves to consider the whole range of musical,
musico-dramatic, and in the case of works without sung text, programmatic
techniques deployed.

In an opera, specifically, these techniques may include the ways in which
individual figures are characterized singly and in relationship to each other:
through revealing contrasts of musical style, distinctive orchestrational com-
binations, and so forth. For example, Cio-Cio San (in Butterfly) is characterized not only by melodic pentatonicism and particular Japanese tunes, but
also by myriad reinforcements, in music and text, of her smallness and fragility. These features are presented not as unique idiosyncrasies, but as characteristic aspects of her Japaneseness, aspects that distinguish her from her
beloved American naval officer, B. F. Pinkerton—nonchalant, jovial, superficial, callous—and also from many other operatic heroines, including three of
Puccini's own: the fiery-tempered Tosca, the sturdy saloon-keeper Minnie (in
La fanciulla del West), and the Chinese "ice princess" Turandot.[47]

Structural manipulations, too, can define character and, especially, establish relationships between characters. Dalila, in Saint-Saëns's opera, dominates the love duet with Samson so thoroughly that he can barely moan, "Dalila, je t'aime," in response, in vulnerable soft notes in high register. The
supposed (feared, desired) power of the Eastern seductress (Philistine, in this
case) over Western man (the Hebrew here, as proto-Christian) has never been
more powerfully portrayed in any art.[48]

5

By now, readers should be well persuaded that operas and other musical works that evoke the non-Western have an oblique relationship to (1) questions of factual truth and (2) the prevailing ideology of their day. How this oblique relationship works in both cases is worth exploring.

First, exotic musical works do not generally claim to represent objectively —as if they were travel books or newspaper reports—the non-Western world as it really is (or the nonmetropolitan world, in the case of "rural European" works). Rather, or also, they present themselves as fictions: objects intended to provide entertainment or invite aesthetic contemplation. This is particularly true of comic operas; one favorable but sassy early review of Adrien Boieldieu's *Calife de Bagdad* specifically noted that it deserved its success because it contained all four essential ingredients of a perfect *opéra-comique*, including "a plot that is not believable" and "words that there is no point in hearing" (the other two were "amusing situations" and "tunes that it is pleasant to recall").[49]

Even so, certain "Oriental" (African, etc.) musical works do demonstrably perpetuate images of that region and its (ancient or recent) inhabitants that range from the wildly idealized, to the true but one-sided, to the noxious and defamatory. Indeed, it can be argued that the very fictiveness of artworks (e.g., of comic operas, as just mentioned) serves to make palatable (by disguising the ungenerous, prejudicial nature of) some slanted portrayals of other peoples and places. In fairness, though, one should also note that some works that invoke a given country or region do, at least in certain moments, capture with precision one or another feature of the group or place being depicted, or at the very least, give a sense of how a distant place—that particular distant place? any distant or unfamiliar place?—feels to a visitor from abroad (from the metropolis, etc.). And the best of them are true in a nonfactual, perhaps mythic sense of the word: they constitute visions of a sometimes beckoning, sometimes scary "nowhere land," a land that Westerners would like to think is quite different from their own, but that may be more a projected self-image, however deformed, to hide the painful resemblance.[50]

Second, similarly complex is the relationship between these works and the "ideology" of their day (in its broadest sense). Many of the works mentioned in this chapter, especially those written in France in the nineteenth and early twentieth centuries, seem deeply imbued with imperialist ideology. As Said has put it, many artworks of this era "happily co-existed with or lent support to the global enterprises of European and American empire."[51] Marilyn Butler rephrases the issue somewhat more concretely, and without the hint of accusation in Said's statement ("happily co-existed"). Because she is speaking only of literature and England, I expand her wording to make explicit its relevance to music and other Western countries: "Poets, travel-writers, novelists [and musicians] undoubtedly belong in a discourse through which the British [as well as the French and others] teach themselves about India [along with the Middle East and North Africa] and acquire the national will to be there"—be there, that is, in a position of command and control.[52] Furthermore, such cultural items can serve imperialism in quite an opposite way: that is, by not seeming to "teach" about the other, indeed—as Said elsewhere observes—by distracting attention from, and/or naturalizing (presenting as inevitable), the imperialist project and its human and social costs.[53]

One might think that these two extramusical factors, truth (verisimilitude) and imperialist ideology, are related in some simple way: namely, that an ideologically justified system of conquest and exploitation that many today would find reprehensible must have been supported by or reflected in cultural images that were counterfactual, and therefore, misleading or fantasy laden and, as Said might call it, mystificatory. In practice, though, the question of ideology cuts across that of falsity or truth in various ways. Works of art can serve the ends of empire not only through false or distorted images, but also or even more through images that are "true" (i.e., more or less accurate reflections of some aspect of the lived reality in the given country), including carefully researched costumes and sets in Orientalist paintings and operas, or relatively faithful transcriptions of dance tunes or sacred chants.

This last possibility—use of ethnographic musical materials within a Western piece—was seized on with eagerness by a few of the composers discussed in the present chapter, such as Saint-Saëns and McPhee. In so doing, they made themselves exceptions to the more general tendency, noted earlier, for composers to conflate various non-Western regions and certain Western ones (the French provinces and Scottish heath, Dutch port cities and Polish villages) into a large and sometimes undifferentiated exotic "zone" in which highly contrasting locations could receive closely similar musico-dramatic treatment. (Many comic operas of Rossini, Offenbach, and Léhar can be relocated to a different setting without creating stylistic incongruity.) Still, the cautious phrase "relatively faithful" at the end of the previous paragraph alludes to a number of crucial problematic issues faced by the more ethnographically inclined composer; perhaps most crucially, the act of transcribing a non-Western musical performance or rendition usually entails straining out some of its most distinctive and characteristic features. The very technological device—Western music notation—that promises the possibility of reproducing accurately the foreign music ends up distorting the way in which the music is conveyed to Westerners. And in any case, whether the exotic details are highly conventional, freshly invented, or (within the limits just stated) minutely observed, it is important to stress that the work's ideological wallop depends not so much on those musical details in isolation, but rather on how these features are *framed* in a given artwork—into what context have they been placed? what aspects of the original have been suppressed in the process of borrowing?—and how they are *received* by a given public.

It should also be stressed that the "cultural work" that is done by the arts when they invoke another society (whether or not that society has been colonized by the West) is not necessarily as repressive and regrettable as the short quotations from Said and Marilyn Butler might suggest. It should not, that is, be assumed that the worldview that musical and other cultural texts of this sort support is necessarily pro-imperialist. Quite to the contrary, as Said himself elsewhere emphasizes: art has the potential for formulating a resistant or "antinomian" response (in part, through modernist irony) to "Western control over the non-Western world." [54] (Or at least—if we accept the possibility of multiple valid readings of a given work—it may allow itself to be interpreted as critical of certain generally accepted policies.)

To put it in less dichotomous terms, a given work may communicate both a measure of enthusiasm for, or at least acceptance of, imperial policies, and also some unease with those same policies and their ramifications. For example, in Léo Delibes's *Lakmé* (1883), the British attempt to rule India is presented as neither heroic and admirable nor utterly vile but something in between: necessary or at least unavoidable, yet also obtuse and misguided. To be sure, many French people must have perceived the tension and folly of colonial efforts more readily when the colonizers were their own hereditary rivals from beyond the English Channel.[55] Indeed, around the same time, Pierre Loti wrote a travel book about India in which he highlighted the unwelcome intrusiveness of the English by pointedly not mentioning them at all except in the introduction and the book's title: *L'Inde (sans les anglais).*[56] Still, this does not rule out the possibility that the eager reception of *Lakmé* in the France of its day and for decades thereafter also reflected some (mostly unspoken) discomfort with the costs and risks of French colonizings, notably in Algeria.

6

We may close this discussion—though this will surely not end it—by posing one last question, one that is implied by several of the questions from sections 1 and 4:

> —How transparent is the exotic veil that the composer and his or her collaborators have cast over their musical work?

The question arises in large measure because certain great operatic trage-dies—e.g., *Aida* and *Madama Butterfly*—achieved high cultural status, thanks to their wide dissemination on stage, in the illustrated press, and in band ar-rangements and salon potpourris and excerpts. One interpretation would be that their exotic settings were often taken allegorically. That is, some people back then would have read "through" the supposed setting (Egypt, Japan) to more universal human issues and conflicts, as indeed some do today.

But another interpretation would hold that the works continued to serve as one of the most potent sources of mental images that Westerners had of the countries supposedly portrayed in them. In that sense, the surface meaning of the allegory may have continued (and may continue today) to operate sepa-rately from the deeper meaning and reinforce—as Said, hooks, and others rightly remind us—various limited, distorted, or indeed entirely fictive and self-serving (frequently colonialist) Western stereotypes of foreign cultures.[57]

And there is no reason to suppose that the same is not also true of lighter or more obviously commercial works of musical theater, such as the aforemen-tioned *Italiana in Algeri* and *Mikado*, Offenbach's pseudo-Chinese *Ba-Ta-Clan*, Leo Fall's *Die Rose von Stambul* (*The Rose of Istanbul*), Léhar's China-based *Das Land des Lächelns* (*The Land of Smiles*), or Rodgers and Hammerstein's *The King and I*. Or of various popular and "folk" songs widely associated with a given country; for example, such Irish (and "Irish") numbers as "Danny Boy" and "Molly Malone." Or of instrumental works, such as Rimsky-Korsakov's *Capric-cio on Spanish Themes* (*Capriccio espagnol*, 1887), which is gypsy flavored, in part; or McPhee's *Tabuh-Tabuhan* (1936), which was inspired by the composer's di-rect and extended involvement with gamelan music during several years spent on the island of Bali.

We must never forget the staying power of some of these cultural products: their continuing vitality for later generations; their lasting ability to leave an impress on the public imagination; and their capacity for surviving all sorts of reinterpretations, manglings, and the like. I am presumably not the only Westerner whose conceptions of Japan remain indelibly marked by repeated viewings of, and listenings to excerpts from, *The Mikado* (despite what I said earlier about the transparent silliness of its Japanese elements) and, even more, *Madama Butterfly*. Television news shots of skyscrapers and subway crowds in Tokyo have never succeeded in convincing me that the country is not still full of (as if just outside the cameraperson's frame) groups of tiptoe-ing maidens with parasols; or that in Nagasaki, another young woman cannot still be seen waiting, in her little house overlooking the port, for a certain pro-foundly unworthy American man to return. Indeed, I am not alone. Friends in Japan report that "Cio-Cio-San's house"—though a total invention—is a big tourist spot for visitors from distant parts. And the images of Puccini's opera were recently reawakened in my head and given a new spin when I saw the 1997 touring production of Miss Saigon, a stagework that is frankly modeled on Madama Butterfly in many crucial respects of character, incident, and musical manner.[58]

I fear that if I ever were to visit Japan, I would come back feeling that I still had never encountered the real Japan. Likewise, some tourists from abroad who visit North America report their disappointment at not encountering "cowboys and Indians." Perhaps we here run up against one of the few true universals in human existence: the need to be reassured (or—as if ritualistically—disturbed and then reassured) by familiar images, however fallacious, seems to surpass all curiosity about how things really are. The specific myths to which we cling are determined by cultural forces; but the general tendency to cling to myth when reality is staring us in the face may be rooted deep in certain protective devices of the nervous system, or—to adopt the language of religion—rooted in the human propensity for the sin of sloth (here: mental laziness).[59]

Still, mythical, phantasmagoric imaginings can of course be real in their own way. How to combine all of this into a theoretically sound critique and appreciation of musical and other artworks evoking the other remains a challenge, and one worth tackling from many different angles. I propose, though, that such a critique/appreciation of musical exoticism, to be adequate and useful, would do well to try to maintain two concepts in a state of creative tension: on the one hand, the essential Westernness of an exotic work—its irrelevance to the East (or whatever other "other" location is being evoked), and the East's to it—and on the other, the work's power to reflect and even shape, perhaps damagingly, the attitude and behavior of Westerners toward the non-Western world. I propose, moreover, that we accept these two concepts as irreconcilable yet equally valid and, at the risk of intellectual messiness (or is it the promise of methodological richness?), take care not to privilege one over the other.

Race before racism: the disappearance of the American

This essay appeared in an earlier form in *Plantation Society* 3, no. 2 (summer 1993): 24–50.

1   Jack D. Forbes, *Black Africans and Native Americans: Color, Race and Caste in the Evolution of Red-Black Peoples* (New York: Blackwell, 1988); and Edward W. Said, *Orientalism* (New York: Pantheon, 1978). All quotations from Forbes's work are cited parenthetically.

2   For the general reader, Martin Bernal, *Black Athena: The Afroasiatic Roots of Classical Civilization* (New Brunswick, N.J.: Rutgers University Press, 1987); Johannes Fabian, *Time and the Other: How Anthropology Makes Its Object* (New York: Columbia University Press, 1983); and Ivan Van Sertima, *They Came Before Columbus: The African Presence in Ancient America* (New York: Random House, 1977) are the best known. Titles are now proliferating in this area of research.

3   It would, for example, be interesting to play this narrative in counterpoint with Hortense Spillers, "The Tragic Mulatta," in *The Difference Within: Feminism and Critical Theory*, ed. Elizabeth A. Meese and Alice Parker (Amsterdam: John Benjamin, 1989), or with the more extensive Deborah E. McDowell and Arnold Rampersad, eds., *Slavery and the Literary Imagination: Selected Papers from the English Institute, 1987* (Baltimore, Md.: Johns Hopkins University Press, 1989). For a more extended discussion of the Foucault material, see Spivak, "More on Power/Knowledge," in *Outside in the Teaching Machine* (New York: Routledge, 1993), 25–51.

4   I prefer this phrase to the more commonly used *poststructuralism* because (1) it does not refer merely to a moment in the history of *forms* of explanation, and (2) it avoids the post-Habermasian confusion between what is called poststructuralism and what is called postmodernism.

5   Edward W. Said, *The World, the Text, and the Critic* (Cambridge: Harvard University Press, 1983), 178–247.

6 Said, The World, the Text, and the Critic, 245.

7 Toni Morrison, Beloved (New York: Plume, 1987), 111. For such limits to scholarship, see also Martin Heidegger, "The Saying of Anaximander," in Early Writings, trans. David Farrell Krell and Frank A. Capuzzi (San Francisco, Calif.: Harper, 1984), 57, translation modified; and Jacques Derrida, Specters of Marx: The State of the Debt, the Work of Mourning, and the New International, trans. Peggy Kamuf (New York: Routledge, 1994), 33–35.

8 The gentle Nambikwara in Claude Lévi-Strauss, Tristes Tropiques, trans. John and Doreen Weightman (Harmondsworth, England: Penguin, 1976); and the Kashinahua in Jean-François Lyotard, The Postmodern Condition, trans. Geoff Bennington and Brian Massumi (Minneapolis: University of Minnesota Press, 1984).

9 Jacques Derrida, Of Grammatology, trans. Gayatri Chakravorty Spivak (Baltimore, Md.: Johns Hopkins University Press, 1976), 107–18.

10 The possibility and limits of doing such a thing are discussed in Stephen Hawking's brilliant A Brief History of Time: From the Big Bang to Black Holes (New York: Bantam, 1988).

11 In fact, Forbes legitimizes deconstruction itself by reversal. He turns brown into an unmixed origin. To do this he has to invoke the ancient Egyptians. For a discussion of Freud's comparable gesture with the ancient Indians, see Jacques Derrida, "To Speculate—On 'Freud,' " in The Post Card: From Socrates to Freud and Beyond, trans. Alan Bass (Chicago: University of Chicago Press, 1987), 369–75.

12 Friedrich Nietzsche, "On Truth and Lying in an Extra-Moral Sense," in Friedrich Nietzsche on Rhetoric and Language, ed. Sander L. Gilman, Carole Blair, and David J. Parent (New York: Oxford University Press, 1989), 246–57.

13 Spivak, "Asked to Talk about Myself," Third Text 19 (summer 1992): 11.

14 The groundbreaking work of Winthrop D. Jordan, beginning with White Over Black: American Attitudes toward the Negro, 1550–1812 (Chapel Hill: University of North Carolina Press, 1968), makes the American contact its starting point. His position on the historicity of racism is comparable to Forbes's, but less radical, confined to difference rather than displacement: "Racial attitudes in this country are very different now from what they were three hundred years ago, and it is very important that we deal with our past, in so far as possible on its own terms" (The White Man's Burden: Historical Origins of Racism in the United States [New York: Oxford University Press, 1974], vii). Whereas Jordan's take on race is scientistic (White Over Black, 583–85), Forbes's is, as I show in my text, deconstructive.

15 Colette Guillaumin, Racism, Sexism, Power and Ideology (New York: Routledge, 1995).

16 Jack D. Forbes, "The Manipulation of Race, Caste, and Identity—Classifying Afroamericans, Native Americans and Red-Black People," Journal of Ethnic Studies 17 (1990): 1–51.

17 Although generally Orientalist in its politics, Louis Dumont's Homo Hierarchicus: The Caste System and Its Implications, trans. Basia Gulati (Chicago: University of Chicago Press, 1981) remains the most accessible study of the social functionalism of the Indian caste system. For an analysis of the colonial/Orientalist construction of caste, see Bernard S. Cohn, India: The Social Anthropology of a Civilization (Englewood Cliffs, N.J.: Prentice-Hall, 1971), especially 124–41.

18 M. Ackbar Abbas, Hong Kong: Culture and the Politics of Disappearance (Minneapolis: University of Minnesota Press, 1997).

19 This argument is generally present in extant scholarship. For a random and superior example, I offer Russell R. Menard, "The Africanization of the Lowcountry Labor Force, 1670–1730," in Race and Family in the Colonial South, ed. Winthrop D. Jordan and Sheila L. Skemp (Jackson: University Press of Mississippi, 1987), 81–108.

20 Daniel Defoe, Robinson Crusoe (New York: Norton, 1975), 205–8.

21 For the general reader, the source books are Samir Amin, *Unequal Development: An Essay on the Social Formations of Peripheral Capitalism*, trans. Brian Pearce (Boston: Monthly Review, 1976), and the last chapter of Perry Anderson, *Lineages of the Absolutist State* (London: New Left Books, 1974).

22 I thank Moustafa Bayoumi for expressing the opinion that allowed me to notice this characteristic. I thank him especially for showing me the record of the Act of 1682, which repeals "a former law making Indians and others free" (W. W. Hening, ed., *The Statutes at Large; being a collection of all the laws of Virginia, from the first session of the legislature, in the year 1619* vol. 2 [New York: R&W&G Barton, 1823], 490), where distinctions by religion are clearly marked.

23 Jack D. Forbes, *Columbus and Other Cannibals: The Wétiko Disease of Exploitation, Imperialism and Terrorism* (Brooklyn, N.Y.: Autonomedia, 1992); and Edward W. Said, *After the Last Sky: Palestinian Lives* (New York: Pantheon, 1986).

Criticism between opposition and counterpoint

Several pages of this essay take their substance from the preface and introduction to *"Huckleberry Finn" as Idol and Target: The Functions of Criticism in Our Time* (Madison: University of Wisconsin Press, 1997), vii–ix, 3–15. My deep thanks to the Press for permission to reprint these materials.

1   Edward W. Said, *The World, the Text, and the Critic* (Cambridge: Harvard University Press, 1983), 29.

2   Edward W. Said, *Beginnings: Intention and Method* (New York: Basic Books, 1975), 378.

3   Edward W. Said, *Representations of the Intellectual: The 1993 Reith Lectures* (New York: Pantheon, 1994), xvii.

4   Edward W. Said, *Culture and Imperialism* (New York: Knopf, 1993), 51.

5   Said, *Culture and Imperialism*, 14.

6   Said, *Culture and Imperialism*, 31.

7   Edward W. Said, "Orientalism and After," in *A Critical Sense: Interviews with Intellectuals*, ed. Peter Osborne (London: Routledge, 1996), 68.

8   Said, *Culture and Imperialism*, 96.

9   Edward W. Said, "The Pen and the Sword: Culture and Imperialism," in Edward W. Said, *The Pen and the Sword: Conversations with David Barsamian* (Monroe, Maine: Common Courage, 1994), 71.

10 Edward W. Said, "Reflections on Recent American 'Left' Literary Criticism," *boundary 2* 8, no. 1 (fall, 1979): 11–30.

11 William Wordsworth, "Essays upon Epitaphs," in *Prose Works*, ed. W. J. B. Owen and Jane Worthington Smyser, vol. 2 (Oxford: Clarendon, 1974), 53.

12 Said, *Beginnings*, 290.

13 Kenneth Burke, *The Rhetoric of Religion: Studies in Logology* (1961; reprint, Berkeley and Los Angeles: University of California Press, 1970), 25. In *Beginnings*, Said cites "this extraordinary and far-too-little-known work," 386 n. 33.

14 Said, *Representations of the Intellectual*, 119.

15 Michel Foucault, *The Order of Things: An Archaeology of the Human Sciences*, trans. unnamed (New York: Pantheon, 1971), 262. Walter Benn Michaels, *The Gold Standard and the Logic of Naturalism: American Literature at the Turn of the Century* (Berkeley and Los Angeles: University of California Press, 1987), 19.

16 Said, *Pen and the Sword*, 69. Was it really impossible for anyone in 1900 to imagine Afri-

can self-rule? The larger theoretical issue here is the question of anachronism: Are there ("modern") forms of human relation that no one in a given (earlier) period of time is capable of conceiving? Richard Strier has argued against the stricture of anachronism, against traditional scholarship and also against both Foucault and new historicism, in *Resistant Structures: Particularity, Radicalism, and Renaissance Texts* (Berkeley and Los Angeles: University of California Press, 1995).

17 Said, "Orientalism and After," 69.
18 Said, "Orientalism and After," 78.
19 Said, *The World, the Text, and the Critic*, 174.
20 Said, *The World, the Text, and the Critic*, 247.
21 Said, *The World, the Text, and the Critic*, 168.
22 William Dean Howells, *My Mark Twain* (1910), in *The Shock of Recognition: The Development of Literature in the United States Recorded by the Men Who Made It*, ed. Edmund Wilson (Garden City, N.Y.: Doubleday, 1943), 741.
23 Jonathan Arac, *"Huckleberry Finn" as Idol and Target: The Functions of Criticism in Our Time* (Madison: University of Wisconsin Press, 1997), 218.
24 Jonathan Arac, "The Politics of *The Scarlet Letter*," in *Ideology and Classic American Literature*, ed. Sacvan Bercovitch and Myra Jehlen (Cambridge: Cambridge University Press, 1986), 262.
25 Edward W. Said, *The Politics of Dispossession: The Struggle for Palestinian Self-Determination, 1969–1993* (New York: Pantheon, 1994), 314.
26 Lionel Trilling, "Huckleberry Finn" (1948), in *The Liberal Imagination: Essays on Literature and Society* (New York: Viking, 1950), 108, 110.
27 John Wallace, quoted in Molly Moore, "Behind the Attack on 'Huck Finn': One Angry Educator," *Washington Post*, 21 April 1982, Metro sec., 1.
28 *Pittsburgh Post-Gazette*, 20 July 1995, A5; *New York Times*, 25 July 1995, B1.
29 Barbara Jeanne Fields, "Slavery, Race, and Ideology in the United States of America," *New Left Review*, no. 181 (May-June, 1990): 113.
30 Toni Morrison, introduction to Mark Twain, *Adventures of Huckleberry Finn*, The Oxford Mark Twain (New York: Oxford University Press, 1996), xxxvi.
31 *Harrisburg (Pa.) Patriot-News*, 3 February 1998.
32 "NAACP Wants Huck Out of Classrooms," *Pittsburgh Post-Gazette*, 3 February 1998, B6.
33 For examples, see my *"Huckleberry Finn" as Idol and Target*, 22, 24–29, 34, 78–80.
34 Sally Kalson, "A Word of Caution about Huck," *Pittsburgh Post-Gazette*, 4 February 1998, A1, A10. Jonathan Arac, "Huckleberry Finn: Not Required Reading," *Pittsburgh Post-Gazette*, 8 February 1998, C1, C4.
35 Said, *Politics of Dispossession*, 359.

The matter of language

1 Edward W. Said, "Orientalism Reconsidered," *Cultural Critique*, no. 1 (fall 1985): 103.
2 For an analysis of the production of the universal "human" and the issues that derive from it, see Cochran, "The Emergence of Global Contemporaneity," *Diaspora* 5, no. 1 (1996): 119–40.
3 The historical links between the grammatical and linguistic notions of this institutionalization have been traced in Cochran, "Culture against the State," *boundary* 2 17, no. 3 (1990): 1–68.

4 Tampering with this configuration poses problems for scholars who have internalized the modern precepts of historical and literary understanding. For example, Said's questioning of this model, which I will deal with in greater detail below, has led to confusion on the part of many of his critics. See Aijaz Ahmad, *In Theory: Classes, Nations, Literatures* (London: Verso, 1992), for a critique that cannot determine whether to qualify Said (and his work) as being too humanist or too antihumanist and therefore claims that he is both at once and unable to resolve the contradiction between the two (164).

5 This is the formulation of Albert Einstein and Leopold Infeld, *The Evolution of Physics: From Early Concepts to Relativity and Quanta* (New York: Simon and Shuster, 1938), 7.

6 Said, "Orientalism Reconsidered," 92.

7 Aristotle described the signifying process of personification as a subcategory of metaphor; it involved what he called "setting before the eyes" (*pro ommaton*) (*Rhetoric*, 3.11.1–4).

8 Hans-Georg Gadamer, *Truth and Method*, 2d ed., translation revised by Joel Weinsheimer and Donald G. Marshall (New York: Continuum, 1994), offers the most complete and best-known account of this historical model.

9 Privileging this aspect, for example, Hans Robert Jauss applies the hermeneutic method specifically to the question of collective reception, a methodological orientation that has played an important role in traditional literary criticism. See his *Toward an Aesthetic of Reception*, trans. Timothy Bahti (Minneapolis: University of Minnesota Press, 1982).

10 Said, "Orientalism Reconsidered," 92.

11 Said, *Orientalism* (New York: Pantheon, 1978), 1. Hereafter, this work is cited parenthetically.

12 The list of such discussions would be lengthy, and I will limit myself to two paradigmatic references to Nietzsche's unfinished essay in the conceptual context of Said's critical reading: the condemnation paradigm in Ahmad's *In Theory*, 194–97, and Homi Bhabha's *en passant* citation of one of Nietzsche's key phrases in *The Location of Culture* (New York: Routledge, 1994), 164.

13 Jürgen Habermas, "The Entwinement of Myth and Enlightenment: Re-Reading *Dialectic of Enlightenment*," *New German Critique* 26 (spring/summer, 1982): 13.

14 Ahmad, *In Theory*, 197.

15 Friedrich Nietzsche, "On Truth and Lie in an Extramoral Sense," in *Philosophy and Truth: Selections from Nietzsche's Notebooks of the Early 1870s*, trans. and ed. Daniel Breazeale (Atlantic Highlands, N.J.: Humanities Press, 1979), 79; for the German edition, see "Ueber Wahrheit und Lüge im aussermoralischen Sinne," in *Sämtliche Werke; Kritische Studienausgabe*, ed. Giorgio Colli and Mazzino Montinari, vol. 1 (Munich: Walter de Gruyter and Co., 1967–1977), 875. Page references for subsequent citations appear in the text, with the first indicating the English translation and the second, the German original; English translations are sometimes slightly modified.

16 Dante, *De vulgari eloquentia*, bilingual (Latin-Italian), ed. and tr. Sergio Cecchin (Turin, Italy: Tea, 1988), chap. 9, 6.

17 Machiavelli, "Che la variazione delle sètte e delle lingue, insieme con l'accidente de' diluvii o della peste, spegne le memorie delle cose" (bk. 2, chap. 5), *Discorsi sopra la prima Deca di Tito Livio*, vol. 2, *Le grandi opere politiche*, ed. Gian Mario Anselmi, et al. (Turin, Italy: Bollati Boringhieri, 1993), 250–51. Machiavelli speculates that the only reason that the linguistic artifacts of classical civilization remained partially extant is because the Christians had no other language to impose and were forced to adopt Latin.

18 Jean-Jacques Rousseau, "Que le p[remi]er langage du être figuré," chap. 3 of *Essai sur l'origine des langues*, ed. Jean Starobinski, in vol. 5, *Oeuvres complètes*, ed. Bernard Gagnebin and Marcel Raymond (Paris: Gallimard, La Pléiade, 1995), 381–82.

19 This passage was a key bone of contention between Derrida's and de Man's conflicting interpretations of Rousseau. See Jacques Derrida, *De la grammatologie* (Paris: Minuit, 1967), 381–97; and Paul de Man, "The Rhetoric of Blindness," in *Blindness and Insight* (Minneapolis: University of Minnesota Press, 1983), 131–36.

20 Rousseau, *Essai*, 381–82.

21 See Starobinski's comments on this chapter, *Essai*, 1544–46.

22 Rousseau, *Essai*, 381. For Aristotle's model of language, the primary substance (*prote ousia*) on which the entire philosophy of language rests, is the absolutely particular: "For example, a particular man or a particular horse" (*Categories*, 2a, 13–14). Aristotle goes on in the *Categories* to draw the logical conclusion that "if these primary substances did not exist, nothing else would exist either" (2b, 5–7). How one conceives of that initial experience enables and limits theories of signification, history, and even political action that necessarily depend on it.

23 To a certain extent borrowing Kantian terminology, this passage indicates the transfer ("metaphor") of a perception (*Anschauung*, or "intuition" in English-language Kantian terminology) into a schema. In explaining the coining of "giant," Rousseau attempts to grasp this visual aspect by relating "passions" to an "idea," which turns out to be erroneously assigned to the expression. For a discussion of figure and *Bild*, particularly in conjunction with Walter Benjamin's use of the latter term, see Cochran, "History and the Collapse of Eternity," *boundary 2* 22, no. 3 (fall 1995), esp. 44–55.

24 Benjamin addresses these same questions, using the same conceptual elements and much of the same terminology, in "The Task of the Translator," in *Illuminations*, trans. Harry Zohn (New York: Schocken, 1969); and in "Die Aufgabe des Übersetzers," in *Gesammelte Schriften*, vol. 4 (Frankfurt am Main: Suhrkamp, 1980).

25 This passage has been translated many times, but there is little agreement about how to express *Bild* in English. The translation I cite, for example, originally renders the phrase in question as "coins which have lost their embossing"; Walter Kaufmann, whose translation is most often cited and is used by Said and his commentators, prefers "coins which have lost their pictures." See "On Truth and Lie in an Extra-Moral Sense," in *The Portable Nietzsche* (New York: Viking, 1968), 47; and Paul de Man provides his own somewhat freer translation: "metaphors that have been used up and have lost their imprint and that now operate as mere metal, no longer as coins" (in *Allegories of Reading: Figural Language in Rousseau, Nietzsche, Rilke, and Proust* [New Haven, Conn.: Yale University Press, 1979], 111).

26 Paul de Man, "Anthropomorphism and Trope in the Lyric," in *The Rhetoric of Romanticism* (New York: Columbia University Press, 1984), 242.

27 Antonio Gramsci, "Quaderno 11," in *Quaderni del carceri*, ed. Valentino Gerratana (Turin, Italy: Einaudi, 1975), 1438. Parts of this passage were included in an earlier notebook, which exists in vol. 2 of Gramsci's notebooks in English (all the volumes are not yet available); I have therefore adopted that translation, incorporating only Gramsci's later modifications to the passage. See *Prison Notebooks*, trans. and ed. Joseph A. Buttigieg, vol. 2 (New York: Columbia University Press, 1996), 159.

28 Gramsci, *Quaderni*, 1438, 1427.

29 Edward W. Said, *Representations of the Intellectual* (New York: Pantheon, 1994), 91.

In responses begins responsibility: music and emotion

This article was first delivered as a lecture at the Institut für die Wissenschaften vom Menschen, Vienna, 28 July 1997. Thanks to my hosts Krzysztof Michalski, Cornelia Klinger, Jochen Fried, and Nancy Blakestad. My special thanks to Paul Bové, Howard Eiland, and Miguel Tamen.

1 Theodor W. Adorno, *Aesthetic Theory*, trans. and ed. Robert Hullot-Kentor (Minneapolis: University of Minnesota Press, 1997), 15, 14.

2 For an exploration of the sorts of issues that the "New Robustness" might have to contend with, see the catalog of the exhibit of Henry Koerner's paintings, a show curated by Joseph Leo Koerner, *Unheimliche Heimat* (Vienna: Österreichische Galerie Belvedere, 1997).

3 See Martha Nussbaum, *The Therapy of Desire: Theory and Practice in Hellenistic Ethics* (Princeton, N.J.: Princeton University Press, 1994), and especially her *Poetic Justice: The Literary Imagination and Public Life* (Boston: Beacon, 1997), in which she promotes the idea of "rational emotions."

4 Walter Benjamin, *The Arcades Project*, trans. Howard Eiland and Kevin McLaughlin (Cambridge: Harvard University Press, forthcoming, 1999), Folder F, sec. 3, pt. 1.

5 James Wood writes, "A critic of leftish persuasion, one who believes that culture is profoundly bound up with society . . . , [Said] clearly finds music an affront. For Said's most genuine experiences of music have been private and solitary, the imperial individual at the piano" (*The Guardian* [Manchester, England], 20 October 1991, 29).

6 Edward W. Said, *Musical Elaborations* (New York: Columbia University Press, 1991), 96. Subsequent references are cited parenthetically in the text.

7 Marcel Proust, *Contre Sainte-Beuve*, in *On Art and Literature*, trans. Sylvia Townsend Warner (New York: Carroll and Graf, 1984; reprint of the 1957 Chatto and Windus ed.), 19–26.

8 Miguel Tamen, personal communication, letter of 4 September 1997.

9 Proust, *Contre Sainte-Beuve*, 26.

10 "Refused" may be too strong, but I think not. He is always wary of the title "theorist," preferring the title "critic." Theory, as pursued by many—even the best theorists, such as Lukács and Foucault—has a predilection for unities and totalities that blind one to history. "Theoretical closure, like social convention or cultural dogma, is anathema to critical consciousness" (Edward W. Said, *The World, the Text, and the Critic* [Cambridge: Harvard University Press, 1983], 242).

11 Benjamin, *Arcades*, Folder B, sec. 9, pt. 4; Paul Valery, quoted by Benjamin, *Arcades*, Folder K, sec. 9, pt. 3.

12 Simon Frith, *Performing Rites: On the Value of Popular Music* (Cambridge: Harvard University Press, 1996), 259.

13 Barbara Herrnstein Smith, *Contingencies of Value: Alternative Perspectives for Critical Theory* (Cambridge: Harvard University Press, 1988).

14 I owe this reference to Jochen Fried. This group wanted to understand what things outside us do to affect us. See Jochen Schulte-Sasse et al., eds., *Theory as Practice: A Critical Anthology of Early German Romantic Writings* (Minneapolis: University of Minnesota Press, 1997).

15 With the exception of Richard Moran, "The Expression of Feeling in Imagination," *Philosophical Review* 103 (1994): 75–106.

16 R. P. Blackmur, *Language as Gesture* (London: George Allen and Unwin, 1954), 372; Edward W. Said, "The Horizon of R. P. Blackmur," *Raritan* 6 (1986): 45–46.

17 Samuel Taylor Coleridge, "The Eolian Harp," in *Poetical Works of Coleridge*, ed. Ernest Hartley Coleridge (London: Oxford University Press, 1967), 100–102, lines 34–43.

18 Proust, *Contre Sainte-Beuve*, 265–70.

19 Emmanuel Levinas, *Totality and Infinity: An Essay on Exteriority*, trans. Alfonso Lingis (Pittsburgh, Pa.: Duquesne University Press, 1969), 58; Annette Baier, "What Emotions Are About," *Philosophical Perspectives* 4 (1980): 18; and David Hume, *A Treatise of Human Nature*, ed. L. A. Selby-Brigge and P. H. Nidditch (Oxford: Clarendon, 1978), 413.

20 Romeo Void, "Myself to Myself," on *It's a Condition* (415 Records [415A-00004], 1981).

21 Marcel Proust, *Swann's Way*, in vol. 1 of *Remembrance of Things Past*, trans. C. K. Scott Moncrieff and Terence Kilmartin (New York: Random House, 1981), 46–48. This passage is cited and commented on by Benjamin, *Arcades*, Folder K, sec. 8a, pt. 1.

22 Merlin Donald, *Origins of the Human Mind: Three Stages in the Evolution of Culture and Cognition* (Cambridge: Harvard University Press, 1991). "External memory media—especially written but also many other forms of symbolic storage [such as the device of the madeleine whose workings Proust describes in *Swann's Way*, 50–51]—are a major factor in human intellectual endeavor" (309).

23 Alex Kozulin, *Vygotsky's Psychology: A Biography of Ideas* (Cambridge: Harvard University Press, 1991), 118–19.

24 Walter Benjamin, *Selected Writings: Volume 1: 1913–1926*, ed. Marcus Bullock and Michael Jennings (Cambridge: Harvard University Press, 1996), 298.

25 Frith, *Performing Rites*, 264–65, 272.

26 Wilfred Sellars, *Empiricism and the Philosophy of Mind*, intro. Richard Rorty with study guide by Robert Brandom (Cambridge: Harvard University Press, 1997), 181.

27 Ralph Waldo Emerson, *Essays and Lectures* (New York: Library of America, 1983), 126.

28 Simon Frith, "Beggars Banquet," in *Stranded: Rock and Roll for a Desert Island*, ed. Greil Marcus (New York: Alfred A. Knopf, 1979), 38.

29 Benjamin, *Arcades*, Folder H, sec. 5, pt. 1.

30 Baier, "What Emotions Are About," 4. Baier continues: "Descartes, Rousseau, and Darwin note and emphasize what no one as far as I would know would deny, but what too few attend to, the fact that our emotions are sensitive both to tone and to rhythm, and are expressed in tone of voice and rhythm of speech. The other important fact about our emotions that Descartes notes is that at least some of them have 'deep' objects, that behind the immediate object stand the ghosts of all the other objects which that specific sort of emotion has had in this person's history, and maybe also the shadows of those that it will have" (4).

31 Baier, "What Emotions Are About," 13.

32 Benjamin, *Arcades*, Folder H, sec. 5, pt. 1.

33 Søren Kierkegaard, *Repetition: An Essay in Experimental Psychology*, trans. Walter Lowrie (Princeton, N.J.: Princeton University Press, 1946), 13.

34 Walter Benjamin, *Illuminations*, trans. Harry Zohn (New York: Harcourt, Brace and World, 1969), 237.

35 Benjamin, *Arcades*, Folder H, sec. 4a, pt. 1.

36 Theodor W. Adorno, *In Search of Wagner*, trans. Rodney Livingstone (London: NLB, 1981), 63.

37 Edward W. Said, *After the Last Sky: Palestinian Lives* (New York: Pantheon Books, 1986), 30, 37, 38, 52.

The sublime lyrical abstractions of Edward W. Said

1 Edward W. Said, *Musical Elaborations* (New York: Columbia University Press, 1991). Subsequent references to this text will be cited parenthetically.

2 Richard Poirier, *The Performing Self: Compositions and Decompositions in the Languages of Contemporary Life* (New York: Oxford University Press, 1971).

3 Edward W. Said, *The World, the Text, and the Critic* (Cambridge: Harvard University Press, 1983), 226–47.

4 Said, *The World, the Text, and the Critic*, 38–39.

5 Rodney joined Parker in the late 1940s, when Gillespie moved on; his playing is featured on some of Parker's most significant recordings (mostly on Savoy Records) during a four-year period that immediately preceded the arrival of a very young Davis into Parker's working group. Rodney's quintet performances in February 1990 and in February and March 1991 in La Jolla, California, are among the greatest he recorded. His remarks on the bandstand were made during the 1991 engagement. For anyone interested, a remarkable essay by Gene Lees, "The Nine Lives of Red Rodney," in Lees's *Cats of Any Color: Jazz Black and White* (New York: Oxford University Press, 1994), presents an accurate and detailed account of a musician who was more improbable, mischievous, and more of a risk taker than anyone likely to survive as long and as well as Rodney did.

6 William H. Gass, *Fiction and the Figures of Life* (New York: Random House, 1971), 248.

7 Kenneth Burke, *Attitudes toward History* (Boston: Beacon, 1959), 107.

8 Said is more sanguine than I am about the current state of music scholarship, although his appreciations are directed toward a body of work on the "high" classical tradition, while my reservation derives from the far more mixed results among the recent splurge of publications concerned with the "other," essentially North American classical tradition. The reach of African American musical energy is, of course, global.

9 Edward W. Said, *Representations of the Intellectual* (New York: Random House, 1996), xii.

10 R. P. Blackmur, *The Lion and the Honeycomb: Essays in Solicitude and Critique* (New York: Harcourt, Brace, 1955), 28.

Uses of aesthetics: after orientalism

1 It is hard not to see the same blurring of aesthetic and ethical stances in Jean Genet, who fought together with Palestinian guerrillas.

2 Kant himself saw the non-Western world aesthetically. He wrote, "If we cast a fleeting glance over the other parts of the world, we find the Arab the noblest man in the Orient, yet of a feeling that degenerates very much into the adventurous." He claimed that the Arabs are "the Spaniards of the Orient"; the Persians are "the French of Asia"; the Japanese are "the Englishmen of this part of the world." Furthermore, he thought that "among all savages there is no nation that displays so sublime a mental character as those of North America." On the other hand, he detected the distortion of humanity in Indians, Chinese, and Negroes of Africa. After all, Kant considered as sublime the mannerisms of the warrior class and the culture centered on it. It goes without saying that his understanding is based on the European representation of the world of his time. See Immanuel Kant, *Observations of the Feeling of the Beautiful and Sublime*, trans. John T. Goldthwait (Berkeley and Los Angeles: University of California Press, 1960), 109–11.

3 The Feuerbachian notion that considers God as the self-alienation of man's generic essence is not a materialistic inversion of Hegel but rather a derivative of the Kantian theory of sublime.

4   Karl Marx, *Capital: A Critique of Political Economy*, vol. 1, intro. Ernest Mandel, trans. Ben Fowkes (New York: Vintage, 1977), 125.

5   Albert O. Hirschman, *The Passions and the Interests: Political Arguments for Capitalism Before Its Triumph* (Princeton, N.J.: Princeton University Press, 1977).

6   The disinterestedness in the aesthetic stance is made possible in the supremacy of economic interest; therefore, it is impossible to escape it by bracketing it. For instance, it is the most mundane and deceptive view to simply distinguish artistic value and commodity value. If a certain work is deemed truly valuable as art, it is valuable as commodity and sold to a collector or museum.

7   See "The Modernist Painting," in *Clement Greenberg: The Collected Essays and Criticism*, vol. 4, *Modernism with a Vengeance, 1957–1969*, ed. John O'Brian (Chicago: University of Chicago Press, 1993), 85.

8   James Baldwin, *The Fire Next Time* (New York: Dial, 1963).

9   Johann Gottlieb Fichte, *Addresses to the German Nation*, trans. R. F. Jones and G. H. Turnbull (Westport, Conn.: Greenwood, 1979), 47.

10 Okakura was clearly aware that art could represent Japan because it was internationally acclaimed. "It is art that represents the spirit of our nation, while things like literature and religion, though truly admirable, are only effective in our country and not the world over. Only art can be our representative vis-à-vis the world; its influence is wide and strong, and incomparable to that of literature and religion. Near the end of the Tokugawa regime, at a time of social unrest, important works inherited from the past were destroyed, trashed, or abandoned like pieces of wood or waste paper. This makes me very sad" (from *Nihon Bijutsu Shi* [The history of Japanese art] [1891], in *Meiji Bungaku Zenshu* [Collections of literary works of the Meiji period], vol. 38 [Tokyo: Chikuma Shobo, 1968], 251–52).

11 Kakuzo Okakura, *The Book of Tea* (New York: Kodansha International, 1989), 31–32.

12 Okakura, *Nihon Bijutsu Shi*, 251–52.

13 For instance, Akutagawa Ryunosuke, who wrote many novels about Christian missionaries and Christ, commented: "About ten years ago I used to love Christianity, Catholicism in particular, as art. The Temple of the Japanese Madonna in Nagasaki still remains in my memory. . . . It is only recently that I have begun to love Christ as a person as described by four biographers" (*A Man from the West* [1927], in *Akutagawa Ryunosuke Zenshu*, vol. 7 [Tokyo: Chikuma Shobo, 1989]).

14 Yanagi Soestu, "Chosen no Tomoni Okuru Sho" (A text dedicated to Korean friends), originally published in *Kaizo* (June 1920) and included in *Mingei Yonju Nen* (Forty years of native crafts) (Tokyo: Iwanami Bunko, Iwanami Shoten, 1984).

15 The comments of both Mui Ing and Kim Hyon are taken from Tsurumi Shunsuke's essay "Ushinawareta Tenki" (The lost moment of turn), written as a commentary for *Yanagi Soestu Zenshu* (The complete works of Yanagi Soestu) (Tokyo: Chikuma Shobo, 1980).

Edward W. Said and the American public sphere: speaking truth to power

1   Edward W. Said, *The Question of Palestine* (New York: Times Books, 1979); *Covering Islam: How the Media and the Experts Determine How We See the Rest of the World* (New York: Pantheon, 1981); *After the Last Sky: Palestinian Lives* (New York: Pantheon, 1986); (edited with Christopher Hitchens) *Blaming the Victims: Spurious Scholarship and the Palestinian Question* (New York: Verso, 1988); *The Politics of Dispossession: The Struggle for Palestinian Self-Determination, 1969–*

1993 (New York: Pantheon, 1994); *Peace and Its Discontents: Essays on Palestine in the Middle East Peace Process* (New York: Vintage, 1996).

2   Recently, Villanova University was assailed by the Zionist Organization of America and the Anti-Discrimination League in the Philadelphia area for listing the site of a summer program as "Ramallah, Palestine."

3   *Harper's* index, *Harper's*, July 1997, 13.

4   Soon after the assassination of Rabbi Meir Kahane, founder of the racist Kach Party, in New York, Said was placed under police protection because the New York Police Department had received credible information that he and others identified with the Palestinian cause were on a hit list compiled by the late rabbi's supporters. In addition, his office was vandalized, his apartment was broken into, and he has been subjected to lesser forms of harassment.

5   Edward W. Said, *The Pen and the Sword: Conversations with David Barsamian* (Monroe, Maine: Common Courage, 1994), 138. Many of Said's comments in response to Barsamian's questions explain why Said has invested so much effort in this arena and why he considers it so important.

6   Edward W. Said, *Representations of the Intellectual* (New York: Pantheon, 1994), 11.

7   Some television programs, such as CNN's *Crossfire*, as well as radio broadcasts, take the construction of these polarities to ridiculous extremes, with the apparent objective of provoking the most violent disagreements possible. *Crossfire's* "moderators" generally add fuel to the fire whenever possible. Conventional news shows such as PBS's *NewsHour with Jim Lehrer* and ABC's *Nightline* construct similarly artificial polarities, although the range of opinions allowed on the air in such shows is generally far more limited and much tamer.

8   It is notable that this media conformity with the government line is generally far more evident regarding foreign rather than domestic policy issues. For a brilliant analysis of how this system of media complicity with authority functions, see Edward S. Herman and Noam Chomsky, *Manufacturing Consent: The Political Economy of the Mass Media* (New York: Pantheon, 1988). For an update on their data on the concentration of media ownership in fewer and fewer hands, see Mark Crispin Miller, "The Crushing Power of Big Publishing," Tom Engelhardt, "Gutenberg Unbound," and Janine Jacquet, "The Media Nation: Publishing," *Nation* 264, no. 10, 17 March 1997, 11–27.

9   According to recent figures released by the Palestinian Authority, the already extremely low gross domestic product (GDP) per capita in the West Bank and the Gaza Strip has decreased by 40 percent since 1993, an average of about 10 percent per year for the past four years. Unemployment, already high, has increased, although different sources cite different figures, ranging from 25 to 40 percent of the labor force. According to an Associated Press story dated 11 June 1997, unemployment in the Gaza Strip has doubled to 38 percent over the past three years.

10   This acknowledgment is more likely to be private than public: In the first six months of 1997, two experienced journalists told me that they have only belatedly come to realize that Said's harsh assessment of the Oslo Accord was accurate. One of these journalists told me: "I was put off at first, but now I realize he was right."

11   This was argued most forcefully in a seminal article, "Permission to Narrate," *Journal of Palestine Studies* 13 (spring 1984): 27–48.

12   Said, *Blaming the Victims*, 18.

13   Sometimes spin control does work: The *New York Times* often appears to operate as a

mouthpiece for Israel. Striking examples include Barbara Crossette, "UN Renews Censure of New Israeli Housing in East Jerusalem," 16 July 1997. Of its fifteen paragraphs, seven conveyed in detail Israeli arguments against the resolution, with ample direct quotes from Israel's ambassador-designate to the UN. The article included no quotations from the text of the resolution itself, no explanation of the motives of the 131 countries that voted for it (including all of the European Union countries except Germany), and no quotations from any of the sponsors or supporters of the resolution. Consistent with such an approach, the article referred to the area in question as "disputed" territory, ignoring Security Council resolutions that declared East Jerusalem an occupied territory. Another example is Stephan Erlanger's front-page article (4 August 1997), which conveys paragraph after paragraph of Israeli criticisms of Arafat's handling of terrorism, with barely one paragraph of lame Palestinian responses. The item is complemented with a sidebar that reproduces allegedly incriminating statements by Arafat (some of them completely anodyne) culled by the Israeli Press Office and the American Israeli Political Action Committee.

14   Said, *Peace and Its Discontents*, 51–53.

15   Among the most prominent were Ghassan Kanafani, Kamal 'Adwan, Abu Yusuf Najjar, Kamal Nasser, Majid Abu Sharar, and Khalil al-Wazir, who were all victims of Israeli hit squads, and Abu 'Ali Iyyad, Dr. 'Abd al-Wahhab Kayyali, Brigadier General Sa'd Sayil (Abu al-Walid), 'Isam Sirtawi, Hayil 'Abd al-Hamid (Abu al-Hol), and Salah Khalaf (Abu Iyyad), who were all murdered by Arab governments or their surrogates.

16   Said's response to some of Arafat's criticisms can be found in an interview with a Cairo magazine, al-'Arabi, reprinted in an appendix to *Peace and Its Discontents*, 165–85.

17   In an interview included in *The Pen and the Sword*, Said himself noted that "after I came back from South Africa I had a much better sense of how the Palestinian national movement, at least in the 1970's and early 1980's, was . . . able to bring Palestinians into the twentieth-century experience of colonization" (52). He mentions his meeting with Mandela in the same interview.

18   Said paraphrases Fanon thus in an interview included in *The Pen and the Sword*, 80.

19   Notably, *The Politics of Dispossession* and *Peace and Its Discontents*.

20   Edward W. Said, *The Palestine Question and the American Context* (Beirut: Institute for Palestine Studies, 1979).

21   Said, *Peace and Its Discontents*, xxiii.

22   See, for example, *Peace and Its Discontents*, "Memory and Forgetfulness in the United States," from February 1995, and "Justifications of Power in a Terminal Phase," from April 1995, 135–46. Said wrote numerous such articles for al-Hayat and al-Majallah over the past decade or so. See also his article "L'Irangate, une crise aux multiples facettes," *Revue d'Etudes Palestiniennes*, 25 (fall 1987): 105–38, for an example of this sort of writing for an Arab readership (in this case, a francophone one).

23   Said makes this point forcefully in an interview reproduced in *The Pen and the Sword*, 118.

24   Said, *Peace and Its Discontents*, 169–70.

25   Said, *Peace and Its Discontents*, 184–85.

Sappers in the stacks: colonial archives, land mines, and truth commissions

This article draws in significant part on research toward *Imperialism and Orientalism: A Documentary Sourcebook*, edited with Mia Carter (forthcoming). That project itself derives importantly from the outstanding example of Edward W. Said and the groundbreaking exempla of *Orientalism* and *Culture and Imperialism*.

1 Edward W. Said, "Speaking Truth to Power," in *Representations of the Intellectual* (London: Vintage, 1994), 73.

2 Jeremy Cronin, *Even the Dead: Poems, Parables and a Jeremiad* (Cape Town and Johannesburg: David Philip/University of the Western Cape: Mayibuye Books, 1997), 29–30. I thank Jeremy Cronin for sharing his poems with me.

3 Rudyard Kipling, "Sappers," in *Works* (Hertsfordshire: Wordworth Editors, 1994), 435–36.

4 Said, "Speaking Truth to Power," 73.

5 *The Letters of Queen Victoria: A Selection of Her Majesty's Correspondence between the Years 1836 and 1861*, ed. Arthur Christopher Benson, M.A., and Viscount Esher (New York: Longmans, Green and Co., 1907).

6 William Howard Russell, *Russell's Despatches from the Crimea, 1854–1856*, ed. Nicolas Bentley (New York: Hill and Wang, 1966).

7 Karl Marx, *The Eastern Question*, ed. Eleanor Marx Aveling and Edward Aveling (London: Swan Sonnenschein and Co., 1897).

8 Florence Nightingale, *Ever Yours, Florence Nightingale: Selected Letters*, ed. Martha Vicinus and Bea Nergaard (Cambridge: Harvard University Press, 1990).

9 Lytton Strachey, "Florence Nightingale," in *Eminent Victorians* (New York: Harcourt, Brace and World, 1918), 154.

10 'Urabi Pasha, quoted in the (London) *Times*, 25 July 1882.

11 Albert Hourani, *A History of the Arab Peoples* (Cambridge: Harvard University Press, 1991), 275.

12 William Gladstone, "Aggression on Egypt and Freedom in the East," *Nineteenth Century*, August 1887.

13 Evelyn Baring, 1st Earl of Cromer, *Modern Egypt*, vol. 1 (London: Macmillan, 1908), 183–84; Sir Alfred Milner, *England in Egypt* (London: Edward Arnold, 1893), 438.

14 See, for example, Wilfred Scawen Blunt, *The Secret History of the English Occupation of Egypt: Being a Personal Narrative of Events* (London: T. Fisher Unwin, 1907); A. M. Broadley, *How We Defended Arabi and His Friends* (London: Chapman and Hall, 1884); Wilfred S. Blunt, *India Under Ripon* (London: T. Fisher Unwin, 1909); Wilfred S. Blunt, *Gordon at Khartoum* (London: Stephen Swift and Co., 1911); and Wilfred S. Blunt, *The Land War in Ireland* (London: Herbert and Daniel, 1913).

15 Cromer, *Modern Egypt*, 1:300.

16 General Charles George Gordon, *Letters to His Sister* (London: Macmillan, 1900), iv.

17 Cromer, *Modern Egypt*, vol. 1, chaps. 22–24, 417–78; Blunt, *Gordon at Khartoum*, 87.

18 *The Journals of Major-Gen. C. G. Gordon, C. B., at Kartoum*, ed. A. Hegmont Hake (London: Kegan, Paul, Trench and Co., 1885).

19 John Buchan, *Gordon at Khartoum* (London: Peter Davies, 1934); Arthur Conan Doyle, *The Tragedy of the Korosko* (London: South, Elder and Co., 1898).

20 See Byron Farwell, *Queen Victoria's Little Wars* (New York: W. W. Norton, 1985).

21 W. T. Stead, "Editorial," *Review of Reviews* 13 (1896); Cecil Rhodes, *Political Life and Speeches*, ed. Vindex (London: Chapman and Hall, 1900); Olive Schreiner and C. S. Cronwright Schreiner, *The Political Situation* (London: T. Fisher Unwin, 1896), 41; Olive Schreiner, *An English–South African's View of the Situation* (London: Hodder and Stoughton, 1899), 76; and J. A. Hobson, *Imperialism* (1902; reprint, Ann Arbor: University of Michigan Press, 1965).

22 Stephen Wheeler, "Sikhs and Boers," *Anglo-Saxon Review* 3 (December 1899): 221–23; Arthur Waugh, "The Poetry of the South African Campaign," *Anglo-Saxon Review* 7 (December 1900): 42–49; and Rudyard Kipling, "The Absent-Minded Beggar," in *Works*, 459–60.

23 Rudyard Kipling, "A Sahib's War," in *War Stories and Poems* (New York: Oxford University Press, 1987), 163.

24 George Witton, *Scapegoats of the Empire: The True Story of Breaker Morant's Bushveldt Carbineers* (London: Angus and Robertson, 1982), 1.

25 Maud Gonne, *A Servant of the Queen: Her Own Story* (1938; reprint, Gerrards Cross, England: Colin Smythe, 1994), 309.

26 Emily Hobhouse, *Reports on the Camps of Women and Children in the Cape and Orange River Colonies* (London: Committee of the South African Distress Fund, 1901), 40; Millicent Garrett Fawcett, *What I Remember* (London: T. Fisher Unwin, 1925), 157; and Arthur Conan Doyle, *The War in South Africa: Its Cause and Conduct* (New York: McClure, Phillips and Co., 1902), preface.

27 Joseph Conrad, *Heart of Darkness*, ed. Robert Kimbrough (New York: W. W. Norton and Co., Inc., 1963), 50.

28 Cited in Brian Inglis, *Roger Casement* (Belfast: Blackstaff, 1993), 96–97. The quotation that follows is from the same work, 97.

29 E. D. Morel, *King Leopold's Rule in Africa* (1904; reprint, Westport, Conn.: Negro Universities Press, 1970), 247; E. D. Morel, *The History of the Congo Reform Movement*, ed. William Roger Louis and Jean Stengers (1910; reprint, Oxford: Clarendon, 1968); Arthur Conan Doyle, *The Crime of the Congo* (Toronto: Musson Book Co., 1910); Mark Twain, "King Leopold's Soliloquy," in *Life As I Find It*, ed. Charles Neider (Garden City, N.Y.: Hanover House, 1961), 280; and Inglis, *Roger Casement*, 159.

30 Said, "Speaking Truth to Power," 68–69, 72.

31 Malcolm X, "Not Just an American Problem," in *Malcolm X: The Last Speeches*, ed. Bruce Perry (New York: Pathfinder, 1989), 180–81.

32 Said, "Speaking Truth to Power," xii.

33 Jeremy Cronin, "Even the Dead," *West Coast Line* 20 (fall 1996): 24–29. This poem also appears in Cronin's collection *Even the Dead*, 39–44.

34 Stanley Cohen, "Government Responses to Human Rights Reports: Claims, Denials and Counterclaims," *Human Rights Quarterly* 18, no. 3 (1996): 542.

35 Anonymous, "Human Rights in Peace Negotiations," *Human Rights Quarterly* 18, no. 2 (1996): 258; Mike Tomlinson, "Can Britain Leave Ireland," *Race and Class* 37, no. 1 (1995): 17.

36 Gino Strada, "The Horror of Land Mines," *Scientific American* 274, no. 5 (May 1996): 40.

37 Kenneth Anderson, "An Overview of the Global Land Mines Crisis," in *Clearing the Fields: Solutions to the Global Landmines Crisis*, ed. Keven M. Cahill (New York: Basic Books/Council on Foreign Relations, 1995), 19.

38 Chris Giannou and H. Jack Geiger, "The Medical Lessons of Land Mine Injuries," in Cahill, ed., *Clearing the Fields*, 138–39.

39 Michael Ignatieff, "Articles of Faith," *Index on Censorship* 5 (1996): 111, 113.

40 Bill Rolston, "Turning the Page without Closing the Book," *Index on Censorship* 5 (1996): 34, 36.

Parts of this essay were presented at various universities: Technische Universität Braunschweig, Universität Hannover, Bremen Universität, and the University of Alberta. I thank the following for inviting me to speak: Prof. Dr. Hans-Joachim Possin, Prof. Dr. Liselotte Glage, Ms. Cecile Sandten, and Dr. Ted Blodgett. For kindness extended to me by Dr. David Hoeniger, who read the manuscript in its entirety, I am deeply appreciative. Finally, all translations, unless otherwise indicated, are my own.

1   Wadie Said, a prosperous businessman, headed a company that made office equipment and published books. Edward was his oldest child and only son. See Edward W. Said, "Cairo and Alexandria," *Departures* (May/June 1990): 1–11.

2   The episode is eloquently narrated in "Cairo Recalled: Growing Up in the Cultural Crosscurrents of 1940s Cairo," *House and Garden* (April 1987): 20–32.

3   Edward W. Said, *Culture and Imperialism* (New York: Knopf, 1993), xxvii. Hereafter, this work is cited parenthetically.

4   Edward W. Said, "East Isn't East: The Impending End of the Age of Orientalism," TLS 3 (February 1995): 4. The essay discusses the characterization of the book *Orientalism* as anti-Western. Said explains that the book presents Orientalism as a miniature symbol for the West and that it therefore presents the entire West as the enemy of the Arab and Islamic world. The second part of this argument, he states, posits that the predatory West and Orientalism have violated Islam and the Arabs and that the book has been read and written about in the Arab world as a systematic defense of Islam and the Arabs, even though he has no interest, much less the capacity, for showing what true Orientalism and true Islam really are. He expresses his regret of so simple a characterization of his book, arguing that he nowhere says that Orientalism is evil, sloppy, or uniformly the same in the work of all Orientalists.

5   Bharati Mukherjee, *Jasmine* (London: Penguin, 1989), 27.

6   Edward W. Said, "Interview," *Diacritics* (fall 1976): 35.

7   Palestine had been a mandated territory of Great Britain since 1920, but in 1947, the British turned over control of the country to the United Nations, which divided it into an Arab state and a Jewish state, and placed the city of Jerusalem under international control. At the age of twelve, Said was forced to use a pass when traveling between his home and school. "The situation was dangerous and inconvenient," he recalled to Dinitia Smith during an interview (in *Current Biography Yearbook* [New York: H. W. Wilson Publications, 1989], 494). In December 1947, the Saids left Jerusalem and settled in Cairo, Egypt. Five months later, war broke out between Palestinian Arabs and Jews after the Arabs rejected the partition of Palestine into Jewish and Arab sections, an event that Palestinians ever since have referred to as the *nakbah*, or disaster. For a detailed view of this matter, see Edward W. Said, *The Question of Palestine* (New York: Vintage, 1992). For Elizabeth Hayford's comments, see *"After the Last Sky: A Review," Library Journal* (December 1986): 36.

8   Said is a man of many parts: A specialist in English and comparative literature, an advocate of the new textual approaches in literary studies, he is also the most prominent political spokesman for the Palestinians in the United States. But he is more than just a literary critic and Arabist. He is a dedicated amateur musician and accomplished pianist, with a particular interest in the great classics of Western music, from Bach to Richard Strauss. Said also has been the music critic for the *Nation* since 1986.

9   Edward W. Said, "Orientalism Reconsidered," in *Literature, Politics, and Theory: Papers from the Essex Conference, 1976–84*, ed. Francis Barker, Peter Hulme, Margaret Iversen, and Diana

Loxley (London: Methuen, 1986), 210; Dennis Porter, "Orientalism and Its Problems," in *The Politics of Theory: Proceedings of the Essex Conference on the Sociology of Literature, July 1982*, ed. Francis Barker et al. (Colchester, England: University of Essex Press, 1983), 34; Bernard Lewis, "The Question of Orientalism," *New York Review*, 24 June 1982, 49; James Clifford, "On Orientalism," in *The Predicament of Culture* (Cambridge: Harvard University Press, 1988), 255–77; Robert Young, "Disorienting Orientalism," in *White Mythologies: Writing History and the West* (London: Routledge, 1990), 135; Jacques Berque, " 'Au-delà de l'Orientalisme': Entretien avec Jacques Berques," *Qantara* 13 (October/November/December 1994): 27–28; and Abdelkebir Khatibi, *Maghreb pluriel* (Paris: Denoël, 1983), 130.

10 Maxime Rodinson, "Fantômes et réalités de l'Orientalisme," *Qantara* 13 (October/November/December 1994): 15. I thank Ms. Samia Annabi for providing this reference.

11 Edward W. Said, *Orientalism* (New York: Vintage, 1979), 327. Hereafter, this work is cited parenthetically.

12 Russell Jacoby, "Marginal Returns: The Trouble with Post-Colonial Theory," *Lingua Franca* (September/October 1995): 32.

13 Bart Moore-Gilbert, "Edward Said: Orientalism and Beyond," in *Postcolonial Theory: Contexts, Practices, Politics* (London: Verso, 1997), 34–74. John MacKenzie, *Orientalism: History, Theory and the Arts* (Manchester, England: Manchester University Press, 1995).

14 Ernest Gellner, "The Mightier Pen? Edward Said and the Double Standards of Inside-Out Colonialism," *TLS* 19 February 1993, 3–4.

15 Moore-Gilbert, "Edward Said," in *Postcolonial Theory*, 65. Moore-Gilbert cites Said, *Culture and Imperialism*, 248.

16 On the tirade against Said, see Edward Alexander, "Professor of Terror," *Commentary* (August 1989): 49–50. For Flaubert's defense of Bouilhet, see *Louis Bouilhet: Lettres à Gustave Flaubert*, ed. Maria Cappello (Paris: CNRS, 1996), 391.

17 "A field of studies in 'colonial discourse' and 'post-colonial theory,' " W. J. T. Mitchell writes, "has now emerged as an academic speciality in large part because of Said's brilliant pioneering scholarship" ("In the Wilderness," *London Review of Books*, 8 April 1993, 12). Moore-Gilbert gives a detailed account of the literature that followed the publication of *Orientalism* in "Postcolonial Criticism or Postcolonial Theory?" and "Postcolonial Criticism and Postcolonial Theory," in *Postcolonial Theory*, 5–34 and 152–85, respectively.

18 This and the preceding quotation are from Said, "East Isn't East," 3, 5.

19 For more details on Said's Arab critics, see "Images-miroirs de l'Orientalisme," *Qantara* 13 (October/November/December 1994): 25–26; Sadaq Jalal al-'Azm, "Orientalism and Orientalism in Reverse," *Khamsin* (London) 8 (1981): 23–40; M. H. A. al-Saghīr, *al-Mustashriqūm wa-l-Dirāsāt al-Qur'āniyya* (Beirut: Dar al-Wahda, 1983); N. al-Bītār, *Hudūd al-Huwiyya al-Qawmiyya* (Beirut: Dar al-Wahda, 1982); and Slimane Zeghidour, "Interview with Mohammed Arkoun and Bencheikh on 'Orientalism and Modernity,' " *al-Fikr al-Mu'asir* (summer 1978): 23–41.

20 Homi Bhabha, "The Other Question: Difference, Discrimination and the Discourse of Colonialism," in *Literature, Politics and Theory*, 157. The next quotation is also from this work, 158.

21 Moore-Gilbert's electric reading of Said in *Postcolonial Theory*, 34–74, is a case in point.

22 Nowhere is this reality more obvious than in colonial urbanism, where the political, economic, and cultural issues that underlie the colonial system are interwoven together. Examples abound, but one stands out. David Prochaska's *Making Algeria French* is the story of one town, Bône (Annaba), from 1830 to 1920, studied in terms of its plural society, internal colonialism, and the effects of settler colonialism. Prochaska argues that the plu-

ral society in the settler colonial city was residentially segregated according to race and ethnicity, and that ethnic and racial factors determined social stratification more than class. Therefore, conducting and preserving a "social distance" between ethnic and racial groups was of extreme importance for the colonial order. This is what Frantz Fanon aptly calls the geography of the colonial city in *The Wretched of the Earth*, trans. Constance Farrington (New York: Grove Press, 1964), 31–32. For a somewhat different but also important view of the colonial city, see Janet Abu-Lughod's masterful study, *Rabat: Urban Apartheid in Morocco* (Princeton, N.J.: Princeton University Press, 1980); Abdelkebir Khatibi gives a compelling mapping of the colonial city in "A Colonial Labyrinth," *Yale French Studies* 2, no. 83 (1993): 23.

23   Homi Bhabha, *The Location of Culture* (London: Routledge, 1994), 70, 81.

24   Arif Dirlik, "The Postcolonial Aura: Third World Criticism in the Age of Global Capitalism," *Critical Inquiry* (winter 1994): 333. As Benita Parry perceptively puts it, "The matter of [Bhabha's] . . . implicated style is not one on which I will dwell, other than to observe the enchantment with troping, punning and riddling all too often sends the signifier into free-fall, rendering arbitrary the link between word and signified. To mean what you say is not the same as to say what you mean." See her "Signs of Our Times: A Discussion of Homi Bhabha's *The Location of Culture*," *Third Text* (autumn/winter 1994): 6–7.

25   Bhabha's gradual recognition of alternative methodological resources to those offered by the European theory that so dominates his early work can be found in the essays "How Newness Enters the World: Postmodern Space, Postcolonial Times and the Trials of Cultural Translation," in *Location of Culture*, 212–36, and "Unpacking My Library . . . Again," in *The Post-Colonial Question: Common Skies, Divided Horizons*, ed. Iain Chamers and Lidia Curti (London: Routledge, 1996), 199–211, which cite Derek Walcott, W. E. B. du Bois, and C. L. R. James, among others.

26   Abdul JanMohamed, "The Economy of Manichean Allegory: The Function of Racial Difference in Colonialist Literature," in *Race, Writing, and Difference*, ed. Henry Louis Gates Jr. (Chicago: University of Chicago Press, 1985), 79.

27   Moore-Gilbert, "Edward Said," in *Postcolonial Theory*, 42–43.

28   Aijaz Ahmad, *In Theory: Classes, Nations, Literatures* (London: Verso, 1992), 178. The quotation in the next paragraph is also from this work, 205.

29   An interesting example is Puccini's *Madama Butterfly* (1900), which was inspired by Philadelphia lawyer John Luther Long's novella and the one-act play, *The Girl of the Golden West*, that David Belasco derived from it. Long's novella appeared in *The Century* in 1897. A sexist aria, *Madama Butterfly* shaped the Western image of the Oriental woman as a sensuous beauty waiting to be victimized by faithless, feckless Pinkertons and GIs. If this sounds too extreme, then we need only recall Claude-Michel Schonberg and Alain Boublil's *Miss Saigon*, a musical inspired by *Madama Butterfly*, which tells of a tragic romance between a Vietnamese bar girl and a U.S. soldier during the tumultuous American withdrawal from Vietnam. To *Miss Saigon* one must add David Bowie's "China Girl," a song turned into a video, and Frédéric Mittérand's film *Madame Butterfly* (1995), shot in Tunisia of all places, since filming in Japan proved too expensive. These images are like a nest of boxes— a pleasure within a pleasure—that continues to show the Oriental woman as mellow, sensuous, daisy-like, ready to be penetrated by the white man. For an insightful view of this matter, see Ruth Padel, "Putting Words into Women's Mouths: The Female Role in Opera," *London Review of Books*, 23 January 1997, 12–18.

30   Said, "East Isn't East," 4.

31   Moore-Gilbert, "Edward Said," in *Postcolonial Theory*, 35. See also "Postcolonial Criticism

and Postcolonial Theory," in *Postcolonial Theory*, 155, where Gilbert shows Ahmad's double standard toward the West.

32 Zakia Pathak, Sawati Sengupta, and Sharmila Purkaystha, "The Prisonhouse of Oriental-ism," *Textual Practice* (summer 1991): 215.

33 Wilson Harris, "Interior of the Novel: Amerindian/European/African Relations," in *National Identity: Papers Delivered at the Commonwealth Literature Conference, University of Queensland, Brisbane, 9–15 August 1968* (London: Heinemann Educational Books, 1970), 62.

34 Wilson Harris, *Tradition, the Writer and Society* (London: New Beacon, 1967), 145.

35 V. S. Naipaul, *India: A Wounded Civilization* (1977; reprint, New York: Vintage, 1978), 133.

36 Edward W. Said, *Beginnings: Intention and Method* (1975; reprint, New York: Columbia University Press, 1985), 289. Michel Foucault, "Nietzsche, Genealogy and History," in *Language, Counter-Memory, Practice: Selected Essays and Interviews by Michel Foucault*, ed. and with an introduction by Donald F. Bouchard, trans. Donald F. Bouchard and Sherry Simon (Ithaca, N.Y.: Cornell University Press, 1977), 142–43.

37 See Edward W. Said, "An Ideology of Difference," *Critical Inquiry* (fall 1985): 38–58.

38 Fanon, *Wretched of the Earth*, 43, 170.

39 Alain Ruscio, *Amours coloniales: Aventures et fantasmes exotiques* (Paris: Ed. Complexe, 1997), 97; Malek Haddad, "La Révolution a-t-elle été trahie?" in "La Guerre d'Algérie: 30 ans après," a special issue of *Le Nouvel Observateur* 9 (1992): 62; Khatibi, *Maghreb pluriel*, 24; on the realization of Arabic, see Mohamed Benrabeh, "La Purification linguistique," *Télérama hors/série* (March 1995); 36–39; and Martin Heidegger, *Cahiers de l'Herne* 45 (1983): 22.

40 Ania Loomba, "Overworlding the Third World," *Oxford Literary Review* 13 (1991): 165. Gauri Viswanathan, *Masks of Conquest: Literary Study and British Rule in India* (New York: Columbia University Press, 1989), esp. "Lessons of History," 118–42.

41 Said, *Beginnings*, 297.

42 Edward W. Said, "Identity, Authority, and Freedom: The Potentate and the Traveller," *Transition* 54 (1991): 8.

43 Michel Foucault, *The Archaeology of Knowledge and the Discourse on Language*, trans. A. M. Sheridan Smith (1969; reprint, New York: Pantheon, 1972), 12.

44 Bruce Robbins, "American Intellectuals and the Middle East Politics: Interview with Edward Said," *Social Text* (fall 1988): 41.

45 Edward W. Said, "The Politics of Knowledge," *Raritan* (summer 1991): 17–32.

46 Edward W. Said, *The World, the Text, and the Critic* (Cambridge: Harvard University Press, 1983), 203, 221–22.

47 Michael Sprinker, ed., *Edward Said: A Critical Reader* (Oxford, England: Blackwell, 1992), 236.

48 Edward W. Said, "War in the Gulf," *London Review of Books*, 7 March 1991, 7.

49 Said, "War in the Gulf," 7.

50 Moore-Gilbert, "Edward Said," in *Postcolonial Theory*, 37.

51 Edward W. Said, *The Politics of Dispossession: The Struggle for Palestinian Self-Determination, 1969–1994* (New York: Pantheon, 1994), 301.

52 Quoted in Clive Fisher, *Cyril Connolly: A Nostalgic Life* (London: Macmillan, 1995), 65.

53 Edward W. Said, *Representations of the Intellectual* (New York: Pantheon, 1994), 23.

54 Mitchell, "In the Wilderness," 12.

55 See Said, *Representations of the Intellectual*, xi. See also Michael Wood, "Lost Paradises," *New York Review*, 3 March 1994, 44–47; and Susan Fraiman, "Jane Austen and Edward Said: Gender, Culture, and Imperialism," *Critical Inquiry* (summer 1995): 805–21.

56 Said, "Traveling Theory," in The World, the Text, and the Critic, 226.

57 Quoted in Moore-Gilbert, "Edward Said," in Postcolonial Theory, 66.

58 Said, Representations of the Intellectual, xi.

59 On the "politics of blame," see Blaming the Victims: Spurious Scholarship and the Palestinian Question, ed. Edward W. Said and Christopher Hitchens (London: Verso, 1988), 23.
    With regard to Camus, see the words of Roger Quilliot, "comme par réflexe, Camus chercha refuge dans son enfance." Quilliot quotes Camus's letter to his teacher Louis Germain, reproduced in full in the appendix to Le Premier homme (Paris: Gallimard, 1994), 327.

60 Edward W. Said, The Pen and the Sword: Conversations with David Barsamian (Toronto: Between the Lines, 1994), 75; Roland Barthes, Le Degré zéro de l'écriture (1953; reprint, Paris: Gonthier, 1964), 10; Roland Barthes, S/Z, trans. Richard Miller (New York: Hill and Wang, 1974), 73; and Nadine Gordimer, Writing and Being (Cambridge: Harvard University Press, 1995), 71.

61 Edward J. Hugues, Le Premier homme, La Peste (Glasgow: University of Glasgow French and German Publications, 1995), 33.

62 The Collected Fiction of Albert Camus, trans. Stuart Gilbert (London: Hamish Hamilton, 1960), 29. Julia Kristeva is quoted in Eloquent Obsessions: Writing Cultural Criticism, ed. Marianna Torgovnick (Durham, N.C.: Duke University Press, 1995), 11.

63 Collected Fiction of Albert Camus, 82. Le Premier homme once again confirms how Camus saw Arabs—as nameless servants who help Jacques Cormery, the main protagonist in the novel, light a fire in the cold, empty house, settle his wife on a mattress near the fire, and find a doctor. Nowhere in the novel does Camus give them names or let them speak for and/or represent themselves. They are spoken about and represented by him and his characters as the following excerpt shows: "We are made to understand each other. They are stupid and rough as we, but have the same human blood. We will continue to kill each other, cut each other's balls off, torture each other. Then we'll start living together again. It's the country that wants that" (Le Premier homme, 45).

64 Collected Fiction of Albert Camus, 67, 74.

65 Albert Camus, Actuelles: Chroniques Algériennes, 1939–1958 (Paris: Gallimard, 1958), 1:48.

66 Said, Pen and the Sword, 74–75.

67 Albert Camus, introduction to The Outsider, trans. Cyril Connolly (London: Methuen, 1946), 9.

68 See Jean Daniel, "Sartre-Camus: L'Itinéraire d'Alger à Jérusalem," Le Matin (May 1980): 30–31.

69 José Lenzini, L'Algérie de Camus (1987; reprint, Aix-en-Provence: Édisud, 1988), 122. Conor Cruise O'Brien, in Camus (London: Fontana-Collins, 1970), argues that the disappearance of the Arab residents of Oran makes the city "a 'never was' city whereas we should be able to think of it as a real city under an imagined plague" (47).

70 Albert Camus, The Outsider, trans. Joseph Laredo (London: Hamish Hamilton, 1982).

71 Olivier Todd, Albert Camus: A Life, trans. Benjamin Ivry (New York: Knopf, 1997), 23, 46, 79.

72 Conor Cruse O'Brien, Albert Camus (New York: Viking, 1970), 104.

73 David Ellison, "Camus and the Rhetoric of Dizziness: La Chute," Contemporary Literature (fall 1983): 322–48.

74 George Savile, Character of a Trimmer (1688; reprint, London: Printed for Richard Baldwin, 1689), 109. Sartre is quoted in Olivier Todd, Albert Camus: Une vie (Paris: Gallimard, 1995), 331. For Camus's comment on politics, see Camus, Actuelles, 3:23. On allegations that

Camus was subsidized by NATO or the CIA, see John Conteh-Morgan, "Albert Camus, Aimé Césaire and the Tragedy of Revolution," *African Literature Today* 14 (1984): 49–59.

75 Horst Frenz, ed., *Nobel Lectures* (Amsterdam: Elsevier Publishing Company, 1969), 567.

76 Camus, *Actuelles*, 1:45.

77 Camus, *Le Premier homme*, 77; my emphasis.

78 I borrow the formula "Vuve la Fouance" from Patrick Chamoiseau, *Texaco*, trans. Rose-Myriam Réjouis (London: Granta, 1997).

79 See, for example, Irene Berelowitch, "Mémoires," in *Télérama hors-série Algérie* (March 1995): 83; Benjamin Stora, "Guerre d'Algérie: les mémoires blessées," *L'Express* 23 (December 1988): 56; Jacques Derrida, *Le Monolinguisme de l'autre ou la prothèse de l'origine* (Paris: Galilée, 1996), 73.

80 Quoted in Lenzini, *L'Algérie de Camus*, 8.

81 Albert Camus, *Carnets* (Paris: Gallimard, 1989), 3:238.

82 Patrick McCarthy, *Albert Camus: A Critical Study of His Life and Work* (London: Hamish Hamilton, 1982), 12.

83 *Collected Fiction of Albert Camus*, 49, 52.

84 A perspicacious portrait of Camus is given in Robert Goodhand, "The Omphalos and the Phoenix: Symbolism of the Center in Camus' 'La Pierre qui pousse,' " *Studies in Short Fiction* (spring 1984): 117–26; see also Robert Goodhand, "Albert Camus," *Lire* 186 (March 1991): 123–34.

85 Todd, *Albert Camus: Une vie*, 543–44.

86 Camus, *Carnets*, 3:183.

87 Todd, *Albert Camus: A Life*, 155, 178.

88 Camus, *Carnets*, 3:397.

89 Imre Salusinszky, *Criticism in Society: Interviews* (New York: Methuen, 1987), 67.

90 "I have been accused," Said writes, "by colleagues of intemperate and even unseemly polemicism. To still others—and this concerns me more—it may seem that I am an undeclared Marxist, afraid of losing respectability and concerned by the contradictions entailed by the label 'Marxist' " (*The World, the Text, and the Critic*, 28).

91 Said, "Cairo Recalled," 32; Said, "Cairo and Alexandria," 6.

92 Said, *Peace and Its Discontents*, 177.

93 Milan Kundera, *The Art of the Novel*, trans. Linda Asher (New York: Grove, 1988), 17.

Auerbach in Istanbul: Edward Said, secular criticism, and the question of minority culture

For Mazen Arafat.

An earlier version of this essay was presented at "After Orientalism," a conference to honor the work and life of Edward Said, organized at his home institution, Columbia University, by his present and former students, and held in October of 1996. I am deeply grateful to the organizing committee and to its ringleader, Qadri Ismail, in particular, for inviting me to participate in what proved to be an experience of a lifetime and an opportunity to begin to acknowledge an unrepayable debt. I am also indebted to Val Daniel for inviting me to present related work at the Program in the Comparative Study of Social Transformation at the University of Michigan, Ann Arbor. For their encouragement at various stages I must especially thank Kamran Asdar Ali, Jean Howard, Tejaswini Niranjana, Edward Said, Milind Wakankar, and Cornel West. My thanks also to the editors of *Critical Inquiry*, and to Homi Bhabha in particular, for the carefulness of their responses and suggestions. The essay has benefited enormously from the close reading of Mazen

Arafat, Qadri Ismail, and Gyan Prakash. It is really an episode in an ongoing conversation with Mazen.

1   See Bruce Robbins, "Secularism, Elitism, Progress, and Other Transgressions: On Edward Said's 'Voyage In,' " *Social Text*, no. 40 (fall 1994): 26.

2   See Edward W. Said, *Beginnings: Intention and Method* (New York: Basic Books, 1975), 68. See also Erich Auerbach, "Philology and *Weltliteratur*," trans. Maire Said and Edward W. Said, *Centennial Review* 13 (winter 1969): 11; hereafter abbreviated "PW."

3   Tim Brennan, "Places of Mind, Occupied Lands: Edward Said and Philology," in *Edward Said: A Critical Reader*, ed. Michael Sprinker (Oxford, England: Blackwell, 1992), 81, 92.

4   See ibid., 80.

5   Quoted in Said, "Reflections on Exile," *Granta* 13 (autumn 1984): 171; hereafter abbreviated "RE." Auerbach leaves out the last sentence.

6   James Clifford, "On *Orientalism*," in *The Predicament of Culture: Twentieth-Century Ethnography, Literature, and Art* (Cambridge, Mass.: Harvard University Press, 1988), 263–64; hereafter abbreviated PC.

7   See Brennan, "Places of Mind, Occupied Lands," 77.

8   Brennan, of course, points to the strategic value of that elitism within the U.S. public sphere.

9   Aijaz Ahmad, *In Theory: Classes, Nations, Literatures* (London: Verso, 1992), 164; hereafter abbreviated IT.

10 On the characteristic "hairshirt attitudinizing" tone of Ahmad's book, see Marjorie Levinson, "News from Nowhere: The Discontents of Aijaz Ahmad," *Public Culture* 6 (fall 1993): 101. Levinson's is by far the most astute and ambitious essay in this special issue on Ahmad's book.

11 Vassilis Lambropoulos, *The Rise of Eurocentrism: Anatomy of Interpretation* (Princeton, N.J.: Princeton University Press, 1993), 4; see also 3, 5. I am grateful to Stathis Gourgouris for first pointing me to this work.

12 Auerbach, *Literary Language and Its Public in Late Latin Antiquity and in the Middle Ages*, trans. Ralph Manheim (New York: Pantheon, 1965), 22; see also 24.

13 Said, *Orientalism* (New York: Pantheon, 1978), 258; hereafter abbreviated O.

14 Auerbach, "Vico's Contribution to Literary Criticism," in *Studia Philologica et Litteraria in Honorem L. Spitzer*, ed. A. G. Hatcher and K. L. Selig (Bern, 1958), 34.

15 Said and Said, introduction to PW, 2.

16 Said, *The World, the Text, and the Critic* (Cambridge, Mass.: Harvard University Press, 1983), 5; hereafter abbreviated WT.

17 Auerbach, *Mimesis: The Representation of Reality in Western Literature*, trans. Willard R. Trask (Princeton, N.J.: Princeton University Press, 1953), 557.

18 Abdul R. JanMohamed, "Worldliness-without-World, Homelessness-as-Home: Toward a Definition of the Specular Border Intellectual," in *Edward Said*, 98–99.

19 Lambropoulos misconstrues Said's meaning entirely when he extracts from this final sentence only the phrase "a massive reaffirmation of the Western cultural tradition" and presents it as Said's characterization of *Mimesis* (quoted in Lambropoulos, *The Rise of Eurocentrism*, 6).

20 Hannah Arendt, *The Origins of Totalitarianism*, rev. ed. (New York: Harcourt Brace Jovanovich, 1979), 289, 297; hereafter abbreviated OT.

21 Adelbert von Chamisso, *Peter Schlemiel: The Man Who Sold His Shadow*, trans. Peter Wortsman (New York: Basic Books, 1993), 14.

22 Works on Joyce and exile are, of course, legion. But I have in mind the kind of paradig-

matic status he has for a number of French critics, such as Hélène Cixous, *The Exile of James Joyce*, trans. Sally A. J. Purcell (New York: D. Lewis, 1972).

23 Emily Apter, "Comparative Exile: Competing Margins in the History of Comparative Literature," in *Comparative Literature in the Age of Multiculturalism*, ed. Charles Bernheimer (Baltimore: Johns Hopkins University Press, 1995), 90.

24 Theodor Adorno, *Minima Moralia: Reflections from Damaged Life*, trans. E. F. N. Jephcott (London: New Left Books, 1974), 39; quoted in "RE," 170.

25 Said, *Beginnings*, 372–73.

26 I assume that Said means Cleanth Brooks. However, it is not clear from Said's text if he means Robert Penn or Austin Warren—I suspect the former—although from my present perspective the meaning here would remain substantially the same in either case.

27 Robbins, "Secularism, Elitism, Progress, and Other Transgressions," 27.

28 "The banner of 'secularism' has for more than a century been the standard of a Westernized elite" (Brennan, *Salman Rushdie and the Third World: Myths of the Nation* [New York: St. Martin's, 1989], 144). See also Ashis Nandy, "The Politics of Secularism and the Recovery of Religious Tolerance," in *Mirrors of Violence: Communities, Riots, and Survivors in South Asia*, ed. Veena Das (Delhi: Oxford University Press, 1992), 69–93, hereafter abbreviated "PS," to which I shall return at length below. The antisecularist gesture has also proved a temptation, surprisingly, in subaltern studies; see Dipesh Chakrabarty, "Radical Histories and Question of Enlightenment Rationalism: Some Recent Critiques of Subaltern Studies," *Economic and Political Weekly*, 8 April 1995, 751–59.

29 See Benedict Anderson, *Imagined Communities: Reflections on the Origin and Spread of Nationalism* (London: Verso, 1983), 19.

30 Albert Hourani, *Arabic Thought in the Liberal Age, 1789–1939* (New York, 1962), p. 259. See also Hourani's classic study of the minority question within the Arab successor states to the Ottoman empire, *Minorities in the Arab World* (1947; New York: AMS Press, 1982).

31 See, for instance, *The Rushdie File*, ed. Lisa Appignanesi and Sara Maitland (Syracuse, N.Y.: Syracuse University Press, 1990), 164–66.

32 Said and Jean Mohr, *After the Last Sky: Palestinian Lives*, (New York: Pantheon, 1986), 142–44.

33 Said, interview by Jennifer Wicke and Sprinker, in *Edward Said*, 232, 233.

34 I am grateful to Shai Ginsburg for this valuable suggestion.

35 Said, interview by Wicke and Sprinker, 232.

36 In this sense not only Clifford's but also Ahmad's reading of Said may be spoken of as poststructuralist.

37 According to Said, an important instance of this process, whereby a critique of second nature itself becomes the basis of a new acquiescence to it, is the institutionalization of theory in the North American literary academy.

38 "We are wholly convinced—and therein lies our *petitio principii*—that social freedom is inseparable from enlightened thought. Nevertheless, we believe that we have just as clearly recognized that the notion of this very way of thinking, no less than the actual historic forms—the social institutions—with which it is interwoven, already contains the seed of the reversal universally apparent today" (Max Horkheimer and Adorno, *Dialectic of Enlightenment*, trans. John Cumming [New York: Continuum, 1972], p. xiii).

39 Anita Desai, *Baumgartner's Bombay* (New York: Penguin, 1989), 51, 104.

40 Gayatri Chakravorty Spivak, "Reading the *Satanic Verses*," *Outside in the Teaching Machine* (New York: Routledge, 1993), 239; hereafter abbreviated "R." See also ibid., p. 217, and Spivak, "Marginality in the Teaching Machine," *Outside in the Teaching Machine*, 60.

41 Karl Marx and Friedrich Engels, *Manifesto of the Communist Party*, in *The Marx-Engels Reader*, 2d ed., ed. Robert C. Tucker (New York: W. W. Norton, 1978), 477; emphasis added.

42 See Gyan Prakash, "After Colonialism," introduction to *After Colonialism: Imperial Histories and Postcolonial Displacements*, ed. Gyan Prakash (Princeton, N.J.: Princeton University Press, 1995), 3. In the present context, see the excellent contributions to this volume by Joan Dayan, Anthony Pagden, Emily Apter, and Homi K. Bhabha.

43 Elsewhere, I have analyzed the interplay of these forces in what is perhaps one of their most dramatic enactments in recent decades, namely, the Rushdie affair. See my "Reading the Rushdie Affair: 'Islam,' Cultural Politics, Form," in *The Administration of Aesthetics: Censorship, Political Criticism, and the Public Sphere*, ed. Richard Burt (Minneapolis: University of Minnesota Press, 1994), 307–39.

44 See Gauri Viswanathan, "Beyond Orientalism: Syncretism and the Politics of Knowledge," *Stanford Humanities Review* 5, no. 1 (1995): 18–32.

45 Jawaharlal Nehru, *The Discovery of India* (Delhi: Oxford University Press, 1989), 382.

46 That syncretism has a Western history, that is to say, that it has played a prominent role in Western projects for negotiating cultural difference, has been amply demonstrated by Peter van der Veer, "Syncretism, Multiculturalism, and the Discourse of Tolerance," in *Syncretism/Anti-Syncretism: The Politics of Religious Synthesis*, ed. Charles Stewart and Rosalind Shaw (London: Routledge, 1994), 196–211.

47 I have discussed this problem with respect to Nehruvian nationalism in my "Secularism and Minority: Elements of a Critique," *Social Text*, no. 45 (winter 1995): 75–96.

48 Partha Chatterjee, *Nationalist Thought and the Colonial World: A Derivative Discourse* (Minneapolis: University of Minnesota Press, 1993), 51.

49 The particular conception of genealogy I am invoking here is due to Foucault's influential reading of Nietzsche; see Michel Foucault, "Nietzsche, Genealogy, History," in *Language, Counter-Memory, Practice: Selected Essays and Interviews*, trans. Donald F. Bouchard and Sherry Simon, ed. Bouchard (Ithaca, N.Y.: Cornell University Press, 1977), 139–64.

50 Chatterjee, "Religious Minorities and the Secular State: Reflections on an Indian Impasse," *Public Culture* 8 (fall 1995): 33, hereafter abbreviated "RM"; see also 32.

51 Homi K. Bhabha, "Dissemination: Time, Narrative, and the Margins of the Modern Nation," *The Location of Culture* (London: Routledge, 1994), 157.

52 It will be clear throughout, I hope, that my debt to Lloyd's work on minority discourse is too comprehensive to be fully acknowledged through individual citations; see, for instance, David Lloyd, "Genet's Genealogy: European Minorities and the Ends of the Canon," *Cultural Critique* 6 (spring 1987): 161–85, and "Violence and the Constitution of the Novel," *Anomalous States: Irish Writing and the Post-Colonial Moment* (Durham, N.C.: Duke University Press, 1993), 125–62.

53 Bhabha, "Unpacking My Library . . . Again," in *The Post-Colonial Question: Common Skies, Divided Horizons*, ed. Iain Chambers and Lidia Curti (London: Routledge, 1996), 211.

54 Said, *The Question of Palestine* (New York: Times Books, 1979), pp. xv, xiii; hereafter abbreviated *QP*.

55 The most influential literary representation of this Palestinian figure is still Ghassan Kanafani's novella *Men in the Sun*; see Ghassan Kanafani, *"Men in the Sun" and Other Palestinian Stories*, trans. Hilary Kilpatrick (Washington, D.C.: Three Continents Press, 1983), 9–56.

56 Said, *Culture and Imperialism* (New York: Knopf, 1993), 45.

The present study derives from a book manuscript in progress, tentatively entitled *Exoticism and Orientalism in Western Music*. Section 5 is freely based on a section from my article "Cutthroats and Casbah Dancers, Muezzins and Timeless Sands: Musical Images of the Middle East," in *The Exotic in Western Music*, ed. Jonathan Bellman (Boston: Northeastern University Press, 1998), 104–36, 326–33; and section 6 expands on two paragraphs from my article "Reflections on Orientalism in Opera and Musical Theater," *Opera Quarterly* 10, no. 1 (autumn 1993): 48–64. A fuller version of the "Cutthroats" piece appeared in *Nineteenth-Century Music* 22 (1998–99): 20–53. See also my "Constructing the Oriental 'Other': Saint-Saëns's *Samson et Dalila*," *Cambridge Opera Journal* 3 (1991): 261–302; another version, revised but shortened by half, appeared in Richard Dellamora and Daniel Fischlin, eds., *The Work of Opera: Genre, Nationhood, and Sexual Difference* (New York: Columbia University Press, 1997), 161–84; and excerpts of "Constructing" are included in Derek B. Scott, ed., *Music, Culture, and Society* (Oxford, England: Oxford University Press, forthcoming).

This article has profited from the advice of Daniel Beaumont, Frederick N. Bohrer, Karen Henson, Heidi Ann Owen, James Parakilas, Michael Pisani, Ted Swedenburg, and Jürgen Thym.

1 Edward W. Said, *The World, the Text, and the Critic* (Cambridge, Mass.: Harvard University Press, 1983), 35.

2 Said, *World*, 39.

3 Said, *World*, 35, 39.

4 All such questions, paradigmatic examples, and the like will be indented to facilitate later reference to them.

5 Two fine examples in the single area of "magazine" culture are Catherine Lutz, *Reading "National Geographic"* (Chicago: University of Chicago Press, 1993); and Wendy Kozol, *"Life"'s America: Family and Nation in Postwar Photojournalism* (Philadelphia: Temple University Press, 1994). In a forthcoming essay collection on *Titanic*, many of the authors reportedly confess to finding the film boring or ideologically repugnant; thus, they are left with explaining the film's overwhelming public success (see Emily Nussbaum, "Tip of the Iceberg," *Lingua franca* [September 1998]: 19). This exploration of public reactions to a frankly lowest-common-denominator cultural product is a valuable task, to be sure, but it can hardly provide a fully satisfactory model for dealing with, say, Ludwig van Beethoven's *Seventh Symphony*.

6 The epigraph comes from a lecture by bell hooks in her videotape *Cultural Criticism and Transformation* (Northampton, Mass.: Media Education Foundation, 1997), which deals primarily with stereotypical images of African Americans and images of violent male-on-female sex in popular culture (film, television news commentary). A shorter version of this quotation appeared in an ad for the videotape in *Lingua franca* 8, no. 4 (May–June 1998): 43. The video is based in part on her *Outlaw Culture: Resisting Representations* (New York: Routledge, 1994). Hooks's remark implies, perhaps for simplicity's sake (as does the first quotation in note 57 herein), a currently unidirectional process, in which "we" are passive receivers that need to become critical and active. I would stress, instead, that we are all involved and complicit to varying degrees, as consumers and citizens, in societally endorsed representations of ethnic, national, gender, and class groups. We nourish and reinforce (and some of us more than others, resist) prevailing representations through our individual decisions and actions: what we purchase, what movies we attend,

how we behave toward other individuals (and respond in turn to their behavior), and so on.

7   See, for example, the polemically "absolutist" writings of nineteenth-century Viennese music critic Eduard Hanslick—notably in the lucid new translation (with commentary) by Geoffrey Payzant, *On the Musically Beautiful: A Contribution towards the Revision of the Aesthetics of Music* (Indianapolis, Ind.: Hackett Publishing Company, 1986)—or twentieth-century composer Igor Stravinsky. I briefly explore (and provide bibliography on) the problem of music and extramusical "meaning" in my articles on "Absolute Music" and "Program Music" in *New Harvard Dictionary of Music*, ed. Don Michael Randel (Cambridge, Mass.: Harvard University Press, 1986), 1, 656–59.

8   Rose Rosengard Subotnik, *Deconstructive Variations: Music and Reason in Western Society* (Minneapolis: University of Minnesota Press, 1996), 158–59. Subotnik emphasizes what she labels "sound" and "style," but states or implies the other considerations (context, etc.). Her importance for a "nonpositivist, nonvenerative position about music in society, rather than music as autonomous art" has been particularly appreciated by Edward W. Said: see his *Musical Elaborations* (New York: Columbia University Press, 1991), xvi, 12, 16, 48; and his words of praise (including the quoted words above) on the back cover of the paperback edition of Subotnik's *Developing Variations: Style and Ideology in Western Music* (Minneapolis: University of Minnesota Press, 1991).

9   Said, *Musical Elaborations*, 75.

10   The opposite kind of repertoire would comprise works in which extramusical meaning is at best implicit (and some would say, nonexistent). Take, say, Wolfgang Amadeus Mozart's string quintets. The original intended social setting for the quintets—an amateur ensemble playing for its own pleasure in a private home or aristocratic palace—must have left the players, and the occasional listener who wandered by, a wide latitude of individual responses to the music; many today would suspect that the original social/performing context does not suffice to explain (does not justify, did not fully motivate) the works' rich aesthetic effusions.

11   Finding the right verb tense for talking about musical phenomena is a sticky matter. The repertoire that we are discussing was largely created in the past, but it remains in active use today, and evokes a sense of playing out in "present tense" when performed or studied. Furthermore, and more generally, the "ethnic other" associations on which it relies blossom perennially in film music, advertising jingles, Broadway musicals, and even some new instances within Western art music, as we will see at the end of section 2. Hence, my use, in the present paragraph and elsewhere, of what I call the "then-and-now" tense: was/is, etc.

12   On problematic terms such as *art music*, *classical*, and *serious*, see two chapters in Ralph P. Locke and Cyrilla Barr, eds., *Cultivating Music in America: Women Patrons and Activists since 1860* (Berkeley: University of California Press, 1997): Ralph P. Locke, "Reflections on Art Music in America, on Stereotypes of the Woman Patron, and on Cha(lle)nges in the Present and Future," 296–336 (esp. 308); and Ralph P. Locke and Cyrilla Barr, "Introduction: Music Patronage as a 'Female-Centered Cultural Process,' " 1–23 (esp. 1–2). Compare with notes 24 and 26 below.

13   Let me quickly stress, though, that Western art music is not the only musical stream—of the many in the world—that could be described as "aesthetically elaborate and demanding": for example, one might cite various subcategories of jazz, such as bebop, or the art music traditions of India or Japan, or various intricately polyphonic musics of central Africa. See Ralph P. Locke, "Music Lovers, Patrons, and the 'Sacralization' of Culture in

America," *Nineteenth-Century Music* 17 (1993–94): 149–73 (esp. 165–66) and 18 (1994–95): 83–84. That article is a fuller version of the first half of my chapter "Reflections on Art Music in America," in Locke and Barr, *Cultivating Music in America*.

14 Edward W. Said, *Culture and Imperialism* (New York: Knopf, 1993), 18–19, 32, 51, 66–68.

15 Said, *Culture*, 18–19, 32, 51, 66–68, 114, 125 (here, *contrapuntal* is used successively in its plain musical sense and then in its Saidian sense), 146, 194, 259, 279, 318, 336. On the relationship between Said's cultural analysis and musical views, see Pegram Harrison, "Music and Imperialism," *repercussions* 4, no. 1 (spring 1995): 53–84; and the chapter by Lindsay Waters in the present book.

16 See, for example, Said's frequent warning that one must not treat a work that is "rich in . . . aesthetic intellectual complexity" (e.g., Jane Austen's *Mansfield Park*) as if it were, for instance, a crudely "jingoistic ditty" (Said, *Culture*, 96).

17 See the discussion in Jonathan Arac's chapter in the present book.

18 On the implications of Said's brief references to the realities of life in the Middle East, see James Clifford, *The Predicament of Culture: Twentieth-Century Ethnography, Literature, and Art* (Cambridge, Mass.: Harvard University Press, 1988), 260–61.

19 "I thought life might be a dream, or I an Angel, and all this world a deception, my fellow-angels by a playful device concealing themselves from me, and deceiving me with the semblance of a material world" (John Henry Cardinal Newman, *Apologia pro vita sua: Being a History of His Religious Opinions*, ed. Martin J. Svaglic [Oxford, England: Clarendon Press, 1967], 15–16).

20 On the immense problems of dating and seeking an origin for the various tales in the *Nights*, and their variously misleading translations into European languages, see Robert Irwin, *The Arabian Nights: A Companion* (London: Allen Lane, 1994), 9–102.

21 I quoted Cardinal Newman earlier in the text partly as a counterweight to the better-known fact that other contemporaries (e.g., the prominent Arabist and translator Edward William Lane) took the *Arabian Nights* as an ethnographic treasure trove. Lane's extensive footnotes to the *Nights* were reprinted as a book, which has been widely consulted ever since: *Arabian Society in the Middle Ages: Studies from the Thousand and One Nights*, ed. Stanley Lane-Pool (London: Chatto and Windus, 1883).

22 This passage is my conflation and summary, from the shooting script and cutting continuity for *Citizen Kane*, as published in *The Citizen Kane Book* (Boston: Little, Brown and Company, 1971), 249–52, 399–401.

23 To be fair, she suddenly found new life in the spunky Princess Jasmine of the Disney *Aladdin* film, and she hovers a bit over Princess Leia and her mother in the *Star Wars* films.

24 One can, for example, live in a medium-sized American city for two decades without having the chance to see a single "classic" play by Shakespeare or Molière, Ibsen or O'Neill, except in an occasional dutiful student performance. Serious (usually nonprofit) theater survives, for better or worse, on novelty, on what is current; unlike serious concert life, it does not view its role as primarily retrospective or curatorial. Similarly, most readers of serious novels (except academics and, again, students) are at least as likely to read something contemporary (Anne Tyler, Toni Morrison, Michael Ondaatje) as something time honored (Austen, Dickens, Proust). I apologize for the use, in this one footnote, of the potentially invidious term *serious*, which can so easily imply that anything else is trivial by definition. Alas, all the other terms available to describe Western art music are likewise problematic: *classical* can imply both "exemplary" and "marked by restraint" (the latter by opposition to *romantic*); *concert music* ignores the fact that rock music, too, often happens characteristically in concerts; and *Western art music* itself seems to suggest that

everything else—George Gershwin, Duke Ellington, Edith Piaf, Willy Nelson—is inartistic, or at best naively, "artlessly" skillful and attractive.

25 Malcolm McLaren, "Madam Butterfly," Island Records O-96915 (a 45-rpm, 12-inch record). The basic version comprises Side A; the "On the Fly Mix" (remixed by John Morales and Sergio Munzibai) comprises Side B.

26 Recent studies—by Lawrence W. Levine, Paul DiMaggio, and others—emphasizing the elite exclusiveness of the institutions of "classical music" contain crucial insights but have also been somewhat one-sided in argument, downplaying the institutional supporters' civic commitment to making expressive culture available to a broad population. See Locke, "Music Lovers."

27 See Lisa C. Arkin and Marian E. Smith, "National Dance in the Romantic Ballet," in *Rethinking the Sylph: New Perspectives on the Romantic Ballet*, ed. Lynn Garofala (Middleton, Conn.: Wesleyan University Press, 1997), 11–68, 245–52.

28 The opera also features (among other characters) Klinghoffer, his widow, and a chorus of Jews in exile parallel to the one for the displaced Palestinians. For a critique of complaints that the work endorses anti-Jewish and anti-Zionist sentiments, see Edward W. Said, "*Die tote Stadt; Fidelio; The Death of Klinghoffer*," *Nation*, 11 November 1991, 596–600; summarized in Herbert Lindenberger, "Opera/Orientalism/Otherness," in his *Opera in History from Monteverdi to Cage* (Stanford, Calif.: Stanford University Press, 1998), 160–90, 311–15 (and specifically, 177–79, 314). The recording, on Nonesuch audiocassettes 9 79281-4 (CDs 9 79281-2), omits the one scene that was most sharply criticized as snidely anti-Jewish (representing a superficial bourgeois American family, presumed to be Jewish, that hears the news of the hijacking on the radio and takes it all lightly).

29 The Gubaidulina is recorded on BMG 74321-49957-2.

30 Jonathan Bellman, "Introduction," in *The Exotic in Western Music*, ed. Jonathan Bellman (Boston: Northeastern University Press, 1998), ix–xiii (quotation from ix). A second book, apparently framing the issues quite differently, is forthcoming: Georgina Born and Dave Hesmondhalgh, eds., *Western Music and Its Others: Difference, Representation, and Appropriation in Music* (Berkeley: University of California Press).

31 Thomas Betzwieser and Michael Stegemann, "Exotismus," in vol. 3 of *Die Musik in Geschichte und Gegenwart*, 2d ed., ed. Ludwig Finscher (Kassel: Bärenreiter and Straßburg: Metzler, 1994-), cols. 226–43 (quotation from col. 226). For further bibliography, see note 36 herein.

32 Frederick N. Bohrer, review of *Europa und der Orient, 800–1900* and *Exotische Welten, Europäische Phantasien* (two exhibition catalogs), *Art Bulletin* 73 (1991): 320–25 (quotation from 322).

33 Frederick N. Bohrer explores the problem of the limits of the exotic ("What was *not* exotic in the 19th century?") in a series of astute articles, including "Eastern Medi(t)ations: Exoticism and the Mobility of Difference," *History and Anthropology* 9 (1996): 293–307 (quotation from 298). On Eugène Delacroix's *La mort de Sardanapale* and similar "Assyrian" works, see Bohrer's "Inventing Assyria: Exoticism and Reception in Nineteenth-Century England and France," *Art Bulletin* 80 (1998): 336–56.

34 The first method (chronological) is sketched out in Betzwieser and Stegemann, "Exotismus"; and in Ralph P. Locke, "Exoticism" and "Orientalism," in *New Grove Dictionary of Music and Musicians*, rev. ed., ed. Stanley Sadie (London: Macmillan, forthcoming). The second (organizing the data according to "nation being evoked") is the primary structural principle in Bellman, *Exotic*. The third is exemplified by the various studies of French, Italian, and other strands of musical Orientalism listed in Locke, "Constructing

the Oriental 'Other,' " nn. 2 and 4. A further bibliographical overview is given in Linden-berger, *Opera in History*, 160–64, 311–12.

35 How do Algerians in France differ in this regard from Algerians in Algeria? For that mat-ter, what about natives of various European countries, like non-Algerian but nonethe-less rap-loving (rap-envious?), and rapping, French? Ted Swedenburg deals with some of these issues in "Islamic Hip-Hop vs. Islamophobia: Aki Nawaz, Natacha Atlas, Akhena-ton," in *Global Noise: Rap and Hip Hop outside the U.S.A.*, ed. Tony Mitchell (Middletown, Conn.: Wesleyan University Press, under consideration); and writing jointly with Joan Gross and David McMurray, "Arab Noise and Ramadan Nights: Raï, Rap, and Franco-Maghrebi Identity," in *Displacement, Diaspora, and Geographies of Identity*, ed. Smadar Lavie and Ted Swedenburg (Durham, N.C.: Duke University Press, 1996), 119–55.

36 Among musicologists (card-carrying or not), one might mention Lindenberger (see note 28), Betzwieser and Stegemann (see note 31), Jean-Pierre Bartoli, Timothy J. Taylor, and Derek B. Scott, all of whom treat exoticism primarily as the incorporation—or at least attempted or seeming incorporation—of musical materials from distant cultures into a Western compositional framework. See the bibliography in my forthcoming articles "Ex-oticism" and "Orientalism," in *New Grove*.

37 A fuller lexicon of exotic stylistic features is given, with selected instances from the reper-toire, in Michael Pisani, "Exotic Sounds in the Native Land" (Ph.D. diss., University of Rochester, 1996), 90–100, 116–19. Pisani condenses this lexicon nicely into seven cate-gories in his " 'I'm an Indian Too': Creating Native American Identities in Nineteenth-and Early Twentieth-Century Music," in Bellman, *Exotic*, 218–57 (esp. 230–31), 343–47. I might gently question or clarify his characterization of one particular "Oriental" (by which he means "Far-Eastern") device: "exaggerat[ing] the intervals of the gapped scales, often 2–4 and 6–8" (231). He seems to be thinking of a black-key pentatonic, starting on C-sharp (which lacks E-sharp and B-sharp, i.e., degrees 3 and 7 of the C-sharp major scale). For those of us accustomed to thinking of black-key pentatonicism as start-ing on F-sharp, the gaps are, of course, those between 3–5 and 6–8 of the F-sharp-major diatonic scale (B-sharp and E-sharp).

38 Listening to an opera on recordings or in concert performance produces an even more radical "dis-Orientation": the operas lose their original visual element and no new one is put in its place, except perhaps through strenuous imaginings.

39 See, for one instance, the discussion of the (partly updated) Frankfurt staging of *Aida* in Samuel Weber, "Taking Place: Toward a Theater of Dislocation," in *Opera through Other Eyes*, ed. David J. Levin (Stanford, Calif.: Stanford University Press, 1994), 107–46 (esp. 107–26).

40 Now available on two videodiscs, HBO Video (Image Entertainment, 1990) ID 7818HB, in Thames Video Collection series.

41 Even in a new work based on *Butterfly*, the aforementioned *Miss Saigon*, the location is kept close to that of the original: an Asian country (now Vietnam) in which American govern-ment officials and armed forces are stationed.

42 On uses of Spanish "local color" in *Carmen*, see Susan McClary, "Structures of Identity and Difference in Bizet's *Carmen*," in *The Work of Opera: Genre, Nationhood, and Sexual Differ-ence*, ed. Richard Dellamora and Daniel Fischlin (New York: Columbia University Press, 1997), 115–29; and James Parakilas, "How Spain Got a Soul," in *Exotic*, Bellman, 137–93, 333–42. In 1943, lyricist Oscar Hammerstein II successfully reworked *Carmen* as *Carmen Jones*, set in the American South among African Americans.

43 Most of the works just named are discussed in Locke, "Cutthroats" (especially the longer

version), or in other people's chapters in Bellman, *Exotic; Aida* is further discussed in Locke, "Reflections." *Samson* is explored at length in Locke, "Constructing the Oriental 'Other.' "

44 Michael Pisani, "I'm an Indian Too," in *Exotic*, Bellman, 194–217. See also Richard Taruskin, " 'Entoiling the Falconet': Russian Musical Orientalism in Context," in *Exotic*, Bellman 194–217 and 342–43; also published (without the subtitle) in *Defining Russia Musically: Historical and Hermeneutical Essays* (Princeton, N.J.: Princeton University Press, 1997), 152–85.

45 For some instances of this, involving borrowings from actual Arab music in the works of Félicien David and Saint-Saëns, see Locke, "Cutthroats," 112–15, 121–23 (revised version: 30–35); and Locke, "Constructing the Oriental 'Other,' " 266–67. Quasi-ethnographic "accuracy" becomes more common in the twentieth century—for example, in certain works by Debussy, Colin McPhee, and Britten that echo the Indonesian gamelan. See Mervyn Cooke, " 'The East in the West' ": Evocations of the Gamelan in Western Music," in *Exotic*, Bellman, 258–80, 347–50.

46 Said's conception of Orientalism, at least as it applies to works of literature, is by no means as purely negative as it appears in summaries by certain other scholars, such as John M. MacKenzie, *Orientalism: History, Theory, and the Arts* (Manchester, England: University of Manchester Press, 1995), 1–42. This misunderstanding may derive from applying Said's remarks in *Orientalism* (which deal mostly with nonfictional representations of the Middle East) to artistic realms. Said's own handling of such works as Rudyard Kipling's *Kim* (in *Culture*, 132–62) displays an unmistakable awareness of the possibility of deep and positive Western identification with the colonized other, though of course it also keeps issues of asymmetrical power in mind.

47 See Kimiyo Powils-Okano, *Puccinis "Madama Butterfly"* (Bonn: Verlag für systematische Musikwissenschaft, 1986), 47–62. To be sure, gentleness does not distinguish Cio-Cio San from the other, more gentle female in *Turandot*, Liù, or from the tender and delicate Parisian seamstress Mimì in *La boheme*. This last resemblance reminds us of why an exotic character such as Cio-Cio San speaks to the listener—does not seem all *that* alien, in the end.

48 Locke, "Constructing the Oriental 'Other,' " 289–98.

49 *Mercure de France*, cited in Georges Favre, *Boieldieu: sa vie, son oeuvre*, 2 vols. (Paris: Librairie E. Droz, 1944), 115.

50 The Middle East, it should be quickly added, had and has its own fascination with the West and various Western musics, and was/is motivated, no less than the West, by various mixtures of innocent curiosity and concrete self-interest. In the nineteenth century, for example, the Ottoman leadership in Egypt and Turkey actively reached out to European government agencies for help in Westernizing not only such things as their agricultural economy, but also their military bands. A recent case is the hiring, by the government of Oman, of the BBC Philharmonic (101 musicians) to play two concerts in honor of the twenty-fifth anniversary of the sultan's investiture and make a fresh recording of the national anthem ("Sultan Seeks Orchestra," *BBC Music Magazine*, March 1996, 9).

51 Said, *Culture*, 186.

52 Marilyn Butler, "Orientalism," in *The Romantic Period*, ed. David B. Pirie, Penguin History of Literature, vol. 5 (London: Penguin Books, 1994), 395–447, 488–92 (quotation from 399).

53 Said, *Culture*, 132–62 (the *Kim* discussion cited earlier).

54 Said, *Culture*, 186 (also 67–68, 240–42). Felicity Nussbaum gives some interesting in-

stances of this, such as in English lesbian writing about harem women: *Torrid Zones: Maternity, Sexuality, and Empire in Eighteenth-Century English Narratives* (Baltimore, Md.: Johns Hopkins University Press, 1995), 135–62.

55 A familiar phenomenon: see Said, *Culture*, 241.

56 See also the widely disseminated English translation: Pierre Loti, *India*, ed. Robert Harborough Sherard, trans. George A. F. Inman (London: J. Pott, [ca. 1910]).

57 "Most of us, no matter how sophisticated our strategies of critique and intervention, are usually seduced, at least for a time, by the images we see on the screen. They have power over us and we have no power over them" (bell hooks, *Reel to Real: Race, Sex, and Class at the Movies* [New York: Routledge, 1996], 3). (I have silently corrected in that sentence what seems a typo: "at last for a time.") Hooks is speaking primarily of the ways that colonialist and white supremacist thinking are reflected in stereotyped portrayals of African Americans (including some by African Americans), but stresses elsewhere that "the field of representation [as a whole] remains a place of struggle" (*Black Looks: Race and Representation* [Toronto: Between the Lines, 1992], 3; see also 1–7).

58 The quiet wedding chorus sung by the Bar-Girls ("Dju vui vai"), for example, fulfills much the same function as Puccini's "O Kami" chorus. Other Puccini echoes in *Miss Saigon* have been repeatedly noted by newspaper critics (e.g., Stephen B. Holden in the *New York Times*).

59 Bell hooks puts the matter more encouragingly in her video: we, blacks and whites alike, must move toward "decolonizing our minds, so that we can both resist certain kinds of conservatizing representations and at the same time create new and exciting representations" (end of part 1 of *Cultural Criticism and Transformation*).

Newman, Cardinal John Henry, 270; *Thousand and One Nights*, 262
Nietzsche, Friedrich, 59, 86–92; "On Truth and Lie in the Extramoral Sense," 93–95
Nightingale, Florence, 166, 169–170
Nussbaum, Martha, 97, 106, 107, 110–112

O'Brien, Conor Cruise, 215
Ôe Kenzaburo, 139
Okakura Tenshia, 147–151, 292n
Ondaatje, Michael, 165, 167
Orient, the, 58, 84–86, 96, 192, 194, 211–212, 234
Orientalism, 7, 69, 140–141, 144–145, 234–235, 242–243, 274–275
Oslo Accord, 3, 11, 28–29, 161–163
Oz, Amos, 28–29

Palestinians and Palestine, 3, 9, 20–23, 27–30, 34–36, 44–45, 253–256, 292n; and the media, 152, 158–164
Persian Gulf War (1991), 26, 210–212, 276
Picasso, Pablo, 34
Picture of Dorian Gray, The, 40
Pisani, Michael, 275
Poirier, Richard: *The Performing Self*, 116
Pollini, Maurizio, 103
Porter, Dennis, 190
Proust, Marcel, 99, 101, 104–105, 107–108, 110–111
Puccini, Giacomo: *Madame Butterfly*, 264–265, 272, 276, 280–281

Ravel, Joseph-Maurice, 273
Renan, Ernest, 18
Rhodes, Cecil (John), 175
Robbins, Bruce, 239
Robertson, James, 169
Rodin, Auguste, 32, 45
Rodinson, Maxime, 191–192
Rodney, Red, 127
Rolling Stones, The, 111
Rolston, Bill, 186
Romanticism, 141–143, 149
Romeo Void, 107
Rorty, Richard, 212
Rosen, Charles, 105
Rossini, Gioachino, 266, 270

Rousseau, Jean-Jacques, 90–91, 268
Ruscio, Alain, 205
Ruskin, John, 145
Russell, Sir William Howard, 169

Said, Edward: *After the Last Sky*, 21–22, 35–37, 188, 243, 240–242; *Beginnings*, 3, 10, 68; criticism of *Orientalism*, 190–203; *Culture and Imperialism*, 6, 67–68, 98, 214; interview with Ricke and Sprinker, 242, 244; memoir, 15–16, 38; *Musical Elaborations*, 23, 98, 106–113, 116, 126, 130, 134–135, 259–260; *Orientalism*, 6–7, 46, 51–52, 68, 84–86, 140, 145, 207, 241–242; "On Originality," 125; as Palestian American, 189; *The Palestine Question and the American Context*, 160; *Peace and Its Discontents*, 160; "politics of blame," 68–69, 202, 215; *The Politics of Dispossession*, 161; *The Question of Palestine*, 253; Reith lectures, 135, 155–156; *Representations of the Intellectual*, 10, 68, 155, 213; *The World, the Text, and the Critic*, 229, 234. *See Also* Affiliation; Contrapuntal criticism; Feminism; Humanism; Identity; Intellectual; Language; Modernism; the Orient; Orientalism; Palestinians and Palestine; Secular criticism
Said, Wadie, 15–16, 38–39, 187–188
Saint-Saëns, Camille, 276
Sapper, 167–168
Schreiner, Olive, 175
Schumann, Clara, 24
Secular criticism, 115, 234, 238–241, 247–248, 250–252
Shahak, Israel, 20
Shakespeare, William, 205; as political/historical figure, 81–83
Shohat, Ella, 20
Shehadeh, Raja: *The Third Way*, 20
Silverstein, Hilda, 19
Simon, Claude, 139–140
Smith, Barbara Herrnstein: *Contingencies of Value*, 100
Spaeth, Sigmund: *Great Composers*, 24
Spivak, Gayatri Chakravorty, 5, 130, 188, 239–240, 245–246
Stead, William Thomas 175
Stone, I. F., 13

Library of Congress Cataloging-in-Publication Data

Edward Said and the work of the critic : speaking truth to power /
Paul A. Bové, editor.

"Boundary 2 book."

Includes index.

ISBN 0-8223-2487-3 (alk. paper)

ISBN 0-8223-2522-5 (pbk. : alk. paper)

1. Criticism—History—20th century.   2. Literature, Modern—
History and criticism—Theory, etc.   3. Power (Social sciences)
in literature.   4. Politics and literature.   5. Politics and culture.
6. Said, Edward W.   I. Bové, Paul A., 1949–

PN51.E34   2000   801'.95'0904—dc21   99-049997